PRINCIPLES OF REMEDIES LAW

Third Edition

Russell L. Weaver

Professor of Law & Distinguished University Scholar
University of Louisville, Louis D. Brandeis School of Law

Elaine W. Shoben

Judge Jack and Lulu Lehman Professor of Law
University of Nevada—Las Vegas, Boyd School of Law

Michael B. Kelly

Professor of Law
University of San Diego School of Law

CONCISE HORNBOOK SERIES™

WEST
ACADEMIC
PUBLISHING

© West, a Thomson business, 2007
© 2011 Thomson Reuters
© 2017 LEG, Inc. d/b/a West Academic
    444 Cedar Street, Suite 700
    St. Paul, MN 55101
    1-877-888-1330

Printed in the United States of America

ISBN: 978-1-63459-686-2

To Laurence, Ben & Kate, with love
RLW

To Ed and Abby, with love
EWS

To Pam, Logan & Preston
MBK

Preface

The purpose of this book is to provide students with a clear and concise guide to the study of remedies. As you will see (or, perhaps, have already seen), remedies is a fascinating course. It involves historical analysis in the sense that historical distinctions between "law" and "equity" condition and limit the availability of remedies today. Remedies also involves modern analysis in the sense that it examines remedial limitations which, whether or not they originated for historical reasons, must have vitality and force today.

In this book, we examine many different types of remedies. In addition to the damage remedies, which you may have first encountered in contracts, torts and property courses, we also examine injunctive remedies. As a result, we focus on permanent injunctions, as well as temporary (a/k/a, "preliminary" injunctions) and temporary restraining orders (a/k/a, "TROs"). We examine the conditions and limitations on these remedies, as well as the methods (principally, contempt) by which they are enforced. We also examine the declaratory remedy which is frequently combined with the injunctive remedy.

A significant portion of the book focuses on damage remedies. Many of these remedies are "substitutionary" in nature because they provide plaintiff with a monetary substitute for her losses. For example, if plaintiff loses an arm in an automobile accident, it is impossible for defendant (or, a court, for that matter) to physically replace the arm. In the face of this impossibility, remedies provides damages to the plaintiff as a limited, and in some respects inadequate, way of compensating for the loss.

The course also focuses on the array of things a court can do for the prevailing party in litigation. Knowing the alternatives is essential to choosing among them. Choosing the wrong remedy may lead you to file the wrong cause of action in the wrong jurisdiction or even to sue the wrong defendant. In some ways, the remedy should be the first thing an attorney considers when contemplating how to help a client. The remedy often is foremost in the client's mind. Focusing on the remedies at the outset of litigation may prevent a number of poor litigation choices.

We give thanks to the many people who assisted us in the creation and revision of this book, including our research assistants and secretaries. Last, but not least, we are thankful to our spouses and children who supported us through the various stages of this project.

RLW
EWS
MBK

Summary of Contents

Table of Contents

PRINCIPLES
OF
REMEDIES LAW

Third Edition

Chapter One

OVERVIEW

A. INTRODUCTION

Even though many schools teach Remedies as a separate and independent course, usually taught at or near the end of a student's legal education, you have studied remedies in a number of other courses. For example, in Contracts, you studied concepts like specific performance, "benefit of the bargain," and restitution, and you probably examined various equitable defenses (*e.g.*, unclean hands, unconscionability, and estoppel). Likewise, in torts, you examined concepts such as "economic loss" and "non-economic loss," "general" and "special" damages, "pain and suffering" and "medical expenses."

So, why do we have a separate Remedies course? There are a number of reasons. First, although you may have been introduced to many remedial concepts (*e.g.*, equity and conscience), Remedies gives you the chance to consider them in greater depth. The time available in a Contracts course or Torts course does not always permit full exploration of each remedial option. Second, there are many remedies which you may not have studied or may have touched on only tangentially (i.e., preliminary injunctions, temporary restraining orders and permanent injunctive relief). Third, Remedies allows you to see the law in a more integrated way. Established subject boundaries are artificial, and although convenient for classification, they are not responsive to the law in practice or to the remedial policies that transcend substantive areas of the law.

Remedies also allows you to see the relationship between "rights" and "remedies." In many of your first year courses, you were focused on whether plaintiff had a legal right. Is this a tort? Is it a contract? If so, what are the requirements? One tends to think of a Remedies course as assuming that plaintiff's rights have been violated and to focus on the remedies to which plaintiff is entitled. In fact, as we shall see, how one characterizes the legal right can affect plaintiff's remedial options. For example, a fundamental principle of equity provides that equitable relief is not available except when the plaintiff's legal remedy is inadequate. As a result, during this course, we will frequently find ourselves focusing on plaintiff's "legal" cause of action and the remedies available under

1

that action. Only after we ask, and answer, those questions is it possible to focus more specifically on plaintiff's remedies.

There are many different ways to categorize remedies. Some distinguish between "substitutionary" and "specific remedies." Others distinguish between "legal remedies" and "equitable remedies." Still others distinguish between "damage remedies," "coercive remedies," "declaratory remedies" and "restitutionary remedies." While all of these categorizations are useful, they often overlap and none necessarily excludes other categorization possibilities.

Substitutionary Versus Specific Remedies. Some commentators distinguish between so-called "substitutionary remedies" and "specific remedies." "Specific remedies" give plaintiff the specific item sought. For example, when plaintiff's ex-husband makes off with her family heirloom (*e.g.*, a family Bible), specific relief might come in the form of a court order requiring the ex to return the Bible. By contrast, "substitutionary remedies" give plaintiff money in exchange for an otherwise non-compensable loss. For example, suppose that plaintiff loses an arm in an automobile accident. Since a court cannot order defendant to replace the arm, it instead orders defendant to pay plaintiff money to compensate him for lost wages, medical expenses and pain and suffering associated with loss of the arm.

Substitutionary and specific remedies are not mutually exclusive. For example, if defendant breaches a contract to sell personal property, specific performance might be appropriate. (The Uniform Commercial Code provides that specific performance can be ordered when goods are "unique" or in "other appropriate circumstances.") Even though specific performance is ordered, a court might also order substitutionary relief in the form of damages to compensate plaintiff for damages incurred during the period between the breach and the time the goods are finally delivered.

Damage Remedies. Damage remedies can take a variety of forms including nominal, statutory, liquidated or compensatory. Each of these damages is designed to serve different purposes. For example, nominal damages are designed to vindicate plaintiff's rights by making a legal declaration of those rights and providing plaintiff with "nominal" compensation. Compensatory damages are supposed to repay plaintiff for any losses she has suffered, making her whole, in so much as the law is capable of doing. When plaintiff has lost an arm, compensatory damages are substitutionary and cannot provide an adequate substitute. On the other hand, when plaintiff is a seller, a damage award equal to the price may be exactly the thing plaintiff lost. In that case, damages are more like a specific remedy.

Compensatory damages can vary depending on the case, but generally are designed to compensate plaintiff for a loss. In property cases, for example, a court might award "general" damages involving a calculation of diminution in market value—*e.g.*, the amount by which plaintiff's real estate has decreased in value due to a nuisance. In some cases, the compensatory measure might focus instead on the cost to repair.

Liquidated and statutory damages represent efforts to tell courts how much to award or how to calculate a damage award. Statutory damages are legislative enactments that specify either an amount or a formula (*e.g.*, three times actual damages) for damage recoveries. Liquidated damages represent efforts by parties to a contract to specify either an amount or a formula (*e.g.*, $100 per day) that a court should use in calculating damages.

Coercive Remedies. "Coercive remedies" involve *in personam* orders that are enforceable through the remedy of "contempt of court." "Contempt of court" is an extremely powerful remedy by which a court can impose jail sentences or fines in order to punish a defendant for violating a court order, to coerce defendant to obey the order, or to compensate plaintiff for violation of the order. In this course, we will focus on various types of *in personam* orders including injunctions, specific performance and the so-called prerogative writs (*e.g.*, mandamus, prohibition, quo warranto, habeas corpus).

Declaratory Remedies. Declaratory remedies are commonly available at both the federal level and the state level. The function of declaratory relief is to provide a judicial declaration regarding the rights, obligations, or responsibilities of the parties relating to a particular situation (*e.g.*, a declaration that plaintiff's picketing activities are protected by free speech principles and that an ordinance that purports to restrict those activities is unconstitutional). No money is awarded, no orders are issued; the court simply declares one party's position to be correct under the law. (Note that every award of damages or coercive relief contains an implicit declaration that the plaintiff is right and deserves to recover. Declaratory remedies provide that declaration expressly, but do not immediately include more tangible relief.)

In providing declaratory relief, the court provides a number of benefits to the parties. First, and foremost, in the example set forth above, if the parties wish to picket and they obtain a legal judgment declaring the statute invalid, the parties can picket without fear of arrest or criminal prosecution. When there is a dispute regarding the meaning of a contract, a declaratory judgment gives the parties a chance to resolve ambiguity early so that neither party is forced to act without full knowledge of his rights and obligations (and thereby incur liability.)

Sometimes, a request for declaratory relief is accompanied by a request for injunctive relief. Even when there is no request for injunctive relief, a declaratory judgment might have the same effect on the parties if they choose to respect and obey it.

Restitutionary Remedies. Restitution is a remedy that is imposed to prevent unjust enrichment. It awards a plaintiff the amount that defendant gained as a result of the wrong, not the amount that the plaintiff lost (as in damages). Restitution includes such remedies as quasi-contract, constructive trust, equitable lien, subrogation, rescission, reformation, accounting for profits, ejectment and replevin. Some of these remedies are specific (*e.g.*, ejectment and replevin give plaintiff specific property to which she is entitled), while others are substitutionary (i.e., quasi-contract gives plaintiff a monetary equivalent for a benefit conferred on defendant).

Legal Versus Equitable Remedies. As we shall see, distinctions are also made between so-called "legal remedies" and so-called "equitable remedies." England created two separate and distinct court systems—"law courts" and "equity courts"—that functioned under quite different principles, rules and procedures. Even though most states have merged their law courts and their equity courts into a single unified system, the distinction between "law" and "equity" remains important because remnants of the rules differentiating law and equity continue to apply today. We will examine this topic in greater detail in Chapter 2.

The historical distinction between "legal remedies" and "equitable remedies" led to fundamental differences in the way that those remedies are enforced. Historically, "equitable remedies" have been regarded as *in personam* remedies—involving a direct order to a defendant to engage or refrain from engaging in a particular act— and have been enforced through the remedy of contempt. In other words, if defendant refused to comply with the personal order, defendant might be jailed or fined for the refusal to comply. By contrast, "legal remedies" do not involve *in personam* orders, but rather monetary judgments in favor of one party or the other. Defendant's failure to pay the judgment did not constitute contempt. Plaintiff was forced to enforce the order through the remedies of attachment and execution. In other words, if defendant refused to pay, plaintiff was forced to seize or place liens on defendant's property and eventually sell it in order to satisfy the judgment.

Preliminary Versus Permanent Remedies. Distinctions also are made between "preliminary remedies" and "permanent remedies." Preliminary or provisional remedies are interlocutory, issued during the pendency of a suit (i.e., a preliminary or temporary injunction, or a temporary restraining order), and are designed to last only until the end of the suit. Permanent or final remedies (i.e., a permanent injunction or an award of permanent damages) are issued at the end of a suit and are designed to last forever (absent modification or dissolution).

These categories are helpful. They offer you a way to file away the lessons you encounter throughout the book. But in some ways, the most important lessons involve the unity of remedies.

Remedies aim at a single goal: to rectify a wrong, to restore a right. Remedies generally seek to place the victim of a legal wrong (typically the plaintiff) in the position that person would have occupied if the wrong had not occurred. For convenience, we may call this the plaintiff's rightful position, the position the person deserves to occupy and would occupy but for defendant's wrong. Courts might achieve that by equitable, specific, coercive relief, ordering plaintiff to return the Bible. They might choose legal, substitutionary, compensatory relief, awarding plaintiff the price defendant promised to pay or the cost to repair the property. But the plaintiff's rightful position forms the starting point for most remedies. Some remedies go beyond, awarding punitive damages in addition to compensation. Some deviate from the basic approach, focusing on defendant's ill-gotten gain instead of plaintiff's loss. But all start with a right—a legally enforceable right—that defendant's conduct threatens to infringe. As you read the chapters that follow, note not only the differences among the remedies, but also the underlying similarities. Both are important as you make strategic choices regarding how to pursue a remedy for your clients.

Chapter Two

EQUITY AND EQUITABLE REMEDIES

The modern law of remedies owes much to its historical roots. This is particularly true for the so-called "equitable remedies." At one point in history, there were two separate and independent court systems referred to as "law courts" and "equity courts." Whereas "law courts" granted "legal relief," "equity courts" granted "equitable relief." Each system proceeded according to its own rules and criteria.

Although the overwhelming majority of states subsequently merged the two court systems into a single system, modern courts still distinguish between "legal remedies" and "equitable remedies," and they use historical distinctions to limit the availability of "equitable relief." For example, as we shall see, modern courts will not ordinarily grant equitable relief when plaintiff has an adequate remedy at law. In other words, despite the merger of the two court systems, historical and limitations distinctions remain important today.

Because of the influence of history, a modern lawyer must understand something about the history and development of equity, and the ancient rules that control the granting of equitable relief, in order to practice effectively today. In this chapter, we trace that history, and we extend the discussion by examining how historical considerations affect the willingness of modern courts to grant equitable remedies.

A. THE DEVELOPMENT OF "LAW COURTS" AND "EQUITY COURTS"

In Common Law England, there was initially only a single court system (referred to as the "King's Courts" and later as the "law courts") which had the power to hear cases and to dispense "justice." This court system actually included three different branches, all of which could be loosely referred to as "courts": King's Bench, Common Pleas and Exchequer. A plaintiff with a grievance sought access to the King's Courts by requesting the issuance of a "writ" authorizing a court to hear the case. There were various categories of writs, including assumpsit, replevin, conversion.

Early plaintiffs also had another venue for seeking redress for their grievances: they could bypass the King's Courts and directly petition the King of England for relief. The King had the power to hear these claims, and had virtually unbridled discretion to grant or withhold the requested relief. This discretionary authority ultimately evolved into a parallel system of "equity" or "chancery" courts.

The creation of equity courts did not come about quickly or immediately. Over time, as the number of petitions to the King increased, the King decided that he was too busy to deal with all of them, and began to ask his Chancellor to hear and decide the petitions. The Chancellor was a minister of the king who also served (at that point, at least) as a high church official. As a minister, the Chancellor performed various functions, including the granting of "writs" authorizing litigants to bring suit in the law courts. When a given set of facts did not fit within the scope of an existing writ, the Chancellor sometimes created new forms of writs which the courts could accept or reject.

Having been delegated the King's discretionary authority to hear petitions, the Chancellor began to hear petitions and dispensed justice on the King's behalf. Because of his dual function as a high governmental minister and an official of the church, the Chancellor seemed particularly suited to hear such petitions. Not infrequently, the Chancellor would listen to the parties in a sort of fact-finding exercise, and would render decisions that invoked pious sounding words like "justice," "equity" and "conscience."

Over time, the English Lords objected to the Chancellor's ability to create new writs for the law courts as an infringement of their rights and prerogatives. The lords were concerned about additions to the scope of federal power at the expense of their own power. In 1258, the Provisions of Oxford were adopted which prohibited the creation of new forms of writs absent the consent of the King and the King's Council (which was composed of Lords). The Provisions had the effect of slowing the development and creation of new writs, and new forms of action, and to some extent froze the number of writs (albeit with such exceptions as the King and King's Council chose to create) as of 1258. Although a later statute relaxed the effect of the Provisions of Oxford somewhat, by authorizing the issuance of new writs that were factually similar to existing writs, the Provisions nevertheless impeded the development of new writs. Statute of Westminster II (1285). As a result, the Chancellor's power remained more circumscribed than it had been prior to adoption of the Provisions of Oxford.

Even though the Provisions of Oxford limited the Chancellor's power to issue new writs, they did not affect the King's equitable power to hear petitions and dispense "justice." Over time, as the Provisions of Oxford began to negatively impact the ability of the law courts to respond to new legal problems, more and more people began to petition the King (or the King's Chancellor) for relief. As the number of petitions became too numerous for even the Chancellor to hear, he began to appoint subordinates to help him hear and decide the petitions. As the number of subordinates working on these petitions grew in number, a separate court system began to develop. This new court system came to be called the "chancery" system or "equity" system, and it was a parallel court system that rivaled the law courts. Chancery judges functioned like other judges in that they developed facts, applied the law to facts, and began to develop legal precedent and procedural rules. However, consistent with equity's origin as an appeal to the King's (and later the Chancellor's) conscience, the Chancery Court system (a/k/a equity court) continued to dispense justice according to principles of equity, justice and conscience.

As equity developed into a separate court system, that system existed side-by-side with the King's Courts. As a result, if a plaintiff wished to obtain a "legal remedy," he was required to obtain a writ which would be taken to a court of law, and which would be governed and resolved by traditional legal principles. By contrast, if plaintiff sought an "equitable remedy," he was required to file suit in a court of equity. The two court systems functioned by very different rules and frequently adjudicated quite different issues. For example, if plaintiff sought damages for a breach of contract, the case would have been filed in a court of law. Since plaintiff sought only damages, a court of equity would not entertain the case. By contrast, if plaintiff sought specific performance, rather than damages, the case would have been brought in a court of equity since the law courts did not grant specific performance.

The dividing line between law and equity was not entirely precise and clean. Indeed, a given case might be heard (in all or in part) in both a law court and an equity court. For example, suppose that plaintiff sought specific performance in a court of equity. As we shall see, the remedy of specific performance was discretionary, rather than automatic, so that the equity court was not required to grant the requested relief. If specific performance was denied, plaintiff might have been relegated to his legal remedies, and forced to return to a court of law to seek those remedies. Even if a court of equity granted the request for specific performance, if substantial damages were involved as well, plaintiff might have been forced to go to the law court to obtain those damages. In other words, plaintiffs might have been forced to bring two separate actions, one in the law courts and one in the equity courts.

At times, courts of equity exercised so-called "equitable clean-up" jurisdiction. Under the doctrine of equitable clean-up, if a case involved both equitable issues (*e.g.*, specific performance) and a request for damages, a court of equity might grant the request specific performance, and then "clean-up" the legal issues by awarding incidental damages.

B. HISTORICAL DISTINCTIONS BETWEEN LAW AND EQUITY

In addition to the fact that equity courts developed differently than law courts, they also functioned differently in terms of their governing principles and the way they issued judgments or decisions.

1. Equitable Relief Was Unavailable Except When Plaintiff's Legal Remedy Was Inadequate

One historical distinction that was applied by equity courts was the notion that equitable relief was not available except when a plaintiff's legal remedy was inadequate. While the King might dispense justice to those who appealed to him, even if the plaintiff might have been able to avail himself of a legal writ or a legal remedy, the later courts of equity were reluctant to do so. As a result, they developed and applied the notion that equitable remedies should be regarded as extraordinary, and that equity courts should not provide relief when the plaintiff's legal remedy (usually damages) would suffice. In other words, when plaintiff's legal remedy was regarded as providing adequate relief, equity would dismiss the case, thereby forcing plaintiff to pursue his legal remedies.

In general, a legal remedy might be considered adequate when it provided plaintiff with equivalent compensation for his loss. For example, suppose that plaintiff sought to purchase a wagon from defendant. When defendant breached, plaintiff sought specific performance. If the wagon were not particularly special or unique, so that an equivalent wagon could easily be purchased on the open market, the legal remedy of damages might have been considered adequate. Once plaintiff was given his damages (essentially, the "benefit of his bargain," involving the difference between the fair market value of the wagon and the contract price), plaintiff could purchase an equivalent wagon on the open market.

Equity courts were forced to determine the adequacy of legal remedies on a case-by-case basis. Even though specific performance might have been denied when sought in connection with a fungible wagon, specific performance might have been available when the contract was for a unique item. For example, if plaintiff had contracted to purchase a one-of-a-kind stallion with champion blood lines, a court of equity might have regarded the damage remedy as inadequate. Even if plaintiff had been awarded damages, he might not have been able to purchase an equivalent horse on the open market. Specific performance might also have been granted for items that might have seemed fungible and replaceable if the item was for some reason particularly unique. For example, if plaintiff sought to purchase a diamond ring, and the cut of the diamond was exceptional or unique, plaintiff might have been entitled to specific performance. As a general rule, because of its significance to the feudal economy, land was regarded as unique rather than fungible, and specific performance was routinely granted for the breach of a contract for the sale of land.

Over time, equity developed a series of rules regarding determinations of adequacy. For example, equity courts routinely held that legal damages constituted an adequate remedy for an ordinary trespass (in that plaintiff could be compensated for diminishment in the value of the land, or any damage thereto). However, even for trespasses, there were circumstances when a court might consider plaintiff's legal remedy inadequate. Suppose, for example, that defendant routinely trespassed across plaintiff's land (because it was easier to get to a neighbor's property), but caused no visible damage to the property. Plaintiff repeatedly sued defendant, and repeatedly prevailed, but received only nominal damages (designed to vindicate his ownership and title to the property) because there was no injury. Because the damages were so low, defendant continued to trespass on plaintiff's property. In this situation, plaintiff's legal damages might have been considered inadequate because a multiplicity of actions would have been required to vindicate his possessory rights.

2. Equity Acted *In Personam*

A second historical distinction between law and equity was that courts of equity granted "*in personam*" relief. In other words, equity courts would enter decrees requiring plaintiffs to engage in, or refrain from engaging in, specific acts (*e.g.*, not to trespass on plaintiff's property). If plaintiff failed or refused to comply, the *in personam* decree could be enforced through the sanction of contempt of court. In other words, a non-compliant defendant could be imprisoned or fined for noncompliance.

By contrast, law courts historically rendered monetary judgments against defendants. In other words, a law court would not command the defendant to do, or refrain from doing, a particular act. Instead, it would simply render a monetary judgment. Since law court decrees generally did not involve *in personam* orders, a law court defendant would not be held in contempt for noncompliance, and therefore would not be fined or imprisoned for failing to satisfy a judgment.

A court of equity's *in personam* decree would, ordinarily, be directed only against the parties to the case before it. Suppose, for example, that A wished to contract with B to purchase 10 bushels of wheat at 2 British Pounds Sterling per bushel (for a total of 20 pounds). However, because of a mistake in drafting, the contract stated that A would pay 20 British Pounds per bushel (or 200 pounds). When A refused to pay the stated price, B sued A in a court of law for 200 pounds. A then sought reformation of the contract in a court of equity (because "reformation" was a remedy that a court of law would not grant) to bring the contract terms into compliance with the agreement of the parties (*e.g.,* so that A will be required to pay 20 pounds rather than 200 pounds). During the pendency of the equitable proceeding, a court of equity might have enjoined the law court proceeding. However, rather than enjoining the law court directly, the court would have enjoined the plaintiff in the law court proceeding (who would, of course, be the defendant in the equitable proceeding) from advancing the case in the law courts until the court of equity could hear and decide the case. As a result, it is theoretically possible that the law plaintiff could have proceeded with the case. However, in that instance, he would have been subject to contempt sanctions in the court of equity.

3.   Equity Was a Court of Conscience

A third distinction between law and equity was that equity courts were historically regarded as "courts of conscience." In the early days, when the people could directly petition the King himself, the petition involved an appeal to the King's conscience, and his sense of right and wrong. After the King transferred his decisionmaking authority to the Chancellor, this focus continued in that the petitions involved an appeal to the Chancellor's conscience. Indeed, since the chancellor was a religious official, one might justifiably have expected him to make his decisions based on principles of "conscience," "justice" and "equity."

As the Chancellor began to delegate his decisionmaking authority to subordinates, and a system of equity courts began to develop, this focus on justice and equity continued. In their decisions, courts of equity would frequently invoke principles of "conscience," "justice," and "equity" in their decisions. For example, equity judges denied relief to some plaintiffs on equitable or moral grounds under the doctrines of "laches" and "unclean hands."

Although early equity decisions might have been based solely on the Chancellor's conscience, and his sense of right and wrong, equity eventually began to develop its own precedent for deciding cases. Like courts of law, which had precedent and rules that suggested how particular types of cases should be resolved, equitable precedent helped to channel and direct equitable decisions. For example, although equity courts had the power to issue injunctions, they developed rules and limitations on the use of the injunctive remedy. For example, rules developed suggesting that courts should not enforce personal service contracts. In addition, equity courts refused to grant equitable relief when plaintiff had an adequate remedy at law.

Equity courts also developed "maxims" that helped them decide cases. Although these "maxims" were generalizations of experience, that were based on the results of prior cases, they eventually developed into a loose set of "rules" designed to bring some coherency to the body of decided cases and some consistency to future decisions. "Equitable maxims" included a variety of principles including the following:

— He who comes into equity must come with clean hands; He who seeks equity must do equity;

— Equity is a court of conscience;

— Equity does not suffer a wrong to go without a remedy;

— Equity abhors a forfeiture;

— Equity regards as done that which ought to have been done;

— Equity delights to do justice and not by halves;

— Equitable relief is not available to one who has an adequate remedy at law;

— Equitable relief is discretionary;

— Equity aids the vigilant, not those who slumber on their rights;

— Equity regards substance rather than form;

— Equity acts in personam;

— Equity is equality;

— Equity follows the law;

— Equity will not aid a volunteer;

— Where the equities are equal, the law will prevail;

— Equity imputes an intent to fulfill an obligation;

— Where the equities are equal, the first in time will prevail.

Even though equitable precedent and equitable maxims existed, it is not clear how much they controlled or constrained the exercise of equitable discretion. Similar maxims and rules exist in other areas of the law, such as the "canons" or "maxims" that are used in interpreting statutes, and commentators have questioned whether these canons or maxims actually drive judicial decisionmaking, or whether they are simply used to justify decisions made on other grounds. Indeed, questions have even been raised regarding whether the maxims are consistent with each other, and whether they provide the actual basis for judicial decisions. *See* Karl Llewellyn, *Remarks on the Theory of Appellate Decision and the Rules or Canons About How Statutes Are to be Construed*, 3 VAND. L. REV. 395 (1949) (suggesting that the canons of judicial interpretation are inconsistent with each other). Similar problems exist with the equitable maxims. As you examine the maxims listed above, consider whether they are entirely consistent. If "equity is equality," can it really be said that "equity delights to do justice and not by halves" or that "where the equities are equal, the first in time will prevail?" In fact, as courts try to apply the equitable maxims, they frequently find that the maxims suffer from inconsistency.

4. Equitable Relief Was Discretionary

When appeals were made to the King or the Chancellor, as noted, they frequently involved an appeal to the King's (or Chancellor's) conscience. Necessarily, the grant or denial of such relief was within the King's (and, later, the Chancellor's) discretion. In other words, the King (or Chancellor) would decide the case as he thought best.

As equity developed as a separate court system, it continued to assume that equitable relief was discretionary. As a result, even though plaintiff might have suffered suffer serious and irreparable injury, a court of equity could nonetheless choose to deny plaintiff equitable relief. For example, courts of equity sometimes denied a plaintiff an equitable remedy when the plaintiff had engaged in unethical or immoral conduct related to the transaction at issue before the court (the so-called "clean hands" doctrine), or had unduly slept on her rights (the "laches" doctrine). While the clean hands and laches doctrines can be traced to the notion that equity is a "court of conscience," they can also be attributed to the notion that equitable relief is "discretionary." These ideas will be discussed in greater depth later in this chapter.

C. EQUITY IN THE AMERICAN COLONIES AND THE DRIVE FOR MERGER OF LAW COURTS AND EQUITY COURTS

Just as the English common law was transplanted to the United States, equity and equitable principles were transplanted as well. All thirteen colonies had chancery courts, in one form or another, and these courts continued to function after the Revolution (despite some resistance since equity courts were associated with Britain's King George). In other words, some states maintained both courts of law and courts of equity, and they continued to function under the ancient rules governing law and equity.

By the nineteenth century, a movement to abolish equity as a separate judicial system was gaining strength. In 1848, the State of New York adopted the Field Code, a civil procedure code, which abolished the distinction between law and equity, and which allowed both equitable and legal claims to be presented in a single cause of action before a single court. Most states followed the Field Code model, and combined their law courts and equity courts into a single judicial system. In other words, instead of maintaining formal distinctions between legal causes of action and equitable causes of action, these civil procedure codes created one form of action known as the "civil action" and allowed plaintiffs to include legal and equitable claims in the same case.

Today, the Federal Rules of Civil Procedure make clear that there shall be "one form of action known as the civil action." In other words, there are no longer "law cases" and "equity cases," but simply civil actions. Moreover, cases are not "law cases" or "equity cases," they are simply "cases."

Despite the fact that the overwhelming majority of states have merged law with equity, a handful of states have resisted the drive towards merger. These states maintain dual court systems.

D. EQUITABLE RELIEF TODAY

Even though law courts and equity courts have been merged in the overwhelming majority of states, and even though there may be only a single cause of action known as the "civil action" in most states, the historical distinctions between law and equity have not completely disappeared. Courts continue to distinguish between "legal remedies" and "equitable remedies," and continue to subject equitable remedies to many of the historical distinctions and limitations that were applied in equity.

1. Equitable Relief Continues to Be Available Only When Plaintiff's Legal Remedy Is Inadequate

Courts continue to deny equitable relief except when plaintiff's legal remedy is inadequate. This principle is also known as the "irreparable harm" requirement. The classic example of an "adequate legal remedy" involves items that are readily purchasable on the open market. For example, in *Fortner v. Wilson*, 202 Okla. 563, 216 P.2d 299 (1950), plaintiff agreed to purchase a Chevrolet automobile from a car dealership, but the dealer breached and refused to sell him the car. When plaintiff sued seeking specific performance, the Court refused to grant the remedy on the basis that Chevrolet automobiles are freely available on the open market. As a result, if plaintiff were awarded damages (calculated by determining the difference between the contract price and the fair market price of the automobile), he could purchase a comparable Chevrolet on the open market. In justifying the denial, the Court stated that a court of equity will not "specifically enforce a contract for the sale of ordinary articles of commerce, which can at all times be bought in the market, such as barroom fixtures, cattle, coal, corn, cotton, logs or lumber, pianos, sauerkraut, whisky, used cars, or an existing business and stock in trade, since the remedy at law for a breach of such contract is regarded as complete and adequate."

Of course, a plaintiff's injury will be regarded as "irreparable" when an award of damages will provide plaintiff with inadequate relief. Inadequacy can exist when the property that is the subject of a contract is "unique" so that plaintiff cannot readily purchase a substitute on the open market. Inadequacy can also exist in a variety of other situations such as when damages are difficult or impossible to calculate, when defendant is insolvent or it is otherwise impossible to collect a monetary judgment, or when plaintiff will be required to bring multiple proceedings to vindicate his rights. In addition, a legal remedy may be inadequate when the plaintiff's injury is of such a nature that the remedy of damages is substitutionary and ineffective. For example, suppose that plaintiff wishes to protest outside of the mayor's office, but is told to "leave or be arrested." Under such circumstances, an award of damages cannot replace fully replace and vindicate plaintiff's First Amendment rights and therefore would be regarded as inadequate.

Today, commentators debate whether it makes sense to maintain the historical requirement of inadequacy as a predicate to equitable relief. One reason for maintaining the requirement is illustrated by the *Fortner* case. If the car buyer can purchase an equivalent vehicle on the open market, a court might justifiably be reluctant to order specific performance. The parties are already at odds with each other. If they are ordered to continue to do business with each other, further disputes are not only possible but likely. If plaintiff can be satisfactorily compensated through a damage award, damages might be regarded as a preferable remedy.

In regard to contracts for the sale of goods, *Fortner's* rule was codified in Uniform Commercial Code, § 2–716, but relaxed a bit: "specific performance may be decreed where the goods are unique or in other proper circumstances." This provision has been interpreted to permit specific performance even though the goods are not unique in the strict sense, but are very scarce or cannot be replaced by alternative sources. *Copylease Corp. of America v. Memorex Corp.*, 408 F.Supp. 758 (S.D.N.Y.1976).

2. Equitable Remedies Continue to Be "*In Personam*" in Nature

Another historical distinction that survives today is the notion that "equity acts *in personam*." When a court renders an *in personam* judgment, it orders the defendant to do, or refrain from doing, some act. A defendant who refuses to comply can be held in contempt of court and subjected to imprisonment or fines. Indeed, in an appropriate case, defendant can be kept in jail until he agrees to comply.

By contrast, law courts historically entered monetary judgments. In other words, for example, they would enter decrees stating that defendant owes plaintiff a sum of money. Such judgments were not automatically enforceable and defendant could not be held in contempt for refusal to pay. On the contrary, plaintiff must try to place liens or attachments on defendant's property, and later to execute on those liens or attachments in order to satisfy the judgment. For example, if defendant is able to impose a lien on defendant's real property, the real estate can be sold and used to satisfy the judgment. Likewise, if defendant owns personal property, the sheriff can seize the property and sell it in satisfaction of the judgment.

Ordinarily, if a court is going to enjoin litigation in another court, it will not attempt to enjoin the other judge or the other court directly. Instead, it will enjoin the parties to the litigation. As at common law, if the party fails to comply (*e.g.*, he/she continues the litigation despite the injunction), he can be subjected to contempt sanctions. There are situations when courts will issue orders against other courts or against governmental officials. However, these orders usually fall under the court's authority to issue prerogative writs such as mandamus and prohibition. These common law writs will be discussed later in this book.

3. Equitable Remedies Continue to Be Based on Principles of "Conscience" and "Equity"

In applying equitable remedies, modern courts continue to assume that equitable relief should be governed by principles of "conscience," "equity," and "justice." However, unlike the early English kings and chancellors, modern judges are not as much "at large" in dispensing equity and justice. Over the centuries, a large body of maxims have been developed, as well as equitable precedent, all of which tends to limit (to a greater or lesser extent) judicial discretion.

Of course, the description of equitable remedies as being based on "conscience" is somewhat misleading. Courts of law have their own "rules of conscience" even though they do not label them as such. For example, we know that an ancient court of equity might have refused to specifically enforce a contract when the plaintiff's hands were unclean. A modern court, applying what might be regarded as "legal principles" might refuse to enforce a contract on "public policy" grounds.

In deciding whether a particular result is "conscionable" or "equitable," equity courts rely on the equitable maxims discussed earlier, as well as the chancellor's own sense of morality or justice. Many modern courts still use the maxims. But many commentators continue to question whether the maxims are consistent with each other, and whether they really provide the basis for judicial decisions, or simply a boilerplate justification. *See* Karl Llewellyn, *Remarks on the Theory of Appellate Decision and the Rules or Canons About How Statutes Are to be Construed*, 3 VAND. L. REV. 395 (1949).

4. Equitable Relief Continues to Be Discretionary

Another equitable principle that survives today is the notion that equitable relief is discretionary. Even if the plaintiff is suffering irreparable injury, and might otherwise have a valid claim to relief, a court has discretion to deny equitable relief.

For example, with some exceptions, modern courts will refuse to grant injunctive relief (an equitable remedy) when the decree would involve courts in continuing supervision of the parties and their activities. For this reason, courts are reluctant to enforce contracts requiring one person to perform personal services for someone else. As a result, if a star football player refuses to play for the team to which he is under contract, a court is unlikely to enter an order requiring him to play for the team. The player, by his refusal, has already indicated his unwillingness to play, and courts are reluctant to require involuntary servitude. In addition, if the court orders the player to return to the field, a variety of problems might result. Suppose, for example, that the player has a really bad game. Should the court regard the bad performance as just an "off day" or is it appropriate for the court to second guess and possibly impose contempt sanctions?

In a similar vein, modern courts are reluctant to enforce so-called "lights on" clauses. Some contracts for the lease of retail property require the lessee to pay rent (sometimes a percentage of sales), and also require that the lessee keep the "lights on" and the business operating. For lessors, especially lessors who operate large shopping centers, these "lights on" clauses are particularly important. A shopping center might give preferential terms to a department store (the anchor tenant) because it believes that the department store will attract lots of shoppers who will patronize other stores as well, and make the overall center much stronger (and, of course, if the lessor receives rent based on a percentage of sales, the Anchor Store increase the owner's take from the center). Correspondingly, if the department store closes, there will be a big hole in the center in the sense that a large tenant is now dark (lights off) and out of business. In the "lights on" situation, even if damages are difficult or impossible to ascertain, thereby rendering the legal remedy inadequate), courts may be reluctant to order the department store to remain open. Not uncommonly, when the owners of a department store decide to close, they are losing money. If a court orders the department store to remain open, there may be endless litigation about whether the store is being operated in compliance with the court order. For example, the shopping center owner may complain that the department store is not open for enough hours per day, that it is not maintaining sufficient (or sufficiently enticing) merchandise, and is not maintaining sufficient staffing. Courts frequently avoid this problem by refusing to grant specific performance of the lights on clause.

Grossman v. Wegman's Food Markets, Inc., 43 A.D.2d 813, 350 N.Y.S.2d 484 (1973), provides a good example of a situation where a court will refuse to grant injunctive relief. In that case, plaintiff sought an injunction requiring defendant to occupy leased premises and operate it as a retail grocery store. Because of the potential for additional disputes, the *Grossman* court denied plaintiff the requested relief noting that "courts of equity are reluctant to grant specific performance in situations where such performance would require judicial supervision over a long period of time." In a case like *Grossman v. Wegman's Food Markets*, a court might be inclined to grant "negative" relief. In other words, even though a court might not order the *Grossman* defendant to keep the store open, it might prohibit defendant from opening a competing nearby store.

Even though courts may be reluctant to enter injunctions that would require ongoing or continuing supervision, the reluctance does not lead to an absolute ban on continuing or supervisory injunctions. For example, courts have issued so-called "structural injunctions" which have involved the courts in regulating prison conditions and in desegregating public schools, and some of these decrees have remained in effect for many years and have required extensive judicial involvement. For example, in Jefferson County, Kentucky, where Louisville is located, the court maintained supervision over school desegregation for twenty-five years, dissolving school district lines and imposing mandatory busing. In Kansas City, Missouri, the court imposed a massive magnet school and capital improvements program at a cost of hundreds of millions of dollars. *See Missouri v. Jenkins*, 515 U.S. 70, 115 S.Ct. 2038, 132 L.Ed.2d 63 (1995). The court also ordered salary improvements for school district employees, the imposition of full-day kindergarten classes, expanded summer school options, before-and after-school tutoring, and an early childhood development program. The court ordered actions were so involved that they were once described as the "most ambitious and expensive remedial program in the history of school desegregation."

5. Balancing of Hardships & Public Interest

Frequently, courts will "balance the hardships," and will also consider the public interest, before deciding whether to grant equitable relief. For example, in *Boomer v. Atlantic Cement Co.*, 26 N.Y.2d 219, 257 N.E.2d 870, 309 N.Y.S.2d 312 (1970), plaintiff sought an injunction against a factory that caused noise and dust and interfered with the use and enjoyment of his home. Despite the fact that plaintiff was using his property as a residence, the court found that the surrounding area was more suited to a factory than a home, and emphasized that the factory provided badly needed jobs to the community. As a result, the court entered a so-called "conditional" or "compensated" injunction. In other words, although the court granted an injunction, it balanced the hardships and concluded that the injunction should be lifted if the factory paid permanent damages to the plaintiff. In other words, in return for the payment, the factory was given a permanent easement allowing it to continue creating noise and pollution at the same level. Likewise, suppose that a large municipal airport causes noise that interferes with nearby landowners' peaceful use and enjoyment of their property. Because of the airport's importance to the community, it is unlikely that a court will require the airport to shut down. If anything, the court might order the airport to alter its operation (*e.g.*, to limit takeoffs and landings to daylight hours and early evening hours, but not in the middle of the night).

In balancing the hardships, or in considering public policy, the issues are not always clear-cut. For example, in *Georg v. Animal Defense League*, 231 S.W.2d 807 (Tex.Civ.App.1950), a court refused to enjoin construction of an animal shelter even though the shelter would likely result in noise and annoyance to neighbors. The denial was based in part on the societal need for dog shelters, and the absence of a suitable alternative site that would not irritate others. It is not necessarily clear that the decision was correct. Another court might have placed much greater value on protecting the home against a private nuisance, and therefore might have been inclined to issue the injunction.

E. EQUITABLE DEFENSES

A number of common law equitable defenses were used historically, and are used today, to prevent an award of equitable relief. The major defenses are unclean hands, unconscionability, laches, and estoppel. All of these doctrines are grounded in equitable principles of conscience, justice and equity, and all reflect the idea that equitable relief is discretionary.

1. Clean Hands Doctrine

The "clean hands" doctrine (a/k/a the "unclean hands" doctrine) states that "he who comes to equity must come with clean hands." The doctrine involves two fundamental ideas: equitable relief is based on principles of conscience and it is discretionary. As such, equitable relief can be denied to those who have acted inequitably or unconscionably in relation to the matter before the court.

Perhaps the most famous unclean hands case, the *Highwaymen's Case,* involved two bandits who agreed to rob travelers and to split the profits. When one of the partners refused to share the profits on the agreed basis, the other sued for an accounting. The Chancellor, after invoking the unclean hands doctrine and dismissing the case, fined plaintiff's solicitors for contempt. *See Everet v. Williams*, Ex. (1725), 9 L.Q.Rev. 197 (1893). The Court concluded that neither bandit was entitled to equitable relief, and neither could call on a court of conscience to provide relief. Equity refused to allow itself to be used as a counting house for thieves.

The "clean hands" doctrine can be raised by a party as a bar to equitable relief, or can be raised by a court *sua sponte*. The doctrine applies to almost any conduct considered to be unfair, unethical or improper—including, of course, conduct that is illegal. However, the misconduct must be serious enough to justify withholding an equitable remedy that would otherwise be available, and thereby relegating plaintiff to her legal remedies.

When the clean hands doctrine is strictly applied, the doctrine can lead to potential inequities. For example, in the *Highwayman's Case*, since the court decided to leave the parties where it found them, then one of the robbers was left with a disproportionate share of the loot. Of even greater concern, the loot was not returned to those from whom it was stolen. Of course, if the judge had decided to divide the loot, he would have aided the robbers in the execution of their illegal scheme. Instead of helping sort out the situation, judges may try to prevent inequity by notifying the police or prosecutors about the parties' actions, and leave it the police try to find an effective solution.

Courts will generally refuse to apply the clean hands doctrine when the plaintiff's misconduct is unrelated to the transaction at hand. For example, even a convicted felon can obtain equitable relief when his criminal conduct is unrelated to the matter before the court *(e.g.,* one who is convicted of embezzlement from his employer might be able to obtain (at a later point) injunctive relief preventing a neighbor (unrelated to the employer or the embezzlement) from trespassing on his property).

In addition, courts will sometimes refuse to apply the doctrine when public policy considerations demand it. One of the classic cases is *Stewart v. Wright*, 147 Fed. 321 (8th Cir.1906). In that case, a gang of swindlers (the "Buckfoot Gang") arranged rigged footraces that were designed to swindle rich people (the "pigeons") out of their money. However, the swindlers cleverly enmeshed the pigeons in such a way that they were susceptible to the clean hands defense. They did so by telling the pigeons that the swindlers wanted to teach someone a lesson, and that they would do so by virtue of a rigged foot race that would allow the pigeons to win a lot of money at the other person's expense. Unfortunately for the pigeons, the races were rigged against them. When one of the pigeons sued, seeking restitution of his lost money, he was met with the clean hands defense. In *Stewart*, the court decided not to apply the clean hands doctrine, concluding that the swindlers were relatively more culpable than the pigeon, and that public policy considerations demanded that the swindlers be required to make restitution. Otherwise, the swindlers would have no incentive to discontinue their conduct.

2. Unconscionability

Since equity developed as a "court of conscience," courts have always exercised discretion to deny equitable relief on the grounds that one of the parties has acted "unconscionability." The doctrine is frequently applied when one party has entered into a harsh and unconscionable contract with another person, and then seeks to enforce the contract through equitable remedies. Courts also deny relief on discretionary grounds.

The holding in *Campbell Soup Co. v. Wentz*, 172 F.2d 80 (3d Cir.1948), involves a classic application of the unconscionability doctrine. In that case, the Campbell Soup Co. contracted to purchase all of the Chantenay red cored carrots being grown on a fifteen acre farm. The contract contained a clause prohibiting the farmer from selling the carrots to others even if they were rejected by Campbell Soup Co. In refusing to enforce the contract, the court stated that "We think that a party who has offered and succeeded in getting an agreement as tough as this one is, should not come to a chancellor and ask court help in the enforcement of its terms."

In addition to being recognized by the common law, the concept of "unconscionability" is codified in UCC § 2–302:

> (1) If a court as a matter of law finds the contract or any term of the contract to have been unconscionable at the time it was made the court may refuse to enforce the contract, or it may enforce the remainder of the contract without the unconscionable term, or it may so limit the application of any unconscionable terms as to avoid any unconscionable result.

> (2) [If] any term [may] be unconscionable [the] parties shall be afforded a reasonable opportunity to present evidence as to its commercial setting, purpose and effect to aid the court in making the determination. UCC § 2–302 (May 2001 proposed revision).

Although the term "unconscionable" is not defined, the UCCs comments offer some clarification: "The principle is one of the prevention of oppression and unfair surprise (*Cf. Campbell Soup Co. v. Wentz*) and not of disturbance of allocation of risks because of superior bargaining power." UCC § 2–302 comment 1.

3. Laches

A third defense that can be used to defeat an equitable claim is the defense of "laches." Laches is associated with the maxim: "Equity aids the vigilant not those who slumber on their rights." Broadly defined, laches involves any unreasonable delay by the plaintiff in instituting or prosecuting an action under circumstances where the delay causes prejudice to the defendant. *See e.g.*, RESTATEMENT SECOND OF TORTS § 939 (1977). The laches defense is applied today in many different types of cases, but particularly in tort and contract cases.

At common law, laches served as the equitable "statute of limitations." Historically, legislatively imposed statutes of limitations were applied only to legal actions and not to equitable actions. Equity courts used "laches" principles to limit the availability of equitable claims. However, the defense of laches functioned quite differently than the statutory statute of limitations. Whereas the statute of limitations was set at a specified and definite period of time, after which an action could no longer be maintained, laches was not tied to a specific period of time. The focus under laches was on "unreasonable delay" and "prejudice" both of which can occur prior to the expiration of the statute of limitations, or, for that matter, much later.

Modern courts consider a variety of factors in deciding whether to apply the laches doctrine. For example, in a case involving specific enforcement of a contract to sell land, a court might consider whether the land's value has remained stable or has been volatile. If there is volatility, plaintiff's delay might be considered unreasonable, and defendant might be able to make a stronger claim of prejudice. As a result, in such a case, laches might run in a much shorter period than under the legal statute of limitations. On the other hand, if land prices have been very stable, laches might run much more slowly than the statute of limitations. Deciding whether the laches doctrine applies, a reviewing court will necessarily consider whether defendant has been prejudiced by the passage of time—as by the loss of witnesses or other evidence.

In some cases, laches might come into play relatively more quickly. Suppose, for example, that plaintiff seeks specific performance of a highly perishable product (*e.g.*, tomatoes). In an ordinary case, courts might be disinclined to specifically enforce such a contract because tomatoes are usually available on the open market, and plaintiff's legal remedy (damages) is usually adequate. But, even when specific performance might be available (because tomatoes are not available on the open market), laches is likely to run quickly. The market for tomatoes can fluctuate significantly in relatively short periods of time, and defendant is more likely to suffer prejudice if plaintiff delays in seeking specific performance.

4. Estoppel

Estoppel is a defense that can be used in both offensive and defensive ways. In general, estoppel applies when defendant made a promise (explicitly or implicitly) to plaintiff on which plaintiff reasonably relied to her detriment. Estoppel operates to prevent defendant from acting inconsistently with the promise.

The doctrines of promissory estoppel and equitable estoppel are very different. Equitable estoppel is purely a remedial device which, when applicable, precludes equitable relief and relegates plaintiff instead to legal remedies. Even when laches applies, plaintiff's cause of action may still be alive. Promissory estoppel, on the other hand, is a substantive cause of action which permits foreseeable reliance to substitute for consideration and thereby supply the basis for a breach of contract action. *Feinberg v. Pfeiffer Co.*, 322 S.W.2d 163 (Mo.App.1959), provides the classic example of promissory estoppel. In that case, a company promised a pension to a long and faithful employee when and if she retired. After she retired in reliance on the promise, the employer reneged on the promise. The court held that the company was "estopped" from refusing to pay the pension because the employee had reasonably relied on the promise to her detriment, and would suffer detriment if the promise were not honored.

Although an estoppel claim is conceptually different from a laches claim, laches and estoppel share similarities. Estoppel assumes that plaintiff (or defendant depending on whether the estoppel is offensive or defensive) made misrepresentations on which the other party relied. Although both defenses require a showing of prejudice, estoppel does not necessarily require the passage of time.

Historically, courts have refused to apply the doctrine of estoppel against the government. Some later cases have relaxed this prohibition and suggest a greater inclination to apply estoppel principles against the government.

F. THE RIGHT TO TRIAL BY JURY

Historical distinctions between law and equity are also important because of the right to trial by jury. The Seventh Amendment to the United States Constitution guarantees the right to trial by jury "[i]n suits at common law, where the value in controversy shall exceed twenty dollars." The Seventh Amendment is reinforced by Rule 38 of the Federal Rules of Civil Procedure which provides that: "The right of trial by jury as declared by the Seventh Amendment to the Constitution or as given by a statute of the United States shall be preserved to the parties inviolate." Although the Seventh Amendment only applies to federal proceedings, many state constitutions also guarantee the right to a jury trial.

Most jury trial provisions "preserve" the right to jury trial as it existed at the time they were adopted. As a general rule, when the Seventh Amendment was adopted in 1791, equity cases were tried to a judge while legal cases were tried to a jury. As a result, on a simplistic level, if the right to jury trial is preserved as it stood in 1791, then a court must seek to ascertain whether a claim was regarded as legal or equitable at that time, and whether it would have been tried to a jury. If it was equitable, no right to jury trial exists.

But a simple distinction between "equity" and "law" is not always determinative. For example, a breach of contract case might have been tried either at law or in equity at common law depending on how it arose. Suppose, for example, that a buyer contracted to purchase an antique piece of furniture from a furniture dealer, but the dealer (seller) breached the contract. If the buyer sought specific performance, and the request were granted, then the matter would have been tried in equity. Moreover, equity would have decided all of the issues, including the following: Was there a contract? What were its terms? Was the contract breached? Should specific performance be granted? Of course, had buyer sought damages rather than specific performance, all of these issues except the last one ("Should specific performance be granted?") would have been decided at law without a jury. If the law court had determined that buyer was entitled to damages, it would also have determined the amount.

Common law practice was also qualified by the so-called "equitable clean-up" doctrine. Under that doctrine, when legal and equitable issues were combined in the same case, and the legal issues were "incidental" to the equitable issues, the equity court could resolve both the legal and equitable issues. In other words, even though a case involved a request for damages, an equity court might decide all of the issues without a jury.

Similar problems would have arisen if two separate cases were filed in law and in equity. Suppose, for example, that buyer contracts to purchase 10 bushels of wheat from seller at 1 pound of British Sterling per bushel. However, the parties draft the contract incorrectly, and erroneously provide that buyer agrees to pay 10 pounds of British Sterling per bushel for all 10 bushels of wheat. Suppose, also, that buyer refuses to comply with the erroneous contract, and seller files suit in a court of law seeking to compel payment as per the written terms. If the case were tried solely at law, then the matter would have been tried without a jury, and the law court would have decided all of the relevant issues. Was there a contract? What were its terms? Was there a breach? Is plaintiff entitled to damages? If so, in what amount? Moreover, since early law courts did not consider requests for reformation of contracts, the law court would have rejected buyer's claims that the contract should be reformed.

At common law, the buyer might have thwarted the law action by filing a request for reformation of the contract in a court of equity. In order to prevent the law court from going to judgment before the equity court could decide the case, the buyer (equity plaintiff) might have sought injunctive relief prohibiting the seller (the equity defendant/law plaintiff) from proceeding with the law case. If the buyer had prevailed in the equity action, the contract would have been "reformed" and the seller would have been ordered to proceed based on the reformed contract in the law case. In other words, the equity court would have decided many of the basic issues. Was there a contract? What were its terms? Should the contract be reformed? If the parties refused to settle at that point, the remaining issues would have been decided in a court of law. Was there a breach of the contract? If so, what damages should seller receive? Of course, in an appropriate case, the equity court might have refused to reform the contract. If that had happened, the matter would have returned to the law court which would have decided all of the issues. As the foregoing analysis reveals, the method by which a case would have been tried at common law (whether in law or in equity) depended in important respects on context.

Applied literally, the Seventh Amendment would have required an exclusively historical analysis of 1791 law in order to decide whether a party had a right to a jury trial at that time. As the year 1791 became more distant, and as the federal courts and most state courts merged their law and equity courts into a single system, that task became increasingly difficult. As time passed, fewer and fewer modern judges were knowledgeable regarding Eighteenth Century procedural practices, and few were equipped to adequately research those issues.

In construing the Seventh Amendment, in *Dairy Queen, Inc. v. Wood*, 369 U.S. 469, 82 S.Ct. 894, 8 L.Ed.2d 44 (1962), the United States Supreme Court adopted a pragmatic approach which largely obviated the need for historical research. *Dairy Queen* held that "where both legal and equitable issues are presented in a single case, 'only under the most imperative circumstances, circumstances which in view of the flexible procedures of the Federal Rules we cannot now anticipate, can the right to a jury trial of legal issues be lost through prior determination of equitable claims.' " As result, *Dairy Queen* abolished the equitable clean-up doctrine (which suggested that, if equitable issues predominate over the legal issues in a case, a reviewing court can "clean up" the legal issues after it resolves the equitable ones). The net effect is that any legal issues, for which a trial by jury is timely and properly demanded, must be submitted to a jury.

Dairy Queen also held that trial courts may reassign claims from legal to equitable. In that case, petitioner brought an action for an accounting. Even though a claim for an accounting would have been an equitable claim at common law, the court concluded that the suit could also have been framed as a claim for debt, a "legal" claim at common law. Since equitable relief is generally unavailable except when the legal claim is inadequate, and since the plaintiff's claim could be recharacterized as one for debt, the Court concluded that the claim should be treated as legal (a claim for debt) rather than equitable (equitable accounting). *Dairy Queen* is regarded as a creating a strong, pro-jury, legal claim first approach.

In *Ross v. Bernhard*, 396 U.S. 531, 90 S.Ct. 733, 24 L.Ed.2d 729 (1970), the Court rendered an additional pro-jury opinion, and seemed to suggest that cases involving requests for damages (as opposed to *in personam* relief) would be subject to the right to trial by jury. In that case, petitioners brought a shareholders derivative action. At common law, a derivative action would have been purely equitable and would have been tried before a judge. Nevertheless, because the underlying claims were legal and there would have been a right to jury trial had the corporation itself brought those claims, the Court held that the right to jury trial applied. Some have construed *Ross* as creating a broad right to trial by jury for any claim involving damages as opposed to *in personam* relief.

Neither *Dairy Queen* nor *Ross* resolved all potential issues relating to the right to trial by jury. One question that came up afterwards is whether a right to jury trial exists for causes of action based on legislation. Strictly speaking, if a particular statute did not exist in 1791 (which is likely to be the case), one can argue that the Seventh Amendment does not require a trial by jury. In other words, there is no antecedent right to trial by jury to be preserved. On the other hand, if the statute merely codifies a common law claim as to which there was a trial by jury, or supplants a common law right, one can argue that the Seventh Amendment still requires a jury trial.

Curtis v. Loether, 415 U.S. 189, 94 S.Ct. 1005, 39 L.Ed.2d 260 (1974), involved section 812 of the Civil Rights Act of 1968 which allowed private plaintiffs to bring civil suits seeking redress for violations of the Civil Rights Act of 1968. The Act authorized the trial court to award various types of relief including damages and injunctive relief, and the *Curtis* plaintiff sought compensatory and punitive damages, as well as injunctive relief. The United States Supreme Court overruled the trial court's denial of respondent's demand for a jury trial, holding that "although the thrust of the Amendment was to preserve the right to jury trial as it existed in 1791, it has long been settled that the right extends beyond the common-law forms of action recognized at that time." The Court rejected petitioner's argument that the Seventh Amendment is inapplicable "to new causes of action created by congressional enactment" noting that the Seventh Amendment applies "to actions enforcing statutory rights, and requires a jury trial upon demand, if the statute creates legal rights and remedies, enforceable in an action for damages in the ordinary courts of law." The Court concluded that § 812 created "legal rights" because it sounded basically in tort.

Even if a statute does not fit within the *Curtis* analysis, so that a right to jury trial is required, Congress may choose to provide a right to jury trial. In deciding whether Congress has chosen to impose a right to jury trial under a given statute, the question is one of congressional intent. *Lorillard v. Pons*, 434 U.S. 575, 98 S.Ct. 866, 55 L.Ed.2d 40 (1978). However, there are limits to Congress' power. In *Lehman v. Nakshian*, 453 U.S. 156, 101 S.Ct. 2698, 69 L.Ed.2d 548 (1981), the Court held that a jury trial was not available under the Age Discrimination in Employment Act (ADEA) (in a suit against the U.S. government) even though the Act authorized suits for "such legal or equitable relief as will effectuate the purposes of this Act." The Court held that "the United States, as sovereign, 'is immune from suit save as it consents to be sued and the terms of its consent to be sued in any court define that court's jurisdiction to entertain the suit.'" *United States v. Mitchell*, 445 U.S. 535, 538, 100 S.Ct. 1349, 1352, 63 L.Ed.2d 607 (1980), *quoting United States v. King*, 395 U.S. 1, 4, 89 S.Ct. 1501, 1502, 23 L.Ed.2d 52 (1969).

Although the Seventh Amendment preserves the right to trial by jury, Rule 38 of the Federal Rules of Civil Procedure requires that a party who seeks a jury trial must demand it in writing. Failure to make the demand can constitute a waiver of the right.

The demand must be made no later than 10 days after the service of the last pleading directed to such issue. In the demand a party may specify the issues which the party wishes so tried; otherwise the party shall be deemed to have demanded trial by jury for all the issues so triable.

Chapter Three

CONTEMPT

Contempt is the enforcement mechanism for equitable orders. The maxim "equity acts in personam" refers to the nature of an equitable decree as a personal directive. Disobedience is punishable as contempt if the order was a specifically detailed, unequivocal judicial command and if the defendant had the ability to obey the order. For example, if a court orders a parent to pay a specific amount of child support at a specific time, the failure to do so is punishable as contempt if the parent has the financial resources or the ability to earn money to pay.

The use of contempt to enforce equitable decrees is fundamentally different in nature from the enforcement of judgments issued by courts sitting at law. Whereas the failure to pay a judgment entered at law can result in the court executing against the property of the defendant, the disobedience of an equitable order can result in the incarceration of the defendant. The failure to pay a judgment at law will not result in the loss of personal freedom; if the defendant has no assets to pay the judgment, then there are no consequences because the person is said to be "judgment-proof." In contrast, one has an obligation to obey orders issued by a court sitting in equity. An equitable order is personal and the defendant may be fined, jailed, or civilly liable for the failure to obey.

A. TYPES OF CONTEMPT

Contempt of court is defined in a leading historical treatise as an "act of disobedience or disrespect" toward a judicial body "or interference with its orderly process, for which a summary punishment is usually exacted." Ronald L. Goldfarb, The Contempt Power 1 (1963). There are two basic types of contempt which differ in form and function: criminal contempt and civil contempt. The primary function of criminal contempt is to vindicate the interest of the state in obedience to court orders. The primary function of civil contempt is to benefit the plaintiff for whose benefit the court issued the order.

Further, there are two types of criminal contempt. The subclassifications are: direct (or summary) and indirect (or constructive) criminal contempt. Direct criminal contempt is the judge's tool to maintain order in the courtroom and to punish disruptive behavior by attorneys, parties, or spectators. It also vindicates the court's authority by summarily punishing any disruption of the orderly administration of proceedings. In contrast, indirect contempt concerns disobedience that occurs outside the courtroom. When a defendant fails to produce documents or refuses to return property as directed by the court, for example, the judge can punish the contemnor if the conduct was willful.

Civil contempt also has two subclassifications: compensatory civil contempt and coercive civil contempt. In contrast to the public function of criminal contempt, the function of civil contempt is to benefit the plaintiff's private interests. Whereas criminal contempt serves to vindicate the state's interest in obedience, civil contempt provides a remedy for the individual litigant to coerce obedience (coercive civil contempt) or to compensate for losses occasioned by disobedience (compensatory civil contempt).

Both criminal and civil contempt are discretionary. A judge is not required to punish contemptuous behavior and may choose to ignore the conduct or to use another sanction if appropriate, such as Rule 11. Alternatively, a court may simply issue a warning or may make a public or private rebuke. For example, in *United States v. Koubriti*, 305 F.Supp.2d 723 (E.D.Mich.2003), the court found that John Ashcroft, then the United States Attorney General, had violated a gag order prohibiting the attorneys and parties from commenting publicly on the trial of men found in the company of terrorists following the September 11, 2001, attacks on the country. The Attorney General said erroneously at two separate press briefings that the men on trial were suspects in the 9/11 attack on the World Trade Center, although such charges were never brought against them. The court distinguished between the dual roles of the Attorney General—the prosecutorial role and the political one—and choose not to pursue contempt charges but only to make a formal and public admonishment of his violation of the gag order.

B. DIRECT (SUMMARY) CRIMINAL CONTEMPT

Direct criminal contempt, also called summary criminal contempt, is used to maintain order in the courtroom. A judge may punish a variety of disruptive behavior with this tool. When someone in the courtroom—an attorney, party, spectator, or other person—is disrespectful or disruptive, the judge may punish willful conduct summarily with direct contempt. The purpose of this powerful tool is to protect the dignity of the court and to maintain the orderly administration of the proceedings.

The basis of a federal court's power to punish behavior with direct contempt is 18 U.S.C. § 401(1). That section provides:

A court of the United States shall have power to punish by fine or imprisonment, at its discretion, such contempt of its authority, and none other, as—

(1) Misbehavior of any person in its presence or so near thereto as to obstruct the administration of justice; * * *

State courts have inherent power to punish contempt but often derive power from statutes as well. For example, Arkansas law provides that state courts may punish "persons guilty of disorderly, contemptuous, or insolent behavior committed during the court's sitting, in its immediate view and presence, and directly tending to interrupt its proceedings or to impair the respect due to its authority." Arkansas courts have concluded that the principal justification for this provision "lies in the need for upholding public confidence in the majesty of the law and in the integrity of the judicial system." *McCullough v. State*, 353 Ark. 362, 366–67, 108 S.W.3d 582 (2003). Another court described the foundation of the contempt power as "the need to protect the judicial process from willful impositions, particularly those designed to hobble the normal machinery of justice." *In re Brown,* 454 F.2d 999, 1007 (D.C.Cir.1971).

1.   Obstruction of the Administration of Justice

One basis for imposing direct contempt is behavior that is disrespectful to the judge or the court that occurs in the courtroom and in the presence of the judge. The nature of the proceeding before the court does not matter.

Even though a judge might regard conduct as disrespectful does not mean that the judge may necessarily treat it as contemptuous. In *In re McConnell*, 370 U.S. 230, 82 S.Ct. 1288, 8 L.Ed.2d 434 (1962), the United States Supreme Court held that ardent advocacy by an attorney for a client is not alone sufficient for contempt. In *McConnell*, even though the judge warned an attorney to desist, he continued to demand that the judge rule on an issue. The Court concluded that the attorney acted in good faith in an attempt to preserve the issue for appeal.

Not all such courtroom arguments are protected. When a judge has already ruled against an objection, an attorney might be held in contempt for continuing to argue despite the judge's order to desist even if the attorney's speech is not aggressive or unrestrained. For example, *McCullough v. State*, 353 Ark. 362, 108 S.W.3d 582 (2003), upheld a contempt sanction in this context despite the attorney's argument that the judge was more disrespectful than the attorney during their exchange. The court concluded that it is the attorney's behavior that is relevant, and the focus should be on whether the attorney was disrespectful to the court. However, if the judge's conduct reveals personal animosity towards the lawyer, rather than just a heated exchange, the judge should appoint another judge to determine the appropriate sanction for the lawyer's contempt. *See Offutt v. United States*, 348 U.S. 11, 75 S.Ct. 11, 99 L.Ed. 11 (1954).

Contempt sanctions might also be imposed for other types of conduct that obstruct the administration of justice. For example, if an attorney, party or other person in the courtroom, prevents the proceeding from going forward, the obstructor can be held in contempt. Interruptions or other disruptive behavior are classical examples. Another form of obstruction is the refusal to testify under circumstances that are not protected, such as refusing to give witness even after one has been granted immunity from prosecution.

Willfulness is a necessary element of criminal contempt, including direct contempt. When an attorney persists in courtroom behavior that the judge finds disruptive, it is not contempt unless the judge places the attorney on notice to discontinue the behavior. In the absence of such notice, either through a warning or other means, the conduct is not willful. Thus, when a defense attorney continues to refer to the original complaint even after the judge has ruled that an amended complaint supersedes the original one, it is not contempt unless the attorney is warned or otherwise has facts that would reasonably lead one to know that the judge has forbidden the discussion. *Doral Produce Corp. v. Paul Steinberg Associates*, 347 F.3d 36 (2d Cir.2003).

2. Disrespectful Behavior

A judge may employ direct contempt to punish behavior that is disrespectful even if the conduct does not interfere with or delay court proceedings. Although *In re McConnell*, 370 U.S. 230, 82 S.Ct. 1288, 8 L.Ed.2d 434 (1962), involved in the use of direct contempt to punish the obstruction of justice, other courts have permitted direct contempt in cases where the misbehavior did not delay proceedings but was simply disrespectful

As with its use to punish obstruction of justice in the courtroom, direct contempt is not the correct tool for disrespectful conduct unless the behavior occurs in the courtroom and in the presence of the judge. In such cases, the judge essentially acts as witness and jury. As a result, the "in the presence" of the court standard is a high one, especially in federal court. It is not sufficient if the judge hears about the conduct indirectly, although federal courts have tended to interpret that requirement more strictly than some state courts.

A variety of forms of disrespectful behavior by attorneys and litigants may be punished. In one case, for example, a defendant was being sentenced before the judge after he had been convicted of a violent robbery. When the defendant was asked if he had any comments, he lashed out against the criminal justice system and suggested that he would get the maximum because he didn't have money to bribe the judge. The defendant also made foul suggestions about what the judge and the judge's wife could do to him sexually. In that case, *United States v. Marshall*, 371 F.3d 42 (2d Cir.2004), the court held that such behavior by a litigant could be summarily punished even without a warning. Although warnings are normally used before a finding of contempt, the defendant's verbal attack on the court was sufficiently severe that the court could punish it by contempt without prior warning.

A trial judge can punish as direct contempt an attorney's refusal to sit down, refusal to approach the bench, repeated in-court statements that the proceeding is unfair or that the judge is untrustworthy. Such conduct, and such statements, constitute an affront to the court's dignity and authority. Behavior that affronts the court's dignity out of court, however, can be indirect contempt (examined in the next section of this chapter). Thus, an attorney's failure to return to court after recess is indirect contempt whereas pejorative statements made about the proceedings in court right before the recess are punishable as direct contempt. *People v. L.A.S.*, 111 Ill.2d 539, 96 Ill.Dec. 66, 490 N.E.2d 1271 (1986).

3. "In the Presence" of the Court

Direct contempt requires the conduct to be in the presence of the judge. This language is used expressly in the statutory authorization for contempt in the federal courts. Section 401(1) refers to the "presence" or the court "or so near thereto to obstruct the administration of justice." 18 U.S.C. § 401(1). In state courts, it is part of the court's inherent power to punish misbehavior in the presence of the judge.

The procedures for a conviction of direct criminal contempt in federal court are governed by Rule 42(a). That rule states: "A criminal contempt may be punished summarily if the judge certifies that the judge saw or heard the conduct constituting the contempt and that it was committed in the actual presence of the court. The order of contempt shall recite the facts and shall be signed by the judge and entered of record."

Courts have sometimes attempted to punish attorneys or parties with direct contempt for disrespectful conduct that occurs outside the courtroom if it is still in the presence of the judge. Although such behavior may be indirect contempt, a finding of direct contempt requires that the behavior occur *inside* the courtroom. In one interesting case, *Ramirez v. State*, 279 Ga. 13, 608 S.E.2d 645 (2005), an attorney violated a gag order concerning a death penalty case when he called into a radio station talk show that was discussing the case. The judge was listening to the radio and held the attorney in contempt. The judge wrongly characterized the contempt as direct contempt on the grounds that he heard the show personally. The contempt was reversed on appeal on the grounds that, although it may have obstructed justice, the conduct did not occur in the presence of the court.

The strict construction of "in the presence" of the court by federal courts is illustrated by *Matter of Contempt of Greenberg*, 849 F.2d 1251 (9th Cir.1988). In that case, the federal judge and an attorney had a dispute about a ruling and the attorney slammed a hand in anger on the counsel table. The judge did not certify that he had actually seen the slamming of the hand, but he cited the attorney for direct contempt. The conviction was reversed on appeal on the ground that the federal judge's failure to see attorney slam book made direct contempt inappropriate.

The *Greenberg* case contrasts with a state court contempt finding in *Ex parte Daniels,* 722 S.W.2d 707 (Tex.Cr.App.1987). In this case a judge had instructed the bailiff to remove a litigant. She went quietly until they got to the door and then she physically attacked the bailiff. The bailiff then struggled to restrain her and there was a sound of disruption in the back of courtroom. The litigant appealed the ensuing finding of contempt on the grounds that the disturbance was far from state judge's physical location behind the bench. The state court disagreed and said that the behavior has to be in the "presence" of the court but not necessarily the "immediate presence." The judge's personal knowledge of the event was sufficient for direct contempt. It is unlikely that these facts would support a finding of direct contempt in federal court under 18 U.S.C. § 401(1).

An older state court case that has perhaps the most curious construction of "in the presence of the court" standard is found in *People v. Higgins,* 173 Misc. 96, 16 N.Y.S.2d 302 (1939). In that case a male deputy sheriff and a woman juror had a private sexual encounter that interfered with jury deliberations. This act was found to be a criminal contempt in the "immediate view and presence" of the court. Both state and federal courts are unlikely to uphold a finding of direct contempt under these facts today.

C. INDIRECT (CONSTRUCTIVE) CRIMINAL CONTEMPT

Indirect criminal contempt is the second type of criminal contempt. In contrast to "direct" contempt that occurs inside the courtroom, this type of contempt is called "indirect" because it concerns behavior that occurs outside the courtroom. The behavior is frequently referred to as "constructive contempt" because it occurs outside of court.

1. Function and Source of Judicial Power

Indirect contempt is regarded as criminal rather than civil when its purpose is to protect the integrity of the court by ensuring respect for and obedience of its orders. In other words, contempt is imposed to punish conduct that constitutes an affront to the court when a lawful order is disobeyed. In the situation of *Ramirez v. State*, 279 Ga. 13, 608 S.E.2d 645 (2005), the proper tool for the court to use in redressing the violation of its gag order by calling the radio talk show was indirect criminal contempt. The failure of the court to have a proper hearing foreclosed that conviction, however.

Courts have inherent power to punish violation of their orders. In federal court, the statutory power is 18 U.S.C. § 401(3) which provides:

> A court of the United States shall have power to punish by fine or imprisonment, at its discretion, such contempt of its authority, and none other, as—
>
> * * *
>
> (3) Disobedience or resistance to its lawful writ, process, order, rule, decree, or command.

Although the primary function of criminal contempt is the state's interest in the dignity and authority of the court, there is a secondary benefit for plaintiffs. Plaintiffs benefit because the threat of indirect criminal contempt deters defendants from violating the court order that was granted for their benefit. When a court orders a defendant parent to pay child support, for example, the threat of indirect criminal contempt provides an incentive for that parent to pay.

2. Specificity Requirement

A finding of indirect criminal contempt requires first that there be a valid order issued by a court of competent jurisdiction requiring the defendant to act or refrain from acting in a certain manner and that the defendant had notice of the specific terms of the order. The specificity requirement for the framing of injunctive orders is contained in Federal Rule of Civil Procedure 65(d): "Every order granting an injunction * * * shall be specific in terms [and] shall describe in reasonable detail, and not by reference to the complaint or other document, the act or acts sought to be restrained[.] * * * "

The lack of a specific order is illustrated by *In re Stewart*, 571 F.2d 958 (5th Cir.1978). In that case, a federal district court judge presided over a jury trial in a matter unrelated to the contempt case. One of the jurors in that case told the judge that he had been demoted at work because he had been on jury duty. The judge believed the juror and told him to inform his supervisor that the judge would not tolerate the demotion of a citizen as a penalty for being on jury duty. The juror repeated this "order" to his supervisor. The supervisor, Stewart, disputed whether the juror had been demoted or simply reassigned, and stated that his action was unrelated to the absence for jury duty. The juror reported this reply to the judge who then held Stewart in contempt.

Among the defects in this finding of contempt was the lack of any specificity in the order. A criminal contempt finding based upon 18 U.S.C. § 401(3) must be premised upon the violation of an identifiable court order. That order must be sufficiently specific that the defendant has an opportunity to know that his behavior is disobedience.

Contempt requires the disobedience of a clear and unambiguous order to give notice of the conduct that may support contempt. In *Gucci America, Inc. v. Weixing Li,* 768 F.3d 122 (2d Cir.2014), for example, a district court wrongly found a bank in contempt for failure to comply fully with a subpoena for documents concerning certain "defendants' accounts." The original complaint had included some "John Does" defendants and was later amended to include names. This change created an ambiguity in the term "defendant." The opinion explains that a party must be able to ascertain from the "four corners" of the order what it must do, and thus the resulting contempt could not stand.

3.   Federal Rules of Criminal Procedure Requirements

Federal courts must follow Federal Rule of Criminal Procedure 42 for a conviction of criminal contempt. Rule 42(a) governs direct contempt, as previously noted. Rule 42(b) covers indirect criminal contempt hearings.

Under Rule 42(b) the notice "shall state the time and place of hearing, allow a reasonable time for the preparation of the defense, and shall state the essential facts constituting the criminal contempt charged and describe it as such." Rule 42(b) also provides: "If the contempt charged involves disrespect to or criticism of a judge, that judge is disqualified from presiding at the trial or hearing except with the defendant's consent." Contrast this provision with Rule 42(a), discussed in the last section, that requires for direct contempt that the judge "certifies that the judge saw or heard the conduct constituting the contempt and that it was committed in the actual presence of the court."

4. Constitutional Requirements

It is also necessary to a finding of indirect criminal contempt that the defendant intentionally or willfully disobeyed the order without a justifiable excuse such as the inability to comply. For example, a judge cannot hold an insolvent defendant in contempt for the failure to make scheduled child support payments unless the defendant willfully refused to seek reasonable employment and then claimed inability to meet the court-ordered payments.

The Supreme Court held in *Bloom v. Illinois*, 391 U.S. 194, 88 S.Ct. 1477, 20 L.Ed.2d 522 (1968), that indirect criminal contempt is a "crime in the ordinary sense." Subsequent cases from the Court have further clarified that criminal penalties for contempt may only be imposed on someone who has been afforded the Constitutional protections for criminal proceedings. Constitutional protections for defendants accused of criminal contempt apply only to indirect criminal contempt—disobedience of a court's order outside the presence of the court—and not to direct contempts.

The Constitutional safeguards for indirect contempt include: the privilege against self-incrimination, the right to a jury trial, the right to proof beyond a reasonable doubt and the right to present a defense. Other rights that apply include double jeopardy, notice of charges, assistance of counsel, and summary process. A federal court's failure to provide Constitutional safeguards, or to follow rules of criminal procedure, is a ground for reversal of a conviction of indirect criminal contempt. This ground frequently arises when the judge erroneously labels the contempt as civil rather than criminal and thereby fails to follow criminal procedures. It is the nature and purpose of the contempt that controls the requirements rather than its label.

5. The Duty to Obey

People who are bound by a court order must either obey the order or seek its dissolution through proper judicial channels. It is not permissible to wait until a contempt hearing to challenge the court's order in the first place. The Supreme Court established this principle in its famous opinion in *Walker v. City of Birmingham*, 388 U.S. 307, 87 S.Ct. 1824, 18 L.Ed.2d 1210 (1967). That case involved a civil rights demonstration in Alabama for racial integration of public places. The demonstration took place prior to the passage of the Civil Rights Act of 1964, which prohibits segregation in public accommodations as a matter of federal law. When the organizers of a demonstration announced their intention to hold protest marches on Easter week-end, city officials became fearful of the possibility of violence that prior civil rights marches of that era had evoked. As a result, city officials obtained an *ex parte* order from a state court judge prohibiting the organizers from violating a city ordinance that imposed a parade permit requirement for street demonstrations.

After being served with the order, the organizers issued a press statement indicating that they would not be intimidated by the "raw tyranny" of the court and that the protests would go forward as scheduled. After they held the demonstration as planned despite the order against it, the trial court held the organizers in criminal contempt.

The demonstration's organizers appealed based on the unconstitutionality of the order. The United States Supreme Court rejected the argument on the following basis: "This Court cannot hold that the petitioners were constitutionally free to ignore all the procedures of the law and carry their battle to the streets. One may sympathize with the petitioners' impatient commitment to their cause. But respect for judicial process is a small price to pay for the civilizing hand of law, which alone can give abiding meaning to Constitutional freedom." *Walker v. City of Birmingham*, 388 U.S. 307, 321, 87 S.Ct. 1824, 18 L.Ed.2d 1210 (1967). The Court noted that the case was not a situation where the petitioners had attempted to seek dissolution and were met with frustration. Nor did the case involve a situation in which the order lacked any pretense to validity or was "transparently invalid." Because of the *Walker* principle, it is not possible to attack an order collaterally by violating it and then challenging its validity in the contempt hearing.

6. Persons Bound

Because the *Walker* principle does not permit collateral attack of a court order, it is particularly important to discern which individuals are bound by it. Federal Rule of Civil Procedure 65(d) provides that an injunction is binding upon the parties to the action, their officers, agents, servants, employees, and attorneys, and upon "other persons who are in active concert or participation with them" who receive "actual notice of [the order] by personal service or otherwise."

The Supreme Court has interpreted this rule to include not only party defendants but those in privity with them, as well as those who aid and abet them. For example, in *Golden State Bottling Co. v. NLRB*, 414 U.S. 168, 94 S.Ct. 414, 38 L.Ed.2d 388 (1973), a bona fide purchaser of a company who acquired it with knowledge that an order to remedy an unfair labor practice had not been fulfilled may be considered in privity with its predecessor for purposes of Rule 65(d).

The federal courts have generally been careful not to read Rule 65(d) expansively. As the Seventh Circuit famously observed: "Rule 65(d) is no mere extract from a manual of procedural practice. It is a page from the book of liberty." *H.K. Porter Co. v. National Friction Products*, 568 F.2d 24, 27 (7th Cir.1977). For example, a federal court could not issue an injunction against trespass that purported to bind the world at large. *Kean v. Hurley*, 179 F.2d 888 (8th Cir.1950). Such an injunction exceeds the scope of Rule 65(d). Further, such an approach functionally turns a court into a legislature because the injunction then acts like a statute, which can bind the world at large.

In contrast, many state courts have been more willing to bind nonparties to an injunction and to find them in contempt for violation of the order when they have notice. One extreme example is *Silvers v. Traverse*, 82 Iowa 52, 47 N.W. 888 (1891), in which the court granted an injunction barring sale of alcohol on certain property and applied it to all the world. Under this order, a nonparty, who was completely unrelated to the defendant, was held in contempt for selling liquor on the premises. Similarly, a few state court opinions have taken the extreme position that once jurisdiction is acquired over the *res,* an order can protect the *res* against all, such as an injunction against trespass on a parcel of land. *See State v. Porter*, 76 Kan. 411, 91 P. 1073 (1907); *State v. Terry*, 99 Wash. 1, 168 P. 513 (1917). In such cases, courts have relied on their inherent power to preserve their orders.

Although the extreme cases obligating nonparties to obey an order have tended to come from the state courts, there is one famous example of a federal court relying on its inherent power to preserve its order. The case arose during the turbulent years after *Brown v. Board of Education* when the federal district courts had to oversee desegregation orders that often prompted violence in the communities. In *United States v. Hall*, 472 F.2d 261, 267 (5th Cir.1972), the court wanted to bind nonparties to an order not to interfere with an orderly desegregation process. Hall was not a party to the suit but he was served with a noninterference order that purported to bind anyone with notice not to obstruct school entrances. In open defiance of the order, Hall blocked a high school entrance. The district court found him in criminal contempt, and the Fifth Circuit upheld the conviction under the court's inherent power to preserve its judgment. In contrast with other federal opinions limiting the power of federal courts under Rule 65(d), the *Hall* opinion said that Rule 65(d) is a "codification rather than a limitation of courts' common-law powers." The opinion, which arose in a time of great stress on the federal courts, has been widely criticized by commentators.

D. CRIMINAL AND CIVIL CONTEMPT DISTINGUISHED

A disobedient defendant may be held in either criminal or civil contempt, or both, for the same act. The justification for allowing both types of sanctions is that they serve different functions. In contrast to criminal contempt, which has the primary function of vindicating the state's interest in obedience to court orders, civil contempt is for the benefit the plaintiff. Compensatory civil contempt gives the plaintiff damages for injuries caused by the defendant's violation of the order and coercive civil contempt ensures compliance designating daily fines or imprisonment until the defendant stops invading the interest that the order protects. For example, if a defendant defies an order not to trespass, criminal contempt might punish the defendant for his disobedience of, and disrespect for, the court. By contrast, civil contempt might be used to compensate the plaintiff for the damage done by a defiant trespass, and might also be used to coerce the defendant to cease the trespass.

The distinction between criminal and civil contempt is not always easy to discern. The distinction is nonetheless a critical one when attacking a finding of contempt on appeal. Before further exploration of the features of the two types of civil contempt, this section will first explore the significance of the differences between criminal and civil contempt.

There are differences in procedure and Constitutional safeguards for criminal and civil contempt. These differences are consistent with the differences between civil and criminal litigation in general. The failure to follow proper procedural and constitutional safeguards for a criminal contempt is a grounds for reversal. For example, if the court did not use the evidentiary standard of proof "beyond a reasonable doubt," a criminal contempt conviction is reversible. By contrast, a civil contempt finding can be imposed based on a lower standard of proof. States differ on which lower standard to use. Many states require proof for civil contempt at the evidentiary standard of "clear and convincing evidence" instead of the usual civil standard of proof by a "preponderance of the evidence."

A judge's decision to label a contempt as "civil" rather than "criminal" is not controlling as to whether the contempt will be treated as civil. The nature of the sanction rather than the label controls the determination. If a contempt is criminal in its character and its purpose, then the court's failure to follow the greater requirements of a criminal contempt will cause its reversal on appeal. *See In re Stewart*, 571 F.2d 958 (5th Cir.1978).

Since criminal contempt is a crime in the ordinary sense, it is treated as a separate offense, independent from the underlying case that produced the order. As such, it is immediately appealable. Moreover, a criminal contempt sanction survives regardless of the success of the underlying case (the one that produced the order that the contemnor violated). By contrast, civil contempt (1) is tied to the underlying case, (2) must be appealed at the same time as the remainder of the case is appealed, and (3) does not survive unless the underlying civil claim is ultimately victorious.

United States v. United Mine Workers, 330 U.S. 258, 67 S.Ct. 677, 91 L.Ed. 884 (1947), illustrates these principles. The case arose during World War II when the federal government took over the coal mines under its emergency powers, and the issue was whether a union could strike against the employer when the United States was the employer. When the federal government sought an injunction against the strike, the union tried to invoke the Norris-LaGuardia Act that prohibits federal courts from enjoining labor strikes. The United States argued that the Act did not apply because it was not an "employer," within the meaning of the Act, and that therefore the injunction was not prohibited. When the district court issued an injunction forbidding the strike in order for it to have time to consider the issues, the union struck in violation of the order. The district court then held the union in criminal contempt.

Although the United States Supreme Court found in favor of the plaintiff on the "employer" issue, it held as an alternative ground that the defendant could be punished criminally for violating the court's order regardless of whether the plaintiff prevailed in the underlying action. The Court distinguished between civil and criminal contempt, and held that the difference in the function of the two contempts justifies the difference in their durability. The Court explained that civil contempt remedies do not survive if the underlying claim fails, but that criminal contempt penalties survive because they are independent and serve to vindicate the authority of the court.

As an illustration of these principles, assume that a court orders a defendant ex-employee not to violate a noncompetition agreement with a former employer. The agreement purports to restrict the defendant from competing against the former employer for a certain period of time in a certain geographic area. The ex-employee violates the order and is held in criminal contempt. On appeal, the court holds that the non-competition agreement is overly broad and unenforceable, and therefore that the ex-employee should prevail on the merits. Notwithstanding the employee's success on the merits, criminal contempt findings will stand regardless of the outcome of the case. By contrast, any civil contempt sanctions will fall when the ex-employer loses the underlying case because civil contempt remedies depend upon the plaintiff's ultimate success on the merits in the underlying case.

E. COMPENSATORY CIVIL CONTEMPT

Compensatory civil contempt provides a plaintiff with compensation for losses caused by the defendant's disobedience of a court order. In seeking compensation, the plaintiff must bear the burden of establishing with specificity that certain losses were occasioned by the defendant's failure to comply with a lawful court order in effect at the time of the losses. Unlike criminal contempt, a finding of civil contempt does not require willfulness but only requires a showing that the defendant actually failed to comply with a court order.

Compensatory civil contempt functions to give the plaintiff damages for losses caused by the disobedience. For example, consider the situation where a court orders the defendant, a former employee of the plaintiff, to cease use of a customer list wrongfully taken when the defendant quit employment with the plaintiff. Assume that the plaintiff is a former employer who can prove that the defendant used the list wrongfully to solicit customers away from the plaintiff. Through compensatory civil contempt, plaintiff may recover damages caused by the continued use of the list after the court's order. Whereas damages caused by soliciting customers before the injunction are recoverable only as damages for the civil wrong, losses traceable to conduct in defiance of the court order are recoverable as compensatory civil contempt.

Like all awards for civil damages, the purpose of compensatory civil contempt damages is to make the plaintiff whole. Unlike common law damages in tort or contract, attorney's fees and costs are a proper element of recovery for compensatory civil contempt. The attorney's fees must be limited to those incurred in pursuit of the contempt claim, and cannot extend to fees incurred in pursuit of the underlying claim that produced the order that the defendant disobeyed.

F. COERCIVE CIVIL CONTEMPT

Coercive civil contempt is a tool that is designed to force a recalcitrant defendant to comply with a court order. The coercion may take the form of daily fines (or other measure of increment) or indefinite imprisonment until compliance. For example, if a defendant refuses to obey a discovery order to produce certain documents for litigation, the court may issue a daily fine until the documents are produced. Or if a parent refuses to disclose the location of a child in order to thwart the visitation rights of the other parent, the court may imprison the defendant until the parent obeys.

1. "Keys in the Contemnor's Pocket"

When the court issues a coercive contempt sanction, the defendant is said to have the "keys to the jail in hand" because release occurs as soon as there is compliance with the court's order. The other expression often used is that the keys are in the "pocket" of the contemnor. Similarly, if a daily fine is ordered, the fine stops as soon as the defendant complies. For example, if a union is fined for each day of an illegal strike, the penalty accrues each day until the strike stops. The essence of the civil nature of this contempt is that the contemnor has the capacity to end the on-going sanction by compliance with the order. By contrast, when a court imposes criminal contempt, it usually imposes a determinant penalty (*e.g.*, a specified number of days in jail or a fixed fine).

In *United States v. United Mine Workers*, 330 U.S. 258, 67 S.Ct. 677, 91 L.Ed. 884 (1947), the United States Supreme Court held that the amount of a daily civil contempt fine should be determined by several factors: "the character and magnitude of the harm threatened by continued contumacy, and the probable effectiveness of any suggested sanctions in bringing about the result desired." *Id.* at 304. Typically such fines are paid to the government and are unrelated to the actual damages suffered by the plaintiff, which may be recoverable as compensatory contempt. A few courts have tailored fines to correspond to daily losses, such as intangible losses suffered by a business, and ordered them paid to the plaintiff. Thus, when a group picketing an abortion clinic is fined daily for recurring violations of a court order restricting the scope of its protests, the coercive fine may be paid to the clinic for the intangible loss caused by the disruptions. Normally, however, a plaintiff's losses are properly addressed by compensatory civil contempt.

2. Ability to Purge

Coercive civil contempt sanctions must be limited to the period of time when coercion is possible. The reason for this limitation is that the penalty becomes punitive, and thus criminal rather than civil, if the defendant can no longer purge the offense. For example, suppose that a court imposes a coercive contempt sanction (imprisonment) against a witness who refuses to testify at a trial even when granted immunity. The sanction is valid as long as the trial continues because the contempt continues each day of the trial and the witness can purge the contempt at any point until the end of the trial. Once the trial is over, the sanction must end because at that point the witness can no longer testify and thus can no longer purge the contempt.

If the circumstances are such that no defendant would be able to purge the contempt, it is improper for the court to order coercive civil contempt in the first place. If the particular circumstances of this defendant make compliance impossible or improbable from inability to comply, then such condition is an affirmative defense that must be proven by the contemnor.

For example, if the defendant has contracted to perform a show where trained elephants fly, the court cannot jail the defendant until such time as the show goes on because elephants simply cannot fly. Damages would be the appropriate remedy if the contract is otherwise enforceable. In contrast, if a painter had agreed to sell a unique and completed painting and refused to do so, resistance to the specific performance order could result in coercive civil contempt until the painter complied. The painter can raise the impossibility defense if the painting has been destroyed or earlier sold to another person. The coercion cannot continue if compliance is impossible, and again the remedy would be damages if the contract is otherwise enforceable. Compare the fact that as a matter of substantive law, impossibility (or commercial impracticability under UCC § 2–615) may also be a defense to the contract itself. Impossibility as an affirmative defense to contempt is explored further in this chapter's Section G on defenses.

3.   The "*Bagwell*" Rule

The third noteworthy limitation on coercive civil contempt is known as the *Bagwell* rule. This term refers to the Supreme Court's decision in *United Mine Workers v. Bagwell*, 512 U.S. 821, 114 S.Ct. 2552, 129 L.Ed.2d 642 (1994), where the Court held that in some cases coercive civil contempt is in spirit criminal contempt and therefore cannot be employed without the Constitutional and procedural safeguards used for criminal contempt.

Bagwell arose out of a labor dispute between the UMW and two coal companies in Virginia. The union engaged in unlawful strike activities, including blocking access to facilities, physically threatening employees, and damaging company property. The companies obtained an injunction against the unlawful activities, but the union violated the injunction with continued violence. The judge then announced prospective penalties for future violations: $100,000 for violent ones and $20,000 for nonviolent ones.

By the end of the strike, the court had found some 400 violations of the order. The cumulative penalties were more than $64 million, of which $12 million went to the companies and $52 million to the state. When the strike was settled, the companies also agreed on the amount of damages to be paid for the findings of civil contempt. Nevertheless, the State of Virginia refused to forgive the fines owed to it. This fact influenced the Supreme Court's conclusion that the line between civil and criminal penalties is not an entirely bright one in this area of contempt.

The United States Supreme Court held that the failure to accord criminal safeguards to the defendant in a case such as this one cannot be automatically excused by the fact that the contempt was based on civil contempt. Although the announcement of prospective penalties for continued violations of the order is a classic form of coercive civil contempt, this case went beyond the bounds of permissible use of civil contempt. The Court noted that the case involved complex fact-finding and severe penalties. Under these circumstances, the Court held that Constitutional protections can apply even to a civil contempt.

The Court left unclear exactly what circumstances trigger these rights and reserved for future cases where to "draw the line" between coercive contempts that require criminal safeguards and those that do not. Cases involving simple orders where disobedience is readily ascertainable appear unaffected by the decision. *Bagwell* applies only to contempt trials that are complex and to situations where the potential penalties are severe.

As *Bagwell* reflects, coercive civil contempt is the most ambiguous type of contempt in terms of its purpose and nature. As with all civil contempt, its primary function is to benefit the plaintiff who secured the original equitable order. The vindication of the court's authority is an important derivative benefit.

G. AFFIRMATIVE DEFENSES TO CONTEMPT

As this chapter has already noted, a finding of contempt can be challenged for its failure to use proper procedure or otherwise for a court's failure to meet statutory requirements. There are also affirmative defenses to contempt, for which the burden of proof rests with the defendant.

The Supreme Court explained in *United States v. Rylander*, 460 U.S. 752, 103 S.Ct. 1548, 75 L.Ed.2d 521 (1983), that the defendant's burden cannot be avoided by claiming the Fifth Amendment right against self-incrimination. In that case, a taxpayer had been jailed in coercive contempt for failure to produce documents required in an IRS summons. He had not contested lack of possession before the enforcement order in which the court found possession. His attempt to defend the subsequent contempt with impossibility was rejected because he refused to be cross-examined on Fifth Amendment grounds. The Court held that the defendant has the burden of proof to show that he lacked possession at the current time and could not relitigate the finding in the unappealed enforcement order concerning possession at the earlier time. The opinion explains that the taxpayer did not meet the burden of proof for this affirmative defense to contempt because "the claim of privilege is not a substitute for relevant evidence."

1. Impossibility

A contemnor can challenge a contempt finding on the grounds that it was impossible to comply with the order. Specific performance of a personal contract to sing, for example, is impossible if the singer has laryngitis, but not if the singer has also contracted to sing for someone else on the same night. If a court orders specific performance when the singer threatens to breach by singing for a competitor on that date, the singer has the defense of impossibility in the first situation but not the second. The court may order the singer not to perform for anyone else on the contract date, through either an express or implied negative covenant not to sing elsewhere. *Lumley v. Wagner,* 42 Eng. Rep. 687 (1852). In that situation, the singer's failure to sing anywhere on the contract date—either from laryngitis or obstinance—is not contempt. Singing for the competitor on the contract date in defiance of the order, however, would be contempt without a defense of impossibility.

In a divorce case, the court may order one spouse to convey certain property, but if the spouse no longer owns the property, the impossibility of compliance with the order is a defense to contempt. The property must already be sold before the order, however, to avoid contempt; selling the property to a third party as soon as the spouse receives the order does not suffice to avoid contempt because it was possible to comply when the order was entered. Indirect criminal contempt would be appropriate in that case.

There have been a number of divorce cases where a spouse still owns the property (such as the family home) but refuses to convey it to the other spouse upon the court's order. Coercive civil contempt is appropriate in such circumstances, where the obstinate spouse chooses to sit in jail rather than convey the property. The spouse can sit in jail indefinitely in defiance of the court. If the property is in the same state as the court, many states permit the court is issue an order that would act on the *res* to make the conveyance. If the property is out of state, however, the spouse may be held in coercive civil contempt for as long as it takes. There is no defense of impossibility in that circumstance because the spouse can get out of jail as soon as the deed is signed.

2. Exhausted Coercion

In the coercive civil contempt context, there comes a point where it appears that the coercion is not working and that there is no possibility that the contemnor is going to comply. At that point, the impossibility defense takes a special twist. The defense is then known as "exhausted coercion." If the contemnor establishes that there is no possibility of compliance because of the long passage of time or other factors, the contemnor may no longer be held. The underlying premise of coercive civil contempt is that the court can force compliance with the order, so when coercion is exhausted, the justification ends.

In a recurring fact situation, recalcitrant witnesses demonstrate by their continued silence that they will never testify even when granted immunity. Such witnesses say that they fear for their physical safety or for the safety of their families when, for example, the government wants them to testify against members of organized crime. Witnesses have stayed incarcerated for as long as the proceeding in which they may testify is still on-going. When the proceeding is done, it is not possible to purge by compliance so the coercion must end. For an on-going grand jury investigation, the period of possible coercion may be indefinite. Some courts permit contemnors to demonstrate that their continued incarceration is punitive because there is no meaningful possibility of compliance. Others have refused to allow such a demonstration because future compliance is always theoretically possible.

In one famous case, a mother physician became convinced that her ex-husband physician was sexually abusing their young daughter and she refused to honor his visitation rights. The trial court in the District of Columbia did not agree that there was evidence of abuse and ordered the mother to allow visitation. The child then disappeared and the mother refused to reveal the child's location (identified much later as New Zealand where the child was with her maternal grandparents). The court attempted to force compliance by jailing the mother under coercive civil contempt until the information was produced. *Morgan v. Foretich*, 564 A.2d 1 (D.C.1989). The mother instead stayed in jail for over two years and the case became highly publicized. In response to this case, Congress enacted the District of Columbia Civil Contempt Imprisonment Limitation Act of 1989. D.C. Code §§ 11–721 *et seq.*, which provided a twelve-month limitation for imprisonment for civil contempt by a D.C. Superior Court in a case involving child custody. Most jurisdictions lack such limitations.

3. Inability to Comply

Another defense to contempt is the "inability" to comply with the court's order. It is distinguishable from "impossibility" in the sense that compliance is theoretically possible, but not practically so. This defense is frequently introduced in cases where a parent is in arrears making child support payments. A child support order is an equitable decree backed by the contempt power. A parent's unwillingness to earn income to make the payments is not a defense in contrast with the inability to do so, such as from disability. The California Supreme Court clarified this difference in *Moss v. Superior Court*, 17 Cal.4th 396, 71 Cal.Rptr.2d 215, 950 P.2d 59 (1998), where the court found no constitutional impediment to courts using the contempt power against parents who willfully refuse to seek available employment that would permit them to meet their support obligation.

The United States Supreme Court agreed in *Turner v. Rogers*, 564 U.S. 431, 131 S.Ct. 2507, 180 L.Ed.2d 452 (2011), but further addressed the due process requirements in cases involving the ability of a parent to pay a child support order. In that case a father was significantly in arrears with child support payments and had been in and out of jail for contempt several times, managing to pay some of the amount due on occasion. In the show cause hearing the father, appearing without counsel, asked the judge for a chance to make amends now that he was "off the dope." The judge held him in contempt for failure to pay arrears immediately and, without making any finding of the father's ability to pay, again confined him in coercive civil contempt. The case was appealed ultimately to the Supreme Court on the issue of whether the father had a due process right to counsel in the show cause hearing for coercive civil contempt. The Court rejected the position that there is an automatic right to counsel for coercive civil contempt, but did reverse on the grounds that the court failed to use safeguards to assure that the father had an ability to pay before jailing him in coercive civil contempt.

The Court listed several suggested safeguards to reduce the risk of erroneous deprivation of liberty. Those safeguards include notice to the defendant of the question of ability to pay at the hearing, a form to ascertain the defendant's finances, and an opportunity for the defendant to address financial questions at the hearing. Finally, the last safeguard is that a judge must make an express finding of "ability to pay" before proceeding with contempt. The Court clarified that its concern is with "accurate decision-making" on the issue of ability to pay. The burden remains nonetheless with the defendant to establish the defense of inability to pay as an affirmative defense.

H. CONSTRAINTS ON JUDICIAL USE OF THE CONTEMPT POWER

The contempt power is an extraordinary weapon to entrust to anyone in a free society. The fact that it is rarely abused is a credit to the country's judiciary. There are nonetheless some restraints on the excesses of some situations and some judges. Three that are discussed below are the right to a jury trial in some cases, the limited right to counsel, and the discipline of overreaching judges.

1. Jury Trial Rights in Contempt Cases

The right to a jury trial depends upon the type of contempt. There is no right to a jury trial in a civil contempt case because the plaintiff receives this remedy as a part of the underlying equitable remedy, such as a specific performance order. The exception to this rule is *United Mine Workers v. Bagwell*, 512 U.S. 821, 114 S.Ct. 2552, 129 L.Ed.2d 642 (1994), as discussed in the Section F. If a coercive civil contempt falls under the *Bagwell* exception, then Constitutional safeguards attach, including the right to a jury trial.

For criminal contempt, the Supreme Court held in *Bloom v. Illinois*, 391 U.S. 194, 88 S.Ct. 1477, 20 L.Ed.2d 522 (1968), that the sixth amendment right to jury trial applies to serious criminal contempts. This Constitutional requirement is applied to the states through the Fourteenth Amendment. Serious criminal contempts are ones where the imposed penalty exceeds six months' imprisonment. This requirement applies to findings of both direct and indirect contempt.

The consecutive imposition of shorter sentences that aggregate to more than six months' imprisonment also triggers the jury trial right. The Seventh Circuit held in *United States v. Seale*, 461 F.2d 345 (7th Cir.1972), that the trial court could not sentence a litigant to three months' imprisonment for each of sixteen acts of misbehavior in the presence of the court. In that case a militant defendant had frequent outbursts during his trial with comments about how the trial was political persecution of him and how the judge was a racist. The right to a jury trial attached because the aggregation of the penalties exceeded six months.

Seale further held that when a defendant is tried for contempt at the end of a trial, the trial judge should avoid the possibility of prejudice by not presiding over the contempt hearing. The possibility of prejudice was particularly acute in that case because the findings of contempt involved personal attacks on the integrity of the judge during the trial. When the judge makes a finding of summary contempt during the course of a trial, however, the contempt is imposed immediately by the trial judge who witnessed the acts. These rules relating to direct contempt are a matter of federal common law on this subject. For indirect criminal contempt, as previously noted, Federal Rule of Criminal Procedure 42(b) disqualifies a judge from presiding at the contempt hearing without the defendant's consent if the behavior charged as contempt "involves disrespect to or criticism" of the judge.

2. Right to an Attorney for Contempt Hearing

The right to an attorney for a criminal contempt hearing is the same as for any criminal proceeding. The full Sixth Amendment rights attach, including the right of indigents to have an attorney appointed.

Whether there is a right to have an attorney appointed for civil contempt is a developing area of the law. The issue has become particularly salient in cases involving incarceration to coercive child support payments as a civil contempt sanction. The Supreme Court found no due process right to counsel for coercive civil contempt in *Turner v. Rogers*, 564 U.S. 431, 131 S.Ct. 2507, 180 L.Ed.2d 452

(2011), but the Court reserved the possibility that it could find such a right in cases where the State is the plaintiff, seeking reimbursement of welfare funds paid to the custodial parent, rather than the custodial parent individually, who usually also appears without counsel.

3. Judicial Abuse of Contempt

In the rare case where a judge abuses the contempt power, there are judicial oversight committees with the power to discipline the judge. Almost all states have codes based on Model Code of Judicial Conduct, adopted by the American Bar Association in 1972 and revised in 1990.

In one interesting case, *In re Inquiry Concerning Perry*, 641 So.2d 366 (Fla.1994), the Florida Supreme Court sanctioned a judge who improperly used the contempt power. He had held in contempt six defendants with suspended licenses who drove away from the courthouse right after the judge had warned them not to drive. The judge arranged to "trap" them and they were arrested immediately and brought back to the court, where the judge was waiting to hold them in criminal contempt for driving with a suspended license. The judge then set bond at the high level of $20,000, which resulted in twenty-six days in jail for one of the six who could not post bond.

The conduct—driving with a suspended license—was treated as direct contempt, but the transgression was not in the court in the presence of the judge and thus was not sustainable as a direct contempt. The Florida Supreme Court found that the judge's failure to follow proper procedures for indirect criminal contempt was an abuse of discretion and not a mere error in law. The court noted the tension between the necessity of maintaining the dignity of the court and the danger of abusing the "awesome power" of contempt. The judge received a public reprimand.

An example of a judge who was removed from office for misuse of the contempt power is *Furey v. Commission on Judicial Performance*, 43 Cal.3d 1297, 240 Cal.Rptr. 859, 743 P.2d 919 (1987). The trial judge in that case had become exasperated with an indigent woman who was a spectator in his courtroom. She had used foul language, had been intentionally disruptive, and had written a false letter to the Commission on Judicial Performance concerning his conduct. The judge summoned her by letter to his courtroom twice. She didn't appear the first time. She appeared in response to the second letter, and the judge then held her in contempt for her previous failure to answer his summons and for her refusal to answer questions by invoking her right to remain silent. The judge instructed that she not be permitted to make a phone call after her arrest for contempt, in an apparent attempt to interfere with her petition for habeas corpus. The California Supreme Court found this use of contempt was willful misconduct that supported removal of the judge from office.

Chapter Four

PREVENTIVE INJUNCTIONS

A preventive injunction is a court order designed to avoid future harm to a plaintiff by prohibiting or mandating certain behavior by the defendant. It is an equitable remedy available only after a full trial on the merits. The next chapter covers the requirements for injunctive relief that is only temporary, before a full trial.

Preventive injunctions are distinguishable from actions for mandamus, which is appropriate only for nondiscretionary duties. Federal courts have jurisdiction over mandamus actions under the Mandamus and Venue Act, 28 U.S.C.A. § 1361, which gives a district court jurisdiction over any action in the nature of mandamus "to compel an officer or employee of the United States or any agency thereof to perform a duty owed to the plaintiff."

For example, a medical provider sued the Secretary of Health and Human Services to compel payment of Medicare claims in *Wolcott v. Sebelius*, 635 F.3d 757 (5th Cir.2011), *aff'd* 497 Fed. Appx. 400 (2012). The opinions explain that federal courts provide different remedies under different statutory authorization. Mandamus was appropriate only for the parts of the complaint that involved successfully appealed claims because payment was then a nondiscretionary duty. The medical provider also sought an order to prevent denial of future claims on grounds previously found invalid. That relief would be under different statutory authority for a declaratory judgment to establish the right (Chapter 8) and a preventive injunction (this chapter) to prevent the future denials.

The preventive injunction, a discretionary remedy, is "preventive" in the sense of avoiding future harm. Once the plaintiff has established a substantive claim, a preventive injunction may be available only if the plaintiff can establish additional requirements. Those requirements for a permanent preventive injunction are examined below.

A. PROHIBITORY AND MANDATORY INJUNCTIONS

A preventive injunction may be either prohibitory or mandatory in its wording. By definition, a prohibitory order forbids certain conduct. In contrast, a mandatory order requires certain conduct. For example, in one case customers caused a problem by blocking the sidewalk when they waited outside a popular restaurant. As a practical matter, the restaurant could not be ordered to stop customer congestion of the sidewalk (a prohibitory injunction), but the court could make an affirmative order requiring the restaurant's sidewalk employees to attempt to enforce an orderly line of customers (a mandatory injunction). *Tushbant v. Greenfield's Inc.*, 308 Mich. 626, 14 N.W.2d 520 (1944).

A prohibitory injunction is generally easier to supervise and to enforce because a court can determine relatively easily if the defendant has engaged in the prohibited conduct. For example, if a defendant has engaged in a copyright violation, the court may issue a prohibitory injunction to prevent future recurrences. If the defendant repeats the behavior, the defendant has disobeyed the order. Equitable orders are enforced by contempt (Chapter 3), so it is desirable for disobedience to be easily ascertained.

In contrast, it is more difficult to supervise a mandatory order because it is often unclear whether a defendant has completed an affirmative act. Consider a situation where a neighbor sues a rancher because cattle keep escaping from the ranch and damaging the neighbor's property. Assume that the court directs the rancher to erect with reasonable care a fence to contain his cattle in order to prevent them from trespassing again on the plaintiff's property. Cattle fences by their nature are subject to compromise and therefore it is not possible to say with certainty that the rancher has disobeyed the court order if the only proof is that cattle again trespassed on the neighbor's property. Even when a fence is erected with reasonable care, the animals may escape at some spot weakened by external forces such as weather, human trespassers, or wild animals. Therefore, it is not possible to hold the rancher in contempt with the mere evidence that the cattle escaped.

The example of the rancher's fence raises another point about the scope of an injunction's wording. The order must be tailored to the degree of protection provided by the substantive law. Jurisdictions vary in their rules with respect to trespassing animals: some do not require ranchers to fence their animals at all; some require ranchers to take reasonable steps to contain their animals; and some provide for strict liability for damage done by wandering cattle. If the jurisdiction provides for strict liability, then the order against the rancher could be a prohibitory one: keep the cattle from trespassing on the neighbor's property. If the jurisdiction does not provide for strict liability for trespassing animals, such a prohibitory order would be inappropriately broad in its scope.

If the jurisdiction in this example requires that ranchers take reasonable efforts to contain their cattle, then an order to erect a fence requires affirmative conduct. This order does not require a guarantee that animals will not trespass, which is beyond the coverage of the substantive law in that jurisdiction. Rather, the order requires the defendant to erect a fence, which may not be foolproof. The court may need to conduct a hearing to determine if the flaw in the fence is contemptuous. Such a contempt hearing for the alleged violation of the mandatory order is relatively more extensive in its nature than a contempt hearing to determine if a prohibitive injunction has been violated. In this example, proof that the rancher did not maintain a reasonably sound fence would be necessary for contempt of a mandatory injunction, but proof that the rancher's cattle trespassed on the neighbor's land is all that would be necessary for contempt of the prohibitory injunction. *See Ex parte Murle and Jane Blasingame*, 748 S.W.2d 444 (Tex.1988) (fence order against ranchers not sufficiently specific to support finding of contempt).

The apparent simplicity of a "do not trespass" injunction against people rather than animals can also be elusive. Consider the case of a student sit-in that disrupted the operation of a college administration building in order to protest the firing of a professor who expressed unpopular political views. In *Board of Higher Education of New York v. Students for a Democratic Society*, 60 Misc.2d 114, 300 N.Y.S.2d 983 (1969), the university confronted this situation and obtained an injunction against further demonstrations. The wording of the injunction had to account for the fact that the administration building is a public building, that the students had legitimate reasons to go there for their academic careers, and that the students could make lawful protests expressing their views. The wording used was to prohibit congregating or assembling in the university's buildings "in such manner as to disrupt or interfere with normal functions" or to block ingress or egress. Notice that a contempt hearing to enforce this order would not require showing the political motivation of the actors but only if they intentionally congregated "in such manner" to disrupt operations.

Although the distinction between prohibitory and mandatory injunctions lies in whether affirmative conduct is required, application of that distinction is not always clear. In the famous case of *Wheelock v. Noonan*, 108 N.Y. 179, 15 N.E. 67 (1888), defendant was ordered to remove large boulders that he had left on the plaintiff's property beyond the period of his license. In that case, the apparently prohibitory order to cease the continuing trespass was tantamount to an affirmative order to remove the boulders. The court nonetheless entered the order because there was no other effective remedy for the plaintiff. Removing the boulders was problematic and the plaintiff had no easy means of self-help. The difficult task of removal belonged properly with the wrong-doing defendant even though the order necessitated court supervision.

B. "EQUITY JURISDICTION"

The term "equity jurisdiction" refers to the appropriate exercise of a court's discretion in granting equitable relief. The term does not refer to jurisdiction in the sense of personal jurisdiction or subject matter jurisdiction, which are separate procedural requirements. "Equity jurisdiction" is a confusing term in that sense and is best regarded as a term of art derived from historical context. Although there was a historical justification for the use of the term "jurisdiction" by Chancery courts, the term "equity jurisdiction" now refers to the appropriateness of equitable relief as a matter of remedial equity. Thus, if a court incorrectly concludes that equitable relief should be granted, it is merely an erroneous order that must be appealed and not a void order from the lack of jurisdiction.

As a term of art, the term "equity jurisdiction" means simply that the plaintiff has established the elements for equitable relief. Those requirements for a preventive injunction are that the plaintiff must show: (1) the inadequacy of the remedy at law, (2) the likelihood of irreparable harm without the injunction, (3) that the balance of hardships tips in the plaintiff's favor, and (4) that the public interest favors the injunction. The sections below detail these requirements. Additional considerations, which are not usually listed as separate requirements but are relevant to the exercise of the court's discretion, include (5) the imminency of the harm and (6) the practicality of supervision.

1. Inadequacy of the Remedy at Law

The inadequacy of the remedy at law is the first requirement for equity jurisdiction for a preventive injunction. The inadequacy rule originated in sixteenth century England where Chancery would not take a case if the King's courts would grant a remedy at law. Although the jealousy of the court systems is no longer a justification for the rule, modern American courts cite the requirement as an explanation for granting or denying equitable relief. For example, in cases involving interests in real property, the uniqueness of each parcel of land makes damages inadequate to compensate losses.

The plaintiff must demonstrate that damages are an inadequate remedy in order to show that the remedy at law is inadequate. A remedy may be inadequate either because an injured party cannot be adequately compensated in damages or because the damages which may result cannot be measured by any pecuniary standard.

(A) Damages Speculative

One way to meet the inadequacy standard is to show that damages might be too speculative to ascertain. The mere existence of speculativeness or uncertainty is insufficient, in and of itself, to render damages inadequate. But, when damages become too speculative, then damages are regarded as unavailable and therefore inadequate for purposes of supporting equitable relief.

In one old case involving the lease of farm land, the lessor had reserved the right to enter and plow a part of the land in the fall but was prevented from doing so by the lessee. The lessor sought an injunction in the grounds that the speculative nature of the damages caused from the inability to plow in the fall made the remedy at law inadequate. The court noted that although it would be difficult to measure the loss caused by failure to plow in the fall rather than the spring, there was nonetheless an adequate remedy at law. Namely, the lessor could have brought an action at law to eject the lessor from the land for violation of the lease. *Carlson v. Koerner*, 226 Ill. 15, 80 N.E. 562 (1907).

(B) Multiplicity of Actions

A second way that plaintiffs can meet the inadequacy requirement is to demonstrate that without an injunction a multiplicity of lawsuits for damages will be necessary. For example, in *Berin v. Olson*, 183 Conn. 337, 439 A.2d 357 (1981), the plaintiff sued for water damage caused by the discharge of surface water onto his land by the adjoining landowner. The plaintiff received damages for past losses and sought an injunction against future diversions of water onto his land. The defendant argued that the plaintiff's recovery of damages proves the adequacy of the remedy at law, but the court properly granted the injunction on the basis that the plaintiff had established the likelihood of future diversions and thus probability of a multiplicity of future damage suits.

In *Phillips v. Wertz*, 546 S.W.2d 902 (Tex.Civ.App.1977), a court rendered a similar decision in a case involving a neighbor's construction project that kept knocking into the neighbor's hedge. The court concluded that plaintiff was entitled to an injunction because the repeated trespasses would necessitate a probable multiplicity of actions. Likewise, in *Thomas v. Weller*, 204 Neb. 298, 281 N.W.2d 790 (1979), the court granted an injunction in a case where a duck hunter made annual trespasses on neighboring land.

In each of the prior cases, the plaintiff established a pattern of repeated trespasses. Moreover, the damage remedy at law would focus on a single trespass, and would be inadequate because it would require a multiplicity of actions to respond to defendant's repeating behavior. Injunctive relief is advantageous because the possible penalties (in contempt) for violation of the injunction are greater than the damages that may be awarded in a damage action.

The inadequacy requirement can also be met by showing that plaintiff's land has been invaded by a continuing trespass. Consider the *Wheelock* case involving boulders left on plaintiff's land. In that case, because the landowner could not easily remove the trespassing boulders because of their size and weight, an injunction was appropriate because the trespass would continue without it and the plaintiff could not employ self-help. The remedy at law thus would be inadequate. Likewise, in *Lucy Webb Hayes National Training School for Deaconesses and Missionaries v. Geoghegan*, 281 F.Supp. 116 (D.D.C.1967), the court reached the same result when a husband refused to arrange for his wife to vacate a hospital room despite repeated demands by the hospital to transfer her to a nursing home.

However, the mere existence of a continuing trespass does not necessarily render the legal remedy inadequate. Suppose, for example, that a landowner licenses the use of his land for a concert on condition that the renter agrees to pay a rental fee and also agrees to remove debris after the concert is over. If the renter fails to remove the trash, he has committed a continuing trespass. Nevertheless, the remedy at law is likely to be deemed adequate because the landowner can hire someone to clean the land and recover damages for the expense.

(C) Intangible Business Interests

The inadequacy requirement can also be satisfied in other ways. Cases involving intangible business interests, such as the unauthorized use of customer lists, often support equitable relief because damages are speculative and irreparable harm results. Courts routinely grant injunctions when the defendant has misappropriated trade secrets or protected customer lists from a business. Cases involving former employees often present this fact situation.

Courts have also traditionally enjoined violations of copyright and patent laws. The federal statutory protections for these forms of intellectual property promote the creative activities that produce things protected by copyright and patents. A lawsuit for infringement is usually premised upon the irreparable harm that is done by taking such property and using or marketing it without permission.

The traditional rule of enjoining patent infringements is not as clear following the United State Supreme Court's 2006 decision in *eBay Inc. v. MercExchange*, 547 U.S. 388, 126 S.Ct. 1837, 164 L.Ed.2d 641 (2006). This case, involving eBay's infringement of a business method patent for electronic markets, specifically addressed the proper application of equitable principles for a permanent injunction in a patent infringement case. The parties had attempted to reach a license agreement but negotiations broke down, so the patent holder sued.

The traditional rule in patent cases has been that, absent special circumstances, an injunction would be issued once a plaintiff established the on-going violation of a patent. The trial court in *eBay* declined to follow the traditional rule after the plaintiff obtained a jury verdict for damages for the patent violation in this case. The trial judge declined to issue the usual injunction on the grounds that the damages were adequate. The Court of Appeals reversed on the grounds that an injunction for patent infringement should always be granted absent exceptional circumstances.

The Supreme Court carved a middle path that is not entirely clear. It reversed the "automatic" approach of the Court of Appeals, but it also declined to adopt the "modern reality" approach of the district court. Instead, the Court listed the traditional grounds for issuing an injunction and told the trial court to follow those benchmarks. This case thus erodes, at least slightly, the traditional rule that patent violations should be enjoined.

The scope of *eBay* is uncertain. On the one hand, it is possible that the opinion is limited to business method patents. *See Bilski v. Kappos*, ___ U.S. ___, 130 S.Ct. 3218, 177 L.Ed.2d 792 (2010) (referring several times to eBay as a case involving "business methods") On the other hand, *eBay* may be affecting the standards for awarding any type of injunction. *See* Mark P. Gergen, John M. Golden, and Henry E. Smith, *The Supreme Court's Accidental Revolution? The Test for Permanent Injunctions*, 112 Colum. L. Rev. 203 (2012).

eBay was appealed from the Court of Appeals for the Federal Circuit, which hears patent appeals. This circuit, whose jurisdiction is based on subject matter rather than geography, develops its own precedent, reviewed directly by the United States Supreme Court.

The existence of the Federal Circuit provides greater certainty and uniformity in patent law because it is not possible to have splits among the circuits on patent law issues. One view of *eBay* is that the Supreme Court was bringing the Federal Circuit into line with other federal law and declining to permit a separate line of equity jurisprudence just for patents. *See* S.J. Plager, *The Price of Popularity: The Court of Appeals for the Federal Circuit 2007,* 56 Am. U. L. Rev. 751 (2007).

A study of pre- and post-*eBay* patent injunctions concluded that after *eBay,* significantly fewer injunctions are granted when the patent holder and alleged infringer do not compete in the marketplace. Lily Lim & Sarah E. Craven, *Injunctions Enjoined; Remedies Restructured*, 25 Santa Clara Computer & High Tech. L.J. 787 (2009).

The Court similarly refused to permit a "thumb on the scale" in favor of injunctive relief in a case involving intellectual property rights to genetically altered plants. In *Monsanto Co. v. Geertson Seed Farms,* ___ U.S. ___, 130 S.Ct. 2743, 2757, 177 L.Ed.2d 461 (2010), the district court had issued an injunction against the further planting of genetically altered alfalfa in the absence of compliance with environmental regulations. Disapproving the basis for the injunction, the Court noted: "It is not enough for a court considering a request for injunctive relief to ask whether there is a good reason why an injunction should not issue; rather, a court must determine that an injunction should issue under the traditional four-factor test set out above." 130 S.Ct. at 2757.

(D) Civil Rights and Constitutional Violations

Injunctive relief might also be justified on the ground that damages are inadequate simply because of the nature of the right involved (*e.g.,* constitutional rights). Cases involving school desegregation decrees provide a prime example of irreparable harm because of this type of harm. In *Brown v. Board of Education,* 349 U.S. 294, 75 S.Ct. 753, 99 L.Ed. 1083 (1955), the United States Supreme Court discussed the necessity of equitable intervention for effective school desegregation. In the second *Brown* opinion, the Court concluded that injunctive relief was necessary to correct violations of equal protection when public schools were intentionally segregated on the basis of race.

Unconstitutional prison conditions is another notable example of the inadequacy of damages to protect constitutional rights. Complex injunctive relief is also appropriate to correct prison conditions that violate the Eighth Amendment guarantee against cruel and unusual punishment. *See Hutto v. Finney,* 437 U.S. 678,

98 S.Ct. 2565, 57 L.Ed.2d 522 (1978). Although damages may be awarded for such deprivations, they are not by nature sufficient to vindicate the loss of constitutional rights.

(E) Nuisance

It is often held that an injunction is the "usual" remedy in nuisance cases. This rule is followed particularly where the nuisance is of a public character and affects health and safety. In such cases, the remedy at law is inadequate and the harm is great and irreparable, so courts grant injunctive relief as a matter of course.

The famous exception to the application of this rule is *Boomer v. Atlantic Cement Company*, 26 N.Y.2d 219, 257 N.E.2d 870, 309 N.Y.S.2d 312 (1970), where the highest state court in New York declined to issue an injunction against a nuisance because of the public interest in operation of the polluting company. In that case landowners sued a neighboring cement plant for injury to their homes from its pollution. Although New York law holds that a court should ordinarily enjoin a nuisance, there would be an injury to the larger community in this case because of the corresponding loss in jobs. Despite the fact that a damage remedy would be inadequate in the usual sense, the court declined to enjoin the multi-million dollar operation. Instead it conditioned an injunction on the failure of the defendant to pay permanent damages to the plaintiffs. The effect thus was to allow only damages and no equitable relief.

2. Irreparable Harm

Irreparable harm is the second requirement for a preventive injunction. Most jurisdictions list it as a separate requirement but some formulations subsume it within the inadequacy rule. As a general matter, the usual reason why the remedy at law is considered "inadequate" is that damages do not suffice when the harm is "irreparable." For that reason the two requirements are often combined.

There are circumstances, however, when the requirement of irreparable harm is distinguishable from the inadequacy requirement. Even if the damages cannot redress the harm, satisfying the inadequacy rule, the irreparability rule further requires that the harm be great. Trivial harm does not merit the remedy of an injunction even if it would support damages. For example, suppose that a child routinely walks to school by going across a neighbor's yard. The child is technically trespassing even if the passage causes no damage to the land. Interests in land are routinely protected by equity because the uniqueness of land makes the damage remedy at law inadequate. The irreparable harm requirement, however, precludes an injunctive remedy if the harm involved is trivial, and the trial court may conclude that such a dispute should be left to a resolution in damages rather than to an exercise of its extraordinary powers in equity. An injunction requires continuing supervision and a judge may be faced with further motions for modification, dissolution, or contempt. When a matter is trivial, it would be a waste of judicial resources to employ the injunctive remedy. The irreparable harm rule reflects this policy.

The trivial nature of the injury may affect the plaintiff's litigation strategy. In one interesting fact situation, one neighbor sued another for ouster of possession by several minor acts of trespass, including parking on the plaintiff's land and shoveling snow on it. The neighbors were at odds previously concerning a failed negotiation for the purchase of the land. The plaintiff sought to bring his action under a statute concerning ouster of possession, which ultimately failed. The statutory ouster claim was more promising than an action for injunctive relief from trespass, which would be likely to fail because of the trivial nature of the invasions. The court noted that the appropriate remedy for the plaintiff in this case was damages, which were likely to be small. *Marder v. Realty Construction Co.*, 43 N.J. 508, 205 A.2d 744 (1964).

(A) Quality of Harm

The great harm required for inadequacy need not be economic harm. Intangible harm, such as an invasion of privacy, may satisfy the rule. The key for the plaintiff is to establish that the harm is by nature incalculable and that it is not trivial.

It is the quality of harm rather than the quantity of harm that is at issue. This principle has been litigated extensively in the environmental context. In a case involving regulations on hunting snow geese and other wild fowl, *Fund for Animals v. Frizzell*, 530 F.2d 982 (D.C.Cir.1975), the D.C. Circuit has explained that the destruction of even one bird would be an irreparable injury if the harvest of excessive numbers would irretrievably damage the species. However, the court concluded that a regulation permitting the harvest of a small percentage of game for sport is not irreparable harm.

(B) Competitive Harm

An intangible business interest that often supports an injunction against a former employee is a violation of a covenant not to compete, also known as a noncompetition agreement.

Jurisdictions have a variety of statutory and common law rules concerning the enforceability of such promises not to compete against former employers, but under all formulations an injunction is not permissible without a showing of irreparable harm. Moreover, the mere fact of competition itself is insufficient to support equitable relief, even if the employee has agreed not to compete. The required showing of irreparable harm can be based on the fact that former employees have special training or talents, or knowledge of protected information.

Although the most highly publicized type of noncompetition case involves athletes with highly-prized skills, the same principle applies to doctors and other professionals, as well as to employees with specialized technological skills. The key for the employer is to show the following: (1) that it would suffer irreparable harm if the former employee works elsewhere, (2) that there is a violation of an enforceable promise not to compete, (3) that the noncompetition agreement is limited to a reasonable period of time following the termination of the former employment and within a reasonable geographic range.

Some jurisdictions have relaxed the required showing of irreparable harm for some business interests. Florida, for example, enacted a statute that creates a rebuttable presumption of irreparable harm when an employer has demonstrated the violation of an enforceable restrictive covenant. Florida Statutes s. 542.335(j) (2001). Similarly, New Hampshire has held as a matter of common law that "[w]henever an employee uses his experience gained from an employer in violation of a reasonable covenant not to compete, irreparable injury occurs and injunctive relief is appropriate." *Highdata Software Corp. v. Kothandan*, 160 F.Supp.2d 167, 168 (D.N.H.2001).

Courts also issue injunctions to protect the interests of former employees as well as former employers when there has been an adequate showing. For example, an employee who is fearful that a former employer will wrongfully try to enforce an invalid noncompetition agreement may try to obtain an injunction against enforcement. However, if there is no proof that the former employer has interfered with the employee's search for new employment, the court may conclude that the irreparable harm requirement is not satisfied. Some courts have found that an employee cannot obtain injunctive relief based solely on a showing that competitors were reluctant to hire him/her, or that clients were fearful of dealing with the former employee because of the existence of a noncompetition agreement. There must also be proof that the employer had taken some action to fuel the fears.

(C) "Substantive Equity" and Irreparable Harm

Claims involving so-called "substantive equity" are not subject to the inadequacy rule and irreparable harm requirements. Unlike remedial equity, substantive equity allows an action in equity for certain interests that historically were not recognized at law. Those interests include trusts, mortgages, bankruptcy, and stockholders' derivative actions. Because historically it was only Chancery that recognized these interests, it did not matter what type of remedy the suitor sought. Remedial equity, by contrast, focuses on the remedy sought in equity because the substantive interest is also recognized at law even though only equity permits the remedy. For example, contractual interests are recognized both at law and in equity, but only equity gives specific performance.

3.   Balance of Hardships

The third requirement for a preventive injunction is that the balance of hardships must tip decidedly in favor of the suitor. An injunction is never a matter of right even when the plaintiff can show the inadequacy of the remedy at law and irreparable harm. The court must exercise its discretion in deciding whether to issue the order by weighing the relative hardships of the parties and the interests of any unrepresented third parties.

(A) Economic and Non-Economic Burdens

The rule that the remedy at law must be inadequate does not mean that all economic interests are foreclosed from equitable relief. Quite to the contrary, economic interests are most frequently what is at stake. However, the damages remedy may be inadequate because the potential losses are too uncertain or indefinite in calculation to permit an adequate damages recovery. For example, a patent holder who seeks to enjoin competitive use by an infringer has economic interests at stake, but the remedy at law is typically inadequate because of the difficulty of ascertaining the dollar loss caused by the unlawful competition.

A company that seeks to enjoin a former employee from disclosing trade secrets is also protecting economic interests when the potential monetary loss would defy calculation at the level of certainty necessary for damages. Similarly, a sports team that seeks to enforce an agreement with a star player not to play for any other team during the contract period is protecting an economic interest that could not be measured in damages. How could the team establish with any degree of certainty the effect of the prohibited competition? It could not show that it would have won a championship or that the other team would not have won it. It also could not even show with certainty any decline in attendance at home games. The losses are simply too intangible.

By the same token, the burden of an injunction on the star player in this example is both economic and non-economic. The player needs to earn a living, of course, but the additional burden would relate to the lost opportunity that an injunction would also produce. As a professional athlete in prime career years, the player will also want to preserve the intangible opportunity of establishing dominance in the sport. Such dominance produces economic benefits in itself, such as product endorsements, but it also brings personal satisfaction that is beyond dollar calculation. If the injunction causes the athlete to have a reduced chance to be in the hall of fame, the harm is not calculable in dollars. Damage law does not even try to address the causal issues nor the calculation issues inherent in such a question. Thus, it is the job of the court sitting in equity to balance such potential losses of both parties.

(B) Relative Burdens on the Parties

The concept of "burden" on the parties is a very broad one and the trial judge needs to assess not only the nature and extent of the burdens on each party but also the relative burdens in this case. For example, in *Muehlman v. Keilman*, 257 Ind. 100, 272 N.E.2d 591 (1971), an Indiana case considered the relative interests of a home-owning family to the use and enjoyment of land and of the neighbors who made excessive noise with trucks used in their business. The Indiana Supreme Court found that the trial court properly balanced the competing interests in formulating a compromise. Even though the court found for the plaintiff family on the facts that established the noise as a nuisance, the injunction did not enjoin the offending truck noise altogether. Noting that equity should avoid destroying a legitimate business with its order if possible, the court issued a decree that restricted the truck noise to normal working hours. Although the order did not give complete relief to the plaintiffs, it did protect them from disturbance of their sleep while still permitting the neighbors to earn a living.

In *Yome v. Gorman*, 242 N.Y. 395, 152 N.E. 126 (1926), Justice Cardozo confronted a very delicate issue of comparing intangible burdens. In that case, the plaintiff was a widow who sought to move the remains of her deceased husband from one cemetery to another following a change in her own religious affiliation after his death. The interests involved could not be compared in any objective way and the judge was required to balance the sentiments as much as possible, including the interests of the deceased husband. In denying the injunction, Justice Cardozo explained that it is not possible to formulate a rule but only to "exemplify a process." *Id.* at 403.

A restraint on free speech is an example of another non-economic burden that courts must sometimes balance against other interests. *Madsen v. Women's Health Center, Inc.,* 512 U.S. 753, 114 S.Ct. 2516, 129 L.Ed.2d 593 (1994), required balancing free speech interests against the freedom to seek lawful medical services. The case involved an injunction against abortion protestors at a health clinic. The Supreme Court held that a narrowly tailored injunction may restrain speech if the rights of the parties are carefully balanced.

The trial court's injunction in *Madsen* had established a 36-foot buffer zone around the clinic and surrounding private property. It also imposed limited noise restrictions and provided for a 300-foot no-approach zone. The Court held that the provisions establishing the buffer zone around the clinic and noise restrictions did not violate the First Amendment, but that the buffer zone on private property and the no-approach zone burdened more speech than necessary. The holding underscored the need for narrow tailoring of any injunction that impinges on free speech.

Similarly, in *Schenck v. Pro-Choice Network of Western N.Y.,* 519 U.S. 357, 117 S.Ct. 855, 137 L.Ed.2d 1 (1997), the Court considered the balance of hardships in an injunction involving the free speech of abortion protestors and the interests of patients walking into clinics. The Court upheld the constitutionality of an injunction establishing a "fixed buffer zone" that prohibited protestors from interfering with patients and counselors within 15 feet of an abortion clinic. The Court found unconstitutional, however, a further provisions of the injunction that imposed "floating buffer zones" that moved with the patients. The Court concluded that such zones burdened more speech than was necessary. See further discussion of First Amendment constraints on injunctions in a variety of other contexts in Chapter Six.

4. Public Interest

Courts must always consider the public interest in the issuance of any injunction. That consideration affects both the decision whether to grant an injunction as well as the scope and nature of it. Public health and safety, as well as public economic interests, are appropriate considerations.

The importance of health and safety is dramatically illustrated by *City of Milwaukee v. Activated Sludge, Inc.,* 69 F.2d 577 (7th Cir.1934). The plaintiff in that case established a patent infringement by the City of Milwaukee in its processes of treating and purifying sewage. Courts at that time routinely enjoined patent infringements, so the trial court issued such an injunction in this case. The Seventh Circuit reversed the injunction, despite the validity of the patent and the proof of infringement. The court noted that if the trial court's injunction were made permanent, it would close the sewage plant and leave the city "without any means for the disposal of raw sewage other than running it into Lake Michigan, thereby polluting its waters and endangering the health and lives of that and other adjoining communities." *Id.* at 581. Because such a prospect endangered the lives of so many people, the court declined to take this risk and limited the plaintiff to monetary recovery.

An equally dramatic illustration of the role of public interest is found in the case of *Boomer v. Atlantic Cement Co.,* 26 N.Y.2d 219, 257 N.E.2d 870, 309 N.Y.S.2d 312 (1970). As previously noted, this famous case involved a polluting cement plant where neighboring home owners sought to enjoin its continued operation. Although precedent in the state established that an injunction was the "usual remedy" for nuisance, the court declined to take direct action that would have the effect of closing the plant. The cement company was a major employer in the community and then-current technology could not have eliminated the pollution without shutting down the plant.

The pollution from the cement company in *Boomer* was a matter of public interest because of the effect of the nuisance on the health of the surrounding neighborhood, as well as because of the potential economic injury to the larger community because of the corresponding loss in jobs. Rather than enjoin the multi-million dollar operation, the court conditioned an injunction on the failure of the defendant to pay permanent damages to the plaintiffs. The practical effect of this approach was to allow only damages. The dissenting opinion characterized the result as an inappropriate inverse condemnation because the permanent damages allowed the company a "servitude on the land" to continue its pollution. He saw no such public benefit in allowing a company to continue to pollute.

Boomer is a favorite topic of law and economics scholars, who generally approve the result. In the absence of a court order specifying the amount that the company must pay the landowners, the parties could negotiate the amount that the landowners would take in exchange for the right of the company to pollute them. Theoretically, the amount of money paid in exchange for the privilege of continued pollution will depend upon the level of pollution. If it is very high, then the amount of money necessary to purchase the right to pollute would be so high that excessive polluters would be driven out of business by the market force.

Public interest is the factor that is most difficult to predict in any given case. In some situations, both sides of a case have a plausible argument that the public interest favors each of them. *Boomer* is a prime example of this problem. The factory argued successfully that its continued operation was in the public interest because the factory contributed jobs and taxes to the local economy. The competing public interest was the environmental pollution and widespread interference with the ability of neighboring landowners to use and enjoy their land. This 1970 opinion pre-dated the era of federal legislative activism in environmental law that occurred during the subsequent decade. Numerous federal statutes now reflect the strong public interest in the environment.

Public safety, particularly as embodied in military needs, was the key to the Supreme Court's 2008 opinion *Winter v. Natural Resources Defense Council, Inc.*, 555 U.S. 7, 129 S.Ct. 365, 172 L.Ed.2d 249 (2008). At issue in that case was were some Navy training exercises off the coast of California that used active sonar, emitting pulses of sound underwater and then receiving the acoustic waves that echo off the target, to identify the location of enemy submarines. The plaintiff conservation group and others sought to enjoin the exercises pending the Navy's compliance with environmental regulations that would require assessment of the impact of the exercises on marine mammals who live in the water where the tests occur.

The district court issued an injunction that required measures to mitigate any possible effect on marine animals, and the Court of Appeals affirmed with modification. The Supreme Court reversed on several grounds, including that the public interest in the training exercises had not received sufficient weight. Although at issue was a preliminary injunction—the topic of the next chapter—the Court emphasized that the consideration of public interest is paramount in any type of injunctive order. The Court noted that although military interests do not always prevail over other public interests, this case did not involve a close question. The Navy successfully argued the public interest in a properly trained antisubmarine force for the safety of the entire fleet and for the preservation of national security.

When the plaintiff is the government, public interest is the centerpiece of the litigation in a much more direct manner. It is for the court, however, rather than the government to determine whether the position of the governmental plaintiff is necessarily consistent with the public interest. The government in such cases is simply a litigant arguing the nature of the public interest as reflected in the legislation empowering the government to bring the case. Nonetheless, it is often true that when the government is a party, the factors of balance of hardship and public interest converge. See *Drakes Bay Oyster Co. v. Jewell*, 747 F.3d 1073 (9th Cir.2014).

5. Imminency

A threatened harm must be imminent before a court will order equitable relief to prevent it. A court will decline to issue an injunction if the harm has already occurred and is not reasonably likely to reoccur. The remedy at law is adequate for past harm.

(A) "Be Good" Orders

The requirement that harm be imminent serves the purpose of assuring that courts do not issue injunctions that amount to orders that the defendant "be good" on general principles. The problem with "be good" orders is that an equitable order is backed by the contempt power. Therefore, an individual who violates such an order faces greater potential penalties, including significant criminal penalties, than if the wrongful conduct occurred in the absence of an order prohibiting it.

Consider, for example, an injunction that prohibits the defendant from trespassing on the plaintiff's land. In the absence of any indication that such a trespass is imminent, the order simply prohibits the defendant from doing something that no one is privileged to do. One might ask why it would matter to have the injunction prohibiting behavior that is already prohibited? The answer is that the consequences of violating the injunction may be significantly greater than the consequences of doing the same prohibited act in the absence of an injunction. Consider someone not bound by the injunction who trespasses on the plaintiff's land. The plaintiff may sue this person for damages in tort (without the availability of attorney's fees) and may file a complaint for criminal trespass if the elements of that crime are met. In contrast, consider someone who trespasses in violation of an injunction. The sanctions for this wrong are not governed by tort and criminal law but by the law of contempt (Chapter 3). The landowner may then recover compensatory civil contempt damages for the trespass, including attorney's fees. Furthermore, the defendant may be prosecuted for criminal contempt, with different elements than criminal trespass and greater possible criminal sanctions.

(B) Preservation of Judicial Resources

The rule that the potential harm must be imminent also prevents the use of judicial resources to supervise injunctive orders when there is no clearly demonstrated need for immediate action. If the harm has occurred in the past and appears to be already completed, then there is no imminent threat of future harm and the proper remedy is damages.

Conversely, if the harm is unsubstantiated and projected in the distant future, then it is not imminent and the court should not issue the injunction until the threat is more substantial. Imminent harm refers to an invasion of the plaintiff's interest that is likely to occur soon, or to continue if it is an ongoing invasion of the interest. It is imminent if is likely to occur in the near future unless equity intervenes.

In *Boring v. Google, Inc.,* 362 Fed. Appx. 273 (3rd Cir.2010), for example, a homeowner objected to the display on Google Maps "Street View" of a picture of his home taken by trespassing on his private driveway. Google Maps removed the picture upon the homeowner's objection. The homeowner sued for damages for trespass and invasion of privacy, and also sought injunctive relief. The court declined to issue the injunction in the absence of imminent harm; in fact, there was no probability of future harm at all under these facts. In contrast, a pattern of fraudulent behavior in *Securities and Exchange Comm. v. Manor Nursing Centers, Inc.,* 458 F.2d 1082 (2d Cir.1972), supported an injunction against a defendant who violated federal securities law; the pattern permitted the inference that it would continue.

(C) Ongoing Versus Intermittent Harms

The imminency test is most easily satisfied if the conduct sought to be enjoined has been ongoing, such as continuous pollution of neighboring lands by a factory. In such a case of ongoing harm, the claimant can prove the necessary immediacy by pointing to the continuous invasion of their interests.

The application of the imminency rule is most difficult in cases where a defendant has engaged in behavior that infringes intermittently upon the plaintiff's rights. The plaintiff must demonstrate a likely invasion in the near future either on the basis of past behavior or on other grounds. A pattern of trespass, such as parking on the plaintiff's property with some regularity even after a request to stop, may establish the likelihood of future trespass. The question is whether the behavior is likely to repeat, so the repetition of the behavior after knowledge of the plaintiff's objection is probative to the question of future likely behavior. An injunction must be based on the court's prediction that future harm is imminent, so the plaintiff must establish a basis for that probability.

A pattern of the same behavior, such as repeated trespass by parking, is a more straightforward matter of proof than a pattern of different types of invasions of the plaintiff's interests. *Galella v. Onassis*, 353 F.Supp. 196 (S.D.N.Y.1972), provides a good illustration of a case where the pattern of past invasions has been varied and unpredictable. In that case, the widow of former President John F. Kennedy sought an injunction to restrain a professional free-lance photographer from violating her rights of privacy. Jacqueline Kennedy Onassis presented evidence that the photographer had repeatedly engaged in harassing behavior toward the family in order to obtain pictures, but each time the invasive behavior was different.

Based upon the pattern of past conduct, as well as public statements by the photographer, the court concluded that his behavior would continue in the future. The evidence of imminency was very strong because the photographer had sent an advertisement to customers announcing future anticipated pictures of Onassis. Even though the plaintiff could not establish what type of invasive conduct was likely to occur in the future, there was sufficient evidence of the abstract pattern of behavior to permit the court to conclude that there would be future invasions even if their exact nature was unpredictable. Equitable intervention was appropriate to prevent the imminent harm.

(D) Fear of Future Harm Without Antecedent Harm

It is particularly difficult to predict future losses when there is no past or current harm caused by the activity that the plaintiff seeks to enjoin. One interesting example is a case where neighbors sued to prevent a landowner from proceeding with an announced future use of the land. In *Nicholson v. Connecticut Half-Way House, Inc.*, 153 Conn. 507, 218 A.2d 383 (1966), the defendant landowner had announced a plan to have a half-way house that would serve as a temporary residence for selected parolees from state prison. The neighbors' suit claimed that the parolees might commit criminal acts in their neighborhood. The court denied injunctive relief because these unsubstantiated fears could not justify the injunction.

Similarly, in *Adkins v. Thomas Solvent Co.*, 440 Mich. 293, 487 N.W.2d 715 (1992), neighbors sought to enjoin the operation of a solvents company when they feared deterioration in their property values because of public fears of ground contamination. The court held that unfounded public perception was not a sufficient grounds for equitable intervention.

6.   Practicality

Practicality considerations affect the issuance of injunctions in two ways. First, it is appropriate for the trial judge to consider issues of practicality in deciding whether to issue an injunction at all. Injunctions consume large amounts of scarce judicial resources and courts must choose their priorities. Second, practicality affects the scope of the injunction. Courts may choose to limit relief in the name of practicality even when the result is to give incomplete relief.

(A) Allocation of Scarce Judicial Resources

Courts regularly decline to grant mandatory injunctions that would be difficult to supervise. It is for this reason that injunctions rarely issue to supervise a construction project. Judicial resources are not plentiful enough to permit the supervision of many complicated orders.

Equity chooses to afford greater protection to some rights— such as civil rights in a complicated school desegregation case—by devoting the judicial time needed for oversight. School desegregation cases and prison reform cases involve complex injunctions that require ongoing supervision over long periods of time. The difference between a court's refusal to supervise the construction project and its willingness to supervise a school desegregation plan is the greater value put on the Constitutional right.

It is not only the protection of Constitutional rights in major public law cases that receive special treatment. Large amounts of judicial resources are devoted to the ongoing supervision of child support cases. The practicality limitation does not foreclose supervision of that type of injunction even though it frequently is reopened and frustrating for the judge to oversee. The public interest supports this use of judicial resources.

The practicality limitation permits the courts to give more attention to the cases involving rights that our society values most highly. Equity leaves the wronged party to a construction contract to receive damages and take care of the problem without further judicial help. It is simply impractical to have judicial supervision for every such case. In contrast, the reform of unconstitutional conditions in schools or prisons, and the support of children by their parents, are cases that are too important to bar equitable relief with the practicality limitation.

(B) Framing the Injunction

The second way in which practicality affects the issuance of an injunction is in the wording or "framing" of any injunction that is issued. Even if the court finds an injunction appropriate, it may reduce the scope of the order such that it affords the plaintiff limited or even inadequate relief. The court may impose such a limitation in the name of practicality.

In a nuisance case, for example, the court may order limited abatement. Fumes or an odor may be reduced by not eliminated; offensive animals may be reduced in number but not removed entirely; or noise may be restricted during certain hours. *See Muehlman v. Keilman*, 257 Ind. 100, 272 N.E.2d 591 (1971). These limited results may be the product of a balance of hardships, or they may be the result of the practicality limitation if the lesser orders are easier to supervise. To the extent that such orders promote settlement and self-regulation between the parties, there is an even greater savings in judicial resources.

One case where the practicality limitation is dramatically illustrated is *Dover Shopping Center, Inc. v. Cushman's Sons, Inc.,* 63 N.J.Super. 384, 164 A.2d 785 (1960). That case involved a contractual provision to "maintain a retail bakery" in a shopping center. Although Cushman bakeries were successful elsewhere in the city, the store did not turn a profit in this particular shopping center. Therefore, the owners ceased operations in this locale in order to cut overhead costs, but they continued to pay rent as provided by the contract. The shopping center sued to keep the bakery open, as required by contract.

The court did not want to enter a "do business" order because, like a construction contract, it would be impractical to supervise the operation of a bakery under an injunctive order. Instead, the order required the defendant to keep the doors open, to display the name "Cushman's" and to maintain someone in charge. Although this particular order was practical to supervise, it did not give the plaintiff an adequate remedy in itself. The basis for the finding of the inadequacy of damages was the cooperative nature of the shopping center. The court determined that the center operated as the sum of its parts, so the detrimental effect of letting one of the stores close its doors could not be measured. The order did not address the need to keep the store open, but the effect of the order was to accomplish the same result. The court noted that it was "willing to rely upon the defendant's self-interest in continuing to preserve its good reputation by conducting its business in a manner which would reflect credit upon its operation." *Id.* at 790.

Injunctions are discretionary and not a matter of right. In the exercise of that discretion, a judge weighs the "equities" of the case. The common law factors in that assessment have been the subject of this chapter to this point. They include not only the inadequacy of the remedy at law and irreparable harm, but also the relative hardships of the parties and public interest. These factors, along with the determination of the imminency and practicality, form the equities of the case. The trial judge's assessment of those equities is upheld on appeal unless there has been an abuse of discretion. The next section will consider the role of these common law factors when the authority for the injunction is derived from a statute.

C. STATUTORY INJUNCTIONS AND CONSTRAINTS ON DISCRETION

The earlier sections of this chapter have focused on common law principles of equitable jurisdiction. It has emphasized that a court never grants an injunction automatically under the common law, even in situations where the claimant demonstrates a right deserving of legal redress. The essence of equitable jurisdiction is that the judge retains discretion as to the propriety of granting or denying relief. Thus, common law injunctions are always discretionary and not a matter of right. In the exercise of that discretion, a judge evaluates the irreparable harm that may result without the injunction, weighs the relative hardships of the parties, contemplates any problems of practicality in enforcing an order, and considers the public interest.

These common law factors may be replaced by a statutory mandate that alters the traditional discretion of the trial court. In some circumstances, a legislature may choose to require an injunction without regard to the judge's evaluation of the equities of the case. In such cases, it is the legislature's predetermination of the equities that governs. This section first examines the general principles of remedies when the plaintiff's claim is statutory, and then examines the particular situation noted here, when statutory remedies constrain equitable discretion.

1. Statutes Providing Injunctive Relief Generally

It is axiomatic that remedies are derived from the same source as the substantive right under which a claimant prevails. When a right derives from the common law, then common law remedies govern. When a claim is brought under a statute, the court looks to the statutory provision for remedies. If injunctions are enumerated, common law principles are generally implied.

The Supreme Court endorsed this principle in *Hecht Co. v. Bowles,* 321 U.S. 321, 64 S.Ct. 587, 88 L.Ed. 754 (1944). This case involved price controls during World War II under the Emergency Price Control Act of 1942. The statute empowered the governmental Administrator to enforce the Act in court, and the Administrator took the position that he was automatically entitled to an injunction upon showing a violation of the Act. Although a company in question, Hecht's department store, had violated certain provisions of the Act, it had demonstrated its substantial good faith efforts in attempted compliance with it. The Administrator nevertheless contended that the statutory language "shall be granted" required courts to issue an injunction automatically upon a showing of any violation.

The Supreme Court rejected that argument, finding room for discretion under the statute to select other remedies that may be more appropriate. Writing for the majority, Justice Douglas noted that the "grant of *jurisdiction* to issue compliance orders hardly suggests an absolute duty to do so under any and all circumstances." *Id.* at 329. With respect to Hecht's department stores, the trial court found that an injunction would be ineffective and not in the public interest.

The Supreme Court agreed and observed that it was unlikely that Congress intended a drastic departure from the traditions of equity by removing discretion from the trial judge. The Court further noted: "The historic injunctive process was designed to deter, not to punish. The essence of equity jurisdiction has been the power of the Chancellor to do equity and to mold each decree to the necessities of the particular case. Flexibility rather than rigidity have distinguished it." *Id.* at 330. The trial court had found that the regulations were complex and confusing to apply, and that the defendant had acted in good faith. The Administrator had discovered the violations upon a "spot check" and the company had corrected them immediately and voluntarily. Moreover, the store took vigorous steps to prevent further mistakes. Under the circumstances, the judge found that the common law factors for equitable relief were not present.

2. Statutes Providing Limited Relief: Implied Injunctive Remedies

Where a statute is silent with respect to equitable relief but expressly provides for legal relief such as damages, the court must determine whether equitable remedies may be nonetheless appropriate. Conversely, when a statute provides for only equitable remedies, the issue is whether a damage remedy is foreclosed. The process of statutory interpretation begins with the plain language of the statute and its reflection of legislative intent. Most jurists will also consult legislative history and other sources of guidance to determine the purpose of a statute. In many cases, the statutory enumeration of particular remedies and the omission of others have led courts to find a negative implication that only the remedies expressed were intended by the legislature and all others excluded.

Title II of the Civil Rights Act of 1964 provides an interesting example of limited remedies where none other is implied. This Act prohibits discrimination on the basis of race in places of public accommodation. Effective in 1965, this Act preempted the "Jim Crow" laws that required racial segregation in some states. The federal statute provides that a court may remedy violations of Title II with injunctive relief and attorney's fees. Damages are not available and courts have not implied a damages remedy under Title II.

Because of the remedial limitation, any plaintiff who brings a claim under Title II is acting as a "private attorney general." The payment of attorney's fees to private plaintiffs who obtain an injunction against those who continue to discriminate is thus an essential remedy to provide an incentive for individuals to bring actions with such limited remedies. The full nature of this remedial scheme was sufficient to meet the goals of the Act without the implication of a damages remedy. The Supreme Court in *Newman v. Piggie Park Enterprises, Inc.*, 390 U.S. 400, 88 S.Ct. 964, 19 L.Ed.2d 1263 (1968), found it necessary to imply that the statute requires attorney's fees to be awarded in the usual case, however, and not just upon a showing of bad faith by the defendant.

Some courts have gone even further in the implication of remedies to statutes that provide only limited remedies. Confronted with an absence of clear guidance from the text or history of a statute, judges have invoked the general policy behind the statute to allow additional remedies. The most famous of these cases is *Orloff v. Los Angeles Turf Club,* 30 Cal.2d 110, 180 P.2d 321 (1947). In this case, a California statute prohibited discrimination on the basis of race in certain public places. This state statute preceded the federal prohibition against racial discrimination in public accommodations in the Civil Rights Act of 1964, and thus it represented a new right at its time. The California legislature created the right of non-discrimination but, unlike the subsequent federal counterpart, did not provide for injunctive relief. The remedial portion of the California statute specified only $100 and compensatory damages.

The opinion of the California Supreme Court in *Orloff* notes that compensable damages would be difficult to measure, and that $100 is not a sufficient deterrent. Defendants may wish to be racially exclusive despite the statute, and they would not have enough incentive to obey the law when there is only a small monetary cost for its violation. The court thus allowed injunctive relief in order to give effect to the object of the statute.

3.   Statutes Constraining Equitable Discretion

Although the provision of a statutory injunctive remedy usually implies the use of common law equitable discretion, there are nonetheless a few statutes that have been interpreted as constraining equitable discretion. Statutes may do so either by a preclusion of an injunction or by a statutory mandate of one. In either instance, the legislative intent must clearly guide courts in their remedial options.

The most famous example of this category of statute is the Supreme Court's interpretation of the Endangered Species Act of 1973 in *Tennessee Valley Authority v. Hill*, 437 U.S. 153, 98 S.Ct. 2279, 57 L.Ed.2d 117 (1978). The Act first empowered the appointed Secretary to make a list of species who were endangered according to certain criteria. It then said that when the habitat of an endangered species is threatened by an activity such as construction, the Secretary must seek an injunction in federal district court to preserve the habitat, and the injunction shall issue.

There was a dam construction project in Tennessee that had been the object of controversy since its inception. When the dam was almost completed, opponents discovered a small species that was endangered, the snail darter. Although many years later it was learned that the snail darter was not properly classified as an endangered species, it was found to meet the statutory criteria at that time.

Following this statutory scheme, the Secretary placed the snail darter on the endangered species list and brought an action in court to enjoin the project. The trial court questioned whether it had discretion to refuse to issue the injunction against such an expensive construction project, expressly funded by Congress and near completion, for the sake of an apparently insignificant species. The Supreme Court determined that the Act required the injunction once the trial court confirmed that the species was protected by the Act and that the project threatened its habitat. The Court held that the absolute language of the Act removed all discretion from the trial court to balance the relative importance of this species with the economic significance of the federal project.

The Court reasoned that the language, history and structure of the Act demonstrated the clear Congressional intent to remove discretion from the trial judge. Congress had already determined that protection of certain species should be given the highest of priorities because their value was "incalculable." The Court further found that because Congress had already considered the public interest and expressed its intent favoring protection of endangered species, the doctrine of separation of powers precluded traditional judicial balancing of equities.

Since *Tennessee Valley Authority v. Hill,* the Supreme Court has not found another statutory scheme that clearly removes judicial discretion in the granting of an injunction. The Court held in *Weinberger v. Romero-Barcelo,* 456 U.S. 305, 102 S.Ct. 1798, 72 L.Ed.2d 91 (1982), that the trial court had discretion not to issue an injunction precluding the United States Navy from releasing military supplies into water near its training site off Puerto Rico. Despite the apparently mandatory language of the environmental statute prohibiting such dumping without a permit, the trial court found that no harm was done to the water and simply ordered the Navy to get a permit while it continued its operations. The Supreme Court upheld the ability of the trial court to fashion this discretionary remedy and overturned the Court of Appeals opinion which had held that the statute compelled an injunction against operations while the Navy sought the permit.

Similarly, in *United States v. Oakland Cannabis Buyers' Cooperative,* 532 U.S. 483, 121 S.Ct. 1711, 149 L.Ed.2d 722 (2001), the Court upheld the trial court's discretion in enforcing the Controlled Substances Act, which prohibits with mandatory language the manufacture and sale of certain drugs. The Supreme Court distinguished *TVA v. Hill* on the grounds that criminal enforcement is the customary means of ensuring compliance with the statute. Thus, Congressional policy under the Act can be upheld without an injunction. The Court noted that discretion is displaced only by a "clear and valid legislative command." 121 S.Ct. at 1720–1722.

State statutes sometimes mandate injunctive relief for particular interests. For example, in 2011 the Texas legislature enacted a statute providing that noncompetition agreements "are enforceable" when they meet certain enumerated standards, not including irreparable harm. Tex. Bus. & Com. Code Ann. § 15.15. That language appears to remove the discretion of the judge in issuing an injunction when the statutory standards are met. Texas courts are struggling to understand the scope of this language and whether it also applies to temporary injunctive relief (Chapter 5).

See *Argo Group US, Inc. v. Levinson*, 468 S.W.3d 698 (Tex.App.2015) (describing split).

In contrast to statutes mandating injunctions, some statutes prohibit injunctions. One example is the Norris-LaGuardia Act, 29 U.S.C. § 104 which prevents federal courts from enjoining labor disputes by removing federal jurisdiction over such issues. Another example is Internal Revenue Code § 7421(a), which effectively prohibits injunctions against the Internal Revenue Service from collecting taxes.

On the state level, there are a few anti-injunction statutes where public interest strongly disfavors interference with the operations of certain local industries. For example, some heavily agricultural states have statutes pertaining to nuisance actions against farming activities where the legislation bars courts from issuing injunctions against normal farming activities.

In conclusion, statutory authorization for injunctive relief may affect the discretionary nature of traditional equitable relief, but it rarely does so. In the few cases where courts have found a legislative intent to remove the court's discretion, the common law standards were suspended. In the absence of such clear intent by the legislature, however, courts have generally interpreted statutes to incorporate the common law standards for injunctions, thus preserving the discretionary nature of the remedy.

Chapter Five

TEMPORARY INJUNCTIVE RELIEF

Any injunction is "extraordinary" relief that requires a strong showing of necessity. The preventive injunction, examined in the previous chapter, is the classic equitable order that is issued after a full trial on the merits. This chapter explores two types of injunctions that are the product of greater urgency. When circumstances do not permit the court to have a full trial on the merits of a claim before acting to preserve a situation, then a temporary injunction may preserve the *status quo* pending further opportunity for future fact-finding.

A. OVERVIEW

Temporary restraining orders and preliminary injunctions are two types of temporary relief that a court may use to prevent irreversible losses before trial. They are forms of interlocutory injunctions, which by definition involve expedited relief for a short term. The term "temporary relief" is used here to encompass both preliminary injunctions and temporary restraining orders as those two terms are used in the Federal Rules of Civil Procedure.

1. Types and Terms

The nomenclature for these injunctions is somewhat confusing across jurisdictions. Many states use the term "temporary injunction" as synonymous with preliminary injunction, or sometimes as a shorthand for temporary restraining orders. This chapter will use the federal terms: preliminary injunction and temporary restraining order.

Federal Rule of Civil Procedure 65 governs preliminary injunctions and temporary restraining orders in federal courts. This rule has been influential in other jurisdictions; many states have identical or similar rules. Some states vary in the procedures and requirements for these two types of temporary relief, but the variations tend to be slight.

2. Purpose and Function

The principal concern underlying any temporary relief is that immediate and irreparable harm may occur before the dispute between the parties can be resolved at a full trial on the merits. The injunction may prevent the commission of an act that threatens to render future remedies ineffectual. For example, a court may issue a restraining order to prevent a defendant from removing or disposing of property for the purpose of defrauding creditors with liens, or to preserve property that will be the subject of the subsequent trial.

Courts often say that the purpose of temporary injunctions is "to preserve the *status quo*" until a hearing on the merits. The "*status quo*" is defined as the "last actual peaceable uncontested status" of the parties to the controversy. The idea is that the temporary relief does not alter the legal relations of the parties but instead serves to maintain their relationship for the duration of the order.

The purpose of temporary relief is different from the purpose of remedies awarded at the end of a full trial on the merits. Preventing further damage pending trial is different from putting the parties in their rightful positions. As such, it is not clear that a statute affecting remedies after a full trial would apply equally to temporary relief. For example, the Texas legislature enacted a statute in 2011 that clarified the enforceability of noncompetition agreements. The act said that they "are enforceable" when they meet certain enumerated standards, not including irreparable harm. Tex. Bus. & Com. Code Ann. § 15.15 *et seq.* Texas courts are uncertain whether these standards also apply to temporary injunctive relief, given its different function and purpose. See *Argo Group US, Inc. v. Levinson*, 468 S.W.3d 698 (Tex.App.2015) (describing split). The issue is whether courts should require irreparable harm for temporary relief when it is not required for permanent relief in the context of noncompetition agreements covered by the statute.

Despite the fact that courts often state that the purpose of temporary relief is to maintain the *status quo*, that purpose is insufficient by itself to justify relief. Rather, a trial court focuses primarily on whether the plaintiff can establish that the absence of immediate relief will cause irreparable harm under circumstances where the court is justified in protecting the plaintiff's interests even at the risk of causing loss to the defendant before there can be a full trial on the merits. As Judge Posner explained, the "premise of the preliminary injunction is that the remedy available at the end of trial will not make the plaintiff whole; and, in a sense, the more limited that remedy, the stronger the argument for a preliminary injunction." *American Hosp. Supply Corp. v. Hospital Products Ltd.*, 780 F.2d 589, 594 (7th Cir.1986).

The *status quo* that the court seeks to preserve through an award of temporary relief may be a state of action or a state of inaction. For example, the order might require a defendant to continue supplying goods pursuant to a distributorship agreement. On the other hand, the order could involve a decree that prevents a developer from razing a building pending determination of its qualification for protection as a historical landmark under a statute. Finally, an order might enjoin a freeway extension, or direct a defendant to comply with state regulations for hazardous-waste facilities.

This chapter examines the differences between two types of temporary relief: preliminary injunctions and temporary restraining orders. The main differences between the two are how long they last and how quickly they are obtained. The chapter also explains the requirement for security for this type of relief. A plaintiff must be prepared to compensate a wrongfully enjoined defendant for losses caused by the expedited order. Such compensation is awarded without regard to the good faith of the plaintiff in seeking the order in the first place. Unless the plaintiff is ultimately victorious in the underlying case, the plaintiff will be liable for the defendant's proven losses associated with the temporary restraining order and/or preliminary injunction. The reason for this rule is that the plaintiff has asked the court to act under circumstances when there was not time for careful deliberation of the full facts of a case.

B. TEMPORARY RESTRAINING ORDERS

A temporary restraining order (TRO) is designed to deal with urgent situations when it is necessary to preserve the *status quo* long enough for a preliminary injunction hearing. It lasts only a few days unless there is consent from the party restrained for a longer period. The TRO is dissolved after the hearing for the preliminary injunction, when the court may decide on other appropriate relief at that point.

1. Duration

Federal Rule of Civil Procedure 65(b) contains specific procedural requirements for a temporary restraining orders. It provides that the order can last only fourteen days, with a second fourteen-day extension for good cause or if the other party consents to an extension.[1] The limits were previously ten days with possible

---

[1]   The relevant portion of Fed. R. Civ. P. 65(b) reads: "Every temporary restraining order issued without notice must state the date and hour it was issued; describe the injury and state why it is irreparable; state why the order was issued without notice; and be promptly filed in the clerk's office and entered in the record.

judicial extension to twenty days, so that older cases reflect the earlier numbers, as in *Sims v. Greene*, discussed below.

These limitations on TROs have been strictly applied by the federal courts. In *Sims v. Greene*, 160 F.2d 512 (3d Cir.1947), the Court of Appeals found that the district court erred in not adhering to the exact time limits. In that case, the trial court issued a TRO against an individual defendant that restrained him from interfering with the plaintiff as presiding bishop of a church. Even though defendant maintained that the plaintiff was no longer the bishop, because he had been defrocked by the General Conference, the court issued the order nonetheless to preserve the *status quo* of the current bishop. After ten days, the court extended the TRO for another ten days without comment. The appellate court reversed noting that, under Rule 65(b), a TRO cannot extend beyond ten days unless cause is shown why it should extend for another ten days. After that it cannot be extended at all without the consent of the party enjoined.

It is an extraordinary remedy to enjoin a defendant when there has been very little opportunity to receive evidence in the matter. The court must set a time for a preliminary injunction hearing as soon as possible in order to minimize the time of restraint without at least such a hearing. In *Sims*, the Third Circuit ordered the district court to begin the hearing for the preliminary injunction at once and to continue that hearing daily until its conclusion.

2.   *Ex parte* TROs

When the threat of irreparable injury is immediate and strong, it is possible to receive a TRO without even giving notice to the opposing party before the court issues the restraint. Such an order requires a very strong showing of necessity because it is another step beyond the usual mode of adjudication. Not only is the court enjoining a defendant when there has been very little opportunity to receive evidence in the matter, but an *ex parte* order does so without even giving notice to the defendant.

Federal Rule of Civil Procedure 65(b) provides for the possibility of an *ex parte* TRO only upon a specific showing that immediate and irreparable harm will result before the opposing

---

The order expires at the time after entry—not to exceed 14 days—that the court sets, unless before that time the court, for good cause, extends it for a like period or the adverse party consents to a longer extension. The reasons for an extension must be entered in the record."

party could be notified and heard.[2] Therefore, the plaintiff must make a showing of extreme necessity.

For example, if an individual is threatening to destroy plaintiff's property, and there is reason to believe that notice of the court action might hasten the destruction, then the plaintiff might successfully petition the court for a restraining order without notice to the opposing party until after the order issues. The advantage to the plaintiff of this approach is that defendant can be punished for contempt if he destroys the property in violation of the TRO. This threatened sanction has two advantages for the plaintiff. First, it reduces the chance that the defendant will proceed with the threatened destruction because contempt can result in a criminal conviction for violation of the court order. Second, even if the defendant proceeds with the destruction, the remedies for civil contempt can be greater than for the tort of conversion.

3. Constitutional Limitations

Many states have adopted identical or similar provisions to Federal Rule of Civil Procedure 65(b). Although states are free to adopt procedures that differ, the Supreme Court has held that there are constitutional limits on the issuance of an *ex parte* TRO under state law, at least when First Amendment rights are at stake.

In *Carroll v. President and Commissioners of Princess Anne*, 393 U.S. 175, 89 S.Ct. 347, 21 L.Ed.2d 325 (1968), an extremist organization held a rally opposing a voluntary school desegregation plan during the period when school boards were responding to the United States Supreme Court's desegregation decision in *Brown v. Board of Education*, 347 U.S. 483, 74 S.Ct. 686, 98 L.Ed. 873 (1954). The speakers at the rally made racially provocative remarks and urged those in attendance to return to a future rally. Town officials feared an explosive confrontation and therefore sought and obtained an *ex parte* TRO to prohibit the second rally. The Court found that the TRO was constitutionally defective because the officials failed to attempt to give notice of the proceedings to the defendants. The Court explained that when First Amendment rights are at stake, it is particularly important to have all parties present. Only if defendants can present their objections to the order and its wording

---

[2]   The relevant portion of Fed. R. Civ. P. 65(b) reads: "The court may issue a temporary restraining order without written or oral notice to the adverse party or its attorney only if: (A) specific facts in an affidavit or a verified complaint clearly show that immediate and irreparable injury, loss, or damage will result to the movant before the adverse party can be heard in opposition; and (B) the movant's attorney certifies in writing any efforts made to give notice and the reasons why it should not be required.

are they able to assure that any order that is issued will be fashioned as narrowly as possible to protect all interests.

C. PRELIMINARY INJUNCTIONS

The Federal Rules of Civil Procedure address the requirements for a preliminary injunction in Rule 65(a)(1). That rule provides that "the court may issue a preliminary injunction only on notice to the adverse party." Then Federal Rule of Civil Procedure 65(a)(2) permits the consolidation of the preliminary injunction hearing with the trial on the merits. Although these rules cover only procedural requirements, without mention of substantive standards, federal courts have interpreted Rule 65 to incorporate the common law substantive requirements that traditionally govern equitable orders.

1. Traditional Test

Common law substantive requirements require the plaintiff to make a showing with regard to four factors: likelihood of success on the merits, irreparable injury, balance of harm, and public interest. The difference between the traditional test and the alternative test is what the plaintiff must show with respect to these factors.

Many federal circuits, as well as most state courts, follow the traditional test for a preliminary injunction. The traditional test takes these four factors and sets a threshold test for each factor. The alternative test, covered in the next section, permits a sliding scale, such that one factor can be demonstrated more weakly if another factor is established as very high.

Under the traditional test a plaintiff must establish each of the factors independently: (1) a probability of prevailing on the merits; (2) an irreparable injury if the relief is delayed; (3) a balance of hardships favoring the plaintiff; and (4) a showing that the injunction would not be adverse to the public interest. The plaintiff has the burden of showing that the threshold has been met or surpassed on each of these four requirements.

If the plaintiff is unable to show that any one of the four elements in the traditional test is satisfied, that failure ends the inquiry in jurisdictions following this approach. In *Narragansett Indian Tribe v. Guilbert*, 934 F.2d 4 (1st Cir.1991), for example, the defendants purchased a lot from a Narragansett Indian for the construction of a private residence. The Tribe filed a complaint alleging that the property encroached on the reservation, but it did so only after the purchasers had completed all the permits and begun construction. The district court denied the requested preliminary injunction and the First Circuit affirmed.

The First Circuit reasoned that although the potential alteration of real property is a classic example of irreparable harm, in this particular case the possibility of irreparable damage in the absence of an injunction was "very faint." The opinion notes that there had already been extensive site preparation work at the time of suit, that trees and underbrush had already been cleared, that the excavation for the foundation was complete, and that the invasive work for the installation of a septic system had been done. Given the significant transformation of the land that was already complete, the plaintiff failed to convince the court that completion of the dwelling would do further irreparable harm. The strength or weakness of any other factors—likelihood of success on the merits, balance of hardships and public interest—was irrelevant because the plaintiff failed to cross the threshold for one factor—significant irreparable harm.

The Supreme Court has emphasized that public interest must be carefully considered in the issuance of a preliminary injunction. In its 2008 opinion *Winter v. Natural Resources Defense Council, Inc.*, 555 U.S. 7, 129 S.Ct. 365, 172 L.Ed.2d 249 (2008), the public interest involved was national security. At issue was the failure of the Navy to file an Environment Impact Statement before conducting some Navy antisubmarine training exercises off the coast of California. The Navy argued that there was no environmental impact in the use of active sonar, which emits pulses of sound underwater and then receives the acoustic waves that echo off the target. The plaintiffs, who had conservation and commercial interests, sought to enjoin the exercises pending the Navy's compliance with environmental regulations. The district court issued a preliminary injunction that required measures to mitigate any possible effect on marine animals, and the Court of Appeals affirmed with modification. The Supreme Court reversed on several grounds, including the particular application of the alternative test sliding scale covered later in this chapter. One of those grounds was that the public interest in the training exercises had not received sufficient weight because a properly trained antisubmarine force is necessary for national security.

A trial court's decision to grant or deny a preliminary injunction is given great deference and is reversible on appeal only for abuse of discretion. This test is satisfied when the trial judge has failed to consider properly all the interests, as in *Winter*, or when the court has made an error in the interpretation of law. For example, in *Infinity Radio v. Whitby*, 780 So.2d 248 (Fla.App.2001), the trial court denied a preliminary injunction against an on-the-air radio personality who went to work for a competitor. The court of appeals concluded that the trial court misinterpreted the effect of the assigned contract that contained the noncompetition agreement and thus had incorrectly concluded that the plaintiff radio station was not likely to succeed on the merits. It therefore remanded the case with an order to issue the injunction.

2. Alternative Tests

Some federal circuits follow alternative approaches. Circuits that deviate from the traditional rule are not in complete agreement about a substitute approach but agree to a basic sliding scale principle. That principle is that plaintiffs may meet a lesser standard than "probability" of success on the merits of the underlying claim when the degree of potential harm is particularly great. In contrast, the traditional approach requires proof of a "probability" of success on the merits in all preliminary injunction cases.

(A) The Sliding Scale in the Ninth Circuit

The circuit that began the movement toward the more expansive approach is the Ninth Circuit, although there were some deeper roots in earlier cases. The sliding scale approach, called the alternative test, allows a plaintiff the choice of establishing the four traditional factors or of satisfying a sliding scale test.

The sliding scale test has evolved in the Ninth Circuit over the decades. Under the current formulation, the plaintiff must show either

(1) that there are serious questions on the merits and that the balance of hardships tips decidedly in plaintiff's favor, or

(2) that there is a probability of success on the merits and that there is more than a possibility of irreparable harm without the order.

In other words, a stronger showing of irreparable harm can offset a lesser showing of likelihood success on the merits. Conversely, a stronger showing of a likely success on the merits reduces the required showing of irreparable harm. *Alliance for the Wild Rockies v. Cottrell*, 632 F.3d 1127 (9th Cir.2011). The Ninth Circuit earlier explained the rule as "not separate tests, but the outer reaches 'of a single continuum.'" *Los Angeles Memorial Coliseum Comm'n v. National Football League*, 634 F.2d 1197, 1201 (9th Cir.1980).

It is notable that the alternative test still has threshold requirements on both the issues of success on the merits and irreparability. Although the scale is a "sliding" one, it is still necessary for the plaintiff to pass the thresholds to get on the scale at all. Although the Ninth Circuit held at one point that a mere "possibility" of irreparable harm was sufficient to pass the threshold test, the United States Supreme Court specifically overturned that standard in *Winter v. Natural Resources Defense Council, Inc.*, 555 U.S. 7, 129 S.Ct. 365, 172 L.Ed.2d 249 (2008), noted previously in this chapter for the case's discussion of public interest. There must be evidence of irreparable harm without the requested injunction and not a mere possibility of harm. In *Winter* there was not sufficient evidence that the Navy's use of sonar during training caused any harm to marine animals.

The threshold provides that a "serious question" must be presented. The threshold for irreparability is that there is some level of irreparable harm. Thus, even if there is an extremely high probability of success on the merits, the lack of any irreparable harm would preclude the preliminary injunction. A contract debt without more, for example, would not support the order because the remedy at law—damages—would remain adequate. The "single continuum" does not extend that far.

The public interest remains a factor even though it is not part of the express formulation of the alternative test in the Ninth Circuit. The circuit explained in *Caribbean Marine Services Co. v. Baldrige*, 844 F.2d 668 (9th Cir.1988), that the public interest is always a factor. In that case, owners of fishing vessels sought a preliminary injunction to prohibit the placement of female observers on commercial tuna boats. The federal Marine Mammal Protection Act requires the National Oceanic and Atmospheric Administration to assign observers on tuna boats to monitor the accidental capture of porpoises during the tuna netting process. Prior to 1987, the observers had always been male because the crews of the tuna boats are all male. In that year the Administration notified the plaintiff boat owners that a female observer was assigned for a future voyage.

The owners sued to prevent the placement and the federal district court granted the injunction. The plaintiffs alleged that the presence of women on ship threatened the privacy of the crew and infringed on the commercial enterprise. The privacy argument was based on the fact that the observers would necessarily see crew members undress and perform bodily functions, such as relieving themselves off the side of the ship. The commercial infringement argument was based on the assertion that they would catch fewer fish. Following the alternative test, the district court judge found that serious questions had been raised on the merits and that the balance of hardships strongly favored the plaintiffs.

The Ninth Circuit reversed on the grounds that the lower court abused its discretion in issuing the preliminary injunction. The opinion explains that the owners were not likely to prevail on the merits and the balance of hardships did not weigh in their favor. The court found the argument that they would catch fewer fish with the presence of the female observers to be remote and speculative. The privacy arguments were more substantial, but the court balanced the privacy interest of the crew against the harm to the government. The government's interest was to carry out the policies of Congress as embodied in these statutes and others. Specifically, the government's interest included not only the protection of marine mammals but also Title VII of the Civil Rights Act of 1964 which forbids discrimination in employment on the basis of sex. The strong public interest tipped the scales against the owners.

(B) Formulations in Other Circuits

Several other circuits have developed alternative tests for preliminary injunctions. Notably, the Second Circuit has developed a "serious questions" test. In *ABKCO Music, Inc. v. Stellar Records, Inc.,* 96 F.3d 60 (2d Cir.1996), the court said that a party seeking a preliminary injunction must show: "(1) irreparable harm in the absence of the injunction and (2) either (a) a likelihood of success on the merits or (b) sufficiently serious questions going to the merits to make them a fair ground for litigation and a balance of hardships tipping decidedly in the movant's favor." *Id.* at 64. Under the facts of that case, a copyright holder of song lyrics sued producers of karaoke compact discs for infringement. Once the plaintiff had established a strong probability of success on the merits, the district court could employ the then presumption of irreparable harm for copyright infringement to justify issuance of a preliminary injunction. (That presumption is now under question following the Supreme Court's 2006 patent injunction case, *eBay Inc. v. MercExchange,* 547 U.S. 388, 126 S.Ct. 1837, 164 L.Ed.2d 641 (2006). See discussion in Chapter 3.)

In contrast, the Second Circuit upheld the denial of a preliminary injunction in another copyright case, *Random House, Inc. v. Rosetta Books,* 283 F.3d 490 (2d Cir.2002), involving alleged copyright infringement by the publishers of e-books who obtained copyright permission from famous authors but omitted the publisher who held the rights to publish the works as "books." Because the district court did not find a probability of success on the merits of the claim, the presumption of irreparable harm (then available) was not sufficient to support the desired order. The tiny publisher of the e-books, who found this lawsuit to be a victory of David over the Goliath publisher, was thus saved from probable business extinction if the preliminary injunction had been issued. The parties ultimately settled after the Court of Appeals upheld the denial of the temporary relief.

After the United States Supreme Court decided *Winter v. Natural Resources Defense Council, Inc.*, 555 U.S. 7, 129 S.Ct. 365, 172 L.Ed.2d 249 (2008), discussed previously in this chapter, the Second Circuit considered whether its "serious questions" formulation was consistent with the Supreme Court's requirements. In *Citigroup Global Markets, Inc. v. VCG Special Opportunities Master Fund Ltd.*, 598 F.3d 30 (2d Cir.2010), the Second Circuit concluded that *Winter* is not inconsistent with its standard because the burden on the movant is not just to show that the balance of hardships tips in its favor when there is only a "serious question" on the merits, but that the balance of hardships tips *decidedly* in its favor. Finding this burden no less that that required in *Winter*, the court noted: "The 'serious questions' standard permits a district court to grant a preliminary injunction in situations where it cannot determine with certainty that the moving party is more likely than not to prevail on the merits of the underlying claims, but where the costs outweigh the benefits of not granting the injunction." 598 F.3d at 35.

The Seventh Circuit also has adopted an alternative test. Judge Posner described the test as a formula in *American Hosp. Supply Corp. v. Hospital Products Ltd.*, 780 F.2d 589 (7th Cir.1986). If $[P \times H_p] > (1 - P) \times H_d$ then the preliminary injunction should be granted. P is the probability that the denial is an error because plaintiff will win on the substance; H_p is the harm to the plaintiff if the injunction is denied; H_d is the harm to the defendant if the injunction is granted.

Judge (formerly Professor) Posner's inspiration for this approach was a famous law review article by John Leubsdorf, *The Standard for Preliminary Injunctions*, 91 HARV. L. REV. 525 (1978). The article notes that the court's function is to protect rights and not just to make utilitarian calculations about projected losses by both parties. Nonetheless, Professor Leubsdorf extrapolated from the history and theory of this remedy the following rule: A court should grant a preliminary injunction if the product of the probability that the plaintiff will prevail and amount of uncompensated harm that the plaintiff might suffer without the order is greater than the defendant's uncompensated costs of complying with the order.

Although Judge Posner characterized his formula as the procedural counterpart to Judge Learned Hand's famous negligence formula in *United States v. Carroll Towing Co.*, 159 F.2d 169 (2d

Cir.1947), it has not acquired an equivalent following. The Seventh Circuit test has since been described as a sliding scale like the alternative test. *Abbott Labs. v. Mead Johnson & Co.*, 971 F.2d 6 (7th Cir.1992).

The Seventh Circuit clarified its standard in a 2015 case, *Turnell v. Centimark Corp.*, 796 F.3d 656 (7th Cir.2015). The court explained that it is a two-step analysis. In the first step, the movant must make a threshold showing that: (1) absent preliminary injunctive relief, he will suffer irreparable harm; (2) there is no adequate remedy at law; and (3) he has a reasonable likelihood of success on the merits. In the second step, the court considers: (4) "the irreparable harm the moving party will endure if the preliminary injunction is wrongfully denied versus the irreparable harm to the nonmoving party if it is wrongfully granted;" and (5) the public interest. The scale is sliding in the sense that the more likely the movant is to win, the less the balance of harms must weigh in movant's favor. Conversely, the less likely movant is to win, the more it must weigh in movant's favor.

3. Traditional and Alternative Test Differences

A plaintiff may be successful with the alternative test in cases where the traditional test would not be met. Consider a plaintiff who has a relatively weak case on the merits but the situation is one where the potential harm would be extremely serious in the absence of an injunction. For such a plaintiff, the sliding scale test may permit a preliminary injunction even though the traditional test would not permit it because there is no probability of success on the merits. Conversely, a plaintiff with a strong substantive claim can receive a preliminary injunction with a lesser showing of irreparable harm and balance of hardships, although the plaintiff must still prove irreparable harm as a threshold matter. Such plaintiffs still bear the burden of proving their cases on the merits at trial, but the preliminary injunction would give them the opportunity to do so without sustaining harm in the interim.

One can speculate whether the plaintiffs in *Narragansett Indian Tribe v. Guilbert*—the case from section one of this section, where partial house construction had already altered disputed land—would have fared better in a jurisdiction that follows the alternative test. The plaintiff tribe lost under the traditional test because of the failure to satisfy the required level of irreparable harm. It would appear that their proof might have crossed the lower threshold of irreparable harm under the alternative test because there was further alteration to the land at issue during the construction of the house they sought to enjoin. If they could make the threshold showing of irreparable harm sufficient to get on the sliding scale, then their case would have turned on the strength of their legal claim. If they could show a high likelihood of success on the merits—that the house infringed on the tribal reservation— then that could have offset their low showing of irreparable harm under the alternative test.

4. Preliminary Injunction Hearing

Regardless of whether a circuit applies a traditional or alternative test, the factual basis for the application of a circuit's standard requires some rudimentary fact-finding. The universal interpretation of Federal Rule of Civil Procedure 65(a) is that it requires a hearing before the issuance of a preliminary injunction. The rule itself says in relevant part: "the court may issue a preliminary injunction only on notice to the adverse party." This brief provision does not mention a "hearing" but the circuits have agreed that the requirement of "notice" implies a hearing. A hearing by definition is something less than a full trial on the merits. It is a matter of the sound discretion of the trial judge how much testimony to admit.

At a preliminary injunction hearing, both sides must have an opportunity to present evidence. The Third Circuit so held in a second round of appeal in *Sims v. Greene*, 161 F.2d 87 (3d Cir.1947). After the first round of appeal, the district court judge held a hearing where only the plaintiff was given a significant chance to present evidence. The Third Circuit again reversed on the grounds that a "hearing" implies a fair opportunity for both sides to present testimony.

The preliminary injunction hearing need not be a full trial on the merits, although Federal Rule of Civil Procedure 65(a)(2) permits consolidation with the trial on the merits. Rule 52(a) requires: "In an action tried on the facts without a jury or with an advisory jury, the court must find the facts specially and state its conclusions of law separately." Further, for an interlocutory injunction: "In granting or refusing an interlocutory injunction, the court must similarly state the findings and conclusions that support its action."

The parties may waive their right to a hearing and submit their case on affidavits for the preliminary injunction. It must be clear, however, that there is a waiver and that the parties are willing to proceed only by affidavits. If the party sought to be restrained requests a hearing, however, it is an abuse of discretion for the trial court to refuse it. *Fengler v. Numismatic Americana, Inc.*, 832 F.2d 745 (2d Cir.1987).

The findings of the court at the preliminary injunction hearing are not binding on the judge at the time of the full trial. The United States Supreme Court explained in *University of Texas v. Camenisch*, 451 U.S. 390, 101 S.Ct. 1830, 68 L.Ed.2d 175 (1981), that because a party is not required to prove his case in full at the preliminary injunction stage, the findings of fact and conclusions of law made by a court granting a preliminary injunction are not binding at trial on the merits. The Court found this result consistent with the principle that the purpose of a preliminary injunction is merely to preserve the "relative positions" of the parties until a trial on the merits can be held.

D. DIFFERENCES BETWEEN TROs AND PRELIMINARY INJUNCTIONS

The time constraints in Federal Rule of Civil Procedure 65(b) for a TRO are strict; it may not last more than twenty-eight days without the consent of the party who is restrained. In contrast, a preliminary injunction lasts until trial or modification, which means that it can last for years.

A TRO is not appealable because of its short duration. In contrast, a preliminary injunction is appealable. When the time limitations of Rule 65(b) have been violated, the order "converts" to a preliminary injunction for purposes of appeal. An overextended TRO thus is reversed because it would not be based on a sufficient hearing to support a preliminary injunction. *Sims v. Greene*, 160 F.2d 512 (3d Cir.1947).

Because Federal Rule of Civil Procedure 65(a) requires "notice" for a preliminary injunction, it is not possible to have such an order *ex parte*. In contrast, Rule 65(b) permits a TRO to be entered *ex parte*. Nonetheless, a court may enter such an order only upon a specific showing that immediate and irreparable harm will result before the opposing party could be notified and heard.

E. INJUNCTION BONDS

Federal Rule of Civil Procedure 65(c) provides that a party seeking a TRO or preliminary injunction must provide security before the court issues such an order. The provision is broad: "(c) Security. The court may issue a preliminary injunction or a temporary restraining order only if the movant gives security in an amount that the court considers proper to pay the costs and damages sustained by any party found to have been wrongfully enjoined or restrained. * * *."

Most courts have interpreted the rule to require the judge to make a decision on the propriety of a bond and not to ignore a demand entirely. Furthermore, it is reversible error to refuse a bond unless there is no risk of monetary loss.

1. Purpose and Function

The purpose of the Rule 65(c) security requirement is to provide redress for wrongfully enjoined defendants. The funds indemnify the party enjoined for damages directly resulting from a wrongfully issued injunction. The bond provides a convenient repository of funds against which the wrongfully enjoined party can collect damages. It removes the risk that the plaintiff might be judgment-proof by the time such a claim is possible.

The bond requirement indirectly preserves the dignity of the court and reflects the hesitation of our judicial system to issue orders in haste. Temporary relief is an extraordinary remedy that permits judges to issue orders without time to hear all the evidence and to reflect on the just result. The function of the security requirement is to guarantee that plaintiffs will compensate defendants for losses caused by that hasty decision. It functions as an exception to the general rule that litigation losses and expenses are borne by the parties themselves. Because the claimant must incur costs in posting the bond, this requirement also serves as a check on the zealousness of plaintiffs in instituting litigation.

2. Setting the Bond

The security can be either a bond or guarantee from the defendant. A court may dispense with the posting of a bond if the party seeking injunctive relief has sufficient assets to assure its ability to pay damages, such as when the defendant is a solvent corporation.

The amount of the bond is a matter for the sound discretion of the court. Because the bond is generally regarded as a ceiling on the defendant's future recovery, the time to question the amount of the bond is at the time it is set. The defendant may request a higher bond in order to protect its interests during the interim period of the temporary relief.

3. Recovery Under the Bond

The bond assures that the defendant will be compensated for any losses occasioned by the order in the event that the plaintiff does not ultimately prevail in the underlying case. The damages must be actually caused by the wrongfully-issued order and the defendant must prove them with specificity.

The test for the defendant's recovery on the bond is whether the plaintiff ultimately loses on the merits of the underlying case. It is not sufficient to show that the temporary relief failed to meet the procedural or substantive requirements for the TRO or preliminary injunction. It is the ultimate merits of the case that matter.

The amount of the bond is generally a cap on the damages potentially recoverable by the restrained party, even if the losses far exceed the amount of the bond. In *Static Control Components, Inc. v. Lexmark Inter., Inc.,* 697 F.3d 387 (6th Cir.2012), the recovery was capped at the quarter million dollars set by the bond even though the actual losses from the wrongful restraint were in the seven to ten million dollar range.

Some bonds are left open without a limit to recovery. Such "open" bonds operate the same as security given without a limitation to recovery. Further, some cases have permitted recovery in excess of a bond cap where the order was secured by fraud or malice. In such cases, the recovery in excess of the bond is recovered from the wrongful party and not from the surety for the bond.

There is a presumption favoring recovery under the bond if the enjoined party subsequently prevails on the merits at trial. Despite the presumption, the wrongfully enjoined party has the burden of proving with specificity the actual losses suffered as a result of the injunction because the bond is not a form of liquidated damages. It is simply a source of funds for the payment of provable losses.

Compensable losses include measurable harms caused specifically by the order, not including distress and humiliation. The wrongfully enjoined party recovers proven losses without any requirement of fraud or bad faith on the part of the moving party. The dignity of the court is thus preserved because the consequences of its hasty action are redressed by the party who sought the relief, even in good faith.

F. STANDARDS FOR REVERSAL

The standard for appellate review of a preliminary injunction is abuse of discretion. *Ashcroft v. ACLU,* 542 U.S. 656, 124 S.Ct. 2783, 159 L.Ed.2d 690 (2004). Despite this simple rule, there are aspects of an appeal of the order that require different tests. First, because the order involves an evaluation of the probability of the plaintiff's success on the merits of the claim, appellate courts address questions of law *de novo.*

Second, other aspects of the substantive standards for a preliminary injunction are factually based. The parties have presented rudimentary evidence relating to irreparable harm, balance of hardships, and public interest. Any findings of fact are reviewable on the clearly erroneous standard.

Third, it is the assessment of the equities themselves that is subject to the abuse of discretion standard. That assessment of the equities is the decision whether to issue the preliminary injunction given the evidence.

Distinguish the review of summary judgments with preliminary injunctions. In both circumstances the judge considers the application of the law, but the grant of summary judgment is the substantive determination of a case. In contrast, a preliminary injunction is an interim determination of the relative merits of the claims of the parties. This determination, combined with the other factors covered in this chapter, produce a decision whether to prevent further harm to the plaintiff pending a full trial on the merits. The Supreme Court noted in *Gonzales v. O Centro Espirita Beneficente Uniao Do Vegetal*, 546 U.S. 418, 126 S.Ct. 1211, 163 L.Ed.2d 1017 (2006), that the standard for review for a preliminary injunction is whether the district court abused its discretion, except that issues of law are reviewed *de novo*.

G. FEE AWARDS AFTER PRELIMINARY INJUNCTION VICTORIES

Following the issuance or denial or a preliminary injunction and its appeal, it is common for parties to settle the case. The process of the interlocutory litigation gives an indication of the strength or weakness of the plaintiff's claim, and further litigation is expensive and lengthy.

After settlement, plaintiffs who prevailed on the preliminary injunction may seek attorney's fees if the underlying claim is one which supports fees, such as a civil rights action.

In the United States the prevailing party in a lawsuit is not ordinarily entitled to recover its costs of litigation from the losing party. The "American Rule" is that each party bears its own costs of suit, including attorney's fees. This rule is in contrast to the rule in Great Britain where the prevailing party is entitled to receive its litigation expenses as a matter of course. A number of exceptions to the American Rule, notably including statutory exceptions in areas such as civil rights, consumer protection, privacy, and environmental statutes. Attorney fees also may be recoverable under the Equal Access to Justice Act when a party prevails in a civil suit against the United States. 28 U.S.C. § 2412. The Act eliminates the financial disincentive and disadvantage otherwise faced by private parties in challenging unreasonable government actions. *Sullivan v. Hudson*, 490 U.S. 877, 109 S.Ct. 2248, 104 L.Ed.2d 941 (1989).

Statutes that permit attorney's fees typically use the standard that courts may award fees to "prevailing parties." One question of interpretation is when a party has "prevailed." In the context of preliminary injunctions, a party has not prevailed for the purposes of a fee award if that party wins a preliminary injunction but loses the ultimate trial on the merits. The problem that has arisen is whether a plaintiff is "prevailing" for the purpose of a fee award if the case is settled after the court grants the plaintiff a preliminary injunction.

In *Select Milk Producers, Inc. v. Johanns*, 400 F.3d 939 (D.C.Cir.2005), the plaintiffs were milk marketing cooperatives who were challenging a regulation of the Secretary of Agriculture concerning the price of a class of butterfat used to make butter and dry milk. The plaintiff cooperatives successfully obtained a preliminary injunction against the Secretary to enjoin the imposition of the separate price for this class of buttermilk. The Secretary did not appeal the preliminary injunction and issued instead a new rule that did not include a separate price for that class of butterfat. The parties then stipulated to the dismissal of the case as moot.

Subsequently, the cooperatives moved for an award of attorney's fees under the Equal Access to Justice Act. That Act provides for such fees to "prevailing parties" in litigation against the federal government unless the government's position is "substantially justified." The district court awarded the fees and the Court of Appeals upheld the award on the grounds that the preliminary injunction was a judgment that resulted in a change in the legal relationship of the parties. Further, the preliminary injunction gave the cooperatives the "concrete and irreversible redress that they sought." *Id.* at 948. The dissenting opinion objects that the preliminary injunction should not support attorney's fees because the function of the order was simply to preserve the *status quo* before the resolution of the dispute on the merits.

This dispute about the availability of "prevailing party" attorney's fees for a preliminary injunction underscores the inherent tension in this area of remedies law. Because this relief is awarded on a showing that is less than a full trial on the merits, it is not a true adjudication of the dispute. The standards for the award nonetheless permit the parties to make a more informed guess about the ultimate outcome of the case and therefore the decision to grant or withhold the temporary relief often determines a final disposition of the case by agreement of the parties.

Chapter Six

INJUNCTIONS IN CONTEXT

The injunctive remedy has been used in a variety of contexts, and specific precedential rules have developed regarding its use in many of these contexts. In this chapter, we examine some of these contexts and rules.

A. INJUNCTIONS AGAINST CRIMINAL ACTIVITY

In general, courts are reluctant to enjoin the commission of crimes. As a result, if Al Capone were still alive and robbing banks, courts would be loath to enjoin him from committing future bank robberies.

Various justifications have been offered for this reluctance, including the fact that courts are reluctant to enter futile decrees, and that the criminal laws are "sufficiently effective in deterring similar conduct of these parties, thereby affording plaintiff an adequate legal remedy" *City of Chicago v. Stern*, 96 Ill.App.3d 264, 51 Ill.Dec. 752, 421 N.E.2d 260 (1981). There are other reasons as well. In *Amalgamated Clothing & Textile Workers Int'l Union v. Earle Industries, Inc.*, 318 Ark. 524, 886 S.W.2d 594 (1994), Justice Dudley, dissenting, offered the following explanation:

"Four potential harms are always present when a case involves an injunction against criminal offenses. First, there is a potential harm in the possible conflict with the constitutional guarantee of the right to trial by jury. Equity does not afford a jury trial, and the absence of that protection is a substantial factor to be weighed against chancery assuming jurisdiction. Second, the proof necessary for a conviction in a criminal court is constitutionally designed to require a high standard of proof, proof beyond a reasonable doubt. The proof necessary to sustain a civil action for contempt is lesser, a preponderance of the evidence. Third, a court of equity can issue a show cause order, and the person cited must show why he should not be held in contempt. In a criminal proceeding the accused cannot be compelled to give evidence against himself. As a result, when a court of equity enjoins the commission of a crime, the person enjoined might be cited for contempt in a court of equity and stands to lose these three constitutional guarantees. Fourth, the person enjoined will suffer some stigma or embarrassment comparable to that suffered by being labeled a habitual offender because, before a court of equity assumes jurisdiction, there must be proof that the person enjoined committed acts of violence with such systematic persistence as to warrant a finding that they would be continued unless restrained."

Despite the prohibition against enjoining criminal activity, courts will frequently enjoin public nuisances even though the enjoined conduct might also be regarded as criminal. For example, in *State v. H. Samuels Company, Inc.*, 60 Wis.2d 631, 211 N.W.2d 417 (1973), defendant's business caused a public nuisance by creating noise and ground vibrations. Notwithstanding the fact that the level of disturbance constituted a crime, the Wisconsin Supreme Court held that injunctive relief was appropriate:

> True, a court of equity will not enjoin a crime because it is a crime, *i.e.*, to enforce the criminal law, but the fact the acts complained of cause damage and also constitute a crime does not bar injunctive relief. The criminality of the act neither gives nor ousts the jurisdiction of equity. In such cases, equity grants relief, not because the acts are in violation of the statute, but because they constitute in fact a nuisance.

Other courts are also willing to enjoin public or private nuisances even though the underlying conduct may constitute a crime.

B. INJUNCTIONS REQUIRING ADMISSION

There has been much litigation regarding judicial authority to enter injunctions requiring private clubs or other organizations to admit individuals to membership. As a general rule, courts are reluctant to order social clubs (*e.g.*, country clubs) to admit members. Courts are concerned about "foisting" unwilling parties on each other in social situations. In addition, courts are reluctant to enter injunctions that are likely to involve continuing supervision problems. If a court orders a social club to admit someone to membership, when the club is opposed to admitting him/her, there may be a significant risk of additional litigation. Suppose, for example, that the club's members refuse to associate with the judicially admitted member and the new member files suit seeking to force them to associate with him/her. Finally, in the social club context, the plaintiff may have no "right" to admission, and therefore no cause of action on which to base a law suit. Membership in such clubs has historically been discretionary.

The prohibition against injunctions requiring admission is not, however, absolute. Courts have ordered some professional organizations to admit individuals to membership. Illustrative is the holding in *Falcone v. Middlesex County Medical Society*, 34 N.J. 582, 170 A.2d 791 (1961). In that case, plaintiff graduated from the Philadelphia College of Osteopathy and the University of Milan, completed an internship, and was certified by the state of New Jersey to practice medicine and surgery. In addition, he was listed as a "duly licensed and duly registered New Jersey physician who meets all of the qualifications prescribed in the written by-laws." Nevertheless, he was denied membership in the Middlesex County Medical Society (MCMS), because he held a Doctor of Osteopathy degree, and MCMS did not admit osteopaths to regular membership. The MCMS denial effectively precluded him from practicing at the two local hospitals, both of which required membership in the MCMS.

In *Falcone*, the court ordered the MCMS to admit Falcone to regular membership. The court made a distinction between "customary social and fraternal organizations" and "trade unions and professional societies." The latter, in the court's view, can involve "deprivation of the invaluable opportunity 'to earn a livelihood.'" The Court held that it would be more inclined to compel such organizations to admit individuals to membership. In ordering MCMS to admit Dr. Falcone, the Court noted that it has the power, "by excluding Dr. Falcone from membership, to preclude him from successfully continuing in his practice of obstetrics and surgery and to restrict patients who wish to engage him as an obstetrician or surgeon in their freedom of choice of physicians." The Court believed that such an important power should be subject to judicial constraints:

> Public policy strongly dictates that this power should not be unbridled but should be viewed judicially as a fiduciary power to be exercised in reasonable and lawful manner for the advancement of the interests of the medical profession and the public generally; the evidence firmly displays that here it was not so exercised and that Dr. Falcone was fairly and justly entitled to the relief awarded to him in the Law Division.

There are limits to the scope of *Falcone's* holding. In *Blatt v. University of Southern California*, 5 Cal.App.3d 935, 85 Cal.Rptr. 601 (1970), a law student sought admission to the Order of the Coif ("Coif"), a society that recognizes scholastic achievement by law students. In order to gain admission, students must be in the top 10 percent of their law school classes at accredited schools. Blatt sued claiming that he was in the top 10% of his class (4th of 135), but was refused admission because he refused to serve on the law review. He claimed that representations had been made to him that law review participation was not a condition of membership. In addition, Blatt claimed that Coif was an organization, like MCMS, that affected educational, professional or financial advantage, and therefore should not be allowed to arbitrarily discriminate in its admission requirements. The court disagreed, noting that prior cases, like *Falcone*, only govern "situations affecting the right to work in a chosen occupation or specialized field thereof." The court noted that membership "in the Order does not give a member the right to practice the profession of law," "has no direct bearing on the number or type of clients that the attorney-member might have or on the income he will make in his professional practice," and therefore does not affect his basic right to earn a living. As a result, the court refused to order admission.

In cases like *Blatt*, a court might be more inclined to order admission if the defendant organization has breached a contract. In *Blatt*, for example, plaintiff argued that he had been "promised" that he would be admitted to Coif if he graduated in the top 10% of his class, and he sought to promissorily estop Coif from refusing him admission. The court rejected his allegation of promise and concluded that there was no breach.

The reluctance to order clubs to admit new members was also qualified by the holding in *Roberts v. United States Jaycees*, 468 U.S. 609, 104 S.Ct. 3244, 82 L.Ed.2d 462 (1984). In *Roberts*, the Junior Chamber of Commerce, refused to admit women to full membership. When the Minneapolis and St. Paul chapters began admitting women as "regular" members, the national organization threatened to revoke their charters. The chapters responded by filing charges under the Minnesota Human Rights Act which applied to "a business, accommodation, refreshment, entertainment, recreation, or transportation facility of any kind, whether licensed or not, whose goods, services, facilities, privileges, advantages or accommodations are extended, offered, sold, or otherwise made available to the public." State officials found a violation of the Act, and ordered the Jaycees to admit women to regular membership.

In affirming the state order, *Roberts* rejected the Jaycees' claim that admission was precluded by the United States Constitution's First Amendment right to association. The Court noted that it has traditionally been more protective of "intimate human relationships" such as the right to marry or to have children. It also has been protective of the right to associate for the purpose of engaging in those activities protected by the First Amendment—

speech, assembly, petition for the redress of grievances, and the exercise of religion. However, the Court did not regard the Jaycees as fitting within the first category because the organization was large and relatively unselective in terms of membership. Indeed, the Jaycees had few membership requirements except for age and sex. Although the Jaycees pursue expressive advocacy, the Court found a compelling governmental interest in eradicating discrimination against women. Moreover, the Act was not directed at suppressing the Jaycees' political views or political activities, but instead reflected the state's desire to protect citizens from the harms of discrimination. Finally, the Court doubted that the admission of women would necessarily affect the Jaycee's positions on social issues related to men.

While the *Roberts* decision is important, it should not be construed as allowing the government to prohibit discrimination by all political or social advocacy groups. The Court's decision seems to have been influenced by the fact that the Jaycees was primarily a business association, and that it was large and basically unselective. If a group were organized solely for political advocacy purposes (*e.g.*, to promote the election of women (or, for that matter, men) to political office), the courts will be less inclined to grant injunctive relief requiring membership, and more likely to be protective of the right of association.

C. EXPULSION

Just as courts are disinclined to require private clubs to "admit" members, they are also disinclined to prohibit clubs from expelling members. In some instances, an expelled member may have greater contractual rights against expulsion than it has in requiring admission. For example, if a club expels a member in violation of its charter or membership rules, the expelled member might be able to establish a cause of action. Nevertheless, courts are reluctant to order social clubs to readmit expelled members because of concerns about foisting unwilling people on each other.

Some expulsion cases arise in the educational environment. When a state university seeks to expel a student, the student might be able to challenge the expulsion by asserting the constitutional requirement of due process. However, even in this context, courts have generally been reluctant to grant relief and have been deferential to academic judgments and decisions. An older case, but a leading one, is *Board of Curators of the University of Missouri v. Horowitz*, 435 U.S. 78, 98 S.Ct. 948, 55 L.Ed.2d 124 (1978). In *Horowitz*, a medical student was expelled for unsatisfactory performance. Because of evidence suggesting that the student's clinical performance and hygiene were inadequate, her performance was evaluated by a "Council on Evaluation" which decided that she should be continued, but only on a probationary basis. When she received an "unsatisfactory" rating the following year, the Council recommended against graduation and suggested that she be dropped from school absent "radical improvement." On an "appeal" of the Council's decisions, the student was allowed to take a series of oral and practical exams, and was allowed to spend time with practicing physicians. Five of the seven physicians recommended that she be dropped from school. The Council on Evaluation agreed with this conclusion, and the Coordinating Committee, the Dean, and the Provost ultimately sustained the decision. As a result, Horowitz was expelled.

In sustaining the expulsion, the Court discussed the meaning of due process in the educational context. The Court concluded that Horowitz had not been deprived of "property" in the traditional sense, but had, at most, been denied a "liberty" interest in continuing her medical education. Relying on *Goss v. Lopez*, 419 U.S. 565, 95 S.Ct. 729, 42 L.Ed.2d 725 (1975), the Court affirmed the idea of "flexible due process" in the educational context. In other words, not every case requires a full trial-type hearing as a precondition to expulsion. On the contrary, in appropriate cases, educational institutions can use less formal procedures that are more suited to the educational process. In *Horowitz*, the Court held that the expelled student had been given all the process that she was due by virtue of the school's informal evaluation process, that the school's decision "was careful and deliberate," and that "academic evaluations of a student, in contrast to disciplinary determinations, bear little resemblance to the judicial and administrative fact-finding proceedings to which we have traditionally attached a full-hearing requirement." Indeed, the Court found that the:

> decision to dismiss respondent rested on the academic judgment of school officials that she did not have the necessary clinical ability to perform adequately as a medical doctor and was making insufficient progress toward that goal. Such a judgment is by its nature more subjective and evaluative than the typical factual questions presented in the average disciplinary decision. Like the decision of an individual professor as to the proper grade for a student in his course, the determination whether to dismiss a student for academic reasons requires an expert evaluation of cumulative information and is not readily adapted to the procedural tools of judicial or administrative decisionmaking.

In addition to being deferential to the academic judgments of University officials, the Court was disinclined to "formalize the academic dismissal process by requiring a hearing." In the academic context, the Court concluded, a hearing may be "useless or harmful in finding out the truth."

In *Tedeschi v. Wagner College*, 49 N.Y.2d 652, 404 N.E.2d 1302, 427 N.Y.S.2d 760 (App.1980), a student was expelled from a private college for disruptive behavior including threats against a faculty member. Even though the college was a private institution, so that the constitutional requirement of due process did not apply, Tedeschi argued that she had been discharged in violation of college rules requiring (in her view) a hearing. The court concluded that the college had complied with its rules, but the court acknowledged that it would examine a non-academic suspension more closely than an academic suspension. In that case, the court concluded that the college's rules were not violated.

D. INJUNCTIONS AGAINST LITIGATION

Another context in which injunctive relief is sometimes sought is against pending litigation. Such injunctions are sought in three separate and distinct contexts: 1) state courts might be asked to enjoin litigation in other state courts; 2) state courts might be asked to enjoin litigation in federal courts; and 3) federal courts might be asked to enjoin litigation in state courts. Because different rules apply in each context, we will examine each context separately.

1. State Court Injunctions Against Foreign State Litigation

State courts have sometimes attempted to enjoin litigation in other states. Of course, following common law equity principles, courts do not actually attempt to enjoin foreign courts, but instead enjoin the parties to the foreign litigation from proceeding with that litigation. Indeed, because of personal and subject matter jurisdiction rules, the court might not have the power to directly enjoin the other court. The foreign court may be outside the court's jurisdiction and not subject to service of process within the enjoining state.

Even when a state court has the power to enjoin litigation in another state, the court should rarely exercise that power. Injunctions against extra-territorial litigation are fraught with difficulties. Perhaps the most famous case is *James v. Grand Trunk Western Railroad Company*, 14 Ill.2d 356, 152 N.E.2d 858 (1958), a case that provides a good illustration of what can happen when a state court attempts to enjoin foreign litigation. In *James*, an administratrix sued the Grand Trunk Western Railroad Company in Illinois state court under the Michigan Wrongful Death Act. The defendant railroad, believing that the case should have been brought in Michigan, obtained an injunction from a Michigan court prohibiting the administratrix from prosecuting the case in Illinois. The administratrix then moved an Illinois court for a temporary injunction enjoining enforcement of the Michigan injunction. Plaintiff was then arrested and advised that she would be imprisoned for contempt unless she complied with the Michigan injunction. Although she wrote to her Illinois attorney discharging him, and directing him to withdraw her case from the Illinois courts, she subsequently advised him that the letter did not express her true desires, but had been coerced by threat of imprisonment by defendant's counsel. A second injunction suit was instituted by defendant in Cass County, Michigan. Plaintiff did not appear and was defaulted, and an order was entered enjoining her from further prosecuting her Illinois action and directing her to withdraw it. The Illinois Supreme Court then denied defendant's motion to vacate the restraining order, and entered an injunction restraining defendant until it disposed of the case.

In *James v. Grand Trunk Railroad*, the court recognized that courts should generally decline to issue injunctions against foreign litigation. Even when courts have the power to enjoin the litigation, the better view is that "the exercise of such power by equity courts has been deemed a matter of great delicacy, invoked with great restraint to avoid distressing conflicts and reciprocal interference with jurisdiction." Indeed, the *James* case itself provided an example of such "distressing conflicts and reciprocal interference." Because of the conflicting and interlocking injunctions, the case was deadlocked. Even though the Illinois court recognized the undesirability of inter-jurisdictional injunctions, it nonetheless issued an injunction against the Michigan plaintiff:

> This court need not, and will not, countenance having its right to try cases, of which it has proper jurisdiction, determined by the courts of other States, through their injunctive process. We are not only free to disregard such out-of-State injunctions, and to adjudicate the merits of the pending action, but we can protect our jurisdiction from such usurpation by the issuance of a counter-injunction restraining the enforcement of the out-of-State injunction.

As a result, the net effect of the Michigan and Illinois proceedings was to create litigational gridlock. The two courts had issued inconsistent injunctions that effectively made it impossible to continue the litigation in either state. If the Illinois plaintiff proceeded with the Illinois case, she would be held in contempt in Michigan. Because of the Illinois injunction, if the Michigan plaintiff proceeded with that case, it could be held in contempt in Illinois. In other words, the case was effectively deadlocked by conflicting injunctions (perhaps a result desired by the railroad).

In general, cases like *James* should be dealt with under the doctrine of *forum non conveniens* rather than by the issuance of an injunction. In other words, if the Michigan railroad felt that Illinois was an improper place to litigate the Michigan accident (as it probably was), the Michigan plaintiff should have moved to dismiss the Illinois litigation. Indeed, the doctrine of *forum non conveniens* provided an adequate legal remedy for accomplishing that objective. As the *James* court stated,

> Where, however, suits by nonresidents have no connection whatever with this jurisdiction, and the selection of this forum is purely vexatious, this court has held that the doctrine of forum non conveniens may be invoked to dismiss such cases. In the instant case, however, no such defense of forum non conveniens was interposed by defendant. Instead, it sought to remove the case from the Illinois court by enjoining plaintiff in the State of her residence from prosecuting the Illinois action.

The Uniform Child Custody Jurisdiction Act (UCCJA) (L.1978, ch. 493, eff. Sept. 1, 1978), provides an alternate method for dealing with inter-jurisdictional conflicts. The UCCJA triggers a separate inquiry designed to determine where custody issues should be litigated. As the court explained in *Vanneck v. Vanneck*, 49 N.Y.2d 602, 404 N.E.2d 1278, 427 N.Y.S.2d 735 (App.1980):

> The UCCJA represents a considered effort to give stability to child custody decrees, minimize jurisdictional competition between sister States, promote co-operation and communication between the courts of different States, all to the end of resolving custody disputes in the best interests of the child. The act offers a standard for determining in the first instance whether the necessary predicate for jurisdiction exists. Custody may be determined in the child's "home state", defined as "the state in which the child at the time of the commencement of the custody proceeding, has resided with his parents, a parent, or a person acting as parent, for at least six consecutive months", or in the State that had been the child's home State within six months before commencement of the proceeding where the child is absent

from the State through removal by a person claiming custody and a parent lives in the State. A jurisdictional predicate also exists in New York when "it is in the best interest of the child that a court of this state assume jurisdiction because (I) the child and his parents, or the child and at least one contestant, have a significant connection with this state, and (ii) there is within the jurisdiction of the court substantial evidence concerning the child's present or future care, protection, training, and personal relationships".

The inquiry is not completed merely by a determination that a jurisdictional predicate exists in the forum State, for then the court must determine whether to exercise its jurisdiction. There, too, the act guides the determination, commanding the court to consider whether it is an inconvenient forum or whether the conduct of the parties militates against an exercise of jurisdiction. Notwithstanding that this State has jurisdiction, a court "shall not exercise its jurisdiction under this article if at the time of filing the petition a proceeding concerning the custody of the child was pending in a court of another state exercising jurisdiction substantially in conformity with this article". Once a court of this State learns of the pendency of another proceeding, the court "shall stay (its own) proceeding and communicate with the court in which the other proceeding is pending to the end that the issue may be litigated in the more appropriate forum and that information be exchanged in accordance with sections seventy-five-s through seventy-five-v of this article" (Domestic Relations Law, § 75–g, subd. 3).

The UCCJA represents a preferable approach because it encourages courts in different jurisdictions to consult and cooperatively decide on the best place to try a case. In addition, the UCCJA helps courts avoid the problem of interlocking injunctions.

2. State Court Injunctions Against Federal Litigation

In general, state courts lack the power to enjoin federal court proceedings. As the Court stated in *Donovan v. City of Dallas*, 377 U.S. 408, 84 S.Ct. 1579, 12 L.Ed.2d 409 (1964), "state courts are completely without power to restrain federal-court proceedings in *in personam* actions like the one here. And it does not matter that the prohibition here was addressed to the parties rather than to the federal court itself." The only exception is for the situation when a state court has custody of property (in other words, proceedings *in rem* or *quasi in rem*), and the state court enters an injunction to preserve its jurisdiction. As the Court recognized in *Donovan*, "in such cases, the state or federal court having custody of such property has exclusive jurisdiction to proceed."

3. Federal Court Injunctions Against State Litigation

Although the federal courts have the power to enjoin state court proceedings, they generally abstain from doing so. In the United States Supreme Court's landmark decision in *Younger v. Harris*, 401 U.S. 37, 91 S.Ct. 746, 27 L.Ed.2d 669 (1971), the Court stated that "Since the beginning of this country's history, Congress has, subject to few exceptions, manifested a desire to permit state courts to try state cases free from interference by federal courts." *Younger's* so-called abstention doctrine, also known as "Our Federalism," stated a rule of policy rather than a rule of jurisdiction. In other words, a federal court is not jurisdictionally precluded from issuing an injunction against state court proceedings, but generally refuses to do so on grounds of judicial restraint.

In *Younger*, the Court justified its decision by resorting to ancient equity rules. The court noted that the "basic doctrine of equity jurisprudence" provides that "courts of equity should not act, and particularly should not act to restrain a criminal prosecution, when the moving party has an adequate remedy at law and will not suffer irreparable injury if denied equitable relief." The Court also found support for its approach in the Constitution, noting that the "fundamental purpose of restraining equity jurisdiction within narrow limits is equally important under our Constitution, in order to prevent erosion of the role of the jury and avoid a duplication of legal proceedings and legal sanctions where a single suit would be adequate to protect the rights asserted." Finally, the Court grounded the abstention doctrine in "the notion of 'comity,' that is, a proper respect for state functions, a recognition of the fact that the entire country is made up of a Union of separate state governments, and a continuance of the belief that the National Government will fare best if the States and their institutions are left free to perform their separate functions in their separate ways."

Younger itself provides an illustration of how the "Our Federalism" doctrine applies. In that case, when Harris was charged with violating California's Criminal Syndicalism Act, he filed suit in federal court seeking to enjoin the District Attorney of Los Angeles County from prosecuting him. Younger alleged that the prosecution, and even the presence of the Criminal Syndicalism Act, inhibited him in the exercise of his free speech rights. In addition to requiring a showing of irreparable injury, the Court held that "in view of the fundamental policy against federal interference with state criminal prosecutions, even irreparable injury is insufficient unless it is both 'great and immediate.' Certain types of injury, in particular, the cost, anxiety, and inconvenience involved in having to defend against a single criminal prosecution, could not by themselves be considered 'irreparable' in the special legal sense of that term. Instead, the threat to the plaintiff's federally protected rights must be one that cannot be eliminated by his defense against a single criminal prosecution." If the defendant can defend the criminal proceeding, injunctive relief is inappropriate. In *Younger*, the "chilling effect" of an allegedly unconstitutional statute was deemed to be insufficient to justify federal court intervention.

Younger recognized that its prior holding in *Dombrowski v. Pfister*, 380 U.S. 479, 85 S.Ct. 1116, 14 L.Ed.2d 22 (1965), would establish a limited exception to the Our Federalism doctrine. In that case, no valid criminal prosecution was pending. Instead, the prosecutor had threatened to enforce statutes, and had seized plaintiff's property in anticipation of such prosecutions, but had never followed through. In other words, the seizures had been made without any expectation of prosecution or any effort to secure convictions. Instead, there was a simple "plan to employ arrests, seizures, and threats of prosecution under color of the statutes to harass appellants and discourage them and their supporters from asserting and attempting to vindicate the constitutional rights of Negro citizens of Louisiana." The plaintiffs' offices were "raided and all their files and records seized pursuant to search and arrest warrants that were later summarily vacated by a state judge for lack of probable cause. Plaintiffs also showed that, despite the state court order quashing the warrants and suppressing the evidence seized, the prosecutor was continuing to threaten to initiate new prosecutions of appellants under the same statutes, was holding public hearings at which photostatic copies of the illegally seized documents were being used, and was threatening to use other copies of the illegally seized documents to obtain grand jury indictments against the appellants on charges of violating the same statutes." The Court concluded that these circumstances revealed injury that could not be vindicated by the defense of a single prosecution. The Court found that the facts "depict a situation in which defense of the State's criminal prosecution will not assure adequate vindication of constitutional rights."

The Our Federalism doctrine applies, not only to requests for injunctive relief, but also to requests for declaratory relief. For example, in *Samuels v. Mackell*, 401 U.S. 66, 91 S.Ct. 764, 27 L.Ed.2d 688 (1971), appellants, who were indicted in a New York state court on charges of criminal anarchy, wanted to challenge the state's anarchy law in federal court on vagueness grounds. Fearing that *Younger* would bar a claim for injunctive relief, appellants sought only declaration that the law was void. The Court held that Our Federalism also precluded the federal court from entertaining a request for declaratory relief.

Injunctive relief might be appropriate when a plaintiff alleges sufficient injury, but no criminal prosecution is pending. For example, in *Steffel v. Thompson*, 415 U.S. 452, 94 S.Ct. 1209, 39 L.Ed.2d 505 (1974), petitioner was distributing handbills on a shopping center sidewalk when center employees asked him to stop handbilling and leave. When petitioner declined the request, the center called in the police who told petitioner that he would be arrested unless he terminated his protest. At that point, petitioner left to avoid arrest. Petitioner and a companion returned to the shopping center several days later and again began handbilling. The police were called and once again demanded that petitioner stop handbilling or face arrest. Petitioner left to avoid arrest. The companion was arrested. Although Petitioner desired to return to the shopping center to distribute handbills, he did not do so for fear that he, too, would be arrested. The Court held that Our Federalism did not apply to a threatened prosecution. Since no state court prosecution was pending, plaintiff did not have an adequate legal remedy for the threatened injury. In addition, since there was no pending state court proceeding, federal court intervention could not interfere with such proceedings.

However, Our Federalism might preclude federal courts from hearing a case when a later criminal prosecution is brought. In *Hicks v. Miranda*, 422 U.S. 332, 95 S.Ct. 2281, 45 L.Ed.2d 223 (1975), plaintiff owned and operated an adult theater. The police seized four copies of one of plaintiff's films, and charged two of plaintiff's employees under a state obscenity statute. They did not file charges against plaintiff. Two weeks later, plaintiff filed a federal action seeking declaratory and injunctive relief regarding the seizure of the films. Shortly before a federal court hearing on the request for injunctive relief, local prosecutors (who were also defendants in the federal suit) amended the state criminal complaint to name plaintiff as a criminal defendant and moved to dismiss the federal suit under *Younger*. The Court held that the case should have been dismissed. Even though no charges had been filed against defendant when the federal court proceeding was filed, the subsequent charges provided him with a state avenue for vindicating his objections.

Younger's Our Federalism doctrine is reinforced by the federal anti-injunction statute. That statute provides that a federal court "may not grant an injunction to stay proceedings in a State court except as expressly authorized by Act of Congress, or where necessary in aid of its jurisdiction, or to protect or effectuate its judgments." The Act is subject to various exceptions including an *"in rem"* exception (allowing a federal court to enjoin a state court proceeding in order to protect its jurisdiction of a res over which it has acquired jurisdiction), and a "relitigation" exception (that permits a federal court to enjoin relitigation in a state court of issues already decided in federal litigation), and an exception which permits an injunction when the plaintiff in the federal court is the United States itself, or a federal agency asserting "superior federal interests."

There is also an "expressly authorized" exception to the anti-injunction statute. In *Mitchum v. Foster*, 407 U.S. 225, 92 S.Ct. 2151, 32 L.Ed.2d 705 (1972), the Court dealt with the exception which permits injunctive relief when "expressly authorized" by Congress. The question was whether 42 U.S.C. § 1983 expressly authorized a "suit in equity" to redress "the deprivation," under color of state law, "of any rights, privileges, or immunities secured by the [Constitution]" The Court held that it did, noting that the law need not specifically mention the anti-injunction statute, or explicitly authorize an injunction against state court proceedings. The Court held that the question is whether "an Act of Congress . . . created a specific and uniquely federal right or remedy, enforceable in a federal court of equity, that could be frustrated if the federal court were not empowered to enjoin a state court proceeding." The Court held that 1983 fit within this concept.

E. STRUCTURAL INJUNCTIONS

Many injunction cases involve relatively discrete matters between private litigants (*e.g.*, plaintiff seeks to enjoin defendant from trespassing on his property). By contrast, other cases can involve broad challenges to the operation of a school district or prison system. In these latter cases, litigants sometimes ask a court to enter "structural injunctions" directed at governmental officials. These structural injunctions are designed to eliminate past violations and regulate the way a school, prison, or police department functions in the future.

There are various reasons why courts are reluctant to grant structural relief. First, as noted in chapter 2, courts are reluctant to grant injunctions that will involve them in continuing supervision of the parties. Structural injunctions, since they affect the very structure and functioning of governmental entities, frequently involve courts in continuing supervision problems. Second, structural cases present courts with separation of powers issues. In most instances, the power to operate schools or prisons is vested in the executive branch of government, rather than the judicial branch, and structural injunctions frequently involve courts in the administration of executive branch agencies. Moreover, administrators are usually more competent to administer entities like schools and prisons than judges.

Despite these concerns, federal courts have found it necessary to enter structural injunctions in an extraordinary array of cases, and these injunctions have dramatically reshaped society and directly regulated and controlled state governmental officials. For example, courts have restructured school districts, and regulated the running of prisons, jails, institutions for the sick, the mentally insane and the mentally retarded. Courts have even mandated state apportionment schemes and reorganized city governments.

The development of modern structural remedies has its roots in the United States Supreme Court's holding in *Brown v. Board of Education (Brown I)*, 347 U.S. 483, 74 S.Ct. 686, 98 L.Ed. 873 (1954). In that case, although the Court held that the Topeka, Kansas, school district was illegally segregated, the Court was unwilling to order immediate desegregation. Instead, the Court adopted a go slow approach and deferred a remedy until its decision in *Brown II*, 349 U.S. 294, 75 S.Ct. 753, 99 L.Ed. 1083 (1955). Playing for time, the Court did nothing to enforce *Brown II's* "all deliberate speed" mandates for many years. Even as late as the mid-1960s, many black children were still attending segregated schools. Finally, in *Swann v. Charlotte-Mecklenburg Bd. of Education*, 402 U.S. 1, 91 S.Ct. 1267, 28 L.Ed.2d 554 (1971), the Court signaled an end to the Court's go slow approach. Although the trial court had allowed school officials to submit three separate and distinct desegregation plans, the trial court rejected all three plans as constitutionally inadequate. In frustration, the trial court decided to desegregate the school system itself based on the advice of an outside consultant.

In the years that followed *Brown II* and *Swann*, the federal courts entered structural injunctions in a variety of cases. Some of these cases involved sweeping orders. *Missouri v. Jenkins*, 515 U.S. 70, 115 S.Ct. 2038, 132 L.Ed.2d 63 (1995), represents the remedy's zenith. In *Jenkins*, the trial court found that the Kansas City, Missouri, school district was segregated. However, since the school district was more than 68% black, it was difficult to reassign students in ways that would create meaningful integration. Unable to sweep suburban school districts into its decree, the court decided against additional intra-district reassignments fearing that such transfers would drive non-minority students away and decrease stability. Instead, the court decided to improve the district's educational programs in the hope that the improvements would make the district attractive to non-minority students and thereby create "desegregative attractiveness." To this end, the Court allowed district officials to "dream" about how to improve their system, and the court then granted their dream by ordering the state to spend vast sums of money on the district. These sums included $220 million on quality education programs, $448 million on magnet schools, $260 million on capital improvements, and nearly $448 million on magnet schools. Although the United States Supreme Court initially upheld aspects of the trial court's order, the court ultimately held that the trial court had exceeded its authority in focusing on the principle of desegregative attractiveness, as well as in requiring the state to finance the program of attractiveness.

In recent years, courts have tended to invoke structural remedies much less frequently, and have begun terminating their control over local school districts. In the process, returning those districts to the control of local officials. For example, in *Oklahoma City Board of Education v. Dowell*, 498 U.S. 237, 111 S.Ct. 630, 112 L.Ed.2d 715 (1991), the Court held that the Oklahoma City school district should be released from a desegregation decree. Likewise, in *Freeman v. Pitts*, 503 U.S. 467, 112 S.Ct. 1430, 118 L.Ed.2d 108 (1992), the Court released a Georgia school district from judicial control. In terminating desegregation decrees, the Court emphasized the importance of returning control over school districts to local officials, and the need for judicial intervention to be of limited duration. As the Court stated in *Jenkins*, "local autonomy of school districts is a vital national tradition" and "a district court must strive to restore state and local authorities to the control of a school system operating in compliance with the Constitution." The Court sounded similar themes in *Freeman v. Pitts* noting that, once desegregation has been implemented, the impetus and need for structural decrees diminishes.

In addition, the Court has placed limits on the availability of structural remedies. For example, in *O'Shea v. Littleton*, 414 U.S. 488, 94 S.Ct. 669, 38 L.Ed.2d 674 (1974), respondents, black citizens who had been advocating for equality in employment, housing, education, and participation in governmental decisionmaking, began an economic boycott of local merchants opposed to equality. Respondents claimed that the county magistrate and judge had singled them out for harsh treatment because of the advocacy and the boycott. Specifically, respondents alleged that the judge and magistrate discriminated by setting higher bond requirements and jury fees in criminal cases, and by imposing higher criminal sentences. The Court concluded that respondents were not entitled to injunctive relief, placing particular emphasis on the fact that none of the respondents could satisfy the Article III case or controversy requirement. The Court concluded that those who had been subjected to the alleged practices in the past could not show a case or controversy because "past exposure to illegal conduct does not in itself show a present case or controversy regarding injunctive relief, however, if unaccompanied by any continuing, present adverse effects." The Court found no "continuing effects" because none of the petitioners was then serving an allegedly illegal sentence or awaiting trial. As to those that had been unlawfully convicted and who were serving illegal sentences, the Court concluded that judicial intervention was inappropriate because "the complaint would inappropriately be seeking relief from or modification of current, existing custody." As to those that were then subject to criminal proceedings, the Court found that federal intervention was inappropriate under Our Federalism principles. The Court did recognize that respondents might be arrested again, and therefore might be again subject to illegal practices. However, the Court found this possibility insufficient to justify judicial intervention noting that there was no allegation that any Illinois law was unconstitutional on its face. As a result, the Court found that the alleged injury was not "sufficiently real and immediate" since the Court was unwilling to "anticipate whether and when these respondents will be charged with crime and will be made to appear before either petitioner takes us into the area of speculation and conjecture." Moreover, the Court emphasized that federalism principles militated against judicial intervention, and that respondents would have numerous judicial remedies available to them.

In *Rizzo v. Goode,* 423 U.S. 362, 96 S.Ct. 598, 46 L.Ed.2d 561 (1976), respondents sued a city and its mayor and other police officials, claiming civil rights violations and seeking sweeping relief, including the appointment of a receiver to supervise the police department and civilian review of police activity. The trial court entered an extensive order imposing procedures for the handling of complaints against the police (requiring ready availability of complaint forms, a screening procedure for eliminating frivolous complaints, prompt and adequate investigation of complaints, adjudication of non-frivolous complaints by an impartial individual or body using fair procedures, prompt notification to the parties regarding the outcome), requiring the revision of police recruit manuals and rules of procedure, and requiring the maintenance of statistical records and summaries designed to allow the court to determine how the revised complaint process was working. In entering the order, the trial court recognized that respondents had "no constitutional right to improved police procedures for handling civilian complaints," but the court imposed the order nonetheless because violations of constitutional rights had occurred in "unacceptably" high numbers. The trial court found that, in the absence of changed disciplinary procedures, unconstitutional incidents were likely to continue to occur, not with respect to respondents, but to the members of the classes they represented. In striking down the trial court's order, the United States Supreme Court invoked justiciability concepts and Our Federalism principles. Relying on *O'Shea*, the Court questioned whether respondents could show a "real and immediate" injury because the claim depended "not upon what the named petitioners might do to them in the future, but upon what one of a small, unnamed minority of policemen might do to them in the future because of that unknown policeman's perception of departmental disciplinary procedures." The Court found the connection too speculative.

F. EXTRA-TERRITORIAL DECREES

A number of cases have focused on the permissibility of injunctions that apply extra-territorially—in other words, to land or conduct outside of the issuing court's jurisdiction. Over the years, courts have formulated special rules governing the permissibility of such decrees.

1. Decrees Affecting Land

In general, decrees affecting land are regarded as local in character. As a result, it would generally be inappropriate for a court in a foreign country (*e.g.*, Canada), or for that matter a U.S. state (*e.g.*, California), to attempt to transfer property located in another state (*e.g.*, New York). For example, in *Fall v. Eastin*, 215 U.S. 1, 30 S.Ct. 3, 54 L.Ed. 65 (1909), when a court in Washington state appointed a commissioner to convey land located in Nebraska, the Nebraska Supreme Court rejected the conveyance as ineffective to convey the land. The United States Supreme Court upheld the Nebraska judgment, concluding that the conveyance was invalid noting "the court, not having jurisdiction of the res, cannot affect it by its decree, nor by a deed made by a master in accordance with the decree, is firmly established."

It is important to note that, even though a foreign court may not convey land located outside its jurisdictional boundaries, it can coerce the parties before it into making such a conveyance. For example, *Deschenes v. Tallman*, 248 N.Y. 33, 161 N.E. 321

(App.1928), involved a Canadian court that coerced a company that owned New York land into conveying the property to a third party. Even though the Canadian court did not have jurisdiction over the property, the New York court sustained the conveyance, brushing aside concerns that the conveyance had been coerced by the Canadian court "A judgment of a foreign court will not avail, of its own force, to transfer the title to land located in this state. . . . But the rule is different where the conveyance is executed by the owner, though he act under compulsion. The conveyance, and not the judgment, is then the source of title. . . . His deed transmits the title irrespective of the pressure exerted on his will."

Although foreign courts are not required to accept out-of-state decrees affecting real property, they can choose to do so, if they wish. For example, in *Burnley v. Stevenson*, 24 Ohio St. 474 (1873), a Kentucky court ordered a transfer of Ohio land, and appointed a master to make the transfer. Although the Ohio court recognized that the Kentucky court did not have the power to make the transfer, the Ohio court chose to give it effect:

> That this decree had the effect in Kentucky of determining the equities of the parties to the land in this state, we have already shown; hence the courts of this state must accord to it the same effect. True, the courts of this state can not enforce the performance of that decree, by compelling the conveyance through its process of attachment; but when pleaded in our courts as a cause of action, or as a ground of defense, it must be regarded as conclusive of all the rights and equities which were adjudicated and settled therein, unless it be impeached for fraud.

A further qualification of the general rule (prohibiting a court in one state from transferring or affecting property located in another state) is provided by the *Salton Sea Cases*, 172 Fed. 792 (9th Cir.1909). In that case, appellee diverted water from the Colorado River into irrigation canals for farming purposes. The water spilled onto appellant's lands which were used for the mining, gathering, and refining salt. Since appellant's lands were below sea level, the water created a lake more than 20 miles in length and several miles in width. Initially, the lake destroyed tons of appellant's salt and submerged its railroad. Eventually, the lake expanded and destroyed appellant's plant, sheds, mill and machinery. Appellant sought injunctive relief, precluding appellee from diverting water "unless suitable headgates were provided to control the water, so that the flow would not be in excess of the amount used for irrigation purposes." Defendant admitted many of the complaint's allegations, but alleged that the waters referred to were diverted from the Colorado river in Mexico by a corporation organized under the laws of the republic of Mexico, and that the Mexican corporation owned all of the canals leading from the Colorado river in Mexico to the town of Calexico, California. As a result, defendant argued that he did not have the power to correct the problem. The court held that defendant could be required to remedy the problem because the most effective place to deal with the problem was in California.

2. Decrees Affecting Personal Property

Similar principles apply to personal property located in other states. In other words, a court might decline a request to enjoin or take control of property located in another state for a variety of reasons. Since the property is not situated within the court's jurisdictional boundaries, the order might be difficult to enforce, and therefore there is a significant risk that the decree will be futile.

Nevertheless, in *Madden v. Rosseter*, 114 Misc. 416, 187 N.Y.S. 462 (1921), a New York court appointed a receiver to take control of a racehorse located in California, and ordered the receiver to transport the horse to Kentucky. This order was problematic since the New York court did not have possession or control over the horse, and the receiver's authority stemmed wholly from the New York court. Had defendant refused to turn over the horse, the receiver would have been forced to apply for assistance from the California courts. Although the New York court acknowledged these difficulties, it concluded that the court felt the "courts of sister states may be relied upon to aid in serving the ends of justice whenever our own process falls short of effectiveness." Ultimately, the decree succeeded and the race horse was transported to Kentucky.

G. DEFAMATION

In general, courts have been reluctant to enjoin defamatory statements. There are old decisions such as *Chaplinsky v. New Hampshire*, 315 U.S. 568, 62 S.Ct. 766, 86 L.Ed. 1031 (1942) which suggest that defamatory speech is not entitled to constitutional protection: there are "certain well-defined and narrowly limited *classes* of speech, the prevention and punishment of which have never been thought to raise any Constitutional problem. *Chaplinsky* included within these classes the lewd and obscene, the profane, the libelous, and the insulting or 'fighting' words ..." *Chaplinsky's* dicta regarding defamatory statements was confirmed in the Court's later decision in *Beauharnais v. Illinois*, 343 U.S. 250, 72 S.Ct. 725, 96 L.Ed. 919 (1952). In that case, the Supreme Court stated that libelous utterances "by their very utterance inflict injury or tend to incite an immediate breach of the peace. It has been well observed that such utterances are no essential part of any exposition of ideas, and are of such slight social value as a step to truth that any benefit that may be derived from them is clearly outweighed by the social interest in order and morality."

However, both *Chaplinsky* and *Beauharnais* were overruled by the Court's later decision in *New York Times Co. v. Sullivan*, 376 U.S. 254, 84 S.Ct. 710, 11 L.Ed.2d 686 (1964). *Sullivan* was preceded by the holding in *Near v. State of Minnesota*, 283 U.S. 697, 51 S.Ct. 625, 75 L.Ed. 1357 (1931), a decision that preceded both *Chaplinsky* and *Beauharnais*. In *Near*, the Court rejected the idea that injunctions could be used to enjoin defamatory statements. In that case, a Minnesota county attorney sought to enjoin a Minneapolis publication, *The Saturday Press*, as a "malicious, scandalous and defamatory newspaper, magazine or other periodical." The complaint further alleged that, on nine different occasions, *The Saturday Press* published articles charging "in substance, that a Jewish gangster was in control of gambling, bootlegging, and racketeering in Minneapolis, and that law enforcing officers and agencies were not energetically performing their duties." The trial court issued a temporary restraining order prohibiting future editions "containing malicious, scandalous and defamatory matter of the kind alleged in plaintiff's complaint herein or otherwise."

In striking down the injunction, the United States Supreme Court established a broad prohibition against prior restraints: "The fact that for approximately one hundred and fifty years there has been almost an entire absence of attempts to impose previous restraints upon publications relating to the malfeasance of public officers is significant of the deep-seated conviction that such restraints would violate constitutional right." The Court suggested that public officials, "whose character and conduct remain open to debate and free discussion in the press, find their remedies for false accusations in actions under libel laws providing for redress and punishment, and not in proceedings to restrain the publication of newspapers and periodicals." In other words, they are not entitled to injunctive relief against publication:

> The fact that the liberty of the press may be abused by miscreant purveyors of scandal does not make any the less necessary the immunity of the press from previous restraint in dealing with official misconduct. Subsequent punishment for such abuses as may exist is the

appropriate remedy, consistent with constitutional privilege.

Despite the decisions in *Chaplinsky* and *Beauharnais*, the Court ultimately concluded that defamatory speech is entitled to constitutional protection. In the *Sullivan* decision, the Court provided special protections to those who make defamatory statements regarding public officials. In order to recover for defamation, a public official must prove that the statements were false, and that they were made with "actual malice" (meaning that the defamer "knew" that the statements were false, or acted in "reckless disregard" for whether they were true or false). Coupled with *Near's* strong anti-injunction stance, *Sullivan* seemed to provide strong protections for defamation defendants, and to clearly indicate that prior restraints against defamatory speech are prohibited.

In *Curtis Publishing Co. v. Butts*, 388 U.S. 130, 87 S.Ct. 1975, 18 L.Ed.2d 1094 (1967), the Court extended *Sullivan's* actual malice standard to defamatory statements made regarding so-called "public figures." *The Saturday Evening Post* alleged that the University of Georgia's Athletic Director had conspired to fix a football game, and a jury returned a verdict for $60,000 in general damages and $3,000,000 in punitive damages. In the companion case of *Associated Press v. Walker*, 388 U.S. 130, 87 S.Ct. 1975, 18 L.Ed.2d 1094 (1967), an Associated Press article claimed that Walker, a private citizen who had been in the United States Army, had taken command of a violent crowd and had personally led a charge against federal marshals. A verdict of $500,000 compensatory damages and $300,000 punitive damages was returned. The Court treated both Butts and Walker as public figures and held that the *New York Times* actual malice standard applied to both of them:

Later cases suggest that private individuals might be treated differently, and that injunctive relief *might* be available to a private individual. For example, in *Kramer v. Thompson*, 947 F.2d 666 (3d Cir.1991), a lawyer (Kramer) asked a Pennsylvania judge to enjoin future libels against him by a former client (Thompson). After concluding that Thompson's statements were false and made in reckless disregard for truth or falsity, the trial court permanently enjoined Thompson from making further similar statements about Kramer. The court of appeals overturned the injunction, rejecting other decisions suggesting that injunctions against libel by private individuals might be permissible. The court noted that "the maxim that equity will not enjoin a libel has enjoyed nearly two centuries of widespread acceptance at common law." In addition, the court expressed concern that, "even if we thought that the Pennsylvania Supreme Court might be inclined to adopt the jury determination exception," it doubted that it would have done so in this case because it involved a directed verdict rather than a jury determination. Nevertheless, in some state court cases, courts have enjoined private defamation. *See, e.g., Willing v. Mazzocone*, 482 Pa. 377, 393 A.2d 1155 (1978).

H. NATIONAL SECURITY

Courts have been reluctant to sustain injunctions designed to prohibit the publication of information that might adversely affect national security. Of course, this issue has come into greater focus with the release of information by the WikiLeaks website. However, the problem is hardly a new one.

The decision in *New York Times Company v. United States*, 403 U.S. 713, 91 S.Ct. 2140, 29 L.Ed.2d 822 (1971), is the seminal decision. Also known as the *Pentagon Papers* case, that case involved a Pentagon employee who stole a classified study entitled "History of U.S. Decision-Making Process on Viet Nam Policy" (The Pentagon Papers), and turned it over to the *New York Times* and *Washington Post* newspapers who planned to publish it. In a *per curiam* opinion, the Court denied the government's attempt to enjoin the publication relying on the prohibition against prior restraints: "Any system of prior restraints of expression comes to this Court bearing a heavy presumption against its constitutional validity." The Court went on to hold that the government "carries a heavy burden of showing justification for the imposition of such a restraint," concluded that the government could not satisfy that burden, and vacated the lower court injunctions.

Even though most justices agreed to lift the injunctions, the case produced a number of concurring and dissenting opinions that expressed a variety of views on the issues presented by the case. Some justices took decidedly pro-free speech, anti-prior restraint, positions. For example, Justice Black, consistent with his sometimes articulated absolutist view of the First Amendment, concurred, arguing that the cases against the *New York Times* and *Washington Post* should have been dismissed without oral argument: the "history and language of the First Amendment support the view that the press must be left free to publish news, whatever the source, without censorship, injunctions, or prior restraints." Justice Douglas also concurred making a similar argument: "[T]he First Amendment leaves, in my view, no room for governmental restraint on the press."

There were other concurring opinions as well. For example, Justice Brennan concurred with the Court's decision to lift the injunctions, but he did not rule out the possibility that it might be appropriate to issue a prior restraint in order to protect national security. However, he would have limited such restraints to situations such as when the government is at war and the press is seeking to publish information like "the sailing dates of transports or the number and location of troops." *Near v. Minnesota ex rel. Olson*, 283 U.S. 697, 716, 51 S.Ct. 625, 75 L.Ed. 1357 (1931). He also suggested that an injunction might be permissible under circumstances that might "set in motion a nuclear holocaust." Justice White's concurrence was essentially similar, focusing on "the concededly extraordinary protection against prior restraints enjoyed by the press under our constitutional system." He would have imposed a "very heavy burden" of proof on the government "in the absence of express and appropriately limited congressional authorization for prior restraints in circumstances such as these." Justice Stewart also concurred, suggesting that he would have been more deferential to the Executive's need to protect state secrets, but he doubted that the predicates for deference were present in this case.

Several justices dissented as well. For example, Chief Justice Burger noted that the Pentagon Papers were stolen and he argued that the newspapers should have promptly informed governmental officials regarding their possession of the documents. He also complained that the case was being decided in haste: "We have been forced to deal with litigation concerning rights of great magnitude without an adequate record, and surely without time for adequate treatment either in the prior proceedings or in this Court." Justice Harlan also expressed concern about the haste with which the cases were briefed, argued and decided. However, he believed that the authority to make decisions regarding the confidentiality of such documents rests with the Executive branch, and "are decisions of a kind for which the Judiciary has neither aptitude, facilities nor responsibility and have long been held to belong in the domain of political power not subject to judicial intrusion or inquiry." He felt that the scope of judicial review should be "exceedingly narrow." Accordingly, he would have vacated and remanded, and he would have continued the injunctions pending further proceedings. Justice Blackmun also dissented, arguing that the First Amendment is "only one part of an entire Constitution. . . . Each provision of the Constitution is important, and I cannot subscribe to a doctrine of unlimited absolutism for the First Amendment at the cost of downgrading other provisions." As a result, he would have weighed the press' right to print against the governmental interest in preventing disclosure. In the short term, he would have remanded the case for further development in the lower courts "on a schedule permitting the orderly presentation of evidence from both sides."

In the final analysis, although the justices could not agree on a rationale, a majority agreed to lift the injunctions against the newspapers and dismiss the cases. As a result, the *Pentagon Papers* case stands as a strong bulwark against the idea that injunctions can be used to prevent the publication of information that might damage national security. At the very least, the government must sustain a high burden of proof, and the government cannot meet that burden merely by showing that the information was stolen.

The *Pentagon Papers* decision was followed by an intriguing lower court decision in *United States v. Progressive, Inc.*, 467 F.Supp. 990 (W.D.Wis.1979). In the *Progressives* case, the U.S. government sought to enjoin the Progressive, Inc., from publishing an article entitled "The H-Bomb Secret: How We Got It, Why We're Telling It." The article provided information on how to build a hydrogen bomb. The government sought injunctive relief under 42 U.S.C. §§ 2274(b) and 2280 which authorized relief against one who would disclose restricted data "with reason to believe such data will be utilized to injure the United States or to secure an advantage to any foreign nation." The magazine responded that it wanted to publish the article to demonstrate laxness in the government's security system. The government responded that much of the article's information was not in the public domain, and that some of the information had in fact never been published. In addition, the article integrated information in ways that would enable others to build thermonuclear weapons. In other words, the article exposed "concepts never heretofore disclosed in conjunction with one another" and would therefore help a medium sized nation build an H-bomb.

The *Progressives* case presented the lower court with an interesting dilemma. The case presented facts which arguably fit, albeit rather loosely, within Justice Brennan's suggestion that an injunction might be appropriate if the government were threatened with great enough harm. By enabling a medium-sized rogue country to build a hydrogen bomb, the *Progressive* article involved a significant threat to human safety and perhaps the nation's security. On the other hand, the government could not demonstrate an immediate or imminent threat. Even if the article were published, there was no assurance that a medium-sized country would build a hydrogen bomb or that it would threaten the United States or its people. Moreover, even if such a threat were to develop, there might be a significant time lag. In the *Progressives* case, although the lower court decided to issue the injunction, it lifted the injunction when a similar article was published by another publication.

I. PRIVACY

Injunctive relief is also difficult to obtain in privacy cases. Because privacy issues arise in so many different contexts, the rules are not as clear-cut and injunctive relief is sometimes appropriate.

In their landmark article *The Right to Privacy*, 4 Harvard Law Review 193 (1890), Justice Brandeis & Samuel Warren forcefully articulated the need to protect privacy:

> Recent inventions and business methods call attention to the next step which must be taken for the protection of the person, and for securing to the individual what Judge Cooley calls the right "to be let alone." Instantaneous photographs, and newspapers enterprise have invaded the sacred precincts of private and domestic life; and numerous mechanical devices threaten to make good the prediction that "what is whispered in the closet shall be proclaimed from the house-tops." . . .

Since publication of the Brandeis and Warren article, the tort of invasion of privacy has undergone much development. It is now viewed as including four separate and distinct branches: 1) intrusion upon the plaintiff's physical solitude or seclusion or on plaintiff's private affairs in a way that would be highly offensive to a reasonable person; 2) publication of private facts about plaintiff's live when disclosure would be highly offensive to a reasonable person; 3) publication of information that places the plaintiff in a false light in the public eye; and 4) appropriation of some element of plaintiff's name, likeness or appearance for commercial use.

In privacy cases, it is not clear that the prohibition against prior restraints will be applied in the same way that it is applied in defamation or national security cases. Privacy cases are treated differently because they implicate different policy considerations than defamation cases. In false light privacy cases (where someone sues because they have been portrayed in a "false light"), involving public officials or public figures, or for that matter topics of public interest, there may be a significant free speech interest in publication of the information. Moreover, there may be a public interest in protecting the publishers of information even though they have portrayed the plaintiff in a false light. This free speech interest might require a higher level of proof. For example, in *Time, Inc. v. Hill*, 385 U.S. 374, 87 S.Ct. 534, 17 L.Ed.2d 456 (1967), the

Court suggested that "false light" privacy cases should be treated like defamation cases for damage purposes, at least insofar as the publication involves public officials or public figures. In other words, when damages are sought, plaintiffs must satisfy the *New York Times v. Sullivan* "actual malice" standard and must prove that defendant knew that the statement was false or acted in reckless disregard for whether it was true or false. The free speech interest might also suggest that prior restraints against invasion of privacy might be impermissible in some cases, particularly false light privacy cases.

However, it is important to realize that privacy cases arise in a variety of contexts, and in some of these contexts the free speech interests might be subordinate to the personal interests. For example, in cases involving intrusion into plaintiff's seclusion, courts have been more inclined to grant injunctive relief in some contexts. Illustrative is *Galella v. Onassis*, 353 F.Supp. 196 (S.D.N.Y.1972), in which a photographer, a self-styled paparazzi, was alleged to have harassed Jacqueline Onassis and her children in an effort to obtain pictures of them. The court described the extent and outrageousness of the photographer's actions as follows:

> 1. *Assaults and batteries.* Galella's physical movements were always unnerving and often frightening. Many witnesses testified to his "jumping", "lunging", "leaping", "rushing out", "snaking in and out", "dashing at me", "touching", "bumping", "scuffling", "blocking", "thrusting" his camera and circling (sometimes with assistants) in close orbit about defendant and her children. [The] constance of this Galella practice, applied by him with such unrestrained and relentless vigor, borders on the cruel.

> At times the threat of physical harm was heightened, as it appeared that the propeller of his boat might cut defendant's legs or that his wash might capsize John's boat or that John would fall from his bicycle or his horse. At other times there were deliberate or predictable contacts or physical consequences—the "flicking" of his camera strap, "pushing", "brushing", after-images of endless flashbulbs, John falling to his knees at night or Caroline falling off her water skis.

> 2. *Offensive mouthings.* Unlike other members of the press, Galella "grunts", "yells", makes "strange sounds", "laughs" and calls to defendant: "How do you like me?"; "The Marines have landed!"; "Ha Ha", "Snuggle up to Santa"; "Glad to see me back, aren't you, Jackie?" And

to Caroline: "I am not making you nervous, am I, honey?" (he was making her cry); "How do you like the great paparazzi being back again!"

3.   *Bogus events.* Galella forces his subjects into ersatz happenings. He hired a costumed Santa to try to force himself close to defendant so as to create an unreal situation. This false, forced, attempted pose echoes the startled expression which Galella seeks to arouse by his assaults and taunts. News is real; Galella promotes the phony.

4.   *Self-aggrandizement.*   Professing   anonymity, Galella actually abjured it. His strength was endless in his quest for the limelight. Galella made a career not only of photographing Mrs. Onassis but of being known as one who has done so. The record before this Court shows that he   has   persistently   arranged   to   have   himself photographed with Mrs. Onassis. He has posed for photographs to be published in nationwide and worldwide magazines   disclosing   the   "disguises"   he   dons   to photograph Mrs. Onassis. He boasts openly of the intimate knowledge he has of her every move. He revels in the attention that comes to him as a result of the extreme measures only he is willing to practice.

5.   *Seeking a "PAYOFF".* No self-respecting reporter will suppress his story for a price. Not so Galella, who offered to cease his activities for money or a job.

6.   *Incessant surveillance.* Reporters diligently track their stories down, but when the story is over, they go away. They do not, like Galella, camp for years at their subject's door and dog their every step. The result of Galella's surveillance is that Mrs. Onassis may not enter or leave her home without Galella's knowledge and is faced with the constant threat that he will follow her hour after hour wherever she goes.

7.   *"Secret Agent" tactics.* Outside of movieland, reporters do not normally hide behind restaurant coat racks, sneak into beauty parlors, don "disguises", hide in bushes and theatre boxes, intrude into school buildings and, when ejected, enlist the aid of schoolchildren, bribe doormen and romance maids. The chases that figure in the trial record here would not be performed by a news reporter when there is no news afoot.

In sustaining a request for injunctive relief, the court noted that Galella's tactics had inflicted severe mental and emotional distress on Mrs. Onassis, and concluded that the surprise events might be particularly upsetting to Mrs. Onassis given her personal history (as the widow of an assassinated President, John F. Kennedy, who witnessed the assassination). The court concluded that the photographer should be enjoined from engaging in certain newsgathering tactics: "The proposition that the First Amendment gives the press wide liberty to engage in any sort of conduct, no matter how offensive, in gathering news has been flatly rejected." "There is no general constitutional right to assault, harass, or unceasingly shadow or distress public figures."

Of course, in cases like *Galella*, the critical question is how to frame the injunctive decree. A court cannot and should not simply enjoin the photographer from reporting on Mrs. Onassis or her children. Even an aggressive photographer has the right to photograph newsworthy people, and to report on their activities. As a result, the court concluded that a prohibition against all photography or publication would be "clearly overbroad." The court emphasized that: "Galella's occupation is lawful and the objective of the order is to modify his conduct, not to prevent his photography."

In a case like *Galella*, the injunctive decree must be sufficiently specific so that it provides protection to the subject, gives the photographer adequate notice of what is to be prohibited, and respects the photographer's general right to report on Mrs. Onassis. In *Galella*, the court held that "the injunction cannot be couched in terms of prohibitions upon Galella's leaping, blocking, taunting, grunting, hiding and the like. Nor have abstract concepts— harassing, endangering—proved workable." The court concluded that an effective decree must include specific proscribed distances, and initially entered an order prohibiting Galella from approaching within 100 yards of Mrs. Onassis' home; 75 yards from her children; 50 yards from Mrs. Onassis; "from performing surveillance" of Mrs. Onassis or her children; and "from commercially appropriating [Mrs. Onassis'] photograph for advertising or trade purposes." The Second Circuit modified the order, finding it broader than necessary. *See Galella v. Onassis*, 487 F.2d 986 (2d Cir.1973). However, it upheld those portions of the order which prohibited the photographer from touching Mrs. Onassis, obstructing her movement in public, or attempting to harm or frighten her.

In some privacy cases, although the courts have shown a willingness to award damages, they will not necessarily sustain requests for injunctive relief. An interesting case is *Zacchini v. Scripps-Howard Broadcasting Co.*, 433 U.S. 562, 97 S.Ct. 2849, 53

L.Ed.2d 965 (1977), which involved an entertainer who performed a "human cannonball" act in which he was shot from a cannon into a net some 200 yards away. When the entertainer performed his act in a fair ground surrounded by grandstands, and a reporter filmed the act and showed it on the news, the entertainer sued for damages claiming that the station unlawfully appropriated his property. The news station claimed that it was immune from suit under the First Amendment. While the United States Supreme Court concluded that the entertainer was entitled to recover damages, it emphasized that the entertainer was not trying to enjoin the station from airing the performance. In dicta, the Court suggested that it might not have upheld a prior restraint on publication.

J. PERMITS AND LICENSING

Relying on the prohibition against prior restraints, courts have also been reluctant to enter injunctions prohibiting individuals from engaging in speech or other protected activities. For example, in *Lovell v. City of Griffin*, 303 U.S. 444, 58 S.Ct. 666, 82 L.Ed. 949 (1938), a city ordinance prohibited the distribution of leaflets or circulars without a permit from the city manager. Concluding that licensing schemes constitute the quintessential form of prior restraint, the Court struck the permit requirement down as invalid on its face. Since the ordinance was invalid, it would have been appropriate for the court to enter an injunction against the ordinance.

Courts will sometimes issue injunctions against leafletting, or for that matter against parades. In general, although people have the right to use public streets, parks and sidewalks for expressive activity, the government has the right to impose "content neutral" time, place and manner restrictions. *See Cox v. New Hampshire,* 312 U.S. 569, 61 S.Ct. 762, 85 L.Ed. 1049 (1941). If a major parade is to occur, the city has the right to advance notice of where and when it will take place so that the city can take appropriate action to control crowds and traffic. Moreover, if the circumstances are such that a parade would be particularly inappropriate at a given time, the city might prohibit the parade at that time. The key is whether the city has articulated content neutral time, place and manner criteria in advance, and whether it is in fact judging the request by such criteria.

By contrast, content-based restrictions on speech are generally unconstitutional. For example, in 2005, the Klu Klux Klan (KKK) sought a permit to hold a protest march on Louisville streets on Derby Day (the day when the Kentucky Derby is run). Under the City of Louisville's parade ordinance, the City was not free to turn down the permit down simply because it disliked the content of the KKK's message. However, it could and did reject the permit on content neutral time, place and manner grounds. Derby Day is an extremely busy day with tens of thousands of people converging on Louisville for the Kentucky Derby. Moreover, city police are diverted to Churchill Downs to help with crowd control. As a result, because of the congestion and the strain on police resources, the City could legitimately deny the KKK the right to march on that day. If the KKK tried to march without a permit, the City could have sought injunctive relief prohibiting the march. Of course, the City would not be able to prohibit the KKK from marching on all days, or because it disliked the KKK's message.

K. LEAFLETTING

Injunctions against leafletting fall into the general prohibition against licensing and prior restraints. For example, in *Organization for a Better Austin v. Keefe*, 402 U.S. 415, 91 S.Ct. 1575, 29 L.Ed.2d 1 (1971), a local ordinance prohibited the distribution of literature within the city limits. Organization for a Better Austin (OBA) was a group committed to limiting integration and stabilizing the community. They alleged that respondent Keefe was engaged in "panic peddling" and "blockbusting" in an effort to sell real estate in the area to minorities. When OBA was unable to persuade Keefe to alter his practices, it peacefully distributed leaflets critical of respondent's real estate practices including his claim that he only sells to "Negroes." The trial court issued an injunction prohibiting distribution of the leaflets.

In striking down the injunction, the United States Supreme Court emphasized that courts may not "concern themselves with the truth or validity of the publication" and it held that the leafleting ban constituted an impermissible prior restraint on publication: "This Court has often recognized that the activity of peaceful pamphleteering is a form of communication protected by the First Amendment. . . . Any prior restraint on expression comes to this Court with a 'heavy presumption' against its constitutional validity." The Court concluded that plaintiff was unable to meet that burden.

Even though leafleting constitutes protected expression, and falls within the general prohibition against prior restraints, leafleting can also be subject to content neutral time, place and manner restrictions. For example, in Louisville, Kentucky, the City of Louisville requires those who wish to distribute leaflets to motorists at busy intersections to obtain a permit. The ordinance is designed to promote traffic safety by limiting the number of leafleters to a manageable number and by imposing other safety restrictions. Such a time, place and manner restriction is probably valid if applied in a nondiscriminatory manner.

L. INJUNCTIONS AGAINST OBSCENITY

In general, the Court tends to apply the prohibition against prior restraints somewhat differently to obscene publications. In a number of cases, the Court has held that the First Amendment does not protect obscene materials, and that government may criminalize the production and distribution of such materials. The Court has been wary about taking the additional step of permitting injunctions against obscenity. Part of the difficulty is that the Court has encountered difficulty in defining obscenity, and in drawing a clear line of demarcation between obscene and non-obscene materials. As a result, if the Court permits injunctions against obscenity, there is the risk that the injunctions will be vague or overbroad and will chill both obscene and protected speech. Moreover, when an injunction is issued as a prior restraint against publication, there is always the risk of error.

Because of these concerns, while the Court permits injunctions against obscenity, it has established elaborate procedural protections. In *Freedman v. State of Maryland*, 380 U.S. 51, 85 S.Ct. 734, 13 L.Ed.2d 649 (1965), the Court considered the constitutionality of a Maryland censorship statute that required submission of motion pictures to a censorship board. Under general free speech principles, this censorship board might have been regarded as a violation of the First Amendment. For one thing, it constituted the equivalent of a licensing scheme of the type struck down in *Lovell*. As a prior restraint on speech, such licensing boards are presumptively unconstitutional. The question in *Freedman* was whether the nature of the speech—obscenity—dictated a difference in result. The Court held that prior restraints on obscenity could be upheld, but only if procedural requirements are satisfied. The Court stated:

A noncriminal process which requires the prior submission of a film to a censor avoids constitutional infirmity only if it takes place under procedural safeguards designed to obviate the dangers of a censorship system. First, the burden of proving that the film is unprotected expression must rest on the censor. As we said in *Speiser v. Randall*, 357 U.S. 513, 526, "Where the transcendent value of speech is involved, due process certainly requires that the State bear the burden of persuasion to show that the appellants engaged in criminal speech." Second, while the State may require advance submission of all films, in order to proceed effectively to bar all showings of unprotected films, the requirement cannot be administered in a manner which would lend an effect of finality to the censor's determination whether a film constitutes protected expression. The teaching of our cases is that, because only a judicial determination in an adversary proceeding ensures the necessary sensitivity to freedom of expression, only a procedure requiring a judicial determination suffices to impose a valid final restraint. To this end, the exhibitor must be assured, by statute or authoritative judicial construction, that the censor will, within a specified brief period, either issue a license or go to court to restrain showing the film. Any restraint imposed in advance of a final judicial determination on the merits must similarly be limited to preservation of the status quo for the shortest fixed period compatible with sound judicial resolution. Moreover, we are well aware that, even after expiration of a temporary restraint, an administrative refusal to license, signifying the censor's view that the film is unprotected, may have a discouraging effect on the exhibitor. Therefore, the procedure must also assure a prompt final judicial decision, to minimize the deterrent effect of an interim and possibly erroneous denial of a license.

In other words, the Court upheld the licensing scheme, and it suggested that an injunction could be entered against the exhibition of obscene films provided that the statutory requirements were satisfied. Since the Maryland statute did not satisfy these criteria, the Court struck it down. However, the Court recognized that an appropriately constructed statute could result in an injunction against obscenity.

Chapter Seven

RESTITUTION

Restitution is an extraordinarily powerful cause of action that provides litigants with unique remedial options that can be used in conjunction with, or substitution for, traditional causes of action and remedies. In addition to monetary recoveries, restitutionary actions provide plaintiffs with the opportunity to "trace" their property into other forms, and to invoke special remedial devices such as constructive trusts, equitable liens and subrogation.

A. GENERAL PRINCIPLES

The doctrinal core of restitution is misleadingly simple: "A person who has been unjustly enriched at the expense of another is required to make restitution to the other." RESTATEMENT OF RESTITUTION § 1 (1937). As the name suggests, the purpose of restitution is simply to prevent defendant from retaining benefits unjustly obtained. Despite the seeming simplicity, there can be definitional problems. For example, courts must determine whether defendant was "enriched," and whether retention of the enrichment would be "unjust". However, when applicable, restitutionary remedies can be extremely powerful and flexible.

Quasi-contract, which presumably you studied in your first-year contracts class, is perhaps the best known restitutionary action. Quasi-contract derives from *Moses v. MacFerlan*, 2 Burr. 1005, 97 Eng.Rep. 676 (King's Bench 1760), in which Chapman Jacob issued four promissory notes to a man named Moses. Moses endorsed the notes to MacFerlan, in order to allow MacFerlan to proceed directly against Jacobs, and MacFerlan expressly agreed that he would not hold Moses liable on the endorsements. In breach of his agreement, MacFerlan sued Moses on the notes and obtained a judgment in what might be called the modern analogue to small claims court. Because of the limited "subject matter" jurisdiction of the court in which the suit was brought, Moses was not allowed to interpose the agreement as a defense. Moses then sued MacFerlan for a refund, and the King's Bench held in Moses favor. Lord Mansfield writing for a unanimous Court stated that "the ground of this action is not, 'that the judgment was wrong:' but, 'that, (for a reason which the now plaintiff could not avail himself of against that judgment,) the defendant ought not in justice to keep the money.'" Lord Mansfield concluded that "the defendant

[MacFerlan], upon the circumstances of the case, is obliged by the ties of natural justice and equity to refund the money."

Early restitution cases were brought in equity. Over time, the law courts developed a restitution action of their own called assumpsit. This action, which initially involved "an action of trespass on the case, brought for a failure to perform an undertaking or for performing negligently the duties of a public calling," eventually expanded in scope and use and came to be referred to as an action in "quasi-contract." However, even after the law courts developed the quasi-contract action, equity courts still heard restitution cases. For example, equity might grant a special restitutionary remedy such as a constructive trust, equitable lien or subrogation.

Today, quasi-contract applies in many different contexts. For example, when a motorist is rendered unconscious and receives emergency medical assistance at a hospital, the hospital can hold the motorist liable for the value of the services rendered. Even though there was no express contract between the hospital and the motorist (because the motorist was unconscious and unable to enter into a contract), and there was no implied contract (because the unconsciousness precluded the implication of an intent to agree), principles of restitution—preventing unjust enrichment—provide the basis for the motorist's obligation to pay the hospital for the value of the emergency services.

However, it is important to realize that restitution extends far beyond quasi-contract, and can provide far more complex forms of recovery. In theory, at least, courts possess broad authority to impose restitutionary relief whenever one person has been "unjustly enriched" at the expense of another.

B. CATEGORIES OF RESTITUTION

Over the centuries, courts have used the vague concept of "unjustness" and developed precedent and rules that help define the doctrinal core of restitution. Because of these rules and precedent, vague concept of "unjustness" are given meaning, and courts have guidance regarding the circumstances under which restitution is appropriate. Nevertheless, given the infinite variety of human conduct and actions which can arise, not all unjust enrichment cases can be easily pigeonholed.

1. Fraud

Restitution is frequently employed in cases of fraud. For example, in *Sieger v. Sieger*, 162 Minn. 322, 202 N.W. 742 (1925), a husband entrusted his wife with the purchase of real estate on their behalf. In violation of the husband's trust, the wife arranged to have the property deeded solely to herself, and she refused to include him on the title. The court concluded that the wife had obtained the property in "bad faith" and by taking advantage of a fiduciary relationship. Because she had obtained the property in an "unconscientious manner," she should not "in equity and good conscience be permitted to keep it."

Numerous other contexts arise in which restitution might involve claims of fraud or quasi-fraud. Suppose, for example, that an insurance company agrees to insure defendant's real estate for the sum of $700 per year. After making payments for eight years, plaintiff incurs a loss and files a claim with the insurance company for $5,000. Defendant insurer denies the claim on the basis that the policy was not properly executed and was never in force. Plaintiff may seek restitution from the insurance company for the payments made under the policy. If the company denies that a policy exists, then it was unjustly enriched by receipt and retention of the premiums.

2.   Criminal Conduct

Restitution might be ordered in criminal contexts as well. For example, suppose that defendant embezzles large sums of money from his employer over a long period of time. When the employer finds out about the embezzlement, it is entitled to claim restitution of the embezzled money on the basis that defendant was "unjustly enriched" at his employer's expense. Likewise, when defendant has forcefully taken plaintiff's property through criminal acts (*e.g.*, armed robbery), it is possible for plaintiff to obtain "restitution" from the robber for the amount taken. Indeed, as we shall see, if the robber is otherwise destitute, but the stolen money can be traced into other forms, restitution might allow the victim to trace his money into those other forms. In that way, restitution may provide plaintiff with the only effective means of recovery.

3.   Appropriation of Benefits

Restitution might also be required when defendant has misappropriated a benefit received from defendant. The case of *Beacon Homes, Inc. v. Holt*, 266 N.C. 467, 146 S.E.2d 434 (1966), illustrates the concept. In that case, defendant's mother contracted with Beacon Homes to build a house on defendant's land, but ultimately refused to pay for it. Even though defendant also refused to pay, she claimed ownership of the house, rented it out, and accepted and retained the rental proceeds. In addition, she rejected plaintiff's offer to remove the house and restore the land to its original condition. The court concluded that defendant had been unjustly enriched:

> The question is, can the owner of a lot upon which a house has been built by another, who acted in good faith under a mistake of fact, believing he had a right to build it there, keep the house, refuse to permit the builder to remove it so as to restore the property to its former condition, enjoy the enhancement of the value of the property and pay nothing for the house? For the owner to do so is as contrary to equity and good conscience as it would be if the builder had believed itself to be the owner of the land."

In a case like *Beacon Homes*, factual analysis is very important. If we change the facts a bit, plaintiff may have no right to a restitutionary recovery. For example, suppose that defendant strongly desires to keep the land in an undeveloped condition. As a result, when she finds out about the house, rather than renting it out and pocketing the proceeds, she immediately demands that the builder remove the house. The builder refuses and demands payment for the house. The owner then decides to tear the house down. Under these circumstances, it is difficult to argue that defendant has been "unjustly enriched" by the presence of the house. Quite the contrary, she ended up with a house that she did not want, that interfered with her preferred use of the property, and she was forced to expend money to tear it down. Indeed, she might be entitled to recover from plaintiff for the costs of removing the house.

In a similar case, *Kossian v. American National Insurance Company*, 254 Cal.App.2d 647, 62 Cal.Rptr. 225 (1967), defendant's tenant contracted with plaintiff to clean-up property that was damaged by fire. After the clean-up was finished, defendant reclaimed the property from the tenant, refused to pay defendant for the clean-up, and even went so far as to seek reimbursement for the clean-up cost under its insurance policy. The Court held that defendant should be required to make payment to plaintiff for the benefit received.

4. Breach of Contract

When the defendant has breached a contract, the plaintiff may have the option of suing on the contract or of suing in restitution. For example, Professor Benjamin Weaver agrees to write a new casebook for South Publishing Co. with compensation to be provided through royalties earned on the book. If Professor Weaver completes his work, but South refuses to publish the book, it is difficult for the professor to recover on the contract. Since the book was never published, it is impossible to know how many copies would have been sold or how much royalties would have been earned. Nevertheless, the professor can recover in restitution based on the amount of effort expended in creating the book. The publisher was unjustly enriched in that amount.

As a general rule, when a plaintiff has fully performed under a contract and is only entitled to payment, he cannot disaffirm the contract and sue in restitution. As a result, suppose that plaintiff agrees to reap defendant's wheat for the sum of $2,000. After plaintiff completes the reaping, defendant refuses to pay. Under such circumstances, plaintiff is generally relegated to an action for the contract price rather than an action for restitution.

5. Swindlers

Restitution of unjust benefits is very fact and case specific. As a general rule, courts might be disinclined to give restitution to someone who tried to cheat others, but who ended up losing money, because courts might conclude that the cheater suffers from "unclean hands." However, restitution might be required if it serves a broader policy goal. For example, in the extraordinary case of *Stewart v. Wright*, 147 Fed. 321 (8th Cir.1906), a group of swindlers specialized in arranging rigged foot races. As part of their scheme, they lured wealthy "pigeons" to bet on the races by claiming that the races were rigged in the pigeon's favor. In fact, the races were rigged against the pigeon. When a defrauded pigeon sued to recover his losses, the swindlers defended, relying on the clean hands doctrine. In *Stewart*, the court balanced the relative equities and concluded that the swindlers should be required to disgorge their profits. Given the relative culpability of the parties, the court overlooked plaintiff's misconduct in an effort to discourage the swindlers from continuing their conduct.

6. Improper Exactions

Restitution might also be required when defendant demands and obtains an improper payment from plaintiff. Under appropriate circumstances, a court might conclude that the extra payment constitutes "unjust enrichment." However, factual analysis is important. In *Sloame v. Madison Square Garden Center, Inc.*, 56 A.D.2d 92, 391 N.Y.S.2d 576 (1977), Sloame held season tickets to Rangers Hockey Club home games. The ticket invoice provided that "risk of loss or theft of said tickets shall pass to [Sloame] and that the Madison Square Garden shall not be obligated to admit subscriber to events unless tickets delivered hereunder are presented at such time." When Sloame lost his tickets, the Garden agreed to sell him a second set of tickets for the same seat provided that he agreed to vacate the seat if someone holding the original ticket tried to claim the seat. The Garden also agreed to refund the second payment if Sloame found the original tickets. When Sloame sought restitution for the second payment, the request for restitution was denied. The court held that, given the agreement and the circumstances, the Garden was not "unjustly enriched" by the second payment. The Garden assumed risks when it issued a second set of tickets (*e.g.*, someone might find the first set of tickets and use them to gain free admission to the arena), and the second payment was regarded as appropriate compensation for this increased risk.

7.   Benefits Conferred by Mistake

Another situation when restitution might be ordered is when plaintiff confers a benefit on defendant by mistake. Suppose, for example, that Steve Bronson, a divorced man, has a legal obligation to pay child support to his ex-wife, Ann Bronson. Steve duly makes the required payment every month. However, one month, he mistakenly pays Ann twice and she cashes both checks and spends the money even though she is well aware of the double payment. Under such circumstances, Steve can obtain restitution from Ann for the second payment. Likewise, suppose that A agrees to convey a particular tract of land (the "Nelson Tract") to B for $250,000. Mistakenly, A conveys both the Nelson Tract, and a second tract (the "Johnson Tract") to B for the same $250,000. Since the agreement extended only to the Nelson tract, and not the Johnson Tract, A is entitled to restitution of the Johnson Tract.

These situations, involving benefits conferred by mistake, can arise in a myriad of circumstances. For yet another example, suppose that John Johnson is under contract to convey real estate to Jane Wyman. However, the real estate attorney mistakenly makes the deed out in the name of Janice Wyman (rather than Jane Wyman). When the mistake is discovered, Johnson asks Janice Wyman to convey the property back to him or to Jane Wyman. Janice refuses both requests. Under the circumstances, Janice Wyman would be unjustly enriched if she were allowed to keep the property, and can be required to make restitution. Finally, if a medical insurer intends to provide reimbursement to an insured, but mistakenly sends double reimbursement, the insurer can recover the second payment.

Whether restitution will be required for property conveyed by mistake depends on the circumstances. In some situations, although there is a mistaken conferral, there may be no "unjust" enrichment. Suppose, for example, that Kate Weaver (defendant) haunts flea markets looking for "bargains." At a recent flea market, she finds an old picture. Weaver likes Impressionists paintings and believes that the picture looks "impressionistic." Because neither the plaintiff-seller nor the defendant-buyer believes that the picture has any particular value, defendant is able to purchase it for only $20. When defendant takes the picture to be reframed, the clerk notices that the painting contains a signature, "Monet," and urges defendant to take the picture to an expert. As it turns out, the painting is an authentic Monet worth $1 million. When the flea market dealer hears about the buyer's flea market "find" (the newspaper published a big article about Kate's "find"), and realizes that he sold the painting for $20, he sues Kate seeking restitution. Under the circumstances, although Kate has been "enriched" at the dealer's expense, the enrichment was not "unjust." The dealer set the painting's price, and defendant paid it. In doing so, both the dealer and the defendant took the risk that the picture might be worth more or less.

As with all restitution cases, mistake cases can be highly fact-specific. Suppose, for example, that Grace Harlow also goes to a flea market. At a booth selling real diamonds, fake diamonds and other baubles, Harlow watches a dealer take out some expensive diamonds, and observes the dealer mistakenly place a valuable authentic diamond worth $100,000 in a bin market marked "Fake Diamonds. $10." Harlow immediately purchases the diamond for $10. When the dealer realizes his mistake, he demands that Harlow sell it back to him for $10. Harlow refuses and the dealer sues her for restitution. Under the circumstances, not only was Harlow enriched, but it would be unjust to allow her to retain the enrichment. Harlow was well aware of the dealer's mistake (in placing the authentic diamond in the "fakes" bin) and sought to take advantage of that mistake.

Now, let's consider one last flea market example. Suppose that defendant Sydney Weaver purchases an old picture at a flea market. The picture did not appear to have particular value, and was being sold cheaply ($2). After Sydney bought the picture and took it home, he decided to reframe it. When Sydney took the back off the picture, he found an original copy of the Declaration of Independence worth $350,000. Plaintiff, the flea market dealer, realizes the true value of the picture when he sees news reports about defendant's "fortunate" discovery of the Declaration of Independence. Under the circumstances, restitution is not required. Although defendant was enriched at plaintiff's expense, the enrichment was not "unjust." In purchasing the picture, defendant did not know that it contained a copy of the Declaration of Independence (as plaintiff presumably did not know as well), and both parties must accept the consequences when it turns out that the picture has great value.

8. Emergency Assistance

In some instances, individuals who provide emergency assistance to others may be entitled to restitution for their efforts. As a general rule, the emergency service must not be provided as a gift, but rather with the expectation of compensation. For example, in *Bartholomew v. Jackson*, 20 Johns 28, 11 Am.Dec. 237 (N.Y.Sup.Ct.1822), plaintiff permitted defendant to store wheat on his property with the understanding that it would be removed in time for plaintiff to prepare the ground for the fall crop. When the time for planting arrived, plaintiff notified defendant that it was time to remove the wheat because plaintiff planned to burn the field. When defendant failed to remove the wheat in a timely manner, plaintiff removed it and sought restitution for his time and effort. Restitution was granted.

Likewise, the proprietor of a bus station might be entitled to restitution if he cares for the property of another. For example, Ann Perry takes a bus trip across the United States. At a stop-over in Hobbs, New Mexico, she negligently leaves her suitcase behind. The proprietor of the bus station stores the bag for Ann until she returns, but then seeks payment for the per-day storage fee. In general, assuming that the proprietor intended to charge for the service, Ann is required to make restitution to the operator for the storage costs. She received a benefit at his expense and should be required to make restitution.

9. Gifts

Ordinarily, when one makes a gift to another, the recipient is under no obligation to make restitution. For example, in *Knott v. Pratt*, 158 Vt. 334, 609 A.2d 232 (1992), plaintiff resided with and cared for her father for thirteen years. Although she lived rent free in the father's house, she maintained and improved the house. She did so as a "labor of love" and because she assumed and hoped that she would inherit the property after her father's death. When the father died, he left the property not only to plaintiff, but also to her siblings. Plaintiff sought compensation for her time and expenditures, claiming that "it is against equity and good conscience to allow the estate of her father to retain the increased value of the property." The court disagreed, finding that plaintiff had donated the time and effort to her father. Although she might have hoped to receive a greater share of the inheritance, this hope was not a legal entitlement.

10. "Volunteers" and "Officious Intermeddlers"

As a general rule, courts are reluctant to permit "volunteers" and "officious intermeddlers" to recover sums expended on behalf of others. As the Restatement of Restitution states, "A person who without mistake, coercion or request has unconditionally conferred a benefit upon another is not entitled to restitution, except where the benefit was conferred under circumstances making such action necessary for the protection of the interests of the other or of third persons." RESTATEMENT OF RESTITUTION § 112.

The concept of "officious intermeddling" has been applied in a variety of contexts. For example, although defendant adequately provides for his children's needs, suppose that his sister (the children's aunt) decides that they deserve a meal at a fancy restaurant. After paying for the meal, she sues the father for "restitution" on the theory that the father is responsible for the children's health and welfare, and should be required to reimburse her for the meal. The aunt will be denied relief as a "volunteer" or an "officious intermeddler."

On the other hand, if the father had failed to provide the basic necessities of life to his children (*e.g.*, food, clothing and shelter), and the aunt supplied them in order to ensure that the kids did not starve or freeze to death, she will be entitled to restitution. As the Restatement provides, "A person who has performed the noncontractual duty of another by supplying a third person with necessities which in violation of such duty the other had failed to supply, although acting without the other's knowledge or consent, is entitled to restitution therefor from the other if he acted unofficiously and with intent to charge therefor." However, she might be entitled to recover only the reasonable cost of food and not the price of a fancy restaurant.

Norton v. Haggett, 117 Vt. 130, 85 A.2d 571 (1952), provides yet another illustration of the "officious intermeddler" concept. In that case, plaintiff, who appears to have had some animosity towards defendant, attempted to purchase the note and mortgage on defendant's house with the goal of making defendant his debtor. However, plaintiff mistakenly paid off and discharged defendant's mortgage thereby relieving defendant of any further obligation. The court rejected plaintiff's argument that he should take the place of the creditor: "No protection is deserved by one who intermeddles by paying another's debt either without reason or to secure rights against the debtor without the consent of the creditor." In reaching its decision, the court emphasized that plaintiff examined the town records for the sole purpose 'of seeing whether possibly Mr. Haggett owed some money to somebody;' the bank had no reason to sell the note and mortgage, and would not have sold it to the plaintiff; the Haggetts had no desire for the plaintiff to own the note and mortgage; the plaintiff had no conversation with the bank or the Haggetts thereabout prior to his attempted purchase; the plaintiff's brief concedes that he is a stranger to the instruments.

As a result, the court treated the payment as a gift to defendant.

Simply because plaintiff has voluntarily conferred a benefit on defendant does not make plaintiff a volunteer or an officious intermeddler. For example, in *Western Coach Corporation v. Roscoe*, 133 Ariz. 147, 650 P.2d 449 (1982), plaintiff, who held a lien against a mobile home, repossessed it and spent money to refurbish it (the mobile home had been vandalized). Afterwards, when plaintiff sued to recover the refurbishment costs from defendant (who was a cosignee of the note), defendant tried to defend on the basis that plaintiff was an officious intermeddler. The court disagreed: "Western was not an 'officious intermeddler.' At the time Western took possession of the mobile home and made the alleged repairs, the payments were in default. . . . Western had an interest in seeing that the security for the debt was preserved and was therefore not an 'officious intermeddler.' "

Likewise, in *Deskovick v. Porzio*, 78 N.J.Super. 82, 187 A.2d 610 (App.Div.1963), two sons paid their father's hospital and medical bills, believing that the father was destitute. The court concluded that there was no contract for repayment because there was no agreement between the father and the sons. However, the court refused to treat the sons as mere "volunteers," noting that a " 'mistaken belief in the existence of facts which would create a moral obligation upon the donor to make a gift would ordinarily be a basic error' justifying restitution." The court concluded that prior precedent

> would apply in favor of sons, who, during their father's mortal illness, believing him without means of meeting medical and hospital bills as a result of what he had previously told them, and wishing to spare him the discomfort of concern over such expenses at such a time, themselves assumed and paid the obligations. The leaving by the father of an estate far more than sufficient to have met the expenditures would, in such circumstances, and absent others affecting the basic equitable situation presented, properly invoke the concept of a quasi-

contractual obligation of reimbursement of the sons by the estate.

Similar principles were applied in *In re Marine Trust Co.*, 156 Misc. 297, 281 N.Y.S. 553 (1935). In that case, the court held that the Roman Catholic Archdiocese of Philadelphia was entitled to restitution from the estate of a deceased priest for money that it had advanced for his support during his lifetime while he was incompetent and seemingly impoverished. A surviving brother had defrayed the remaining expenses of maintaining the decedent out of the latter's own substantial funds of which the brother had been acting as trustee. The Archdiocese did not know of the trust fund until after the incompetent's death, and therefore decedent's estate was unjustly enriched at the expense of the Archdiocese. However, recovery was denied because the statute of limitations had run.

11. Bona Fide Purchasers for Value

There has been much litigation regarding whether purchasers of property can or should be required to make restitution. A bona fide purchaser (BFP) is an individual who "gives value for property" without notice that the property belongs to another. RESTATEMENT OF RESTITUTION § 172 (1937). As the Restatement provides:

> The principle that a person who innocently has acquired the title to property for which he has paid value is under no duty to restore it to one who would be entitled to reclaim it if he had not been innocent or had not paid value therefor, is of wide application, being a limitation upon the principle that a person who has been wrongfully deprived of his property is entitled to restitution.

Id., at § 172, Comment a (1937).

A BFP might prevail, for example, when defendant steals a prize bull from plaintiff, sells it, invests the money in gold and silver which he then sells to a third party (the BFP). Ordinarily, while plaintiff might be allowed to "trace" the bull into different forms, including the gold and silver, tracing might not be permitted if the purchaser of the gold and silver is a BFP. The purchaser becomes a BFP if he pays value for the gold and silver and takes it without notice of plaintiff's equitable claim. As a result, although plaintiff can recover against the thief, as well as against the purchaser of the bull, he might be precluded from recovering against the purchaser of the gold and silver.

In order to be treated as a BFP, a purchaser must take without notice of the critical facts. A purchaser is regarded as having "notice" "if he knows the facts or should know them." For example, in the case of the stolen bull referred to in the prior paragraph, assume that JoAnn Olson purchases the bull from the thief for $5,000. That price is reasonable for a bull of good quality, but is on the cheap side for a bull of prize winning quality. Assuming that Olson is regularly engaged in the purchase and sale of cattle (and bulls), and should know that a comparable bull would cost much more (*e.g.*, $25,000), she should be aware that something is amiss in the sale. As a result, she cannot be regarded as a BFP.

C. MEASURING THE ENRICHMENT

When a court finds that defendant has been unjustly enriched, it must then decide how to measure the enrichment. As we shall see, there is no set measure of recovery in restitution cases, and the actual measurement can vary depending on circumstances.

In general, and subject to exceptions, restitutionary recoveries are based on the amount that the defendant received. RESTATEMENT OF RESTITUTION, Comment to § 1, at 13 (1937), provides for the following measure of recovery: "*d.* Ordinarily the benefit to the one and the loss to the other are coextensive, and the result of the remedies given under the rules stated in the Restatement of this subject is to compel the one to surrender the benefit which he has received and thereby to make restitution to the other for the loss which he has suffered."

However, restitution is not always measured by defendant's gain. In many instances, the determination of damages is a policy choice which turns on the nature of the benefit received (*i.e.*, money, property, profits, services, etc.), the nature or degree of defendant's wrongdoing, and the substantive policies underlying the claim or defense.

Suppose that Sydney Rascal steals 3 mahogany trees from James Mail's property. Mahogany wood is particularly valuable, and the trees are worth $100,000. Rascal mills the trees into lumber, and uses the lumber as studs in a new house that he is building. Since the studs cannot be seen, Rascal could have used much cheaper lumber (that would have been equally sturdy and effective) in place of the mahogany. This other wood could have been purchased for $4,000. In a case like this one, there are numerous options for measuring the recovery. One could argue that, since Rascal stole trees worth $100,000, he was unjustly enriched in that amount. On the other hand, Rascal could argue that, since he used the trees in a way that provided him with only $4,000 worth of benefit, he was unjustly enriched only in that amount. In fact, a court would provide the former measure of recovery ($100,000). Given Rascal's status as a thief, the higher measure of recovery is preferable because Rascal should bear the loss of value rather than Mail.

However, the policy-based nature of restitution would suggest that, on similar but slightly different facts, plaintiff might be limited to the lower level of recovery. Suppose that Jacob Weber owns a lumber yard, and Debbie Shoemaker orders lumber for use as studs. Ordinarily, such wood would cost $4,000. Weber mistakenly ships Shoemaker mahogany wood (worth $100,000). Shoemaker does not notice the mistake, and uses the mahogany for studs. When Weber realizes his mistake, he demands payment of $100,000. Shoemaker refuses to pay claiming that Weber is only entitled to $4,000. Like the thief example in the prior paragraph, one could say that Shoemaker received lumber worth $100,000, and therefore was enriched in that amount. However, one could also say that, since Shoemaker only used the lumber in a way that gave her only $4,000 worth of benefit, and therefore that she was only enriched only in the amount of the contract price. In this situation, since Weber was at fault, he would be forced to bear the loss. Shoemaker was not "enriched" in the sense that she received more than she contracted to receive.

A more difficult assessment would be required if both defendant and plaintiff acted in good faith. Consider the prior example involving Rascal's theft of mahogany trees, but assume that Rascal took the trees mistakenly and in good faith. He thought that the trees were on his own property because of a surveyor's mistake. As a result, when Rascal cut down the trees, he thought that they were his own. Again, Rascal uses the trees as studs in his new house, and again the value of the studs is only $4,000 as opposed to the $100,000 value of raw mahogany timber. Under these circumstances, although Rascal has a much stronger case for assessing the value of the lumber at $4,000, the court is still likely to adopt the higher valuation. Mail was completely faultless in the transaction and should not be required to bear the loss. By contrast, although Rascal acted in good faith and under an honest mistake, he was nonetheless mistaken. Between the two, Rascal should be required to bear the loss.

Because of the infinite variety of contexts in which "unjust enrichment" can arise, the measure of recovery is necessarily vague. Reconsider *Beacon Homes v. Holt, supra,* in which plaintiff built a home on plaintiff's property at the request of plaintiff's mother (but without plaintiff's permission or consent). After the sale, plaintiff appropriated the benefit, began renting out the property, and pocketed the proceeds. In theory, there might be more than one way to measure the enrichment. One way is to measure the benefit is by the contract price. However, since plaintiff was not bound by her mother's contract, the contract price is not binding on her. A second way is by an assessment of how much the improvement increased the land's value. In *Beacon Homes*, the court adopted this measure.

Likewise, in *Iacomini v. Liberty Mutual Insurance Co.*, 127 N.H. 73, 497 A.2d 854 (1985), a Mercedes Benz 450-SL was stolen and ultimately wrecked by the thief who took it to defendant for storage and repairs. The repair shop had no knowledge of the theft, and in fact was deceived by the thief who presented a fraudulent certificate of ownership. An insurance company took ownership of the car after compensating the owner, and eventually located it at defendant's repair shop. The shop owner refused to produce the car unless and until he was compensated for the cost of the repairs. The court held that, because the insurance company received the car in a repaired condition due to the shop owner's labor, the shop owner was entitled to compensation to prevent "unjust enrichment." However, because of the unusual and involuntary circumstances, the court held that the measure of recovery should be based on the value of the repairs to the insurance company rather than on the shop's hourly rate. So, the shop owner was only entitled to "the difference between the value of the vehicle before and after the plaintiff worked on it."

For another example, in *Sheldon v. Metro-Goldwyn Pictures Corp.*, 309 U.S. 390, 60 S.Ct. 681, 84 L.Ed. 825 (1940), plaintiff sought an accounting when defendant infringed the copyright on his play "Dishonored Lady," in producing the play, "Letty Lynton." The question was how to measure the infringement. Plaintiff claimed that it was entitled to defendant's gross profit of $587,000. Defendant disagreed, claiming that plaintiff was only entitled to the amount that was attributable to plaintiff's work. Since the infringement was arguably deliberate, an argument could have been made for awarding plaintiff all of the profits from the play. However, the Court refused to adopt that measure of recovery, concluding that it would, in effect, be regarded as a penalty: "we perceive no ground for saying that in awarding profits to the copyright proprietor as a means of compensation, the court may make an award of profits which have been shown not to be due to the infringement." The Court noted that there was proof that a significant portion of the profits were attributable to the names of the stars who played in the film, as well as to defendant's "artistic conception" and production skills.

However, the extent of any offset may vary from case-to-case. For example, in *Hill v. Names & Addresses, Inc.*, 212 Ill.App.3d 1065, 157 Ill.Dec. 66, 571 N.E.2d 1085 (1991), defendant's counterclaim alleged that plaintiff had breached a covenant not to compete and solicited business from defendant's customers. As a result, defendant sought restitution of commissions earned (approximately $126,000+) from the breach. The question was how to measure the damages. The court held that defendant could recover based on lost profits. In addition, to the extent that plaintiff had made profits exceeding defendant's loss, so that the "lost profits" approach would be insufficient to deprive plaintiff of his gain, recovery could be based on plaintiff's gain: "The imposition of a constructive trust in such circumstances reflects an implementation of the 'wise public policy that, for the purpose of removing all temptation, extinguishes all possibility of profit flowing from a breach of the confidence imposed by the fiduciary relation.'" Although the court allowed plaintiff to offset costs attributable to the increased business, it only allowed plaintiff to recover direct costs and not overhead: "Net profits are to be determined by reducing the gross revenues generated from the wrongfully-obtained business by those cost-of-sale items and other expenses which the court concludes were not fixed."

Finally, recall the prior example in which Professor Weaver agrees to write a property casebook for South Publishing Co. Professor Weaver dutifully prepares a wonderful book, but South refuses to accept it because the casebook market has changed (publishers are now producing electronic casebooks rather than hard copy books). As we saw in the prior section, Professor Weaver is entitled to restitution, but how should the "unjust enrichment" be measured? The contract price does not provide an adequate measure because it based the compensation on royalties. Since the book was never published, no royalties will be produced. As a result, the professor can probably recover based on an hourly rate for time spent in preparing the manuscript.

D. SPECIAL RESTITUTIONARY REMEDIES

The equitable side of restitution includes a number of special restitutionary devices including the constructive trust, equitable lien, tracing and subrogation. Because each of these devices is powerful and flexible, they can provide a plaintiff with unique advantages.

1. The Constructive Trust

A constructive trust is created and imposed by courts to prevent "unjust enrichment." RESTATEMENT OF RESTITUTION § 160 (1937). "Where a person holding title to property is subject to an equitable duty to convey it to another on the ground that he would be unjustly enriched if he were permitted to retain it, a constructive trust arises." *Id.* Once a constructive trust is imposed, defendant "holds title to property subject to an equitable duty to hold the property for or to convey it to another, and the latter has in each case some kind of an equitable interest in the property."

A constructive trust is readily distinguishable from an express trust or a resulting trust. An express trust is usually created by the explicit intention of the parties, and a resulting trust arises by an implication given the nature of the transfer—in other words, the transfer is made under circumstances suggesting that the trustee is not being given the "beneficial interest" in the property. By contrast, a constructive trust can be imposed without regard to the trustee's intent, and, indeed, against the trustee's wishes where the trust is needed to prevent unjust enrichment. "A constructive trust is imposed upon a person in order to prevent his unjust enrichment. To prevent such enrichment an equitable duty to convey the property to another is imposed upon him." RESTATEMENT OF RESTITUTION § 160, Comment c (1937).

Illustrative is the holding in *Nockelun v. Sawicki*, 197 A.D.2d 507, 602 N.Y.S.2d 190 (1993). In that case, Plaintiff Amelia Nockelun, the 86 year-old maternal aunt of the defendant, Constance Sawicki, prepared a will leaving her entire estate to the defendant. Subsequently, defendant told plaintiff that, should she enter a nursing home, social services and creditors would attach the plaintiff's house for the payment of debts. Defendant asked plaintiff to convey the house to her to ensure that the house passed to her. Defendant promised to help plaintiff with the bills pertaining to the house and to reconvey the house to the plaintiff should she so desire at a future date. In 1991, the plaintiff sought to obtain a home equity loan to enable her to make repairs to the house and also to pay several debts she owed. The bank required that she obtain legal title to the house before she could get the loan. However, defendant refused to reconvey the house to the plaintiff. Defendant admitted that during the 15 years the deed was in her name, she did not help the plaintiff with the payment of taxes on the property or with any other bills pertaining to the property, with the exception of $200 to assist the plaintiff in repairing the roof. The court imposed a constructive trust on the property.

Comment a to the RESTATEMENT OF RESTITUTION § 160 explains how a "constructive trust" differs from an "express trust." The Restatement suggests that the term "constructive trust" is "not altogether a felicitous one. It might be thought to suggest the idea that it is a fiduciary relation similar to an express trust, whereas it is in fact something quite different from an express trust. An express trust and a constructive trust are not divisions of the same fundamental concept. They are not species of the same genus. They are distinct concepts. A constructive trust does not, like an express trust, arise because of a manifestation of an intention to create it, but it is imposed as a remedy to prevent unjust enrichment. A constructive trust, unlike an express trust, is not a fiduciary relation, although the circumstances which give rise to a constructive trust may or may not involve a fiduciary relation."

A constructive trust also differs from an express trust in that, in the ordinary case, it is not expected that the "trust" will continue for a significant period of time. In most cases, it is assumed that the constructive trustee will promptly be required to turn the property over to the beneficiary.

Special restitutionary devices might be applied in an array of contexts. For example, in *Sieger v. Sieger*, 162 Minn. 322, 202 N.W. 742 (1925), a husband, who was unable to read or to write, entrusted his wife with the power to purchase real estate on their behalf. Of the $3,400 purchase price, $2,000 came from plaintiff's separate funds and the remaining $1,400 came from defendant's separate funds. Although both parties subsequently lived on the land, the wife arranged to have the property titled solely in her own name. When plaintiff learned what his wife had done, he demanded that he be added to the title. The court held that plaintiff was entitled to an undivided share of the property, and ordered defendant to hold the property in trust for plaintiff.

However, a constructive trust is generally inappropriate when plaintiff cannot claim an equitable interest in the specific property on which the remedy would be imposed. In *In re Bull*, 48 Or.App. 565, 617 P.2d 317 (1980), a husband suffered severe physical injuries in an automobile accident and received a sizeable financial settlement. The man had fathered a child by a prior marriage and was behind on child support payments at the time he received the settlement. As a result, the ex-wife sought to impose a special restitutionary remedy on the settlement. The court refused the request noting that such remedies are imposed only to prevent unjust enrichment, and that the unjust enrichment "must result from the receipt of the particular property upon which the lien is imposed."

2.   Equitable Liens

An equitable lien is similar to a constructive trust, but, instead of requiring defendant to hold the property in trust, the court imposes a "lien" against property as security for plaintiff's interest. RESTATEMENT OF RESTITUTION § 161 (1937). If defendant pays plaintiff the amount of the imposed lien, the equitable lien is discharged. If defendant refuses or fails to pay, the court will usually order a sale of the property and compensate defendant out of the sale proceeds.

In some situations, plaintiff may be entitled to choose whether to impose a constructive trust or an equitable lien on property. For example, if defendant steals $100,000 from plaintiff and uses the money to pay the purchase price for real estate, plaintiff might be entitled to impose a constructive trust on the real estate (which would require defendant to hold it in trust for plaintiff) or to impose an equitable lien (which would allow defendant to retain the property, but impose a lien on plaintiff's behalf for the amount of his interest). Which remedy the plaintiff will choose will depend on circumstances. If the real estate is worth more than $100,000, plaintiff might prefer to receive the real estate. On the other hand, if the real estate is worth less than $100,000, plaintiff might prefer the equitable lien. In the latter situation, he can force a sale of the property and still pursue defendant for the remainder of the debt.

In some situations, plaintiff will have the option to impose either a constructive trust or an equitable lien. In other situations, plaintiff can impose only an equitable lien. For example, suppose that Tom Biltmore steals $5,000 from Jane Edwards and invests it in real estate that he already owns. The real estate has a value of $30,000. Under these circumstances, an equitable lien would be appropriate: "A person whose property is without his consent used in making improvements on the other's land or chattels is entitled to an equitable lien for the value of his property so used. This is true not only where materials of the claimant are used in making the improvements, but also where the wrongdoer uses money of the claimant in paying for improvements." RESTATEMENT OF RESTITUTION § 206, Comment (1937).

3. Subrogation

Subrogation is yet another special restitutionary remedy. The RESTATEMENT OF RESTITUTION § 162 (1937), provides that: "Where property of one person is used in discharging an obligation owed by another or a lien upon the property of another, under such circumstances that the other would be unjustly enriched by the retention of the benefit thus conferred, the former is entitled to be subrogated to the position of the obligee or lien-holder."

Wilson v. Todd, 217 Ind. 183, 26 N.E.2d 1003 (1940), illustrates the concept of subrogation. In that case, Todd defrauded Wilson and used the proceeds to pay off a mortgage on his real estate. After Wilson obtained a judgment against Todd, he asked the court to subrogate him to the original mortgage holder's rights against the real estate. The court allowed the subrogation, noting that: "Subrogation is the substitution of another person in the place of a creditor, so that the person in whose favor it is exercised succeeds to the right of the creditor in relation to the debt."

Tracing can be used in subrogation cases to give the plaintiff the benefit of a secured interest and/or a preferred position. However, one who tries to subrogate takes subject to the rights of the original creditor, and is subject to all defenses the defendant might have raised against the discharged creditor. In addition, an individual's subrogation rights are no better than those held by the original subrogee. As a result, if the original claim was secured and was deserving of priority over other creditors, then the subrogated claim may be treated as secured and entitled to priority. On the other hand, if the original claim was unsecured, the subrogated claim will be unsecured as well. Likewise, if the original claim was not entitled to priority over creditors, then the subrogated claim will not be entitled to priority either.

E. SPECIAL ADVANTAGES OF CONSTRUCTIVE TRUSTS AND EQUITABLE LIENS

Both constructive trusts and equitable liens offer plaintiffs special advantages over other remedies. The three most important advantages are that both devices allow plaintiffs to "trace" their property into other forms, can be used to give plaintiffs priority over other creditors, and can be used to circumvent special debtor exemptions such as the homestead exemption.

1. Tracing

"Tracing" is the idea that plaintiffs can trace their property into different forms and impose a constructive trust or equitable lien on the property reflected in those other forms. As the Restatement provides, "Where a person wrongfully disposes of property of another knowing that the disposition is wrongful and acquires in exchange other property, the other is entitled at his option either (a) a constructive trust of the property so acquired, or (b) an equitable lien upon it to secure his claim for reimbursement from the wrongdoer." RESTATEMENT OF RESTITUTION § 202 (1937).

Tracing is similar to replevin in that plaintiff can "follow" and reclaim property. However, tracing differs significantly from replevin because it allows plaintiff to follow the property into different forms. If defendant steals plaintiff's diamond ring and sells it to a pawn shop, replevin might allow plaintiff to reclaim the ring from the pawn shop. However, if defendant takes the pawn shop proceeds and invests it in real estate, replevin would provide plaintiff with no remedy regarding the real estate. Restitution, combined with tracing, might allow plaintiff to follow the diamond into the proceeds and ultimately into the real estate.

The concept of tracing is illustrated by the holding in *G & M Motor Company v. Thompson*, 567 P.2d 80 (Okla.1977). In that case, an accountant embezzled money from his employer, combined it with some of his money, and invested it in life insurance for his wife and child. The employer was allowed to trace the embezzled money into the life insurance policy and to impose a constructive trust on the proceeds of that policy. In imposing the constructive trust, the court relied on the RESTATEMENT OF RESTITUTION § 160, Comment c (1937), "Where a person wrongfully disposes of property of another knowing that the disposition is wrongful and acquires in exchange other property, the other is entitled to enforce a constructive trust of the property so acquired."

Tracing is also illustrated by the holding in *In re Allen*, 724 P.2d 651 (Colo.1986). In that case, a husband embezzled money from his employer during the pendency of his marriage. The employer did not learn about the embezzlement until after the man had divorced his wife and she had received a portion of the embezzled funds as "marital property." By that time, the now ex-wife had transferred her share of the marital assets into a bank account, and then used the money to purchase a piece of real estate in Florida. Since the bank was able to trace the embezzled proceeds from the marital home (in which they were originally invested) into the bank account and eventually into the Florida real estate, the employer was allowed to trace its funds into the Florida property.

(A) Measurement for Tracing Purposes

One issue that arises in tracing cases is how to measure the enrichment. In an ordinary case, the plaintiff might be allowed to recover only the amount that can be traced. For example, suppose that defendant Jimbo Nelson defrauds plaintiff Bill Dusch of $3,000. Nelson deposits the $3,000 in a bank account, and then he uses $2,000 from that account to buy a new car worth $20,000. The remainder of the purchase price comes from his wife's bank account and his wife is a co-owner of the car. Nelson fritters away the remainder of the $1,000 left in the bank account. While Dusch can trace his money into the car, he cannot trace the entire $3,000. Since he can only trace $2000, he can only assert an equitable lien against the car for that amount.

Tracing, combined with other restitutionary principles, might lead to a higher recovery in some cases. Suppose, for example, that Nelson took the $3,000 that he obtained from Dusch and "invested" it in lottery tickets rather than in an automobile. The entire purchase price of the lottery tickets was $3,000. If Nelson happened to win the lottery, thereby netting himself a jackpot of $340 million, Dusch might be allowed to recover some or all of the proceeds. Since the lottery does not require any particular "skill" to win, and if all of the lottery tickets were purchased with Dusch's money, it might be regarded as "unjust enrichment" to allow Nelson to retain any of the proceeds.

A different result might obtain if defendant's skill and labor contributed to the dramatic increase in value. Suppose, for example, that Nelson invested $3,000 of Dusch's money in a new restaurant that he was opening. Working extremely long hours over several months (before Dusch realizes what happened to the money), Nelson manages to create a thriving business worth a considerable sum of money. If Dusch attempts to trace his money into the restaurant, he will be entitled to impose a constructive trust or equitable lien for at least his $3,000 and might be permitted to claim more than that amount. However, he might not be allowed to recover the entire business because the success is due in part to Nelson's hard work and ingenuity and therefore is not entirely attributable to "unjust enrichment."

The *G & M Motor Company* case, *supra*, presents interesting measurement issues. In that case, the plaintiff-employer (from whom money had been embezzled) sought to recover only the amount that had been embezzled. In other words, $1,000 had been embezzled from the employer and invested in an insurance policy that produced a death benefit of $10,000, and the employer therefore sought to recover only 1/10th of the policy's value. In an appropriate case, the recovery might be significantly higher or might extend to the entire value of the policy. Suppose, for example, that the entire premium for the policy was $1,000. In that scenario, absent the embezzlement and the investment of plaintiff's money in the policy, no benefit would have been produced. As a result, plaintiff can make a legitimate claim to the entire policy premium as an "unjust enrichment." Undoubtedly, the employer did not seek the higher recovery in *G & M Motor Company* because the embezzling employee had died and was survived by a spouse and minor children. Since the spouse and children were innocent, the employer chose to allow them to keep the windfall.

(B) Co-Mingled Funds

Tracing issues can be particularly difficult when plaintiff has co-mingled "trust" assets with his/her own funds. In theory, at least, when plaintiff's funds have been mingled with defendant-wrongdoer's funds, they no longer retain their separate identity. Nevertheless, when the money is traceable to a particular fund, plaintiff is usually allowed to trace into that fund and reclaim his monies. As the Restatement of Restitution provides, "Where a person wrongfully mingles money of another with money of his own, the other is entitled to obtain reimbursement out of the fund." *See* RESTATEMENT OF RESTITUTION § 209 (1937). "The person whose money is wrongfully mingled with money of the wrongdoer does not thereby lose his interest in the money, although the identity of his money can no longer can be shown, but he acquires an interest in the mingled fund." *Id.*

Similar rules apply when defendant has mingled plaintiff's money with her own in purchasing other property. In this situation, the plaintiff is generally entitled to an equitable lien in the amount of her funds in the new property. In addition, plaintiff might be entitled to claim a proportionate share of the entire property.

Tracing can be more difficult when the fund of money is in transition with money being continuously deposited and withdrawn. In this situation, the Restatement adopts the "lowest intermediate balance" method in determining the plaintiff's interest: "Where a person wrongfully mingles money of another with money of his own and makes withdrawals from the mingled fund and dissipates the money so withdrawn, and subsequently adds money of his own to the fund, the other can enforce an equitable lien upon the fund only for the amount of the lowest intermediate balance, unless (a) the fund or a part of it earns a profit, or (b) the subsequent additions were made by way of restitution." RESTATEMENT OF RESTITUTION § 212 (1937).

In *Knatchbull v. Hallett*, L.R. 13 Ch. D. 696, the court applied a similar but slightly modified rule: "where a fund was composed partly of a defrauded claimant's money and partly of that of the wrongdoer, it would be presumed that in the fluctuations of the fund it was the wrongdoer's purpose to draw out the money he could legally and honestly use rather than that of the claimant, and that the claimant might identify what remained as his res, and assert his right to it by way of an equitable lien on the whole fund, or a proper pro rata share of it."

However, there are limits to the ability of a plaintiff to trace his monies into other forms. In *Cunningham v. Brown*, 265 U.S. 1, 44 S.Ct. 424, 68 L.Ed. 873 (1924), Charles Ponzi ran a "Ponzi Scheme" in which he encouraged individuals to invest in his operation in exchange for exorbitant rates of return. Ponzi was not investing the money, but instead was paying prior investors out of money received from by later investors. When the scheme was revealed as a fraud, plaintiffs sued trying to rescind their contracts and "trace" their monies into the money remaining in the bank account. The Court refused to permit the tracing, noting that "to succeed they must trace the money, and therein they have failed." In *Cunningham*, the Court refused to apply "the fiction of *Knatchbull v. Hallett* [noting that the] rule is useful to work out equity between a wrongdoer and a victim; but, when the fund with which the wrongdoer is dealing is wholly made up of the fruits of the frauds perpetrated against a myriad of victims, the case is different. To say that, as between equally innocent victims, the wrongdoer, having defeasible title to the whole fund, must be presumed to have distinguished in advance between the money of those who were about to rescind and those who were not, would be carrying the fiction to a fantastic conclusion." In essence, the court held that all of the defrauded investors should be treated equally since they were all defrauded creditors.

2. Priority over Other Creditors

A second advantage of the special restitutionary remedies (*e.g.*, constructive trust, equitable lien and subrogation) is that they can be used to gain priority over other creditors. RESTATEMENT OF RESTITUTION § 161, Comment C (1937). In other words, rather than being treated equally with other creditors, and receiving pennies on the dollar, plaintiff can assert a constructive trust or equitable lien against the property and receive priority over other creditors.

The concept of priority is illustrated by the case of *In re Radke*, 5 Kan.App.2d 407, 619 P.2d 520 (1980). In that case, plaintiff was defrauded into purchasing real estate, and the proceeds were invested in other real estate. Because defendant was otherwise insolvent, plaintiff sought to rescind the contract, trace the money into the other real estate, and impose an equitable lien on the real property. The court granted the equitable lien noting that: "Equity permits the tracing of assets and the impression of a trust or equitable lien on them without the showing that a money judgment against the party who precipitated the fraud would be uncollectible. I PALMER, LAW OF RESTITUTION § 3.14(a) (1978)."

3. Circumvention of Debtor Exemptions

An additional advantage of special restitutionary remedies is that they can be used to circumvent debtor exemptions. Each state provides debtors with certain "exemptions" that allow them to protect assets against creditors. Special restitutionary remedies allow creditors to circumvent the exemptions and assert a claim against the property that is the subject of the exemptions.

Chapter Eight

DECLARATORY JUDGMENTS

The declaratory judgment is a remedy that declares the rights or legal relations of the parties to a situation or expresses the court's opinion on a question of law. The declaration does not order anything to be done, but it is reviewable as a final judgment and has *res judicata* effect. Its primary function is to end uncertainty.

The remedy of declaratory judgment is created by statute and is available under both federal and state statutory schemes. It is a remedy that is neither legal nor equitable in character. Because it is a creature of statute, it is *sui generis* and not governed by common law doctrine. It first appeared early in the twentieth century as a response to a deficiency of common law in that it could not clarify the rights of the parties before the occurrence of an actual loss or of a greater loss than has already happened.

The declaratory judgment remedy does not create new rights but simply offers another remedy in appropriate circumstances. Its advantage is that it determines a legal question or the legal relationships of the parties at an early stage of a dispute. For example, in a patent dispute, the possible infringer faces potential treble damages and attorney fees for willfully infringing the patent. If the threat of liability is "sufficiently immediate," a declaratory judgment may resolve the rights of the parties. *MedImmune, Inc. v. Genentech, Inc.*, 549 U.S. 118, 127 S.Ct. 764, 166 L.Ed.2d 604 (2007). The parties may then choose to act with that knowledge in order to avoid future liability. Failure to meet the immediacy standard makes the request for a declaration of rights inappropriate because courts do not issue advisory opinions.

When criminal prosecution is particularly threatened to an individual more than to citizens in general, a declaratory judgment may be appropriate to resolve the legality of the individual's conduct in advance of any prosecution. The principle is that a potential criminal defendant should not have to violate the law—risking arrest and prosecution—to test its validity. *Steffel v. Thompson,* 415 U.S. 452, 94 S.Ct. 1209, 39 L.Ed. 505 (1974).

This remedy is thus a valuable tool for saving the time and expense of more extensive litigation. As the sections below explain, this remedy is available under both federal and state law.

A.   THE FEDERAL DECLARATORY JUDGMENT ACT

In 1934 Congress enacted the Federal Declaratory Judgment Act [FJDA], now codified as 28 U.S.C.A. §§ 2201, 2202. The first section of the Act permits a party to use a declaratory action to obtain an "authoritative judicial statement of legal relationships." It is an "enabling" Act that confers discretionary jurisdiction on courts. Further, § 2202 permits "necessary or proper relief" based on the declaratory judgment after notice and hearing to the adverse party.

Congress enacted the FJDA following the Supreme Court's opinion the year before in a tax case, *Nashville, Chattanooga & St. Louis Ry. Co. v. Wallace,* 288 U.S. 249, 53 S.Ct. 345, 77 L.Ed. 730 (1933). In *Nashville,* the Court upheld its power to review a state's declaratory judgment and rejected the challenge that such an action violated the Constitutional "case of controversy" limitation on federal court jurisdiction. Refusing to let form triumph over substance, the Court said that the essential question is whether there exists a case or controversy and not the label on the action.

A declaratory judgment is never adjudicated as a matter of right. In *Public Affairs Associates v. Rickover*, 369 U.S. 111, 82 S.Ct. 580, 7 L.Ed.2d 604 (1962), the Supreme Court found that the Act was an authorization, not a command. As such, the Act does not compel the courts to act. Instead, it gives courts the ability to make a declaration of rights "using public interest as their guide." *Rickover* made clear, however, that courts cannot decline to consider declaratory judgments "as a matter of whim or personal disinclination." As the Ninth Circuit has explained, the Act is "cast in terms of permissive, rather than mandatory, authority." *Government Employees Insurance Co. v. Dizol,* 133 F.3d 1220, 1223 (9th Cir.1998) (en banc).

The FJDA does not confer jurisdiction on federal courts. Thus plaintiffs must establish subject matter jurisdiction for a declaratory judgment as with any other case in federal court.

1.   Case or Controversy

Article III, section 2, clause 1 of the United States Constitution confers jurisdiction on federal courts to hear "cases and controversies." Courts have construed this grant of power as limiting federal courts to the adjudication of live disputes between parties. The Supreme Court has declared that no principle is "more fundamental to the judiciary's proper role in our system of government than the constitutional limitation of federal-court jurisdiction to actual cases or controversies." *Simon v. Eastern Ky. Welfare Rights Org.*, 426 U.S. 26, 37, 96 S.Ct. 1917, 48 L.Ed.2d 450 (1976).

The case or controversy requirement would appear at first blush to preclude the declaratory remedy. The Supreme Court nonetheless held constitutional the Federal Declaratory Judgment Act [FDJA] despite the fact that it acts before the parties incur a loss. The Court concluded that the FDJA successfully incorporates the case or controversy requirement. The key is that the parties cannot receive this relief with only speculative concerns; they must have a justiciable controversy. A dispute ceases to be abstract and becomes a "controversy" when it is a substantial and immediate controversy between the parties. This line is often blurry and requires courts to exercise considerable discretion.

The Supreme Court's 1952 opinion in *Public Service Commission of Utah v. Wycoff Co.,* 344 U.S. 237, 73 S.Ct. 236, 97 L.Ed. 271 (1952), explains when a dispute may be too broad or abstract to satisfy the constitutional requirement of a "case or controversy." In *Wycoff* a company sought a determination that its activities were outside the authority of the state's Public Service Commission and filed suit in federal court for a declaratory judgment and an injunction to prevent the state from interfering in its activities. The Supreme Court found that this dispute would involve a determination of whether the company's activities were within the definition of interstate commerce in order to be outside the reach of the state commission. Because such a ruling would reach "far beyond the particular case," the opinion observed, courts must use "a maximum of caution." The broad inquiry was not ripe for determination and thus the case was inappropriate for declaratory judgment relief.

2.   Other Factors

In addition to the requirement that there must be a live and ripe controversy, there are other factors that courts properly consider in deciding whether to issue a declaratory judgment. One such factor is the facts extant when the complaint is filed.

Another factor is the filing of other suits arising from the same set of facts. If a criminal action commences shortly after the defendant files for a declaratory judgment, courts are likely to abstain and defer to the other action. *Hicks v.* Miranda, 422 U.S. 332, 95 S.Ct. 2281, 145 L.Ed.2d 223 (1975). If another civil action exists before a declaratory judgment action is filed, the court may consider the problem of duplication. Even if another suit is dropped, a declaratory judgment may appropriately resolve a ripe conflict unless a covenant not to sue makes it "absolutely clear" that the matter is mooted. *Already, L.L.C. v. Nike, Inc.,* 133 S.Ct. 721 (2013).

Finally, it is a relevant factor whether there is an alternative effective remedy. Federal Rule of Civil Procedure 57, which governs procedures for relief under 28 U.S.C.A. § 2201, specifically provides that the existence of another remedy does not preclude declaratory relief, although the Advisory Committee's Note provides illustrations of when courts might appropriately decline jurisdiction for that reason.

These factors help the court resolve the key questions: (1) whether a declaration will serve a useful purpose, and (2) whether it will effectively settle the controversy.

B. THE UNIFORM DECLARATORY JUDGMENT ACT

Most states have adopted the Uniform Declaratory Judgment Act [UDJA] to permit state courts to make declaratory judgments. Its purpose is like that of its federal counterpart. State legislators have adopted the act in order to provide the state courts with a remedy that would resolve disputes efficiently and quickly by a declaration of rights.

The UDJA provides in section 1 that courts shall have power to declare "rights, status, and other legal relations whether or not further relief is or could be claimed." Further, the court's declaration may be either affirmative or negative in form and shall have the force and effect of a final judgment or decree.

Its coverage, as provided in section 2, includes interpretation of "a deed, will, written contract" as well as "rights, status or other legal relations." Like the federal act, the UDJA makes the declaratory judgment remedy entirely discretionary.

C. FUNCTIONS AND LIMITATIONS ON DECLARATORY JUDGMENTS

The declaratory judgment has a wide range of uses. Illustrated below are some of the most common functions of this remedy as well as some more novel ones. What they all have in common is the need for the resolution of a dispute at an early stage of disagreement.

1. Interpreting Criminal Laws

Potential criminal defendants have usefully employed declaratory judgments to determine if their intended behavior violates criminal statutes. The availability of a declaratory judgment permits citizens to know if their conduct is in violation of the law before prosecution. It thus prevents the "catch-22" of not knowing if it is possible to engage in behavior before being punished for engaging in it.

In *Steffel v. Thompson,* 415 U.S. 452, 94 S.Ct. 1209, 39 L.Ed. 505 (1974), Steffel sought a declaratory judgment that his distribution of anti-war leaflets in a shopping center was not criminal trespass. If he had filed this action simply because he wanted to test the law, there would not have been a ripe controversy for declaratory relief. In this case, however, Steffel had been warned twice to stop trespassing in the shopping center, and a companion had been arrested when he continued to distribute leaflets there. Thus the threat of enforcement of the law against him was imminent because he wished to continue the activity which he believed to be lawful. The Supreme Court agreed that declaratory relief would be appropriate here and that its effect would have a less intrusive effect on the administration of justice in the state than the reversal of a conviction for its unconstitutionality.

2. Patent Infringement

A classic use of declaratory judgment is to resolve patent disputes before the accumulation of significant damages. When there is a dispute as to the coverage of a particular patent, a court can resolve the infringement issue before the alleged infringer has invested significant funds in equipment or infrastructure on the assumption that there is no infringement. The declaratory judgment action may be resolved more quickly than a full trial and thus prevent the accumulation of damages for infringement over a long period of time.

The availability of a declaratory judgment thus encourages commercial development of arguably infringing products when a business might otherwise be reluctant to expose itself to extensive potential liability. In *MedImmune, Inc. v. Genentech, Inc.,* 549 U.S. 118, 127 S.Ct. 764, 166 L.Ed.2d 604 (2007), the Supreme Court adopted the "totality of the circumstances" approach concerning possible patent infringement to determine whether an actual controversy existed.

3. Insurance Coverage

The declaratory judgment is commonly used by insurance companies in anticipation of third party litigation against one of its insureds. One common use is to determine whether the insurer has a duty to defend a particular claim. Such a duty arises from the insurance contract itself, so the issue is whether events have triggered the contractual obligation. In the usual circumstance, the insurer may file an action for declaratory judgment seeking a ruling that there is no duty to defend the insured in the separate action filed by a third party because of the nonexistence of coverage or the application of a policy exclusion.

In *Argonaut Great Central Ins. Co. v. Mitchell*, 482 Fed. Appx. 477 (11th Cir.2012), for example, the issue was whether an insurance policy covered the death of a county sanitation employee working on a garbage truck when he was struck by a car. The decedent's job required him to ride on the platform at the back of the truck and to jump off and retrieve garbage cans from the side of the road. The evidence showed that he was facing the platform next to the truck when he was struck from behind.

The policy covered persons "occupying" the vehicle, and that term was defined as "in, upon, getting in, on, out or off" of the vehicle. The question was whether the worker was "occupying" the truck at the time of the accident. The insurer could have denied coverage and waited to be sued, but that strategy would risk a later finding that it had acted in bad faith toward its insured. The court found that no reasonable jury could conclude that the worker was not "occupying" the truck at the time and thus resolved the insurance dispute at an early stage with the declaratory relief.

4.   Determination of Parental Rights ·

Another modern use of the declaratory remedy is to declare parental rights. This complex area of family law has produced many lawsuits after the birth of a child where courts have considered both contractual and constitutional issues to resolve the parental rights of intended parents and surrogate mothers. Parties who are nervous about future disputes over parental rights may seek a declaratory judgment if the controversy is sufficiently ripe.

In one case involving surrogate motherhood, for example, the intended parents sought a declaratory judgment designed to ensure their parental rights even before the birth of the child. In *Johnson v. Calvert*, 5 Cal.4th 84, 19 Cal.Rptr.2d 494, 851 P.2d 776 (1993), a married couple entered into a contract with a woman to serve as a surrogate mother. The contract provided that an embryo created by the gametes of the couple would be implanted in the other woman's uterus, that the baby would be the couple's child, and that the surrogate mother would relinquish all parental rights to the child. The surrogate received the contractual compensation and became pregnant, but then quarreled with the intended parents. When she made a demand that implied that she might refuse to surrender the baby, the couple sued for a declaration they were the legal parents of the unborn child. The surrogate mother then filed her own declaratory action to ascertain her parental rights, and the cases were consolidated.

The trial court found the contract to be legally enforceable. After the child was born and tested genetically, the court ruled that the couple was the child's genetic, biological, and natural father and mother, and that the surrogate mother had no parental rights to the child. The Supreme Court of California distinguished these facts from other cases finding parental rights in a surrogate mother and affirmed. The use of the declaratory judgment remedy thus permitted resolution of the dispute at the earliest possible stage.

D. RELATION TO OTHER REMEDIES

A declaratory judgment does not create monetary obligations nor does it order specific conduct—unlike judgments at law and coercive orders in equity. It simply makes a declaration. Nonetheless, declaratory judgments can be used in tandem with other remedies, notably including injunctive relief. It has a *res judicata* effect on other actions arising from the same facts.

Because declaratory judgments are statutory actions not arising from law or equity, they are governed by their own procedural law. Although they appear more equitable than legal in form, there is no requirement that the plaintiff demonstrate the inadequacy of other remedies. Moreover, factual issues may be tried before a jury if the relevant issue would be triable before a jury at the time of the ratification of the Seventh Amendment.

Chapter Nine

DAMAGES

A. PLAINTIFF'S RIGHTFUL POSITION

Compensatory damages seek to place the plaintiff (the victim of a legal wrong) in the position that she would have occupied if the defendant had not committed the wrong (sometimes called her "rightful position"). This general rule, properly applied, can produce the right recovery in the vast majority of cases. There are exceptions. Courts exceed the plaintiff's rightful position when awarding punitive damages. Courts may undershoot the plaintiff's rightful position when applying limitations, such as certainty, foreseeability (in contract), and the economic loss doctrine (in tort). Still, the rightful position offers the starting point for nearly all calculations of damages. Most of this chapter addresses specific factors courts consider in applying this one, central rule.

The rightful position standard also applies to injunctions. Preventive injunctions seek to prevent the wrong (or the harm it might cause), preserving the plaintiff's rightful position. Reparative injunctions seek to undo the harm, restoring the plaintiff's rightful position. Damages pursue the same goal. The means differ in one critical way: damages use money as the mechanism for redressing the wrong. As discussed in relation to the irreparable injury rule, damages may be an imperfect substitute, making an injunction the preferred remedy. But when an injunction fails (often because the harm cannot be prevented any longer), money may be the only remedy available. On the other hand, restitution does not employ the rightful position standard, even when awarding money. Restitution focuses on the benefit to the defendant, not the loss to the plaintiff.

The similar goals for damages and injunctions explain one other important point: Damages and Injunctions can be combined to produce the rightful position. Where an injunction prevents some, but not all, of the harm, courts can award damages to compensate for the residual harm. For example, a court may order specific performance of a real estate contract. But if the property is delivered after the date specified in the contract, the court would add damages for the delay. Similarly, if a court orders a party to stop manufacturing products that infringe a plaintiff's patent, damages for the period of infringement preceding the order would be available. An order to promote a person denied a promotion for discriminatory reasons might be accompanied by an order of backpay for the period during which the promotion had been wrongfully denied. In each case, the injunction prevents future harm, but will not make the plaintiff whole unless the court also awards damages. Damages and restitution, on the other hand, pursue entirely different goals. Adding one to the other usually produces an incoherent judgment. While some statutes seem to permit that result, courts rarely apply them literally.

Before addressing specific components of damage calculations, a few general observations may help avoid some common misconceptions about the rightful position standard.

First, the rule looks forward, seeking to recreate the position the plaintiff would have occupied if the wrong had not occurred—including prospective losses caused by the wrong. The rule is not limited to plaintiff's position before the wrong occurred, though occasionally courts carelessly state the rule that way. For example, a pedestrian hit by a car may recover earnings she would have received after the date of the accident (and even after the date of judgment). The fact that she had not earned that money before the wrong occurred makes no difference. Future losses are encompassed by the rightful position standard.

Second, the rule looks to the position the plaintiff would have occupied, not the position she hoped to occupy. Damages seek to compensate a party's realistic prospects, not a best case scenario. They reflect, to the extent possible, objective reality, not subjective expectations. In this way, the rightful position standard includes an element of causation. The position the plaintiff would have occupied but for the wrong will not include losses that would have been suffered even if no wrong had occurred. These losses (or the absence of these gains) are not attributable to the defendant's wrong. The fact that losses followed the wrong does not mean that the wrong caused the losses. Plaintiff may have expected significant gains, but these gains might not have materialized even if defendant had not committed the wrong. For example, most contract plaintiffs expect to earn a profit on their transactions. They are entitled to profits they would have made if the wrong had not occurred, but not to profits they would not have made even if the wrong had not occurred.

Third, the rule does not permit double counting any element of recovery. Plaintiff should not be placed in a better position than she would have occupied if the wrong had not occurred. Double counting is most likely to happen in multiple count complaints, where the losses in each count overlap. For example, an employee may allege that her discharge breached the contract and also constituted discrimination. While a jury may return a verdict for plaintiff on both counts, she lost only one job with only one set of wages. Adding the damages for the two counts is likely to include the wages twice. Courts must take care to eliminate duplication before entering judgment. Double counting can happen in a single count complaint, where similar components of a damage award overlap. For instance, lost enjoyment of life may overlap with pain and suffering. Similarly, the subjective value of property may overlap with emotional distress suffered as a result of damage to the property. In analyzing closely related elements of damage, keep an eye open for overlapping components.

Fourth, the rule looks to the plaintiff's net loss. The rule precludes putting plaintiff in a better position than she would have occupied if the wrong had not occurred. Damages make up the difference between the position the plaintiff now occupies and the position she should have occupied. That will not necessarily include all the costs associated with a wrong. Some losses may be offset by benefits that resulted from the transaction. For instance, a seller who has not yet delivered the promised goods cannot collect the full price and keep the goods. If no wrong occurred, seller would have the price, but would not have the goods. The difference between the price and the value of the goods retained is recoverable; that is the net loss caused by the wrong. Similarly, damages will not cover the full value of a damaged car, only the difference between the value it would have if not injured and its current value—the net loss. Net loss might be even less than the difference in value. If the value of the car can be restored by repairs that cost less than the difference in value, the repairs represent the net loss. Any more than that would allow the owner to repair the car and keep the additional money, a position better than she occupied before the wrong. Net loss can affect the recovery in many settings. Costs a plaintiff would have incurred even if the wrong had not occurred may not be recoverable. For example, a plaintiff promised a job in a new city usually cannot recover expenses incurred moving to that city in an action for breach of the promised employment contract. Plaintiff would have incurred moving expenses even if the contract had been performed. She can recover the benefit of the job (pay, fringe benefits), but not the investment she would have made to obtain those benefits. Similarly, losses often are (or can be) offset by efforts to minimize the loss or by benefits the breach bestowed. For example, if the employee takes another job in the same city, she can recover the difference between the pay she would have received from the first job and the pay she does receive from the substitute job. That difference is her net loss.

Finally, the rule applies to all kinds of damage actions. Whether the underlying wrong sounds in contract or in tort, the rightful position standard governs damage recovery. Differentiating remedies for torts from remedies for breach of contract—or remedies for sales of goods from remedies for employment contracts or construction contracts—may help identify the way the rule applies differently in different factual settings. Occasionally, the rules differ with context. Some differences significantly affect the way one should plead a case. For instance, the easier availability of emotional distress and punitive damages in tort leads many attorneys to stretch wrongs into a tort mold, where a contract action would be more straightforward and intuitive. The differences, however, should not obscure the fundamental unity of compensatory awards. The basic rule applies across all settings. Even statutory provisions, which may specify their own remedial rules for a new cause of action, usually adhere closely to the rightful position standard.

B. EXPECTATION, RELIANCE, AND RESTITUTION

In some cases, it is possible to characterize the plaintiff's rightful position in slightly different ways. For instance, in contract cases a choice between expectation and reliance (and sometimes restitution) receives considerable attention. Both expectation and reliance seek to put the plaintiff in the position plaintiff would have occupied but for the wrong. They define the wrong a little differently.

Expectation seeks to place the plaintiff in the position she would have occupied if the contract had been performed (that is, if no breach occurred). For example, if a seller breached a contract to deliver a television, expectation would provide buyer enough money to obtain an equivalent television from another seller, limiting buyer's total cost to the amount buyer would have paid if the breaching seller had performed.

Reliance seeks to put the plaintiff in the position she would have occupied if the contract had never been made (that is, if no duty arose). For instance, if a seller breached a contract to deliver a television, reliance would provide any expenses the buyer incurred to obtain the television, including any deposit paid to the seller and any costs incurred for delivery of the television. Reliance costs might include other expenditures if breach deprived the seller of the benefit of those expenditures—say, if buyer paid for cable service for several days when she had no TV to enjoy the service.

Restitution—not really a measure of damages at all, but the subject of a different chapter—seeks to put the *defendant* in the position she would have occupied if the contract had never been made. (A fourth choice—seeking to put the defendant in the position if the contract had been performed—receives less attention and has no settled name. This chapter will refer to it as disgorgement. Courts rarely choose this measure intentionally.) Restitution and disgorgement focus on the defendant's gain, not the plaintiff's loss.

The rightful position standard embodies the expectation interest. It focuses on the position the plaintiff would have occupied if the breach had not occurred. Whether the breach involves a duty in tort or the nonperformance of a contractual promise, damages look first to the position if the breach had not occurred. Nonetheless, the reliance interest receives significant attention, both in academia and in practice. The differences deserve a little attention.

1.   Expectation and Reliance in Contract

The distinction is most important in contract cases. Unlike tort duties, which society imposes on everyone, contractual duties are voluntary. Because people have the option to refuse to make a promise, it might make sense to consider the position the parties would have occupied if the promise had not been made (that is, if the contractual duty never arose), as the reliance interest suggests. If the promise had not been made, plaintiff would not have enjoyed any of the benefits of the contract, but also would not have incurred any expenses related to the contract. The reliance interest, then, allows the plaintiff to recover the expenses incurred pursuing the project, but none of the benefits the project might have provided. This, effectively, makes the contract a break-even proposition, with no profits and no losses.

The expectation interest, on the other hand, allows plaintiff to recover the benefits of the project, but not the expenses. If the benefits exceed the expenses, plaintiff recoups a profit. Thus, plaintiffs usually prefer the expectation interest. But if the expenses exceed the benefit, the expectation interest may leave the plaintiff with a loss.

In theory, plaintiffs would recover more under the reliance interest when a contract would have produced losses. However, courts awarding the reliance interest subtract any losses defendant can prove the plaintiff would have suffered from the amount of expenses plaintiff incurred. RESTATEMENT (SECOND) OF CONTRACTS § 349. Thus, in losing contract situations, reliance awards cannot exceed the expectation interest. This limitation suggests that reliance is not a separate remedial interest, but an effort to approximate expectation when technical difficulties make expectation unavailable. That approach was endorsed by the recently approved RESTATEMENT (THIRD) OF RESTITUTION AND UNJUST ENRICHMENT § 38.

The reliance interest proves most useful in situations where the plaintiff cannot prove the amount of profit it would have earned. Instead of recovering nothing, plaintiff recovers expenses, producing a profit of zero, but also no losses (unless defendant proves plaintiff would have incurred losses). In effect, this recovery puts the plaintiff as close to her expectation interest as the evidence allows. Without evidence of profit, these cannot be awarded. But a profit of zero seems as good an assumption as a loss, absent evidence to the contrary.

2. Expectation and Reliance in Tort: Communication as the Wrong

Tort cases rarely refer to the reliance interest. Because tort duties are imposed by law, there is little reason to ask where plaintiff would have been if the duty had not existed. Tort remedies focus on the plaintiff's position if the breach had not occurred, which corresponds to the expectation interest.

Some tort cases produce remedies that resemble the reliance interest, in that they base recovery on unwinding a transaction (as reliance damages do) rather than completing it (as expectation damages do). This commonly occurs when torts involve wrongful communication, such as fraud, upon which a plaintiff relies in making a subsequent decision (often, but not always, entering a contract). Liability depends on plaintiff showing that, but for the wrongful communication, she would have made a different decision. The remedy involves the difference between the decision plaintiff did make and the decision that she would have made if accurately informed. At a minimum, this means reversing the bad decision. Where fraud induced a contract, that means unwinding the transaction, putting the plaintiff in the position she would have occupied if the contract had not been made. That sounds like reliance in contract. Courts following this logic award out-of-pocket costs incurred in relation to that transaction. For instance, where a false statement led a plaintiff to buy property (land, stock, goods) that she otherwise would not have purchased, she can recover the price paid (out of pocket) minus the value of the property received (Expenses – Value Received). (Instead of damages, a plaintiff may elect to rescind the transaction and seek restitution: she must return the property received, in exchange for a full refund of the price she paid. If the property she received had no value at all, these two measures produce the same result.)

Many states prefer the benefit-of-the-bargain rule, which may exceed out-of-pocket losses. This approach treats the misleading communication as true. Thus, plaintiff recovers the value the property would have had if the statement had been true minus the value of the property received (Value as Stated – Value Received). In effect, the benefit-of-the-bargain rule treats the communication as a warranty, a promise to provide property that lives up to the communication, instead of treating the communication as a misrepresentation, justifying rejection of the deal. The plaintiff secures her profit, not just her expenses.

This measure of damages is slightly more generous than the rightful position standard would justify. The explanations are pragmatic. The more generous recovery offers a disincentive to misrepresentation. (If the only cost to defendant were a refund of the excess price, there would be no harm in trying to deceive. If not caught, defendant keeps the unjust profit; if caught, she keeps the just profit, but loses nothing more than attorneys' fees.) It also eliminates the difference between fraud and warranty. Plaintiffs can elect to treat some misrepresentations as promises to deliver goods of certain quality. *See, e.g.,* UCC § 2–313 (allowing express warranties to arise from "affirmation[s] of fact"). Thus, a plaintiff could sue for breach of warranty, collecting expectation damages: the position she would have occupied if the goods had been as promised. That is indistinguishable from the position if the statement had been true. Moreover, misrepresentation often is a greater wrong than breach of contract. It seems anomalous to offer a more generous remedy for breach contract than for the tort of deception.

3.   Problems Proving Expectation Losses

The general rule favors expectation—the position if the wrong did not occur, where the wrong is the breach. In some cases, however, it may be difficult to prove expectation damages, particularly when the law requires reasonable certainty in the calculation. *See* section G.6., *infra.* In these situations, it may be possible to calculate the reliance interest and, thus, to allow some recovery rather than deny all recovery. This approach, though called reliance, often reflects an effort to come as close as possible to the expectation interest. For example, in a contract action a plaintiff may recover unavoidable expenses (usually those incurred before breach) plus lost profits. (The same measure may apply where a tort destroys a business venture.) If plaintiff cannot prove the amount of its lost profits, she nonetheless should recover expenses to date. This result may assume the promise would not have been made (and thus no expenses incurred—reliance) or that profits would have been zero (and thus sales would cover expenses, but not exceed them—expectation). The recently approved RESTATEMENT (THIRD) OF RESTITUTION AND UNJUST ENRICHMENT § 38 treats cost-based recoveries as a proxy for expectation, eliminating reference to reliance as a separate remedial interest in contract damages.

4. Special Contexts

In some contexts, expectation recoveries may seem excessive. In those settings, recourse to the reliance interest or a similar measure based on plaintiff's expenditures has some appeal.

(A) Problems with Title to Real Estate

When a defendant promises to sell real estate, but cannot deliver good title, some courts reject expectation, limiting recovery to expenditures plaintiff made in preparation for the transaction (such as title searches or surveys). This limitation originated in England and is sometimes called the English rule. It denies plaintiff the full profit on the transaction. It contrasts with the American rule, which allows plaintiff to recover the market value of the land minus the contract price of the land (in addition to a refund of any portion of the price already paid)—the expectation interest.

The English rule assumes that mistakes about title are understandable and forgivable, so that only the harm generated by wasted preparations should be recovered. The English Rule comes with several exceptions, designed to limit its clemency to those who acted in good faith. The exception cannot be invoked by defendants who know their title is bad at the time they enter the contract. In effect, this exception retains the benefit-of-the-bargain rule when defendant entered a fraudulent sale contract. Similarly, the English rule will not protect a party who merely changes its mind about the sale. Thus, a seller who has good title but refuses to deliver it must pay expectation damages. (Specific performance usually is available in this situation, even if damages would be limited to reliance.) A seller who caused the problem of title (such as by deeding the property to someone else after entering the contract with the plaintiff) also is liable for expectation damages. Whether the second sale was a sham (to avoid specific performance) or bona fide (usually at a higher price than the contract with plaintiff), plaintiff is entitled to the benefit it would have enjoyed if seller had performed as promised. The English rule covers inability to perform, not unwillingness to perform.

The American rule assumes that recording statutes make mistakes of title less understandable or forgivable. It also adheres to the general premise that plaintiff should be placed in the position she would have occupied but for the wrong. Defendant, not plaintiff, should bear the risk of failure to deliver good title. More states adhere to the American rule, but some of the largest states (*e.g.*, California, Michigan, New York, Pennsylvania, Texas, and Virginia) follow the English rule, with the limitations noted here.

(B) Fantastic Promises

Sellers sometimes make warranties that are impossible to fulfill. In effect, they promise to deliver a product that does not exist, a fantasy. Because the product as warranted does not exist, assessing the value of the product if it did exist poses serious difficulties. Awarding the plaintiff the benefit of the bargain—the value of a fantasy—often seems excessive. Limiting recovery to reliance damages moderates the excessive recovery. Because the UCC does not include provisions for reliance damages, courts often award the benefit of the fantastic bargain. *See, e.g., Chatlos Systems, Inc. v. National Cash Register Corp.*, 670 F.2d 1304 (3d Cir.1982) (purchaser of a $46,000 computer awarded over $200,000 because only computers costing more than that could possibly perform as warranted).

If courts were willing to limit recovery to reliance in cases involving fantastic promises, one might expect to see exceptions similar to those that limit the English rule for inability to deliver good title to real estate. A party who knowingly promises an impossible result may be held to the expectation interest. In effect, that person sold an insurance policy. Similarly, one who could provide the fantastic product may be required to do so or to pay the cost of fulfilling the fantasy.

(C) Disproportionate Recoveries

Sometimes the gain plaintiff expected from a transaction grossly exceeds the price plaintiff paid for the transaction. When defendant received so little in the transaction, it may seem harsh to ask it to pay the full cost of its default. Disproportionate recovery may help explain why full recovery seems unjust to some in both of the preceding discussions (title to real estate and fantastic promises). It also helps explain other limitations on damages, such as foreseeability. *E.g., Hadley v. Baxendale*, 9 Ex. 341, 156 Eng. Rep. 145 (1854) (plaintiff paid 2*l.* 4*s.* to ship mill shaft; when negligent delivery delayed reopening of mill, plaintiff sought £300 in lost profits; jury award of £25—over 10 times price of shipping— reversed). Some secondary sources invite courts to limit disproportionately large awards to the reliance interest. *See* RESTATEMENT (SECOND) OF CONTRACTS § 351(3). Given the prevalence of contract clauses disclaiming liability for consequential damages, *see* UCC § 2–718, relatively few courts today find it necessary to invoke this invitation.

C.   APPLYING THE RIGHTFUL POSITION STANDARD

In assessing the amount of damages recoverable, it may help to break the losses down into component parts. This permits one to focus individually on the elements that comprise a damage award. In the process, however, all kinds of complications can be introduced. For one thing, some losses can be classified in more than one component, risking either omission or double recovery. For another, the names for each component may vary with context, producing a confusing array of formulae, all aimed at the same result. Nonetheless, we need some way to categorize and describe damages. The approach here tries to remain sufficiently specific to be useful, yet sufficiently general to avoid memorization of countless formulae, one for each type of case that might arise.

1.   Categorizing Damages

In general, damages can be divided into three categories: (a) direct loss; (b) incidental loss; and (c) ensuing loss.

(A) Direct Loss

Direct loss involves harm to or deprivation of the thing itself. When someone damages a car or a house (or any other property), direct loss is the loss in value of the car or house. The same would be true if the loss involved failure to deliver a car or house (or any other property or service) under a contract. Loss of its value is a direct loss. The value of the thing or service usually is measured by the cost to replace it with a substitute, though the cost to repair it sometimes works as well or better. Damage to a person also involves direct loss to the individual harmed. Medical expenses, analogous to cost of repair, measure the direct loss.

(B) Incidental Loss

Incidental loss refers to costs reacting to the wrong. For example, when a buyer backs out of a sales contract, the seller's direct loss centers on the lower price she receives when selling the goods to a different buyer. In order to resell, however, she may need to store the goods temporarily, perhaps to insure the goods, and to incur some expenses trying to resell them (*e.g.*, advertising or auction costs). Each involves expenses that the seller would not have incurred if the buyer had performed. Even if the seller suffered no direct loss (because she resold the goods for the same price buyer would have paid), seller must recover the incidental losses to achieve her rightful position. The same expenses can occur with property damage. If a car is damaged or destroyed, the owner must spend time obtaining suitable repairs (or a substitute vehicle), and perhaps a towing charge or storage fees pending repairs. The cost of repairs (or a substitute) is a direct loss, but the other costs are incidental losses. They do not represent damage to the thing itself, but costs incurred in dealing with the wrong. Personal injuries also may involve incidental costs, though they normally are not labeled that way. For instance, ambulance charges (or even a cab to a doctor's office) is an incidental cost.

One could classify some incidental costs as direct losses. The ambulance charges or, on the car, the towing charges could be treated as part of the cost of repair. The border is not always well defined. In some ways, it doesn't matter which way you classify the loss, as long as recovery includes it once (and only once). The categories seek to help you identify losses that might otherwise elude attention. The example, with its slippery edges, should not prevent you from considering whether plaintiff incurred any costs that don't fit under direct loss. Incidental loss provides a category to include components that might escape the other categories.

(C) Ensuing Loss

Ensuing loss—more commonly called consequential damages (in contract) or loss of use (in tort)—involves losses that result from the plaintiff's inability to use the property as intended. For example, a buyer might intend to resell goods at a profit or to use them in its business, increasing profits. Replacing the goods might prevent these losses, if done quickly enough. But if the wrong prevents the planned use, that consequential loss is real. Similarly, an owner of a damaged car loses its use while it is being repaired. Repairs restore the property, but without compensation for the interim loss plaintiff is not restored to the position she would have occupied if the wrong had not occurred. In personal injuries, the inability to work imposes a loss on the plaintiff. Even if medical care restores the plaintiff to full health, the interim loss of income requires compensation.

Ensuing losses can expand the recovery to activities somewhat remote from the original wrong. For instance, if an actor withdraws from a movie, the entire film might be cancelled. The loss of profit on the film, not just the loss on the actor's contract, would ensue from the breach. Similarly, a tort that cut off electricity to plaintiff's factory might reduce annual production. The loss of profits in the venture, not just the value of the electricity, may be needed to make the plaintiff whole. As losses become more and more remote from the wrong, courts become more and more skeptical that the defendant actually caused the losses. Limiting doctrines such as causation, certainty, foreseeability, and avoidable consequences intervene to limit efforts to expand losses beyond the loss fairly attributable to the defendant.

(D) Multiple Categories

Some items of damages might fit more than one category. Most courts speak of earnings lost due to personal injury as a direct loss rather than an ensuing loss. Indeed, if the value of a body is the ability to earn income, the loss of that value is a direct loss. Similarly, consequential losses can be framed as direct losses. Consider the buyer of a machine, after seller breaches the promise to deliver it. Buyer's use of that machine in its business invokes consequential lost profits. But buyer also lost the market value of the machine. That market value can be estimated by the present value of the future income stream a person could earn using the machine—in other words, the lost profits. This transmutation is simple economic sense, not merely a game to avoid the consequential label.

How one categorizes an element of damage holds significance in very few settings. Two cautionary notes seem apt. First, be sure to include an item in one, but only one, category. Neglecting it altogether produces undercompensation. Including it twice produces overcompensation. Second, beware of contract provisions that exclude some elements of damages but not others. For instance, contract provisions excluding consequential damages make it vital to define consequential damages clearly. Similarly, if a limitation on damages applies only to consequential damages, determining whether a loss is consequential or direct takes on importance.

(E) Nominal Damages

Nominal damages technically are not compensatory damages at all. Nominal damages permit a plaintiff who suffers no loss to recover a trivial amount (say, $1) if she establishes defendant's liability. In a contract action, for instance, after seller's nondelivery, a buyer may buy goods for less than the contract price, saving money on the substitute contract. If buyer sues, she would be entitled to judgment and nominal damages even if she had no actual damages. Nominal damages often result from a mistake: plaintiff misjudges the extent of the likely recovery and does not realize the error until after trial. Some wrongs, however, affect rights that are important enough to justify litigation, even if difficulty assessing the loss makes it hard to recover actual damages. For instance, violating a plaintiff's constitutional right to due process may not affect the plaintiff in any measurable way. Nonetheless, nominal damages allow a plaintiff some vindication that may be worth seeking.

Nominal damages are not available if the wrong includes loss or injury as an element of liability. No liability attaches for these wrongs unless plaintiff suffers actual harm. Some torts and statutory wrongs require injury as an element of liability. For example, the Sherman Antitrust Act requires proof of injury as an element of liability. Similarly, the tort of fraud typically is actionable only if injury occurs. Negligence, too, typically requires injury. Thus, negligent driving that does not injure anyone is not actionable at all. These "no harm, no foul" rules preclude nominal damages.

2.   Net Loss and Avoidable Consequences

Commonly, books address the avoidable consequences doctrine together with other limitations on damages (foreseeability, certainty, economic loss) after discussing basic damage calculations for direct loss. This approach obscures the way the basic rules often incorporate the limitations on damages. In determining the net loss, basic damage formulae include an offset for losses that have been avoided or reasonably could have been avoided. These basic rules governing direct loss are easier to understand after introducing the avoidable consequences doctrine, which provides that a plaintiff cannot recover for losses that it could have avoided by reasonable effort or expenditure. RESTATEMENT (SECOND) OF TORTS § 918; *see also* RESTATEMENT (SECOND) OF CONTRACTS § 350. The rule awards damages as if the plaintiff had minimized its losses, even if the plaintiff actually (but unreasonably) suffered larger losses.

The rightful position standard seeks to place plaintiff in the position she would have occupied if the wrong had not occurred— not a better position, not a worse position. If plaintiff avoids some of the losses the wrong appeared to cause, then recovery for those losses would overcompensate plaintiff, putting her in a better position than she would have occupied if the wrong had not occurred. Thus, plaintiff cannot recover for losses that she has avoided.

Contract cases provide the easiest illustration for this point. If a buyer breaches, how much has seller lost? The answer starts with the contract price: but for the wrong, seller would have received that amount. But the answer cannot end there. If seller has not yet performed, she has avoided part of the loss; she retains, and can resell or otherwise reuse, the performance not yet delivered. Awarding the full contract price will overcompensate her. If the contract had been performed, she would have received the contract price, but given up her performance. Allowing her to keep both the price and the performance puts her in a better position than if the wrong had not occurred. Instead, she recovers the contract price minus the value of the performance she retains. If she resells the performance to another, that resale avoids at least part of the loss. She has not lost the full contract price, just the difference between the contract price and the resale price. By subtracting the amount earned on resale from the contract price, plaintiff is made whole. The damages plus the resale price equal the contract price.

Even if seller does not resell the performance to another, she still retains the benefit of not performing. Her choice to use the performance herself instead of reselling it to another does not negate the benefit retained. That benefit is offset against the recovery. If this seems odd, imagine that the sale involved a work of art. If, after buyer's breach, seller keeps the work instead of reselling it, full contract price would overcompensate her. Whatever value the art has, seller retains it. That value must be subtracted from the promised price.

The same rule applies to buyers. A buyer is entitled to a refund of the price paid so far plus the cost (or value) of a reasonable substitute performance, minus the contract price promised to the breaching seller. Full substitute costs might permit buyer to retain both the price and the performance, a position it never could have occupied if the contract had been performed. Subtracting the price it would have paid offsets the award for the loss avoided by not paying the contract price.

Tort claims can present the same issue. Suppose defendant damages the fence on plaintiff's ranch. Plaintiff sees the accident and quickly moves her cattle to a different pasture until the fence can be repaired. The cost of that move is recoverable (probably as an incidental loss). But no recovery is required for cattle who would have escaped through the gap if they had not been moved to another pasture. Plaintiff avoided that loss. Similarly, an injured person may elect surgery to prevent a permanent disability. The cost of the surgery is a direct loss. But the damage from permanent disability was avoided, making recovery for that loss unnecessary.

The avoidable consequences doctrine extends the result to losses that should have been avoided, even if plaintiff did not avoid them. A plaintiff cannot recover for losses that it could have avoided by reasonable effort or expenditure. (Some authorities state the reasonableness a little differently, referring to losses a plaintiff "could have avoided without undue risk, burden, or humiliation." RESTATEMENT (SECOND) OF CONTRACTS § 350. This formulation is unlikely to produce different results. Burdens or risks become "undue" or excessive when they are unreasonable.) In effect, the doctrine removes any incentive a plaintiff might have to keep her losses larger in order to maximize recovery. Even if the plaintiff does not minimize her own loss, the law will limit damages as if she had.

The rule does not require successful mitigation. As long as the plaintiff makes reasonable efforts to minimize the loss, no reduction in damages is required. Thus, a reasonable effort that fails to avoid the loss will not affect recovery. Similarly, the existence of alternative measures that might have reduced the loss more effectively will not affect recovery, as long as the course plaintiff elected was reasonable.

Ideally, the rules on avoided and avoidable losses would coincide precisely. In practice, differences arise. One recurring issue involves the burden of proof. The avoidable consequences doctrine is an affirmative defense. Defendant must plead the defense and prove its elements: (1) that plaintiff acted unreasonably; and (2) that had plaintiff acted reasonably the losses would have been lower by a proven amount. But when the basic damage rule includes offsets for avoided or avoidable consequences, the plaintiff's burden to prove damages as an element of the case in chief may require it to prove that no offset is required (or the amount of the offset, if one is required).

D. DIRECT LOSS

Direct loss refers to the thing injured by the wrong. It may be physical property (a car, a building), a legal right (a patent, a contract right), or a person's body.

Isolating direct loss from incidental and ensuing loss helps focus on the ways to evaluate that component of the plaintiff's loss. In each case, however, incidental and ensuing losses may need to be added to produce the appropriate damage award.

Discussion of direct loss is broken down into specific contexts. In each section, the ultimate goal remains the same: to identify how much money it will take to restore plaintiff to his rightful position. Different contexts generate different terminology and different components—and in some cases involve different economic concerns. In many ways, however, each section is an example of the general rule. You may be able to master the rule without every single example.

1. Reduced Value

When property is damaged, direct loss may be measured by the change in its value: the value of the undamaged property minus any value the property retains despite the damage (Value if Undamaged – Actual Value (as is)). This rule incorporates concern for the net loss. Plaintiff is entitled to the full value of the uninjured property. But any value the property retains should be subtracted. Plaintiff could sell the injured property for that amount. If she did, damages measured by the difference in value would restore the full value to which she is entitled. If property has been so fully demolished that it lacks even a minimal scrap value, this approach subtracts zero from the value of the undamaged property. In any other situation, some offset is required.

This measure applies in a wide variety of settings. It works when real property (such as a building) is damaged or destroyed. It works when personal property (such as a car or computer) is damaged or destroyed. It works when an intangible right (such as a license under a patent or a right to recover under an insurance policy) is damaged or destroyed.

The measure is not limited to physical damage. It can apply to cases where property is misappropriated (conversion). (When plaintiff no longer has the property, the value retained is zero.) It also works when property is delivered in unsatisfactory condition (or not delivered at all), as occurs in some contract actions. The Uniform Commercial Code codifies this approach for goods that do not live up to a warranty, if buyer keeps the goods instead of rejecting them. *See* UCC § 2–714 (the value of the goods if they had been as warranted minus the value of the goods as delivered). The same rule works for construction contracts, where courts may award the value the building would have had if properly built minus the value it has as actually built. (Remember *Jacob & Youngs v. Kent*, 230 N.Y. 656, 130 N.E. 933 (1921), where damages for the failure to use "pipe of Reading manufacture" did not allow recovery of cost to replace the pipe, but only the difference between the value the house would have had with Reading pipe and its value with the pipe actually used.)

Contract cases often allow plaintiff a choice of remedies. Plaintiff might reject the performance and cancel the contract, at least when the shortcoming is serious. (The requirement of material breach may preclude termination in some settings.) Rules governing restitution govern those claims. Alternatively, a plaintiff may establish a right to specific performance, compelling the defendant to perform as promised (replace the goods with goods as warranted or repair the building to conform to the contract). Rules governing injunctive relief govern those claims. When the plaintiff claims damages, however, the equation here applies.

Value may be determined in any of several ways. Each technique follows from a simple definition of value (or fair market value): the amount that a willing buyer would give and a willing seller would accept in exchange for the property in an arm's-length transaction, each party being reasonably informed and neither being under any compulsion to enter the transaction. In other words, things are worth whatever people will pay for them. The law affords some room to consider subjective value (often called value to the plaintiff), even if that exceeds the value others would pay. That topic will be discussed below.

Each aspect of the definition helps identify reasons that some transactions may not reflect fair market value. The definition emphasizes actual transactions as evidence of market value. Mere offers are less reliable. At least one party had not yet agreed and might have insisted on better terms. A bona fide offer may set a minimum value—even if rejected, it suggests the property was worth at least the amount offered. But beware sham offers, made with no intention ever to enter the deal. An offer made knowing the other party would reject it does not reflect how much the offeror really was willing to pay. An offer made by someone who could not perform it provides little evidence of value. Similarly, a collusive offer, one a party induced another to make, may not reflect fair market value.

The definition of fair market value also excludes forced sales, where one party cannot await a better offer. The market might have paid more, if the seller's urgency did not require it to take an early offer. Similarly, a relationship between buyer and seller reduces the probative value of the transaction. When dealing with family members or old friends, a party might be willing to deal on terms more advantageous to the other, producing better (or worse) terms than a true arm's-length sale would produce. Finally, the price agreed to by a deceived party may not reflect fair market value.

Courts accept evidence of three different techniques when calculating value: (a) market value, (b) replacement cost less depreciation, and (c) capitalization of earnings. Each pursues the same definition of value. Each should produce about the same result. Calculations based on book value, a concept useful in tax law, have no use in calculating remedies. Full replacement cost will not be ordered by a court as a remedial measure. Some contracts, however, may require a party to pay full replacement cost, as where a fire insurer promises to pay the full replacement cost of a house or its furnishings. Where that amount has been promised, that amount will be awarded.

(a) Market Value focuses on actual market transactions involving similar property to determine the value of the damaged (or undamaged) property. In theory, market transactions are the best, most direct evidence of fair market value. In practice, a number of problems may interfere with direct comparisons. For one thing, transactions in similar property may be hard to identify. Similar includes similar age, similar condition, similar features, etc. Any aspect of the property that might affect its price in the market should be taken into account, if possible. Transactions also must occur on or near the date of valuation. A transaction one year before or after the injury may imperfectly reflect the market value at the time of the injury. Appraisers may offer estimates of current market value based on recent market transactions. Given the range of factors involved, estimates may vary significantly.

(b) Replacement Cost Less Depreciation starts with the cost to buy new property (or services) similar to those lost, then adjusting the cost to reflect differences in age and condition. Particularly when actual transactions in similar used property are limited, this technique provides an alternative method of calculating value. It aims at the same goal. How much a person will pay for a used item will depend on how much new items would cost and how much better the new item might be. Full replacement cost (with new property) would give the plaintiff the thing she lost. But unless her damaged property was brand new, full replacement cost provides something better than what she lost, overcompensating her. Adjustments often subtract a percentage of the price based on the amount of useful life the original property had left at the time of injury compared to the amount of useful life in the new property.

For example, assume plaintiff's car had a useful life of 10 years, but that it was already seven years old when defendant destroyed it. The car had already lost 70% of its value through use and age; defendant did not take that 70% away from plaintiff. A new car of similar size, type, and features costs $30,000 (and also would have 10 years of useful life). Plaintiff may recover $9,000: $30,000 (replacement cost) minus $21,000 (depreciation, 70% of $30,000).

The example illustrates the technique, but may raise some objections. First, used cars are relatively common, so similar vehicles may be available in the market without recourse to replacement costs less depreciation. Even so, it might be useful in practice to calculate replacement cost less depreciation. It serves as a reality check. If plaintiff's appraiser testifies that similar used cars sold for $18,000, pointing out that a new one, which would last three times as long, only cost $30,000 probes the credibility of the estimate.

The example also assumes straight-line depreciation. That is, it assumes that the first three years of a car have the same value as the last three years. That probably is inaccurate for cars. Cars lose most of their value in the first two or three years, then depreciate at a slower rate. In some cases, evidence of this kind may make a big enough difference to justify the expense in proving the point. Without evidence, however, courts are likely to simplify the calculation as illustrated above.

Courts may consider other adjustments to replacement cost less depreciation. For example, differences in quality between newer products and older ones might justify an adjustment. For instance, if defendant destroyed plaintiff's laptop computer with a Pentium II chipset and an 80 MB hard drive, replacement at today's prices will produce not only a machine that will last longer than the original property, but will have substantially more power. (A machine as slow as plaintiff's cannot be replaced in the market today. If replacement cost is calculated at all, it must be based on the closest machine available.) To put plaintiff in the position she would have occupied if the wrong had not occurred requires some adjustment for those differences.

(c) Capitalization of Earnings applies to property that produces (or could produce) income. Value depends on how much income it will produce over time. The amount a person will pay today depends directly on the amount of net income the property will produce, how long it will take to generate that income, and the risk that the property might produce less income than projected. For example, property (a machine, a shopping mall) that might produce $50,000 in profit in each of the next five years might be worth about $190,000 today (to a purchaser who wants a 10% return on investment). See table, below.

Table 1: Capitalization of Earnings

Year	Expected Income	Discount Rate	Present Value
2011	$ 50,000	0.909090909090909	$ 45,454.55
2012	$ 50,000	0.826446280991736	$ 41,322.31
2013	$ 50,000	0.751314800901578	$ 37,565.74
2014	$ 50,000	0.683013455365071	$ 34,150.67
2015	$ 50,000	0.620921323059155	$ 31,046.07
Total	$ 250,000		$189,539.34

The calculation is easier than it looks. The first two columns show the expected income flow: $50,000 per year for the next five years. The third column contains the discount rate, here based on 10% interest (in effect, assuming that a person would prefer a different investment unless he can earn that much interest from this property). The last column shows the present value of the expected income ($50,000) that many years in the future. Adding them together yields the present value of a machine that will produce that income. That is, given $189,538.34, a person could invest it at 10% and withdraw $50,000 each year for five years, at which point the fund would be exhausted. For some property, buyers will consider a much longer time frame. Power plants generate profits for 30–50 years. Apartment buildings or shopping malls may last even longer. At some point, diminishing returns (and potentially expensive future maintenance or renovation) may make predictions less important to the present value.

The only obscure part of the formula is the discount rate, a calculation of the portion of an amount needed today in order to produce that amount after investing for a period of time. The .909 in the 2011 line says that to get any particular amount after one year of investing at 10%, you need to award 90.9% of that amount today. The discount rate is calculated by the formula $(1+i)^{-n}$, where i is the interest rate (0.10) and n is the number of years in the future the return will be received (1 for 2011, 5 for 2015). You can plug these figures into a spreadsheet or, even simpler, use a financial function calculator to skip to the bottom line. Or, if your client can afford one, you can hire an expert to do all the work for you. When it comes time to cross-examine opposing experts, however, the concepts here may help you see the weak links.

This calculation may look like an effort to award a party lost profits in the guise of fair market value. In fact, it simply acknowledges that value depends on the benefit a person expects from the thing purchased. A person who wanted a 10% return on investment would not consider paying more than $190,000 for this property. The benefit would not be worth the cost. Some benefits defy calculation, such as the joy a consumer will experience from a luxury good. But when a buyer expects property to produce a stream of income, the benefit becomes calculable. The value today does not depend on how much profit the property actually produces, but on how much the parties expect that it will produce. Their willingness to buy or sell depends on their estimates of future returns.

Capitalization of earnings calculations are identical to calculations of the present value of a future income stream, commonly employed when a person is injured and deprived on the ability to earn a living. In those cases, however, interest rate depends on what the plaintiff can earn on the damage award by investing it safely. We will return to this topic in section E.4.

Repairs as Evidence of Value. Usually, cost of repair arises as an alternative to calculating reduced value, as discussed below. In some cases, however, the cost to repair the property can help determine the value of property in its damaged state. This can be important if other measures work poorly for damaged property. While undamaged property may have a market value, replacement cost, or earnings, damaged property may not fit those techniques as well. Subtracting repair costs from the value the property will have once repaired approximates the value of the property in its injured condition. (Value if Repaired − Cost of Repair = Value Damaged). For example, if spending $3,000 on repairs would produce property worth $22,000, it seems likely that the damaged property is worth about $19,000. Anyone offering much less than $19,000 is likely to be outbid by someone willing to take a slightly smaller profit on the repairs. If the property remains useful or valuable without repairs, the value might exceed $19,000. Otherwise, anyone offering much more than $19,000 will lose money on the deal. In many cases, value once repaired minus cost of repair will approximate value of damaged property.

Valuation Date. Prices change over time, making the date on which values are assessed important. The most common date will be the date of the injury. On that date, the plaintiff should have had, but did not have, undamaged property. In contract, this usually means the date for delivery, but sometimes means the date defendant repudiated a contract. In tort, it often means the date the damage or conversion occurred. In some situations, however, the date of injury will not settle the question. In others, the date of injury will not serve the rightful position standard. Thus, exceptions are likely.

When loss in value occurs suddenly, the date of injury works quite well. One minute the car was working fine, the next minute the rear end crumpled. One minute, plaintiff didn't have the goods because delivery was not yet due, the next minute plaintiff's right to possession matured but was stymied by defendant's nondelivery. These wrongs occur on a specific day, sometimes a specific minute.

The date of injury is not only the easiest valuation date, but also the fairest. At that time, plaintiff knows to begin efforts to repair or to replace the property. If plaintiff does not act promptly, subsequent price changes result from her delay as much as from defendant's wrong. (Note the avoidable consequences doctrine working its way into the valuation date.) If plaintiff could elect to recover the value as of the date of trial, she might be tempted to gamble with defendant's money. Instead of repairing or replacing promptly, she can wait. If the price goes up, defendant pays more in damages. If the price goes down, plaintiff repairs or replaces at a bargain (and perhaps seeks damages measured on the date of the injury, collecting more than she lost). The rule encourages plaintiffs to act reasonably by putting the risk of future changes on them. They get the benefit of a subsequent decrease, but also pay the cost of a subsequent increase.

Two problems arise where property damage occurs over time. First, it may be extremely difficult to ascertain the date that damage began to occur. Thus, rules that refer to the value "before the injury" present some difficulty in finding the proper date. Where damage is continuing (for example, subterranean flow of toxic waste onto plaintiff's property), there may not be a clear date for determining value "after the injury," either.

Second, when the day before the injury and the day after the injury are separated by long periods of time, differences in value may reflect more than just the damage caused by the defendant. Property may appreciate or depreciate in the interim, making it hard to isolate the harm caused by the defendant from other losses or gains in property value. For example, cars depreciate over time, even if not subjected to the injury. Value before minus value after would include both the harm done by defendant and any depreciation. Yet defendant should not pay for depreciation it did not cause. Similarly, art or land may appreciate over time, despite being subject to the injury. Thus, some of the damage defendant caused may be offset by appreciation that would have occurred (and perhaps been even greater) if the wrong had not occurred. Defendant should not pay less because of appreciation it did not cause.

Damages should reflect the value the property would have had if not injured minus the value the property does have in its injured condition (Value Undamaged − Actual Value), measured on the same day. The date the injury is complete should correct for depreciation defendant did not cause. The date the injury was discovered (or should have been discovered, to avoid manipulation), also should serve fairly well. Courts unduly devoted to formulating the rule in terms of before and after the injury may require some careful persuasion to recognize the need for exceptions in these cases.

Another problem involves appreciation after the injury. Damaged property may not appreciate as much as undamaged property would have appreciated. Evaluating the loss on the date of injury will not include the lost appreciation. For example, real estate damaged by spilled toxic chemicals may not appreciate as much as it would have but for the spill (as evinced by comparisons to nearby real estate not injured by the spill). Perhaps repairs (cleaning the spill) will eliminate the difference in value, but some residual concerns may remain. People might pay more for land that had never been contaminated than for land that had been contaminated then cleansed. Prejudgment interest on the loss, measured from the date of the injury to the date of judgment (plus any appreciation to the damaged property, which plaintiff retains) may compensate plaintiff for lost appreciation in the value of the property. But the prejudgment interest rate may not match the difference in appreciation between damaged and undamaged property, producing an inappropriate result. Evaluating the loss (both value if undamaged and value as damaged) at the time of trial would include the lost appreciation, even if it differed from the market interest rate. The approach presents problems in other settings, making it uncommon for courts to express the rule this way. For instance, where future appreciation depends on additional investment or effort by the plaintiff (as when a business or a crop is damaged), assessing the value the property would have had after additional investment poses difficulties. The problem is exacerbated when the tort obviates the investment (as by destroying the business or crop).

Damage to crops (for example, caused by misuse of pesticides) illustrates these problems. A crop damaged in the middle of the growing season might be valued at any of several possible times: (a) the date of injury; (b) the date of harvest; or (if different) (c) the date the owner would have sold the crop. In theory, the last is correct: an effort to put the owner in the position it would have occupied if the wrong had not occurred should focus on the amount the owner would have earned on the sale, which in turn depends on the value of the crop at the time the owner would have sold. That date, however, may be subject to manipulation by the owner, who has the benefit of 20–20 hindsight of actual price changes by the time she must testify at trial. Rather than let the owner pick the best price of the year, some courts require valuation on the date of harvest. If the owner wants to speculate that prices will increase after that date, she can buy more of the crop from others and speculate with her own money. This may be reasonable for some plaintiffs, but is distinctly unrealistic for others. As a result, some courts have allowed recovery based on the date the owner actually would have sold, at least when that date is supported by objective evidence (such as the date the owner sold the undamaged portion of the crop or the date the owner sold its crop in previous years). In each case, any savings caused by the damage (such as reduced cost to harvest or tend the crop) reduces the recovery.

The date of the injury does not figure prominently in the cases. Commodities markets allow the sale today of crops to be delivered in the future. Thus, no matter what day the injury occurs, a value of the crops on that day is likely to be ascertainable. The owner could either sell or buy in the futures market on the date of injury— though she may not know how much to sell or to buy until harvest, when the extent of the loss can be determined. Because futures markets specify not only the crop but also the date of delivery (November soybeans, March soybeans), the court still would need to determine which futures market to use, making the date of injury no easier to apply than the more realistic alternatives.

2. Cost of Repair as an Alternative to Reduced Value

Often plaintiffs will (or should) repair their damaged property. Rules governing cost of repair also apply in contract cases, where the cost to complete performance (for example, to finish an unfinished building or to correct a defect in goods) offers an alternative to the value of full performance minus the value of the actual performance. In all of these situations, awarding the cost of repair (plus incidental and ensuing losses) will place plaintiff in the position she would have occupied if the wrong had not been committed. Cost of repair directly measures the actual, out-of-pocket cost plaintiff incurred. (This differs from using repair costs as evidence of the diminution in value.) Repairs also offer an easier measure of recovery. Repair bills are simpler than testimony from appraisers concerning the market value of damaged and undamaged property on a particular day. In addition, repairs often cost less than the reduction in value, minimizing the damages defendant must pay.

Even if plaintiffs do not intend to repair, these advantages may lead a plaintiff to request damages based on the cost of repair. (The decision not to repair does not affect the usefulness of cost of repair as a method of calculating damages. Damage calculations determine the amount the plaintiff deserves to recover, but do not limit the way in which plaintiff spends the money.) In other cases, plaintiff may prefer diminution in value, even though repairs would be cheaper. Objections to the cost of repairs may raise several issues.

Market Value of Repairs. Defendant may object that plaintiff spent too much on repairs. A plaintiff has little incentive to shop around for the best price on repairs if defendant ultimately will pay the bill. Courts often limit recovery to the fair market value of repairs, regardless of how much the plaintiff actually spent. Alternatively, courts may award actual repairs unless unreasonable—using the avoidable consequences doctrine to make defendant prove the cost was unreasonable. If treated this way, a plaintiff who spent more than the market price nonetheless might recover the full cost by showing that her efforts to seek out a better price were reasonable, even though unsuccessful.

Unjustified Repairs. In some cases, repairs are so costly that they make no sense. Courts usually impose some limit on the plaintiff's ability to recover the cost of repair when that cost is excessive relative to the benefit of repairs. When courts reject repairs as excessive, they award reduced value instead. Courts might reject recovery of the cost of repairs using any of several tests:

i. When the cost of repairs exceeds the value of the property before the injury;

ii. When the cost of repairs exceeds the value of the property after the repairs are completed;

iii. When the cost of repairs exceeds the amount of increased value the repairs will provide;

iv. When the cost of repairs is disproportionate to the diminution in value of the property.

Each approach has some merit. The Restatements (both torts and contracts) opt for the last.

The first two approaches make no economic sense. They would allow repairs based on the total value of the property, not on the benefit of the repairs. Thus, costly repairs might be awarded even though the damage to the property was slight. Consider a car accident causing minor cosmetic damage to a vehicle that already had a few dents. The cost to repair the new damage might be several hundred dollars, even if the accident had no effect on the value of the car and the repairs added nothing to its value. If a court focuses on the total value of the car, either before the accident or after the repairs, that value almost certainly will exceed the cost of repairs, allowing plaintiff to elect this measure of damages. While court cases involving a few hundred dollars are rare, the same issues can arise in more costly contexts.

The third measure makes economic sense: where repairs increase value by more than the cost of the repairs, a reasonable person would undertake the repairs. In effect, this test asks what plaintiff would do if she had to pay for the repairs herself instead of having them paid by defendant. If the cost exceeded the benefit, plaintiff probably would not repair. The rule combats moral hazard—the tendency of people to be more liberal when spending someone else's money than when spending their own.

Despite this logic, courts frequently recite the first rule. The third rule, for all its economic sense, does not handle situations where plaintiff unreasonably but sincerely wants to repair the damage. Consider the same example if the car had no dings and the owner paid meticulous attention to its condition. The first ding still might not reduce the value very much; the cost to repair it still might be quite high. Awarding the reduction in value leaves plaintiff in the financial position she would have occupied but for the wrong (a car plus some cash worth the same amount the car was worth before the accident). But it may not feel the same as the position she would have occupied but for the wrong—a car with no damage. To restore that position, cost of repair is required.

The fourth rule strikes some balance between these competing concerns. It looks to the benefit of the repairs, not total value of the property, to determine reasonableness. But it does not mechanically insist on the least expensive alternative, leaving some room for a plaintiff to recover cost of repair even if that exceeds the increase in value the repairs provide. It draws the line when repair costs become disproportionate to the increased value, not when they exceed the increased value.

This compromise has appeal for two reasons. First, it allows some room for plaintiff to err when arranging for repairs. A plaintiff will not always be able to predict the amount of diminution a court eventually will find. As long as repairs are not disproportionate to the loss in value, some leeway for miscalculation may be justified. Second, it leaves some room for subjective value. Plaintiff may value the property more than the market does. (Consider the sincere but unreasonably meticulous car owner.) Even if repairs exceed the value of the property to others, they may not exceed the value of the property to the plaintiff. Thus, when repairs are not disproportionate to the loss in value to the plaintiff, awarding the cost of repairs may be justified. Thus, the last approach has substantial support. *See* RESTATEMENT (SECOND) OF TORTS § 929; RESTATEMENT (SECOND) OF CONTRACTS § 348(2).

The last approach (like the first two) leaves some room for strategic behavior. A plaintiff may assert subjective value in an effort to collect repair costs not justified by the market (that is, costs that exceed the increase in value that repair will achieve). Once awarded, plaintiff might sell the property without repairing it, ending up in a better position than she would have occupied but for the wrong. For example, suppose plaintiff owns a farm worth $500,000. Defendant floods part of the land, reducing the value of the farm to $400,000. By spending $130,000, plaintiff could recover the land and return the value of the farm to $500,000. As the ancestral homeland of plaintiff's family, plaintiff might persuade a court that repairs, to him, are subjectively worth the cost, even though an objective, reasonable owner would not spend $130,000 to increase the land's value by $100,000. If plaintiff can recover $130,000, then sell the land for $400,000 without repairing it, plaintiff ends up with $530,000—more than the value of the land before the injury. For this reason, courts scrutinize claims of subjective value with some skepticism. Some courts reject the disproportionality test altogether, preferring one of the other approaches. Note that the first approach—whether repairs exceed the value before the wrong—would still allow plaintiff to recover repair costs: $130,000 is less than $500,000, even though it exceeds the value repairs will add to the land.

Incomplete Repairs. Most rules assume that repairs will restore the property to its original value. That is not always true. Where repairs do not restore property to its full value, courts must award cost of repairs plus any residual lost value. That is, the difference between the value the property would have had if never damaged and the value the property has as repaired must be added to the award (Cost of Repair + (Value if never damaged − Value as repaired)). For example, a car worth $30,000 before an accident may require repairs that cost $10,000. Even if repairs make the car fully functional, buyers may fear latent problems. If so, the repaired car may be worth only $22,000 after repairs, even though cars of similar make, model, age, mileage, features, etc., would be worth $30,000. Significant repairs frequently reduce the amount a willing buyer will pay for goods. In situations like this one, awarding the cost of repairs leaves plaintiff short of her rightful position (a fully functional car worth $30,000). To make plaintiff whole, the court must award an additional $8,000 to cover the residual loss in value.

3.   Undelivered Value

Sometimes the wrong does not damage property already possessed by the plaintiff, but prevents plaintiff from obtaining additional property. This can happen in tort. Defendant may destroy or divert property en route to plaintiff or may interfere with another's performance of a contract. More commonly, undelivered value involves a breach of contract. Damages should allow the plaintiff to obtain the things promised at no greater cost than if the wrong had not been committed. The value of the property itself is direct loss. (In addition to the value of the property, ensuing losses may result if plaintiff would have been able to use the property to create additional gains.)

The discussion above applies reasonably well to undelivered value. Plaintiff is entitled to the value she would have had but for the wrong minus the value she received despite the wrong. Undelivered property, like destroyed property, usually provides the plaintiff with no value, so the offset usually is zero. Partial deliveries, on the other hand, will provide an offset for the value actually provided. In this context, cost to repair refers to obtaining a substitute for the undelivered value (sometimes called "cover" in contract settings). The same choice between market value and the actual cost to obtain a substitute confronts courts.

Given the similarities, much of what follows may seem redundant. It applies the same rule to several different contract contexts. Indeed, the examples below may illustrate fairly well the central point with which the chapter began: that damages usually can be derived from the basic rule stated in the rightful position standard. Mastering that rule may make more detailed formulae unnecessary.

Still, detailed formulae direct attention to specific components of loss that otherwise might be overlooked. The details below seek to identify the elements of loss deserving attention in different contexts. Whether they reinforce what you already understand or fill in gaps that help you apply the general rule better, they deserve some attention. The examples focus on contract cases, though the elements of loss remain identical if a tortious wrong prevents delivery.

General Approach. Most contract remedies can be reduced to a simple approach: the value the plaintiff would have received if the contract had been performed minus any costs the plaintiff avoided because of the breach. Costs avoided because of the breach typically involve any performance plaintiff would have needed to provide under the contract, but had not yet provided (and, because of the breach, no longer needs to provide). This statement risks being too inclusive: "the value the plaintiff would have received" is broad enough to include ensuing losses. When ensuing losses will be awarded anyway, it may not matter whether they are included in the basic statement here or added later. Two potential mistakes require some care. First, do not add ensuing losses again if they already are included in the basic calculation. Second, limitations on or exclusions of ensuing losses may require omitting some of the value the plaintiff would have received. The examples below take some care to avoid including ensuing losses in the calculation, leaving room for their addition.

The statement above starts with the gross benefit the plaintiff would have received and adjusts by subtracting those the recovery need not include. Alternatively, one could approach the calculation from the opposite direction: starting with the unavoidable costs and adding the profit. The approaches are functionally identical: unavoidable costs plus profits must equal gross benefits (revenue) minus avoidable costs. You can derive either version from the truism that Revenue minus Costs equals Profit. (Again, as used here, profit may be limited to direct gains rather than including ensuing lost profits.)

An example may clarify the point. Buyer ordered 100,000 reams of paper for $500,000. Buyer paid 10% ($50,000) to Seller in advance, with the balance due after delivery. On the date set for delivery, the price for plaintiff to buy similar paper was $600,000. Seller breached. One can start with the value Buyer would have received ($600,000) and subtract the avoided costs ($450,000, the balance due after delivery, but never paid), to arrive at a recovery of $150,000. Alternatively, one can start with the costs already incurred ($50,000) and add the profit buyer would have obtained if the paper had been delivered ($100,000) to reach exactly the same result. Note that in neither case does the calculation include the profit Buyer might have realized by reselling the paper (or by using it). That ensuing loss could be added. The lost profit here refers only to the benefit buyer would have received by paying $500,000 for paper worth $600,000.

Nonperformance vs. Partial Performance. The issues below focus on nonperformance rather than partial performance. Partial performance, at most, forces the inclusion of one additional offset, but does not fundamentally change the calculation. Three techniques may help deal with the complexities partial performance adds.

First, contract problems sometimes can be divided into two parts: a portion of the contract has been performed fully, and another portion that has not been performed at all. If so, courts can simply deal with the unperformed half of the deal. For instance, in the paper example above, assume that Seller delivered half the paper before breaching and that Buyer paid $250,000 for that paper (including the $50,000 down payment). One can treat the problem as if the contract involved 50,000 reams of paper at $250,000, but now worth $300,000. Subtracting the avoided costs ($250,000) from the expected benefit ($300,000) produces damages of $50,000. No damages for the other half of the contract are required. (If buyer had not paid for the paper actually delivered, the judgment should reduce the damages Seller owed Buyer by the amount Buyer owed Seller for the paper already delivered.)

Some contracts cannot be divided or should not be divided. Courts treat contracts as divisible only if it is fair to view the various portions of the contract as corresponding pairs of part performances. Where the whole is greater than the sum of its parts, a party may object to divisibility of the contract. Thus, if the failure to complete performance affects the value of the performance already delivered, dividing the contract may be inappropriate. Similarly, where the price cannot be partitioned among the various parts of the performance, division may be impractical. In these situations, plaintiff often seeks rescission and restitution rather than damages. These situations require one of the alternatives below.

Second, one can account for partial performance by treating the value received as a cost avoided. Thus, the benefit of performance received reduces the recovery. In the paper example (where each party performed the first half of the contract before Seller breached), plaintiff expected to receive a benefit of $600,000, but avoided costs of $550,000 ($300,000 of benefit already received plus the $250,000 she would have paid for the paper she didn't receive), for a recovery of $50,000—the same result produced by treating the contract as divisible.

Third, one can apply the rule for damaged property from the section above: value undamaged minus value damaged. The partial performance gives plaintiff some value that must be offset, unlike cases of nonperformance. In the example, the value undamaged was $100,000 (Buyer received $600,000, but paid $500,000 for that right.) Partial breach damaged, but did not destroy, that right. It reduced it to $600,000 minus $550,000 (the $300,000 received plus the $250,000 not paid), or $50,000.

The second and third approaches are identical. One deals with the gross gain less savings, the other with the net gain. Properly calculated, either will produce the proper result. Care may be required to be sure that all important elements of the calculation find their way into the calculation of the net benefit. When possible, working with the gross benefit (or dividing the contract) may be easier to manage.

(A) Sales of Goods

Article 2 of the Uniform Commercial Code codifies contract remedies for sales of goods. These provisions usefully illustrate how contract remedies work. Reviewing these provisions should help illuminate the way the principles apply in other contract contexts, such as employment and construction.

Nondelivery by Seller. Buyer is entitled to receive a refund of any amount paid to seller, UCC § 2–711(1), plus cover price (the cost to obtain substitute goods in good faith, without unreasonable delay, in a reasonable transaction) minus the contract price promised to the original seller and minus any other expenses saved as a result of the breach (Refund + (Cover Price – Contract Price) – Expenses Saved). UCC § 2–712. Alternatively, if buyer does not make a substitute deal, it may recover any amount paid to seller plus the market price of the goods (the amount it would have cost if he had made a reasonable substitute purchase) minus the contract price promised to the original seller and minus any other expenses saved as a result of the breach (Refund + (Market Price – Contract Price) – Expenses Saved). UCC § 2–713. (The UCC could have awarded the cover price or market price minus the unpaid portion of the contract price. That measure would be slightly less generous to buyers. If, at the time for performance, the goods cost less than the contract price, defendant might keep a portion of buyer's down payment. Allowing a full refund, then subtracting the entire contract price, codifies a restitution component of these remedies.) Of course, a plaintiff could seek specific performance if "the goods are unique or in other proper circumstances." UCC § 2–716. (Other proper circumstances probably encompass any reason the remedy at law would be inadequate.) In each case, plaintiff receives the goods or their money equivalent, minus any amounts saved (such as the contract price). Incidental or ensuing losses—such as the time required to make substitute arrangements and profits lost if substitute goods arrive later than those promised by the seller— would be added.

The limitations on a cover transaction deserve emphasis. To qualify, cover must be:

- in good faith;

- reasonable; and

- without unreasonable delay.

If any one of these descriptions fail, the cover transaction will not qualify and plaintiff will instead be limited to damages computed based on market value less contract price. Requiring a prompt cover transaction limits the plaintiff's ability to speculate that the price might decline. If the price instead goes up, plaintiff cannot collect more from defendant based on the delay. Rather, the market price on the date of delivery will be used, not the postponed cover transaction. Good faith and reasonableness seek to combat the possibility that plaintiff will cover unwisely because the cost will be borne by defendant. The goods must be a reasonable substitute for the goods defendant promised, not a step up in quality. If an exact substitute is unavailable, reasonableness and good faith may permit recourse to the least expensive alternative that is at least as good as the promised goods, even if it is somewhat better than the promised goods. Similarly, good faith and reasonableness limit the price a plaintiff may agree to pay for the substitute. A plaintiff who pays more than is reasonable for the substitute goods appears to succumb to moral hazard, wasting defendant's money in ways that plaintiff probably would not waste its own money.

In practice, cover can be more complex. For example, a business may make frequent purchases of similar goods. If so, it may be difficult to identify which purchase was a cover transaction and which were purchases that plaintiff would have made even if defendant had delivered. If prices fall after the breach, plaintiff may argue that none of the purchases were cover, hoping to use the market value formula to justify a larger recovery.

The UCC also makes provision for calculating damages when buyer keeps goods that do not conform to the contract. These are not undelivered value, but follow the basic rules for the damaged property from the preceding section. Thus, damages for breach of warranty are measured by the reduced value of the goods (value as warranted minus value as received). UCC § 2–714(2). Alternatively, the cost to repair the goods might be recovered under § 2–714(1), which allows damages "determined in any manner which is reasonable" for nonconforming goods.

Nonpayment by Buyer. When a buyer refuses to pay for goods, seller may refuse to deliver the goods—including recovering the goods from a third party, such as a transportation company or warehouse. UCC § 2–703. In addition, buyer may recover the contract price minus the resale price (the amount seller realized in a good faith and commercially reasonable sale of the goods to another buyer) and minus any expenses saved because of buyer's breach ((Contract Price – Resale Price) – Savings). UCC § 2–706. If seller decides not to make a substitute deal, she recovers the contract price minus the market price (the amount she would have received if she had made a reasonable substitute sale) and minus any expenses saved because of buyer's breach ((Contract Price – Market Price) – Savings). UCC § 2–708(1). In some cases there will be nothing to subtract from the contract price; the market value the seller could receive will be zero. For instance, perishable goods may spoil before resale is possible, goods may have been destroyed in transit (after the risk of loss shifted to buyer), or buyer may already have accepted the goods, precluding resale. In some cases, seller may have the goods, but may be unable to resell them at any reasonable price. In these cases, seller may recover the entire contract price, but must hold the goods (if she has them) available for buyer. UCC § 2–709. Savings to the seller might include the cost of shipping the goods or insuring them during transit. Some sellers (such as car dealers) may save the cost of warranty service on the goods. Regardless of the remedy chosen, seller may recover incidental and ensuing losses, such as the cost incurred trying to resell the goods and of storing and insuring them pending resale. The UCC does not include consequential damages for seller, but the definition of incidental damages for sellers covers most ensuing losses sellers might incur. UCC § 2–710.

As with cover transactions, a resale transaction will satisfy these rules only if it is made in good faith and in a commercially reasonable manner. This limits the seller's ability to resell the goods at a steep discount and recover the difference from the breaching buyer. If permitted, seller could nearly give the goods to a relative or make no effort to obtain a realistic price. Section 2–706 contains some specific requirements sellers must meet to satisfy the commercial reasonableness test, such as giving the buyer notice of the sale (thus allowing the buyer to bid at the sale if the goods are being undervalued). If a resale transaction does not satisfy the requirements, then seller's recovery will be based on contract price minus market price, not resale price.

Resale price may not be subtracted from the recovery of a lost volume seller, one who could have performed both the sale to the plaintiff and the resale transaction. The rules stated above assume that a resale by the seller was a substitute for the sale to the buyer. Thus, if seller sold the goods to another buyer at the same price, direct damages would equal $0. Some sellers have the capacity to make both sales. For instance, a manufacturer of computer chips might have been able to fill both the order of the new buyer and the order of the original buyer. By breaching, the original buyer reduced the seller's total profit. If seller could have earned profits on both the original sale and the resale, the breaching buyer must pay the profit (plus reasonable overhead) on the contract breached, plus incidental costs, but minus any savings (such as shipping costs or warranty service) in relation to the contract. UCC § 2–708(2). This remedy puts seller in her rightful position, collecting the profit on two sales: one via the resale, the other via the damage award.

Buyer's remedies parallel seller's remedies very closely. The chart below illustrates the similarities. Either buyers or sellers can make a reasonable substitute transaction and collect the difference between the substitute transaction and the transaction to which they originally were entitled. Either can forego substitute transactions and recover based on market price—the price at which a reasonable substitute transaction would have been made. Either can recover exactly what it bargained for—the goods (via specific performance) or the price (as damages) in an appropriate case. The buyer, unlike the seller, can recover for the reduced value of nonconforming delivery. This remedy may never apply to sellers. If the price is money, seller cannot easily claim that the money isn't green enough. If buyer paid too little, seller may recover the unpaid balance under these provisions. If buyer was to provide something other than money, seller would be treated as a buyer of that something, able to invoke buyer's remedies. (Problems can arise when the currency in which the price is paid proves less valuable than anticipated. That risk is one the parties should address in the contract by specifying the currency.)

Summary of UCC Damage Remedies

SELLER may recover:

Contract Price – Resale Price + Incidental – Savings (§ 2–706)

Contract Price – Market Price + Incidental – Savings (§ 2–708)

Contract Price + Incidental – Savings (§ 2–709)

BUYER may recover:

Refund + Cover Price – Contract Price + Incidental + Consequential – Savings (§ 2–712)

Refund + Market Price – Contract Price + Incidental + Consequential – Savings (§ 2–713)

Value Warranted – Value Received + Incidental + Consequential (§ 2–714)

Specific Performance + Damages Not Avoided by Specific Performance (§ 2–716)

(B) Employment Contracts

In employment contracts, employees sell services and employers buy them. Most of the remedies will be identical to sales of goods. In addition, the damages an employee suffers are largely identical whether the wrong consists of breach of contract, tortious discharge (such as retaliatory discharge), or statutory violations (such as discrimination claims). Some wrongs may justify punitive damages, some wrongs may include distress, but the direct loss to the plaintiff is measured in much the same way regardless of the wrong.

When an employee breaches, the employer may need to hire a substitute (in good faith and reasonably). If the substitute costs more than the contract with the employee, the employee should be liable for the difference—cover price minus contract price. Price should include both wages and fringe benefits. (If the employer covers by paying overtime to other employees, it may save money on benefits, an offset against the damages.) Incidental and ensuing losses, such as the cost to find a new employee and any damages caused in the interim, may fill out the remedy.

When an employer breaches, the employee may need to find substitute employment (similar to reselling the goods). If the new job pays less (considering both wages and fringe benefits), the employer should be liable for the difference—contract price minus resale price. Incidental losses, such as the cost of finding a new job, supplement the recovery. Ensuing losses, though justifiable, face serious obstacles. Because the employer's breach consists of a failure to pay money, ensuing loss usually is limited to interest on the unpaid amount. Thus, even if an employee lost her house to foreclosure because of the breach, recovery for that loss probably is unavailable. That limitation is addressed under ensuing losses.

In either case, problems with the substitute transaction may produce a recovery that resembles market price minus contract price. For example, if an employer, in bad faith or unreasonably, overpays the substitute worker, the court may limit recovery to the amount that the employer could have paid had it entered a reasonable substitute transaction. Similarly, an employee who remains idle rather than taking reasonable substitute employment may find the market value of her services subtracted from the price the employer agreed to pay. On each side, courts usually base this result on the avoidable consequences doctrine. Plaintiff's unreasonable conduct (overpaying the substitute employee or refusing substitute jobs) increases her loss, justifying an offset against the amount that the plaintiff may recover. Avoidable consequences poses some obstacles that may limit the occasions on which a court will resort to market price. Thus, reasonable but unsuccessful efforts to find a new employee or a new job may justify awarding full losses. For employers, ensuing losses—the profit lost by operating without the employee—seem likely to provide full compensation, without regard to the market value of a hypothetical employee it did not hire. Without ensuing losses, the decision not to replace the employee suggests the employer actually saved money as a result of the breach.

If the new employment does not substitute for the old—if the employee would have worked both jobs, not just one—the new wages are not subtracted from the amount owed under the employment contract. The employee is a lost volume seller, one who would have worked two jobs (earning two salaries instead of only one). This rule applies if the employee *would* have worked both jobs but for the breach. If she *could* have worked both, but *would* have worked only one, the new job is a substitute for the old.

Partial performance of employment contracts often resembles the reduced value situation. Where an employee does not work as long or as hard as promised, the employer theoretically could seek the value as promised minus the value as delivered. When the employee is late or absent, employers commonly adjust pay for time not worked, usually without any court proceedings. Suing a lazy employee for damages caused by inactivity, while theoretically possible, is relatively rare. Employers usually fire and replace poor quality employees instead of suing them for damages. Other breaches, such as trade secret violations or breach of a noncompetition agreement, involve the same principles: putting the plaintiff where she would have been if the breach had not occurred. Employers generally prefer injunctive relief, when possible. Damages in these cases usually fall within ensuing losses.

(C) Construction Contracts

Construction contracts, like employment contracts, involve services. Construction services primarily relate to creating or repairing buildings, usually on real estate owned by the buyer of the services.

When the seller (contractor) breaches, the buyer (landowner) may need to make substitute arrangements. These may involve the entire contract or the unfinished work. The owner recovers the cost to complete the project minus the unpaid portion of the contract price (savings from not paying the original contractor what she would have collected had she finished the job). The substitute transaction must be reasonable and made in good faith. Ensuing losses may be recoverable, though many construction contracts exclude damages for delay.

When the landowner breaches—dismissing the contractor without cause—the contractor resembles a discharged employee. It may recover the contract price promised for the full job, minus any expenses saved by not needing to complete the job. (This may include salvage value of materials already purchased for the job.) The full price necessarily includes any profit the contractor would have earned on the project; subtracting savings prevents the profit from exceeding the profit the contractor would have earned completing the contract. Unlike employment, the amount the contractor earns or could have earned on other jobs usually is not subtracted from the award. Most courts treat contractors as lost volume sellers: contractors can handle many projects at one time, simply hiring more laborers as they work more sites. Other jobs, then, are not substitutes for the job the owner breached. The courts award the price on this job and assume that the builder could have performed the other jobs, too.

Construction contracts can be quite complex, involving numerous subcontractors, an architect representing the landowner, issuers of performance bonds, lenders, and other parties (such as prospective tenants of the completed project). The complexities do not change the basic rules. More disputes and more parties complicate liability issues more than damages. Once liability is determined, each wrong can be analyzed under these rules.

(D) Real Estate Contracts

The same principles apply to real estate, but with some differences.

When seller fails to deliver real estate, buyer normally is entitled to specific performance. Where damages are awarded instead, buyer may recover a refund of any payments, plus the market value of the land minus the contract price of the land. For example, suppose buyer and seller had agreed to sell an undeveloped lot on a lake for $100,000 and buyer paid a $10,000 deposit upon acceptance of the offer. Buyer could prove that the lot was worth $140,000 (an appraisal based on actual sales of similar lots). Upon breach by seller, buyer could recover $50,000: $10,000 for the deposit, plus $40,000 for the difference between the market value ($140,000 that buyer would have received) and the contract price ($100,000 that buyer would have paid).

Courts almost never award cover price minus contract price, even if plaintiff enters a substitute transaction. The uniqueness of each parcel of real estate makes it difficult to discern whether the cover price is higher because the substitute parcel is better or because the promised parcel was priced below market value. Plaintiff is entitled to the profit from making a good deal (a contract price lower than the value of the parcel). If the substitute parcel is better than the promised parcel, a remedy based on cover price would overcompensate plaintiff, leaving her better off than if the contract had been performed. The rightful position standard does not permit plaintiff to buy a better parcel at defendant's expense. Thus, even a good faith and reasonable substitute purchase will not be used as the measure of recovery in most jurisdictions. The second parcel, if sufficiently similar, might be evidence of the market value of the promised parcel. (Appraisers generally use the price of similar land in the vicinity to determine market value.) But the substitute transaction has no direct effect on the measure of damages.

As noted above, some states permit a seller who *cannot* deliver good title the benefit of an exception to this general rule. The English rule limits recovery to plaintiff's reliance losses, expenses incurred in reliance on the contract (down payment, title search costs, perhaps surveys relating to use of the land). The exception is not available to a seller that knew it could not deliver good title, that caused its inability to deliver good title (such as by selling to another instead of delivering the land to plaintiff), or who could perform but decided not to perform. In these cases, the rule described in the preceding paragraph (sometimes called the American rule) applies, even in states that follow the English rule. The exception protects sellers from honest mistakes about ownership. Courts reject it when used to facilitate fraud or intentional breach.

When buyer refuses to take delivery and pay for a parcel, seller can resell the parcel and collect the original contract price minus resale price, minus any savings (*e.g.*, brokerage commissions, if lower because of the resale—and perhaps the value of retaining possession of the land, as where it produces a crop before it is resold). Here, the parcel is exactly the same, so any difference in the resale price must reflect the deal itself. For example, reconsider the sale of a lakeside lot $100,000. If buyer breached, seller might look for another buyer. After reasonable efforts, seller might accept the best offer it receives, say $85,000. Seller can recover $15,000, the difference between what it should have received ($100,000) and what it did receive ($85,000). (If seller kept the $10,000 deposit, that would count as the first part of the recovery, leaving only $5,000 owed by buyer.) If seller owed a 6% commission to a broker, it may have saved some money on the resale. Commissions on the second sale at $85,000 would be only $5,100, $900 less than commissions on the original sale at $100,000. That is $900 that seller didn't lose, reducing damages to $4,100.

If seller does not resell, the contract price minus the market value (on the date of the breach) remains a viable remedy—again, taking account of any savings and any ensuing losses. For example, seller might decide to wait for a better time to resell. The absence of an actual resale makes it harder to prove the value of the lot. But assuming that market value can be ascertained, contract price minus market value would be awarded. If the lakeside lot were worth $87,000, seller could recover $13,000—again, less the amount of any deposit seller retained. If no commission was due because the sale fell through, then that saving also would be subtracted. If, however, the broker's contract vested a right to a commission when the contract was signed, seller may not save the commission, making it inappropriate to subtract it. (Nor would that be added to the recovery. The commission would have come from seller's share if the contract had been performed. Seller would not collect both the price and the commission.)

As always, incidental and ensuing losses (such as cost of resale, insurance while resale was pending, etc.) may be necessary to fill out the remedy. If an uninsured event damaged the property in the interim, that might be an ensuing loss; the parcel is different, so the lower resale price may not reflect how good a deal the first contract was. But defendant would have suffered the uninsured loss but for the breach, making it appropriate to use this measure anyway.

Sales can involve estates less than fee simple—life estates, leases, remainders, etc. The rules apply equally well, using the value of the estate at issue. Thus, the fair rental value might substitute for the fair market value in the formulations offered above. The same concerns arise if a tenant enters a substitute transaction for a different property. The actual transaction will not be used to measure the loss, though it might be evidence of the fair rental value of the original premises. If the fair rental value of the original exceeds the contract price, the tenant might recover the difference from the breaching landlord. In these situations, a tenant may prefer specific performance. As an interest in real estate, leases may qualify for injunctive relief under the irreparable injury rule.

Where tenant breaches, the landlord is entitled to the rent promised minus any savings that result from the breach. The savings attributable to the breach vary greatly, not only from state to state, but from context to context. Commercial leases sometimes differ from residential leases. The type of breach—whether the tenant abandons the property, the landlord evicts the tenant, or the tenant retains possession but does not pay rent—may affect the offset. Even the cause of action the landlord brings (an action for rent, which covers only rent already due on the date the action is filed, as opposed to an action for damages, which covers rent due until the lease term expires) may affect the rules.

One generalization seems clear: if the landlord does lease the premises to another, the tenant's obligation to pay rent for that period is offset by the actual amount the landlord receives in the substitute transaction. If the actual transaction was not a reasonable substitute, the court might offset the amount the landlord would have received in a reasonable substitute lease.

By the same token, if the tenant retains possession of the leased premises, the landlord receives no benefit from the breach. It cannot lease the premises to another until the breaching tenant is removed, leaving no justification to subtract the value of the premises.

In most cases, the avoidable consequences doctrine will limit a landlord's ability to recover damages (measured by future rent) for residential leases. In effect, courts now treat the tenant's abandonment of the premises as returning them to the landlord. The rent a landlord would have received by making reasonable efforts to find a new tenant will be subtracted, if the landlord did not make reasonable efforts. On the other hand, a landlord who makes reasonable but unsuccessful efforts to relet the premises may recover the entire rent. Some states reject the last sentence, stating that the landlord can recover the rent promised minus the fair rental value of the premises. If the defendant can prove the fair rental value of the premises, it will not matter that reasonable efforts failed to produce a new tenant. In effect, this adopts contract price minus market price as the basic formula, rejecting the avoidable consequences doctrine.

A few courts may allow the landlord to recover the entire promised rent, without offset. At common law, that approach applied to all leases. The lease entitled the tenant to use the premises for the full lease period. The landlord had no right to convey the premises to another during this period. The parties could negotiate for the return of the premises. But the tenant could not return them to the landlord without the landlord's consent, any more than the landlord could confiscate the premises without the tenant's consent. Under this rule, the landlord recovers the full rent promised. This rule is in decline. Some jurisdictions continue to apply this rule to commercial leases or when a landlord brings an action for past rent after the lease has expired. Even then, some states will apply the avoidable consequences doctrine if the landlord did not make reasonable efforts to find a new tenant.

The focus on rent should not obscure the other promises a lease may include. A landlord may have a right to collect utilities—or utilities may represent a savings if, by abandoning the premises, the tenant reduced the amount the landlord had to pay for utilities. Taxes also may be allocated in a lease. Finally, leases often include provisions governing damages. Those provisions may alter the rules discussed here.

4. Loss of Intangible Property

Some losses involve intangible property, such as contract rights, patent rights, insurance, stock certificates. Where these rights have a market value, the techniques described above can apply with full force. Failure to deliver a stock certificate can be compensated by cover price minus contract price or, if buyer does not cover, market price minus contract price. Failure to pay for the stock can be compensated by contract price minus resale price or, if seller does not resell, contract price minus market value. Thus, direct loss for many intangibles presents no new issue. In some cases, however, intangibles raise new wrinkles.

Insurance Policies. When defendant breaches a promise to obtain insurance for plaintiff, cover price minus contract price will suffice only if plaintiff discovers the problem with enough time to obtain insurance coverage elsewhere before an insured loss occurs. After an insured loss, no one will issue a policy covering the risk of that loss. Thus, to put plaintiff in the position she would have occupied if the breach had not occurred, the law must award the full amount of insurance plaintiff would have received under the policy promised by defendant. Defendant promised to deliver intangible property (an insurance policy), but failed to deliver it. The value of the policy might have been very small (if no insured loss occurred), but turns out to be large (compensation for the insured loss). If the thing itself is not delivered, its value should be provided. This loss could be classified as an ensuing loss.

Intellectual Property Rights. While direct loss for intellectual property violations are possible, often the ensuing losses dominate the cases. In addition, injunctive relief and restitution (or disgorgement) of the defendant's ill-gotten profits form a backbone of intellectual property statutes. Nonetheless, direct loss can result from intellectual property violations in several ways.

The failure to pay for intangible rights may arise from breach of a contract promising to pay for those rights (such as a patent license) or from a tort (such as taking rights without a contract), or from violation of a statute protecting those rights. Breach of contract poses no new difficulty. Damages equal the promised payments minus any savings that result from the breach. Practical difficulties often arise. Price may depend on volume, as where a patent license measures royalties by the quantity sold. If buyer breaches before selling any units, proving the volume it would have sold may be difficult. To a large extent, however, the damages here are governed by contract law.

Taking intangible rights without permission typically produces the same remedies employed when taking tangible rights. Statutory provisions protecting intellectual property refer to plaintiff's actual damages, without defining them specifically. Thus, courts apply the same remedial principles to intellectual property as to other conversions. In some cases, the loss will be measured by the market value of the rights taken. Thus, the patent statute specifies that the amount of a reasonable royalty is the minimum amount a patent holder may recover for infringement. The royalty represents the market value of the right to use the invention during the period it was misappropriated. (Because intellectual property often is unique, injunctions may compel defendants to stop their infringement. The royalty covers the loss until the infringement stops.) A royalty will not preclude the recovery of ensuing losses, such as profits the plaintiff lost as a result of the infringer's sales or other misuse of the invention. The patent statute also permits courts to increase damages up to three times the actual loss, at least in cases of willful infringement. 35 U.S.C. § 284.

The copyright law also provides for damages that may exceed compensation. For instance, it permits plaintiff to recover "any additional profits of the infringer," if they are not accounted for in the plaintiff's actual damages. 17 U.S.C. § 504. Often, any profit the defendant earned by violating copyright will be a profit that the plaintiff lost. But in some cases, defendant will manage to make a profit that the plaintiff could not have made (and thus did not lose). Adding that profit to the plaintiff's recovery puts him in a better position than if the infringement had not occurred. In this way, the copyright statute appears to combine damages and restitution in a manner that penalizes infringement. The copyright law also allows plaintiff to elect statutory damages (sometimes called presumed damages), a useful provision when actual damages defy proof.

Trademark law includes many of the same provisions. It starts with a restitutionary recovery, allowing plaintiff to recover the defendant's profits, but adds "any damages sustained by the plaintiff" to the recovery. In addition, the court is authorized to increase awards up to three times. Treble damages or treble profits (but apparently not both) are available for intentional use of counterfeit trademarks. Statutory (presumed) damages are available for counterfeit trademarks and cyberpiracy. These provisions appear to allow dramatic overcompensation. But the statute also allows the court to reduce the award of lost profits (but not damages) if justice so requires and specifies that the awards must comport with the principles of equity. Courts interpret these provisions to require that recovery be compensatory, not punitive, rejecting recovery that would provide the plaintiff a windfall. 15 U.S.C. § 1117.

Failure to deliver promised rights pose a different story. In some cases, delivery will not be necessary; the intellectual property may be a matter of public record, which plaintiff can use without further input from the owner. The contract establishes the right to use the property, becoming a defense to infringement. But some situations may require further conduct from the owner, particularly where trade secrets are involved. The failure to deliver the promised intellectual property may result primarily in ensuing losses: the profits plaintiff would have made by using the promised rights. In other cases, however, rights may have a market value. This is particularly true where they can be resold (for example, the movie rights to a book). While resale sounds like just another use (and thus another ensuing loss), plaintiff is deprived of a piece of property, however intangible, that has measurable value. This is direct loss, as much as the destruction, damage, or nondelivery of tangible property is a direct loss.

5. Personal Injury

Personal injury, whether physical or emotional, tends to be seen as *sui generis*. The terminology varies, but the concepts remain largely the same. The approaches detailed here can apply with equal force, but some of the questions raised simply don't arise in the context of personal injuries.

Physical Injury to a Person is much like physical injury to property. Courts generally do not attach a market value to the person. Instead, courts award medical costs plus pain and suffering plus any ensuing losses (such as lost earnings). Medical costs are analogous to the cost of repair. Medical costs are relatively easy to measure, unlike the diminution in value of a human body. (With no legitimate market for humans, market value lacks any reference point.) Unlike cost of repair, no one argues (not seriously, at least) that the medical costs were excessive in light of benefit produced. In some ways, medical costs are not direct loss, but incidental costs incurred in an effort to minimize the loss caused by injury to the person. Still, medical costs are the best approximation available for the harm done to a body.

Medical costs measure the direct losses that medical science can repair. Damage that medicine cannot heal often entails loss of use—the inability to pursue activities formerly enjoyed, whether work or leisure. Even successful medical treatment may not instantly restore the body to health, requiring some compensation for interim losses. Some damage may fit neither category: medical treatment is unavailable, evading inclusion as medical costs; but the injury does not preclude other activities, defying quantification as loss of use. Without some compensation, plaintiff remains worse off than if the wrong had not occurred. Absent measures for value of the person, the law resorts to other categories to try to capture these losses.

Anguish Accompanying Physical Injury. Physical injuries may cause pain. But for the wrong, plaintiff would have had a body with no pain (or less pain). Courts, therefore, award recovery for pain and suffering. Pain defies categorization as direct or ensuing. Pain treated by medicine falls within medical costs. Pain that precludes activities could fall within ensuing losses. In some cases, pain may do neither. Courts treat pain as a separate heading, without trying to categorize it as direct or ensuing. *See* section F., *infra.*

Emotional Injuries Without Physical Injury. Some personal wrongs do not injure the victim physically, but nonetheless cause emotional harm. Repair costs (such as counseling, rebutting libelous accusations, or rebuilding relationships) may reduce the future effects. But repair costs may not be effective in some cases— and in any event may not counteract the suffering that occurred before the repairs began. Thus, the damage to a person when a wrong causes emotional injury requires some compensation as direct losses—at least if an actionable wrong caused the emotional injury. *See* section F., *infra.*

E. ENSUING LOSS (CONSEQUENTIAL DAMAGES, LOSS OF USE)

As noted in many places above, awarding the plaintiff the direct loss often falls short of the position he would have occupied if the wrong had not occurred. Repairing a damaged car or house does not compensate for the inability to use the property while repairs are performed. Buying substitute goods may not compensate for the inability to use (or resell) the promised goods between the promised delivery date and the time plaintiff manages to cover. In short, replacing the thing lost does not always compensate for the inability to use the thing for a period of time. And where replacement is impossible—as with many physical injuries—loss of use may be the primary element of damage.

Courts describe ensuing losses in different terms, depending on the context. In contract, the inability to use the performance is called consequential damages (or lost profits, which is one specific example of a consequential loss). In tort, especially property torts, the ensuing loss is called loss of use. Again, lost profits are a common example, though the cost to rent replacement property (and thus avoid losing profits) often suffices. In personal injury actions, courts usually refer to loss of earning potential or loss of income, specific examples of ensuing losses, rather than use a general name for ensuing losses. Loss of enjoyment of life, discussed under intangible loss, is another ensuing loss that is not generally described in this way.

Special Damages. Courts sometimes distinguish general damages from special damages. These terms are used in several different ways, without much consistency. On one level, they refer to a pleading requirement. The complaint must identify with particularity items of special damage, but may plead general damages without itemizing them. That doesn't help decide which damages are general and which are special until the court states which ones must be plead with specificity. In tort, special damages refers to monetary losses, such as medical expenses and lost wages. These are more easily quantified, unlike general damages, which include pain and suffering. In contract, on the other hand, the more easily quantified market measures for loss of value (such as cover price minus contact price or value as warranted minus value as delivered) are called general damages. Special damages refers to elements that are more remote and harder to prove, such as lost profits—damages that might apply in special cases, but not to all cases generally. These variations in usage make the terminology confusing. In general, it is safer to avoid the terms general damages and special damages.

1. Failure to Pay Money: Interest as Damages

Traditionally, courts apply two different rules to late payments. One states that consequential damages are not available for failure to pay money. The other states that prejudgment interest is available for damages if the amount is liquidated—that is, either a sum certain or an amount capable of calculation once the inputs are known (such as price and quantity), even if disputes about the inputs require resolution by the finder of fact. These two rules, in combination, function as a single general rule: consequential damages for failure to pay money are limited to interest on the sum that should have been paid. The rule allowing prejudgment interest is not limited to the failure to pay money. Any loss may be subject to prejudgment interest, subject to limitations such as the liquidation requirement. For example, if defendant damages plaintiff's car, forcing plaintiff to pay for repairs (a direct loss) and rent a substitute vehicle (an ensuing loss), interest on both expenses from the date they were incurred would be recoverable. For nonpayment of money, however, interest is the only consequential loss. Other breaches may produce a different measure of ensuing losses—and then add prejudgment interest to that measure.

When defendant's breach deprives plaintiff of money, a judgment that included only the amount owed would not restore plaintiff to her rightful position. Money received when due would be more valuable than money received after trial (or settlement), perhaps years later. Plaintiff could have used the money in the interim, either earning investment income or paying off interest-bearing debts. Without damages for ensuing loss, defendant in effect receives an interest-free loan of whatever amount it owes plaintiff.

Plaintiffs generally cannot recover for the lost opportunity to invest the money, had it been paid on time. Identifying the investment that the plaintiff would have made often poses a serious problem for courts. Plaintiffs seeking to quantify the lost gains can use 20–20 hindsight when identifying the investments they would have made but for the wrong. Such testimony risks exposing defendants to large and sometimes imaginary losses plaintiffs claim to have suffered. To avoid this risk, the law limits plaintiffs to interest on the amount due (with some exceptions discussed below).

Rationale and Critique. Failure to pay money arguably need not prevent a plaintiff from using the money as planned. Plaintiff can avoid lost use of the money by borrowing the sum defendant should have paid. In effect, this suggests plaintiff should cover with a different source of money, much the way rules on direct loss encourage plaintiff to cover with a substitute transaction for other performances. Plaintiff can invest the borrowed money as planned, earning the same profit (or loss) that she would have earned if the wrong had not occurred. Interest on the loan would not have been incurred but for the wrong. Interest, however, fully compensates plaintiff for the loss defendant caused. The rationale also applies to any loss that can be converted to a loss of money. A plaintiff injured and unable to work theoretically could borrow the amount she would have earned and use the money to avoid any losses that might ensue from loss of income. A plaintiff whose property is damaged can borrow money to make repairs and thus reduce any loss of use to the property. Interest on the amount borrowed could be substituted for the actual ensuing losses.

This rationale resembles the avoidable consequences doctrine. Plaintiff could have minimized the loss by borrowing money and using it as planned. Failure to do so prevented investment gains, increasing the losses rather than minimizing them. (In cases where defendant breached a promise to loan money, the difference between the cost of the original loan and the cost of the substitute loan would be the loss.) This converts the ensuing loss into direct loss. The loss of use of the money no longer measures the loss; the loss of the money itself is the measure.

The rationale misses the rightful position in two situations. First, plaintiff may have been unable to obtain a substitute source of funds in time to pursue the original venture. Some plaintiffs cannot borrow at all, others may be unable to replace the money in time to pursue the lost investment. The avoidable consequences doctrine not only would inquire into the reasonableness of plaintiff's failure to replace the money, but also would place the burden of proof on that issue on the defendant. Limiting damages to interest by rule eliminates those inquiries, effectively assuming that everyone can borrow money.

Second, prejudgment interest rates may not reflect the rates plaintiffs would need to pay—or, in some cases, actually did pay—in order to borrow money. Whether fixed by statute or left to judicial discretion, interest rates sometimes reflect the ways a plaintiff might have invested the money, such as by buying U.S. Treasury Bills. These rates may be much lower than the rate lenders charge for funds. Lenders tend to charge interest rates that exceed the amount they can make by investing the money.

New York offers an alternative rationale: defendants have no reason to foresee (at the time the contract is made) that plaintiff might suffer losses from the inability to use the money in a particular way. Interest, on the other hand, flows naturally from the failure to pay money on time. This rationale offers room for some exceptions to the rule, discussed below.

Prejudgment vs. Postjudgment Interest. Judgments earn interest from the date of judgment to the date of payment. Prejudgment interest covers the period from the date of the injury to the date of judgment. Courts traditionally limit prejudgment interest to liquidated claims. Liquidated means the amount of plaintiff's loss could be ascertained, either as a sum certain or by application of a simple formula. The rule frequently allowed prejudgment interest on claims involving property (breach of contract or injury to property), but denied interest on personal injury actions, where no formula could project pain and suffering. Liquidation usually refers to the entire claim. Thus, even if parts of a tort claim may be liquidated (medical expenses and lost income), intangible losses (pain and suffering) prevented the claim from being liquidated. Requiring liquidation may fit the rationale: borrowing an ascertainable amount makes sense, but borrowing a completely indeterminate amount may not. (All judgments are liquidated amounts. The limitation has no effect on postjudgment interest.)

Limiting prejudgment interest to liquidated claims precludes interest in too many cases. Plaintiff bears losses immediately, but recovers the cost later without any compensation for the delay. The defendant benefits from an interest-free loan for as long as judgment can be deferred. Courts and legislatures have begun to expand the availability of prejudgment interest beyond liquidated claims. The resulting array of rules lacks any clear pattern. The issues can be identified, but research for each jurisdiction will be necessary.

Prejudgment interest for intangible losses (such as past pain and suffering or loss of consortium) receives inconsistent treatment. In admiralty cases, where prejudgment interest is a matter of discretion, federal courts commonly allow interest on past intangible losses. In cases under the Federal Employer's Liability Act (covering railroad workers), interest on pain and suffering is unavailable. Texas allows interest on pain and suffering. (Texas starts interest running from a date after the injury, to account for the fact that not all losses—neither pain nor lost income—accrue instantly upon the injury in tort cases.) South Dakota, by statute, precludes prejudgment interest on intangible losses.

Calculating Interest. Interest rates vary significantly among jurisdictions. Interest rates often are set by statutes. Statutes may fix the rate at a particular percentage or may specify an index that allows the rate to float with the economy. The most common choices for floating rates are Treasury Bills and the prime rate for borrowing. Occasionally, states will specify the rate of interest on judgments, but leave the prejudgment interest rate unspecified. Courts in these jurisdictions tend to use the judgment rate for prejudgment interest, rather than set a different rate. In some jurisdictions, interest rates are committed to the discretion of the courts. Even in these jurisdictions, the freedom to set the rate may be circumscribed by judicial decision. For instance, some states hold that it is an abuse of discretion to pick a rate other than the Treasury Bill rate (or the prime interest rate), unless substantial evidence justifies a different rate.

Interest typically accrues from the date of the loss. Frequently, this will be the date of the injury. For the failure to pay money, this would be the date the payment was due. When interest is awarded for other losses (such as property damage), the date the plaintiff incurred expenses might be chosen instead of the date of the injury. In some states, interest may run from the date that plaintiff submitted a demand stating the liquidated amount claimed. The date of filing the complaint also has been used; the complaint serves the same function as a demand letter.

Compensation seems to require use of the date the loss occurred. From the moment the plaintiff suffers an out of pocket loss—when he has not received money, has paid money, or has borrowed substitute money—the obligation to pay interest on that money or the inability to use that money for other purposes starts to mount. Later dates sometimes reflect the use of interest for different purposes, such as to deter litigation delay or refusal to settle. In other situations, however, it amounts to a simplifying assumption that avoids complex calculations. Where payment would have been received (or costs incurred) on multiple occasions spread over a period of time, calculating interest on the entire amount from a single date simplifies the math. In theory, the date should fall somewhere between the first and the last occasion for the loss. In some cases, the simplification is not just an effort to avoid calculating the amount due on each installment. If interest is due on intangible losses, such as pain and suffering or lost services of a parent or spouse, the timing and amount of each loss may be unknowable. Selecting a single date for interest to start accruing on these losses is no less precise than pretending that the pain or services could be quantified for each day and interest assessed on that amount from that date.

Prejudgment interest applies only to past harms; future harms must be discounted to present value. (In effect, this reduces the claim by the amount of interest the plaintiff will earn on the award until the time the loss actually occurs—the logical opposite of increasing recovery for past losses by interest that would have been paid to borrow the amount of the harms.) Nonetheless, some statutes appear to authorize prejudgment interest on future damages. Sometimes, prejudgment interest on future damages begins to run on the date of a verdict or other significant ruling. For instance, in one New York case, interest on future pain and suffering ran from the date the appellate court reversed the trial court's denial of the plaintiff's motion for partial summary judgment.

Distinguishing past harms from future harms can pose difficulty. For example, destruction of an apartment building deprives the owner of the value of the property. But the value of the property typically is based on capitalizing the future income stream, reducing it to present value. (That is how much another owner would likely pay for the apartment building.) The future income stream, measured directly, would be a future loss, the loss of income before trial would be a past loss. But the lost value of the property is an immediate loss. Similarly, a tort victim unable to work suffers a loss of past income before trial and future income after trial. But in some jurisdictions, the entire loss is treated as a loss of earning capacity, a loss the plaintiff suffered immediately when the disability occurred. Because loss of earning capacity is measured by the future income stream, treating it all as a past loss seems unrealistic. The error can be minimized by reducing the income stream to present value as of the date of the disability. In effect, this takes interest (at the discount rate) out of all earnings (whether before or after the trial) and adds interest (at the prejudgment interest rate) back into the earnings from the date of the disability. The difference between the two rates may cause some injustice. Because discount rates contain an element of speculation (concerning the appropriate interest rate for unknown future events), it seems better not to apply that rate to the relatively certain past losses.

Allowing Recovery to Exceed Interest. In several situations, courts have allowed plaintiffs to recover consequential damages for the nonpayment of money, even when the result exceeds interest on the sum due. While some cases fit general patterns, others are more ad hoc.

Bad Faith. When a party who owes money lacks a good faith justification for not paying, courts may award damages that exceed interest. Insurers frequently face judgments of this sort. A bad faith refusal to pay a claim leads courts to allow consequential damages in excess of interest. (Bad faith also may justify emotional distress and punitive damages, despite the rule that these recoveries do not apply to contract actions. Calling bad faith breach of insurance contracts a tort circumvents these restrictions.) Liability insurers face the same result if they lack good faith in refusing to settle litigation against the insured. Consequential damages typically include the entire judgment against the insured, even if it exceeds the policy limits specified in the insurance contract. Courts do not limit recovery to interest on the amount not paid.

Other cases of bad faith, especially bad faith by banks that refuse to let depositors withdraw their money, extend the principle. These other examples have not achieved the widespread acceptance of insurance cases.

Lenders. Lenders who refuse to fund specific projects face damages beyond interest in some states. Both parties contemplate a specific investment opportunity. Losses the plaintiff suffered from losing that investment opportunity are fairly attributable to the lender. Plaintiff cannot identify some other investment that might have proven profitable, thus reducing concerns for 20–20 hindsight.

For example, defendant may breach a promise to provide plaintiff a mortgage for purchase of specific land. Consequential damages may include appreciation on the land. This principle could extend to other investors, such as partners. These cases usually involve investments that are relatively easy to measure. Real estate investments, where appraisal is fairly standard and reliable, produce judgments for ensuing losses more readily than business investments, where the profit of the business might be difficult to prove.

Actual Interest Losses. If plaintiff did borrow substitute funds, courts sometimes substitute that amount for interest at the legal rate. This accords with the basic goal: to put plaintiff in the position she would have occupied if the wrong had not occurred.

2. Loss of Use

Loss of use refers to the inability to use a thing that has been damaged or destroyed (or not delivered), pending repair or replacement. Repair or replacement will restore the value of the thing to the plaintiff; the loss of use in the interim requires separate attention. Loss of use pending repair or replacement may be temporary, but in other cases loss of use will be permanent. For instance, land submerged beneath a lake or a freeway may never be restored. Physical injury may disable a person permanently, preventing some or all employment. Where cover cannot occur in time, a special opportunity to make a profit (or get a business off to a good start) may disappear entirely, rather than merely being delayed.

Three common techniques help measure loss of use:

(1) the reasonable cost to plaintiff of obtaining (usually renting) a substitute, if plaintiff reasonably can obtain a substitute.

(2) the amount of additional profit plaintiff would have earned using the original thing, if plaintiff cannot reasonably obtain a substitute.

(3) the lost rental value (the amount plaintiff might have received by renting the thing to another), if lost profits are unavailable (usually because uncertain).

All three measures share a focus: how much is it worth to have the property for a period of time.

Cost of a Temporary Substitute. The cost to rent a substitute offers the easiest approach to loss of use. By renting a substitute, plaintiff prevents other losses, such as profits lost because the property was unavailable. Thus, where a business's delivery van is damaged, renting a substitute will allow the company to continue to make deliveries (and profits). The rental value of similar property may be easy to calculate—easier, at least, than estimating the amount of profit plaintiff would have earned if the property had not been damaged. The benefit is even greater when the property was not used to generate profit, but simply provided pleasure to the owner. Works of art, consumer electronics, recreational vehicles (snowmobiles, speedboats), furniture, kitchen gadgets (espresso machine, blender), and hundreds of other possessions produce no profit for the owner, but make life more pleasant. Using the rental cost of these possessions obviates difficult efforts to estimate in dollars the utility (joy) that these items provide.

Temporary substitutes affect a range of possible cases. Rental cars (or cabs and buses) substitute for a damaged car. A hotel or apartment may substitute for a damaged house. A temporary employee may substitute for a regular employee pending her return or replacement. A cleaning service may help a family while awaiting the return to health of a family member.

In each case, the cost of a substitute may be offset by savings. While staying in a hotel pending home repairs, plaintiff's utility bills may be lower than they would have been if the house was occupied. While taking the bus to work, plaintiff may save on parking that she would have incurred if driving to work. The net loss is recoverable, not the gross cost of the substitute.

Courts prefer to award the cost of a substitute when possible. By avoiding lost profits or other consequences of the loss, a substitute often reduces the total loss. Thus, the avoidable consequences doctrine may limit recovery to the cost of a substitute. The cost of a substitute usually can be ascertained relatively easily by looking at the market or, better still, at the actual substitute transaction plaintiff made. Lost profits, on the other hand, can be difficult to measure. Similarly, if no substitutes are available in the market, estimating the amount plaintiff could have obtained in the market by leasing the one she had to someone else (the third technique here) poses difficult issues.

Plaintiff may recover the cost of a reasonable substitute. If plaintiff makes substitute arrangements, that transaction will quantify the loss if it was reasonable and made in good faith. If plaintiff does not make substitute arrangements, the market price of a reasonable substitute should prevent excessive damages. Two problems can arise. First, the substitute might give the plaintiff more than she had before. If defendant damaged a 10-year-old

Yugo, renting a new Ferrari will put plaintiff in a better position than she would have occupied but for the wrong. Second, the substitute might cost more than necessary. For instance, a defendant who expects defendant to pay may agree to terms above market price. In either case, the court may not allow the full cost of the substitute.

In some cases, a vastly superior substitute may be reasonable. It might be the least expensive substitute that is at least as good as the original. For instance, few rental companies carry 20-year-old cars. To obtain a substitute, plaintiff may be forced to rent a better (at least newer) vehicle.

Paying more than the market price for a substitute may be reasonable. Spending more time looking for a better substitute price may increase both the incidental cost of seeking a substitute and the losses pending the arrival of the substitute. Courts probably award the actual cost of a substitute, as long as plaintiff had good reasons to accept an offer. Even a substitute that turns out to be above market price (in hindsight) may suffice. Plaintiff need not find the least expensive substitute, only a reasonable substitute, one within the range of prices acceptable in the market. A deal may be good enough to make it unnecessary to keep looking for a better price.

Lost Profits. Lost profits refers to the financial benefits the plaintiff would have obtained by using the damaged thing. In theory, the concept can include lost utility or joy, though the difficulty of quantifying nonpecuniary gains and converting them into a dollar amount weakens efforts to recover intangible gains. Because a substitute for the damaged thing usually will allow a plaintiff to avoid all or some of these losses, courts often need not measure lost profits directly. In many cases, however, a plaintiff lacks a reasonable way to avoid lost profits. The rightful position standard then compels efforts to include these losses in the recovery. For example, manufacturing equipment may be difficult to replace, especially for a short time. If defendant injures plaintiff's equipment, production may cease, reducing profits for the year.

Lost profits raise several intricate factual issues. A plaintiff with excess capacity or a limited market may not lose any sales despite a temporary halt to production. In this case, profits might be no lower, despite the injury. Similarly, sales might be delayed rather than lost. Additional effort after obtaining a substitute may produce as much profit as plaintiff would have received if no wrong ever occurred. For example, once a machine is back in service, a manufacturer may be able to increase production for a few days, eventually selling as much product as it would have but for the injury. If no sales were lost and no costs increased (*e.g.*, production increased without paying extra for overtime), the profit may have been delayed rather than lost. (If plaintiff could have sold both the production from the lost days and the increased output with the substitute, it is a lost volume seller. The later production did not substitute for the earlier production because plaintiff could have done both and earned even more profit.)

The issues surrounding lost profit often involve accounting. A basic understanding of how a business runs and how accountants calculate profits would help. In most cases, however, a careful, thoughtful comparison of how much the business earned compared to how much it would have earned but for the wrong will produce a good answer. *See* section E.3., *infra.*

Rental Value. The inability to obtain a substitute or to show lost profits does not mean the thing had no value to the plaintiff. The owner of a thing can rent it to another, at least in theory. Being deprived of the thing deprives the owner of this ability. If a court can determine how much the plaintiff might have received if it had leased the property to another for the period of deprivation, it can compensate plaintiff for the lost use of the property. This may be hard to ascertain. If a rental market were available, the first measure (cost for plaintiff to rent) would apply. Thus, courts may need to use the capitalization of earnings technique to appraise the rental value. Capitalization of earnings, however, uses the earning potential of property to estimate its rental value. In effect, this simply shifts the focus from the plaintiff's lost profits to the profits that a hypothetical lessee might have made using the thing. But if reliable data on lost profits were available, plaintiff probably could prove its own profit without recourse to this measure. The technique might work well if plaintiff claims an unusual profit, where lack of foreseeability or certainty precludes recovery. Moving to a hypothetical lessee's profit (expressed in the amount it would pay to rent the item) permits the court to include some recovery for this loss, without allowing recovery of unusual (and perhaps unrealistic) amounts that plaintiff claims.

Archaic Limitations. Traditionally, courts awarded loss of use when property was damaged, but not when it was destroyed. Repairs obviously required some time, but courts seemed to infer that replacement would be immediate. Courts have begun to recognize that replacement also requires time, at least under some circumstances. A new car can be replaced in a matter of hours, once the owner knows the old one cannot be repaired. But an armored car, a garbage truck, or an airliner may take weeks, months, or even years to replace. The more specialized the property, the less likely it is that sellers keep a large inventory on hand for immediate delivery. Thus, many courts now award loss of use for damaged or destroyed property. To the extent that replacement takes less time than repair, loss of use will be smaller in these cases, but not denied.

Courts traditionally denied recovery for loss of use if it exceeded the value of the damaged property. If the cost of a substitute pending repairs exceeds the cost to replace the property, a reasonable person probably would forego repairs and simply replace the property now—at least if they were spending their own money instead of another's. Thus, ensuing loss might affect the decision regarding the reasonableness of undertaking repairs in the first place. In some cases, however, unforeseen delays may extend the period for loss of use. A decision that seemed reasonable when repairs began may seem unreasonable in hindsight, once delays are factored into the calculation. Courts that cap recovery at the value of the property often fail to put plaintiff in as good a position as if defendant had never damaged the property. Plaintiff paid for the repairs and the substitute (pending repairs), both reasonable decisions when made, but recovers less than these costs. The remedial goal does not support this limitation in all cases. Courts are beginning to recognize this problem and treat cases individually, rather than mechanically apply the traditional cap to all cases. Applying the avoidable consequences doctrine allows plaintiff to recover these costs if they are reasonable, but denies them where plaintiff acted unreasonably.

3. Lost Profits

Lost profit begins with the realization that some property may be more valuable to the plaintiff than it is to the market. That surplus might be included in the value of the thing itself, particularly if plaintiff simply values having the thing (as a collector might). Often, however, the value to the plaintiff reflects the way the plaintiff intended to use the thing. The use would have generated additional benefits to plaintiff. Where the additional benefits take the form of money, plaintiff suffers lost profits.

As discussed above, loss of use of property may deprive a plaintiff of financial gains. Courts, therefore, measure loss of use by the amount of lost profit. Lost profits also arise from nondelivery, as in breach of contract cases. Nondelivery under a contract and destruction in tort produce the same effect: plaintiff could have used the property but for the wrong, but cannot do so after the wrong. The differences in terminology produce very little difference in result. Nonetheless, a few issues arise more often in contract than in tort. This section deals with lost profits more directly and in somewhat more detail.

Courts and legislatures historically exhibited hostility to lost profits. The further removed from the value of the thing itself, the more other factors intervene to limit the loss. Courts found rationalizations for this reluctance: causation, remoteness, uncertainty, foreseeability, avoidability, etc. Most of the surviving doctrines are addressed later in this chapter. Even today, the Uniform Commercial Code excludes consequential losses unless explicitly mentioned in the code. UCC § 1–305 (formerly § 1–106). Growing economic sophistication has led courts to permit recovery of lost profits, as long as the evidence sufficiently establishes that, but for the wrong, plaintiff would have benefitted from the project.

Losses to a Project. Lost profits depend on the project in which plaintiff planned to use the item. The simplest project involves resale of the item. Depriving the plaintiff of an item prevents plaintiff from selling it to another at a higher price. The difference (minus the cost of resale) represents the lost profit. That gain often appears in the value of the property itself, if value is based on the amount the plaintiff could realize by selling the property, as opposed to the amount it would cost to buy substitute property. The difference may reflect the difference between markets: plaintiff might sell retail but buy wholesale, with market price differing depending on the market. Where market price reflects the gains a plaintiff might have realized, direct losses may fully compensate the injury. Where market price does not reflect plaintiff's potential gains, lost profits must supplement the direct loss based on market price.

In other cases, the project may be less direct. A bootmaker buys leather, but does not resell it until converting it into boots. Depriving the bootmaker of the leather may reduce profits on boot sales, not on the resale of leather. Thus, merely compensating the buyer for the value of the leather (even retail value) will not capture the entire loss. Similarly, a plaintiff may buy or rent land as part of a business (whether farming, ranching, retail, or manufacturing). If defendant deprives plaintiff of the land, the entire project may suffer. Simply awarding the value of the land may not restore the plaintiff to the position she would have occupied if the wrong had not occurred. When plaintiff intends to use defendant's services as part of a larger project, depriving plaintiff of those services may threaten an entire project (whether a movie, a concert, a lecture, or some other service). In some cases, direct loss will permit plaintiff to replace the key element in time to prevent loss to the venture.

When that is not possible, loss to the project, not just loss of the services, is necessary to put plaintiff in the rightful position.

Courts have recognized the necessity of awarding lost profits in almost every context. Yet courts fear that plaintiffs often exaggerate their profits. Limitations on remedies, discussed below, take on great significance in this context. If a plaintiff reasonably could have avoided lost profits by reasonable use of substitutes, recovery will be limited. If the profits claimed were unforeseeably large, recovery may be limited. If the evidence of lost profits leaves uncertainty, profits may be limited. Where the link between the wrong and the lost profits becomes too remote, profits may be limited. Naturally, any loss that would have been suffered despite the breach will not be included in recovery.

Measuring lost profits often involves issues of accounting rather than of law. Arguments focus on the accuracy of revenue projections, the inclusion of all appropriate costs, allowance for any costs saved as a result of the wrong, proper calculation of overhead, and similar issues. Plaintiffs occasionally include in lost profits elements already compensated in other components of the remedy. Defendants occasionally seek to double count the savings. Careful attention to detail pays off.

Considerations of lost profit will vary from context to context, yet some generalities may help you identify all the important considerations. Generally, profit consists of revenue minus costs. Revenue depends on the quantity sold and the price for each unit (each widget, each text message, each hour worked, each share of stock, etc.) Costs depend on both variable costs and fixed costs. Variable costs include items that increase as the quantity increases: raw materials, labor, perhaps electricity consumption, sales commissions, etc. Fixed costs consist of overhead, costs that are incurred regardless of the quantity produced: the cost of the business location (rent or debt service), the management costs (including staff such as human resources and accounting, which do not depend on the quantity produced), most utilities, office supplies, etc. A share of the overhead is attributable to each unit of production. Costs also can be divided among those incurred despite the wrong and those saved because of the wrong. For example, if breach by a leather supplier precludes a bootmaker from producing boots, it not only saves the cost of the leather, but might save labor by laying off employees and might save electricity by shutting down the production line (until a substitute supply is found). But contracts with employees may preclude saving money on labor, even if no production work is done. Fixed costs typically are not saved as a result of breach.

Any profit that would have been earned in the years following judgment must be reduced to present value. Plaintiff will be able to invest the award and earn returns on it. Present value estimates how much the plaintiff must receive today in order to have the right amount, after investment income, in the year the profit would have been earned. For example, suppose that plaintiff would have earned $100,000 in profit in the third year after judgment and can invest the money safely at a 4% return. If awarded the full $100,000 in the judgment, after two years she would have $108,160—more than the profit she would have earned in the third year. Instead, the court should award $92,455.62. After two years at 4%, this will produce $100,000, the amount plaintiff deserves in the third year. Calculation of present value is illustrated above, in the discussion of capitalization of earnings.

4. Lost Earning Potential

Physical injuries may reduce earning potential. Temporary injuries may prevent plaintiffs from earning income while they heal—or perhaps simply because the wrong delayed the plaintiff. Those costs are relatively easy to calculate and uncontroversial. Lost earnings from a long-term disability that prevents plaintiff from pursuing her career pose larger issues. The same calculation issues can arise from breach of an employment contract, wrongful discharge torts, or discrimination suits.

Future Increases. Plaintiff's current income is some evidence of future income, but not a limit on it. Raises, promotions, moves to a new company, and other changes might produce future improvements in the plaintiff's income. Even if plaintiff's current job offered limited chances for increased pay, that may not limit lost income claims if future career changes seem likely. The rightful position standard does not allow recovery for amounts plaintiff *might* have earned, but only amounts that she *would* have earned. Thus, mere speculation of career changes has little place in the calculations. But amounts plaintiff would have earned but for the wrong include any career changes plaintiff would have made.

In some cases, especially children, earning potential may be destroyed before plaintiff's career path was set. Courts must make some effort to project future income, even though certainty is impossible. The average income for similarly situated people may be as close as a court can come.

Ending Liability. Defendant's liability for future losses of income may not extend indefinitely. Depending on the wrong and the injury, liability may end at some future date.

If plaintiff suffers a permanent disability from any work, defendant's liability probably extends to the date the plaintiff would have retired. If the wrong also deprived the plaintiff of retirement benefits that she would have received, the award might include loss of those benefits for the duration of plaintiff's life expectancy. Some experts rely on actuarial tables showing work-life expectancy, which projects how many months a plaintiff would have worked during the rest of her life. The projections include not only retirement, but also the likelihood that layoffs or other events might interrupt the plaintiff's work life, reducing the number of months during which she earned income.

Injured plaintiffs often can resume work, perhaps after rehabilitation or by changing careers to one they can still perform. Lost income in this setting requires an estimate of both when plaintiff will return to work and how much plaintiff will earn after returning. Estimates of the time required to recover from the injury or to retrain for a more suitable position will vary with each case. For the period before return, courts award the full lost income (subject to avoided or avoidable consequences).

Once a plaintiff returns to work, damages should include the difference between the amount plaintiff actually earns and the amount she would have earned if the wrong had not occurred. In some cases, plaintiff's earnings following return will equal the amount she would have earned if there had been no interruption. That is particularly likely if the plaintiff pursues the same career path, she was on before the wrong. Income seems likely to follow the same pattern it would have followed but for the wrong, in effect eliminating losses following return. A period of absence may harm plaintiff's subsequent advancement. For example, seniority may be lower, promotion and raises may be slower, pensions may take longer to vest, 401k investments may have less time to grow, etc. If residual losses exist, damage calculations should include the difference between income if uninjured and income projected following the injury.

Projecting earnings poses more difficulty if plaintiff pursues a new career, particularly a career that exhibits large variations in income potential. Consider a surgeon who, after an injury to her hands, pursues a law degree. The differences between starting salaries in big law firms, small law firms, government offices, and public interest law groups make it difficult to project future income. If the projected new income stream is lower than the projected original income stream, then residual losses should be included in the damage calculation.

Courts differ over how to treat a new income stream that exceeds the old. The benefit rule (*see* section G.2., *infra*) would offset the increased income against other pecuniary harms caused by the wrong. Alternatively, some courts decide that pursuing a more lucrative career puts an end to defendant's liability. No further losses or gains (at least to income) require calculation thereafter. In effect, this assumes that the plaintiff would have changed careers even if uninjured, so that any additional benefit is not a result of the breach, but independent of it. Ending liability is a double edged sword, cutting off both subsequent harms and subsequent gains. If the higher earnings in the new career are temporary, ending liability precludes a demand for the difference between the earnings in the original career and the new career.

Discharge from employment deprives a person of income from one employer, but does not disable the plaintiff. Context may dictate the period during which defendant remains liable for lost income. In contract claims, the contract duration term will set the end of liability. Defendant promised income to the plaintiff for a particular time, not indefinitely. Losses beyond that time are not attributable to the wrong. Defendant could have refused to renew the contract without committing a wrong. (Where the contract does not specify an end date, it is terminable at will by either party. Discharge in this setting usually is not a breach at all. In jurisdictions that allow recovery for discharge in bad faith or for retaliatory discharge, the analysis of tort claims fits contracts at will fairly well.)

In tort claims and discrimination claims, the duration is not so easily fixed. Plaintiff might have remained defendant's employee indefinitely; no term fixes a time when defendant could refuse further employment without liability. Yet employment for life was never promised. It seems unrealistic to assume that defendant never would have fired plaintiff for a legitimate reason. The assumption converts defendant into a guarantor of plaintiff's future employment—something plaintiff never could claim but for the breach. While the duration of employment could be left to the evidence, proof (with reasonable certainty) that a plaintiff would have retained this job until retirement may not be possible.

The avoidable consequences doctrine can help to fix the end date for liability. Once plaintiff obtains substitute employment of similar nature (or would have, if she had made reasonable efforts to find substitute employment), defendant's liability ends. See *Ford Motor Co. v. E.E.O.C.*, 458 U.S. 219, 102 S.Ct. 3057, 73 L.Ed.2d 721 (1982). The avoidable consequences doctrine was not designed for this task and may be difficult to apply. First, defining similar employment may prove troublesome. The avoidable consequences doctrine often produces very restrictive applications, which would allow a plaintiff to reject a large number of plausible substitute jobs. While arguably appropriate when liability ends at the conclusion of a contract, use in this new setting may produce excessively long liability terms. Second, cutting off liability might preclude recovery if substitute work pays less than the position with defendant.

Present Value. As with lost profits, courts must discount future wages to present value. Awarding full future wages today would overcompensate plaintiff, once he earned investment income on the award. Several techniques have been devised for discounting, usually in an effort to simplify calculations and increase accuracy. Understanding the basic procedure facilitates discussion of the differences in these techniques.

The calculation below involves a plaintiff who would have earned $50,000 a year at the time of judgment and would have received a 5% raise each year until retiring five years after the judgment. (Any income lost before trial would be augmented by prejudgment interest, not discounted to present value.) The calculation assumes that safe investments will pay plaintiff a 2% rate of return on the judgment. Both the rate of increased earnings and the likely future interest rates require evidence. Experts hired by each party may differ in the numbers selected for these two aspects of the calculation.

Year	Salary	Discount	Award
Judgment + 1	$ 52,500.00	0.98039216	$ 51,470.59
Judgment + 2	$ 55,125.00	0.96116878	$ 52,984.43
Judgment + 3	$ 57,881.25	0.94232233	$ 54,542.79
Judgment + 4	$ 60,775.31	0.92384543	$ 56,146.99
Judgment + 5	$ 63,814.08	0.90573081	$ 57,798.38
Total	$290,095.64		$272,943.18

The Salary column shows the amount plaintiff actually would have earned. A table of discount rates provides the Discount column. Multiplying Salary times Discount gives an amount that, if invested at 2% for the number of years available (one for Judgment + 1, five for Judgment + 5, etc.), will produce a total equal to the Salary column. In other words, if awarded $272,943.18, plaintiff can invest it at 2% and, after one year, withdraw $52,500, after two years withdraw $55,125, etc. After the fifth year, when she withdraws $63,814.08, nothing will be left. Plaintiff will have withdrawn $290,095.64 over the years, exactly what she would have earned if the wrong had not occurred.

This calculation uses the traditional method. It projects actual increases in future wages and discounts by an actual interest rate at which the plaintiff might invest. Thus, increases in wages include increases for inflation and the interest rate includes an amount believed necessary to account for inflation. Inflation, however, is notoriously difficult to predict. Projections often underestimate or overestimate actual increases in income. Changes in inflation will affect interest rates. Thus, projections of investment income also may be too high or too low. If plaintiff's investments perform better or worse than the rate assumed in the present value calculation, then the compensation may be excessive or inadequate. Problems projecting inflation increase as the time period increases. With 20 years to go before retirement, the risks of error increase dramatically. Despite these concerns, courts continue to accept expert testimony employing the traditional method.

The partial offset method seeks to remove inflation from the calculation of present value. It performs the same calculation using real rates for increases in wages and interest. (Real means the extent to which income increases and long-term interest rates exceed the inflation rate.) Income increases that exceed inflation are called productivity increases, reflecting the tendency of wages to increase as productivity (of an individual, of a particular industry or of the economy as a whole) increases. Rather than increasing income by 5%, it would subtract the rate of inflation (say, 2%) to determine how much income really increased—in this example, 3%. The method also uses a long-term real interest rate—the difference between interest rates and inflation rates, over the long term. While plaintiff might earn 2% on an investment, some of that would offset inflation. The real interest rate might be 1% or so. (If inflation has been 2%, people receiving only 2% on their investments merely break even. They get more dollars, but the dollars are worth less. That rate is unstable; over time, people will demand more than a break-even interest rate on their investments, even if the interest rate, for now, is less than the inflation rate. This kind of anomaly illustrates why the long-term real interest rate is used.) On these assumptions, the calculation would produce a slightly smaller recovery.

Year	Salary	Discount	Award
Judgment + 1	$ 51,500.00	0.99009901	$ 50,990.10
Judgment + 2	$ 53,045.00	0.98029605	$ 51,999.80
Judgment + 3	$ 54,636.35	0.97059015	$ 53,029.50
Judgment + 4	$ 56,275.44	0.96098034	$ 54,079.59
Judgment + 5	$ 57,963.70	0.95146569	$ 55,150.48
Total	$273,420.49		$265,249.47

The smaller recovery reflects, in part, the use of a long-term interest rate (1%) rather than the short term real interest rate (0%, where inflation of 2% eats up the entire 2% investment income). On different assumptions, the result could be larger rather than smaller. The partial offset method has been approved, but not compelled, by the U.S. Supreme Court.

The total offset method assumes that real increases in wages will exactly match real interest rates. If so, projecting wage increases and discounting to present value serves no purpose. Instead, courts could multiply current wages times the number of years of remaining work to produce future lost wages. In this example, the award would be $250,000—current income times five years. Parties may stipulate to this method. The Supreme Court rejected efforts to use this method over a party's objection. *Jones & Laughlin Steel Corp. v. Pfeifer*, 462 U.S. 523, 103 S.Ct. 2541, 76 L.Ed.2d 768 (1983).

Selecting an appropriate interest rate vitally affects calculations of present value. A higher interest rate produces a smaller damage award; a high interest rate assumes plaintiff will earn more money by investing the award, requiring less initial money from defendant to make plaintiff whole. Plaintiffs argue for low interest rates, while defendants' experts typically use higher rates. Invariably, a plaintiff can find investments that return a reasonably high rate of return—and might choose those investments in an effort to maximize the ultimate recovery. If plaintiff does elect investments at a higher rate of return, using a lower rate in the calculation of present value overcompensates plaintiff. But using a higher interest rate undercompensates plaintiff unless she invests the money at that higher rate of return. Higher rates of return often involve higher risk; the investment may decline. (Junk bonds pay high yields, but the issuer may fail, leaving the holder with nearly worthless paper.) If her investments do not pay as expected, plaintiff faces undercompensation.

Courts normally resolve this dilemma in favor of an interest rate that allows plaintiff to invest safely—that is, a lower interest rate. Once the court determines that plaintiff is entitled to receive a particular amount in damages, courts ensure that plaintiff can receive that amount, without forcing plaintiff to engage in risky investments to achieve his rightful position.

F. INTANGIBLE LOSS

Some losses defy market classifications. The most obvious are pain, distress, and indignity. Similar losses can ensue from property damage, especially where the property has special significance to the owner. The subjective value of property relates closely to emotional distress, making it useful to treat them together.

Intangible losses are real. People generally prefer to live without pain (for example) rather than to suffer through it. Assigning monetary values to intangibles presents difficulties. Unlike goods that people buy and sell regularly, few people ever bargain their way out of (or into) pain, distress, indignity, or other intangible losses. Thus, no market sets the price for pain, distress, and indignity. Juries do their best to estimate the value of intangibles based on limited testimony and experience. The resulting awards vary wildly—whether wildly excessive or wildly inadequate. With no benchmark against which to compare the award, one cannot reach a definitive conclusion as to whether an award is too high, too low, or just right. This section raises some of the techniques that have been or might be used to bring a measure of order to intangible losses.

Aside from cases where plaintiff did not in fact suffer any pain, distress, indignity, or other intangible loss, assigning a value of zero seems inherently wrong. An award that covers all of the other losses but includes nothing for pain and suffering leaves plaintiff worse off than if the wrong had not occurred. Finding the right number may be impossible. If awards for pain invariably exceed the right number, perhaps zero will be closer to right than any other number a court can produce. But efforts to include pain have some chance of getting closer to the right level. So far, at least, courts have not resorted to the one number they know is wrong.

1. Terminology

One difficulty discussing intangibles arises from the array of terms used to describe various aspects of these losses. No precise usage governs how people describe feelings of this sort. Thus, the terms mean different things to each writer. A few definitions may help to keep the meanings consistent within this text, even though others may use them in slightly different ways.

a. Pain refers to the unpleasant (or worse) physical sensation felt as a result of a physical injury.

b. Suffering refers to both pain and the unpleasant (or worse) thoughts that accompany a physical injury. Thus, suffering includes thoughts about the injury. This may include the anticipation of future pain, worry about supporting one's self or family, worry about how to pay doctors, despair over disabilities (related either to work or to leisure activities), and a myriad of other thoughts that may plague a victim of physical injury.

c. Distress refers to unpleasant (or worse) thoughts produced by wrongs that do not initially cause a physical injury to the distressed person. Thus, relatives of an injured person may suffer distress. So may individuals exposed to insults, libel, humiliation, or other indignities.

d. Loss of joy (or lost enjoyment of life) refers to the reduced ability to experience joy. It may result from injuries that preclude awareness of the joys of life, but also applies to disabilities that prevent a person from participating in activities that previously provided joy.

e. Subjective Value refers to value of something to an individual, particularly where the person attaches more value to the item than a reasonable person would. Thus, the value to the person may exceed the market value.

2. Subjective Value

Market value is objective value—the amount a reasonable person would pay. Often, items have greater value to one person than to the market. That value to the individual is subjective value. Examples include wedding photos, pets, or the family farm. Few others would pay much for your wedding photos or your cat; for the farm, market value might be higher. But a person might refuse enormous sums for any of these because these things bring her more joy than the money could provide. When defendant deprives plaintiff of property he values more than the market, compensation at the market rate may not make plaintiff as well off as he would have been but for the wrong.

Subjective value can apply to almost any property plaintiff was not actively trying to sell. (Subjective value may not be limited to property. Leisure time may have subjective value that exceeds the market rate at which others would pay for the person's time.) The preference to keep the property may reflect a value that exceeds what plaintiff thought she could receive in exchange for the property. In other cases, however, the decision not to sell does not reflect subjective value, but an underappreciation of market value. The owner may be mistaken in believing that no one would pay enough to make it worth the effort to look for a buyer. Thus, subjective value generally requires proof; courts will not assume it exists.

Plaintiff's claim that property had special value to him is hard to prove or to disprove. If an owner recently rejected a bona fide offer for the property, that refusal evinces the subjective value. (Subjective value probably exceeds the offered amount, though by how much remains uncertain.) Similarly, if a person recently offered to buy the property for an amount above market price, that offer (if bona fide) evinces subjective value. But without direct evidence of this sort, efforts to estimate subjective value may leave plaintiff better off than if the wrong had not occurred. Consider two examples.

Defendant damaged plaintiff's car, worth $10,000 before the injury but only $3,000 after. Repairs will cost $15,000, but plaintiff argues repair is justified because the car has special value to him. If allowed to recover $15,000, plaintiff might repair the car, achieving the position but for the wrong. But plaintiff might instead sell the car for $3,000 and use that money plus the award to buy an $18,000 car. If so, plaintiff is better off than if the wrong had not occurred: he should have a $10,000 car, instead he has an $18,000 car.

Defendant destroyed plaintiff's antique watch, which had a market value of $1,000. Plaintiff claims that watch was worth more to him, because it had belonged to his great grandfather. If true, awarding subjective value would compensate plaintiff. But if plaintiff really doesn't care about the watch and would have sold it if offered the opportunity, anything more than $1,000 makes plaintiff better off than if the wrong had not occurred.

Defendants have little chance to counter plaintiff's testimony concerning subjective value. This makes overcompensation hard to prevent. Courts exercise caution before accepting plaintiff's estimate of subjective value, even when the claim seems credible.

Measuring Subjective Value. Courts use several approaches to claims of subjective value. In evaluating property, courts may award: (a) market value; (b) cost to replace, to repair, or to reproduce; (c) value to the plaintiff; or (d) emotional distress. The last does not measure subjective value, but uses a different approach to providing compensation.

Market value does not measure subjective value, but rejects it. It denies subjective value for any good available in the market. This will not apply to unique items, such as photographs, keepsakes, heirlooms, etc. Because these items usually are not traded in the market, courts resort to other approaches. But market value might apply to claims that a car has sentimental value. If the same year and model is available on the market, that price will prevail.

The cost to replace or to reproduce property substitutes for subjective value in a few cases where reproduction will include subjective value. For example, if the wedding photographer has the negatives, new prints can be made to replace those destroyed by defendant. The new prints will have a market value near zero (to anyone but the plaintiffs). Awarding the cost to reproduce the property provides better compensation. Plaintiff has what she had before (wedding pictures of her wedding, though not the original prints). Damages should not be limited to the (lower) market value the prints would have once made. Similarly, injury to a companion animal can be compensated by the amount of veterinary bills. No matter how low the market value of the animal (and, thus, how unreasonable it may seem to repair rather than to replace the companion), cost to repair comes closer to reflecting the subjective loss the family would feel without the companion animal.

The value to the plaintiff includes the subjective value. In theory, it awards the lowest amount for which the owner would sell, if anyone would offer that amount. Estimates can get outrageously high because they cannot be subjected to market scrutiny. No one will offer these amounts. In addition, if defendant has destroyed the property, plaintiff no longer has it to sell, making it impossible to test the plaintiff's estimates by making a bona fide offer for the property. Thus, courts cannot put plaintiff to the test to see if he would really reject $50,000 for the wedding pictures and hold out for $1 million.

Some courts limit value to the plaintiff by awarding personal value, but rejecting sentimental value. That line lacks any clear application. All subjective value involves some sentiment or attachment beyond what reason would dictate. Excluding affected or mawkish sentimentality seems the goal. This language leaves room for juries to recognize personal value, while also leaving room for courts to reject outrageously large awards.

Another approach to subjective value focuses on the cost to obtain the item. Some property is worth less than the cost to get it. In effect, parties who obtain that property lose net worth by exchanging valuable money for things that lack market value. Their willingness to enter the transaction in the first place demonstrates that the goods have subjective value beyond the cost to obtain them. Wedding pictures must be worth at least the cost to obtain them (and to protect them in an acid-free paper album, etc.) Video tapes of family must be worth at least the cost of the blank tape, plus some portion of the cost of a video camera. Compensating the cost to obtain the property provides a minimal estimate of sentimental value. It will always undercompensate, but perhaps by less than other measures.

Subjective Value and Distress. Emotional distress closely relates to sentimental value, at least in some cases. When wedding pictures or companion animals are destroyed, the emotional impact on owners may dominate the case. Putting the issue in terms of the amount plaintiffs would accept to sell the pictures or companions converts an essentially emotional response into economic terms. In some situations, courts do not make that transition, dealing instead with the distress directly.

Treating subjective value in terms of distress usually disfavors plaintiffs. Normally, emotional distress over the loss of property would not be compensable. Even emotional distress over injuries to family members usually are not compensable, absent additional considerations. It would be odd to allow recovery for distress over injury to one's dog but not for distress over injury to one's child. Courts have awarded damages for distress in cases involving malicious or intentional property damage. Thus, when defendant maliciously killed plaintiff's dog, plaintiff might recover for the distress of the act. (This borders on converting the entire action into one for intentional infliction of emotional distress.) Courts resist distress claims when the property damage was merely negligent. Plaintiffs seeking recovery probably need to address subjective value directly.

Even when plaintiffs frame the case in terms of subjective value, courts sometimes move from a discussion of subjective value into a discussion of emotional distress. Because the rules on distress limit recovery severely, bypassing the subjective value works badly. It disregards the economic reality that returning the market value of property does not restore plaintiff to her rightful position.

3. Pain & Suffering

Juries may award a victim of physical injury compensation for the pain and suffering that result from the wrong. Trial courts may reject the award if it is against the great weight of the evidence. If a trial court does not remit the award or order a new trial on damages, an appellate court may intervene only if the award is so excessive that it shocks the conscience, as when the award is so large that it evinces passion, prejudice, corruption, whim, or caprice on the part of the jury. The exact language of the standard of review will vary among jurisdictions, but generally allows the jury considerable room to make awards. Some judges tend to defer to almost any amount a jury awards. Other judges seek to put more teeth into the test.

Consistency with Prior Awards. Courts often compare awards for pain and suffering with prior awards in the same jurisdiction. Courts sometimes reject or reduce an award when it seems outside the parameters set by earlier cases. For example, if earlier cases involving worse injuries produced smaller judgments for pain, a court may feel more confident in reducing the award.

This analysis has intuitive appeal, but confronts some difficulties. First, it must account for changing times. The amount appropriate 40 (or even 5) years ago may be inadequate today, whether due to inflation or changing societal values. Second, it assumes, without basis, that the earlier awards were correct. There is no benchmark by which to validate the earlier awards. They easily could have been too low and the present jury just right. Third, comparisons cannot account for individual differences in sensitivity to pain. Pain that some shrug off others find debilitating. Compensation for the same injury the same year might differ based on these differences among people.

Limit to Consciousness. Pain and suffering imply some element of awareness. Plaintiffs in a coma may be unable to recover for pain and suffering. Without some consciousness of their state, they may feel no pain and may have no thoughts courts recognize as suffering. See *MacDougald v. Garber*, 73 N.Y.2d 246, 536 N.E.2d 372, 538 N.Y.S.2d 937 (1989). Even conscious victims may suffer injuries that involve no pain, such as injuries that sever the nerves that convey pain to the mind. In other cases, a patient in a persistent vegetative state may react in ways that evince some level of awareness and pain. See *Wagner by Wagner v. York Hosp.*, 608 A.2d 496, 499 (Pa.Super.1992).

Per Diem Arguments. Plaintiffs' lawyers often ask juries to think of pain in terms of relatively small periods of time—for example, how much would compensate the plaintiff for one day (or hour or week) of this pain? Arguments of this sort are called per diem arguments. Typically, they result in much larger awards for pain than would result from considering the entire period as a whole. Small differences in the amount per day produce large differences when multiplied by many years.

Many courts allow per diem arguments, despite several concerns with the technique. Absent any testimony that a day of pain is worth a particular amount, the argument lacks any foundation in the evidence. Absent any market for pain, no evidentiary basis is possible. On the other hand, without any basis to call one amount wrong and another right, no one can say whether per diem arguments persuade jurors to award too much or prevent them from awarding too little.

Golden Rule Arguments. Plaintiffs sometimes suggest that jurors consider how much they would want if they suffered the plaintiff's injuries. This is called the golden rule argument—award unto plaintiff as you would have others award unto you. Courts almost always hold such arguments improper. By inviting jurors step into plaintiff's shoes, it undermines their role as impartial decisionmakers, evaluating the merits of the argument.

4. Lost Enjoyment of Life (Hedonic Damages)

Some injuries reduce a plaintiff's joy without causing physical pain. For example, spinal cord injuries and injuries that induce coma may produce no pain—even eliminating preexisting pain. These injuries, however, may severely reduce the plaintiff's capacity to enjoy life. Activities that once brought pleasure (tennis, dancing, reading) may be impossible following the injury. To put plaintiff in the position she would have occupied if the wrong had not occurred, compensation for the joy she will not experience seems necessary. Though logical, courts have not settled on a way to handle lost enjoyment of life in damage awards.

One issue focuses on whether to treat loss of joy as a separate heading of damages or to include it in the general category for pain and suffering. Logically, loss of joy is distinct from pain and suffering. A person in pain may nonetheless experience the same joys she always felt. An unconscious person may feel no pain, but nonetheless experience none of the joys he would have felt but for the injury.

In practice, however, getting juries to segregate these two aspects of loss may be difficult, particularly in cases where both are present. In many cases, the two will merge. A paraplegic denied the opportunity to pursue the delights of tennis may suffer anguish over that loss. That anguish could be treated as lost joy or as suffering. Awarding lost joy separately from pain and suffering creates a danger that the jury might include the same loss in both categories, effectively double counting that loss. The imprecise nature of these concepts makes it nearly impossible for a court to discern whether the jury award double-counted the loss of joy, raising the possibility that awards overcompensate.

Cases that award lost enjoyment of life usually involve injuries where pain and suffering are not available, thus eliminating concerns for double counting. Early awards for lost joy involved federal claims for violation of civil rights by depriving the victim of life. (Unlike wrongful death actions, no statute precluded recovery of nonpecuniary losses.) Even if the death was painless (or continued life would have been full of pain), death deprived the deceased victim of the joy future years might have brought. Confronted with living victims, whose injuries deprive them of some but not all of the joy the future holds, lost enjoyment has proven less appealing to courts. Measuring joy is as difficult as measuring pain—though perhaps joys have a market value. (The cost of substitute joys is measurable. One denied the ability to pursue tennis might take up fine wine or other joys the disability does not prevent.)

Juries can (and almost certainly do) consider loss of joy in evaluating pain and suffering. A paraplegic's inability to pursue activities she once enjoyed fits readily into the definition of suffering. Properly applied, no separate component for lost joy seems necessary. Courts can instruct juries on lost joy and pain and suffering together, allowing the jury to assess them as a whole. Evidence and arguments concerning lost joy would remain appropriate.

Combining lost joy with pain and suffering poses one danger: Limitations appropriate to pain and suffering may not apply to lost joy. For instance, a person with no consciousness may lose joy, even if she feels no pain. To apply the rule denying pain and suffering to lost joy may produce inadequate compensation for the plaintiff (or, more importantly, inadequate deterrence for defendants, since the unconscious plaintiff is unlikely to benefit from the award).

5. Indignity and Emotional Distress

Some wrongs inflict emotional harm (indignity or distress) without causing any pain or suffering. Torts such as intentional (or negligent) infliction of emotional distress recognize the importance of these harms. Some traditional torts, such as defamation and trespass, awarded damages even when no tangible loss could be proven. More recently, deprivation of constitutional rights may give rise to a cause of action, but the harm may consist of nothing more than an abstract sense of loss.

Awards for distress and indignity raise many of the same problems discussed under pain and suffering. If anything, distress and indignity may be even more subjective. All jurors have experienced pain from physical injury and can devise some manner of comparing it to the plaintiff's pain. But indignity and distress relate entirely to the plaintiff's reaction. Some let insults roll off their backs, others mull over them for years (or generations—some Irish still point to land that was theirs before Cromwell took it away in the 1650s). The severity of the harm depends largely on the mind of the plaintiff—and, in some cases, lies within the plaintiff's control. Dwelling on the injury may increase the harm (and hence the recovery). Getting on with one's life can be a conscious choice, albeit one that may reduce recovery.

Torts Involving Indignity. If a tort causes distress or indignity, courts include compensation for this injury. Like pain and suffering, courts allow juries wide discretion to determine an appropriate amount. Like pain and suffering, courts review the amount for excessiveness. Like pain and suffering, golden rule arguments are forbidden, but per diem arguments generally allowed (though not without controversy).

Plaintiffs generally try to prove actual damages. That is, they recount their distress, their reaction to the injury. Juries then award an amount to compensate for these harms. Distress and indignity are not measured and calculated. In affirming awards, however, courts tend to consider the outrageousness of defendant's conduct. That focus has some objective appeal: a reasonable plaintiff would suffer less from a minor affront than from an outrage. The focus on defendant's conduct, however, shifts focus away from the effects on the plaintiff. If the law seeks to put plaintiff in the position she would have occupied but for the wrong, the effects on the plaintiff may deserve more attention. The focus on defendants may reflect concern that plaintiffs exaggerate their emotional state, while defendants lack any means of rebutting their claims.

In some torts, plaintiffs seek presumed damages: an award unrelated to any actual harm plaintiff suffered, given to vindicate the right at issue. When available at all, presumed damages substitute for actual damages. For instance, when libel involves defamation per se, plaintiff may recover presumed damages. (Defamation per se applies to attributing a crime involving moral turpitude, a loathsome or contagious disease, or conduct that may injure a party's trade or occupation.) Presumed damages avoid concerns that plaintiff may suffer losses that cannot be proven or linked to the defamation. Similarly, trespass often produced presumed damages, even if no harm to the property occurred. Some statutes, such as the copyright act, allow presumed damages. *See, e.g.,* 17 U.S.C. § 504(c) (statutory damages). The amount of presumed damages varies with jurisdiction and context.

Distress in Contract Actions. Emotional distress in contract actions remains rare and limited. In most settings, courts limit recovery to tangible losses. Plaintiffs are expected to bear the emotional effects on their own. (It isn't personal, it's business—or, at least, it's contract.)

Courts occasionally award distress in several situations involving a contract:

1. where the breach also constitutes a tort;

2. where the breach causes physical injury;

3. where the breach or the contract is of a type that makes serious emotional distress particularly likely to occur.

The first is not really a contract action, at its root. The second involves pain and suffering more than emotional distress. The third group deserves some discussion.

Originally, courts created a very limited exception for distress in contract cases. It applied to cases where the entire loss seemed emotional. One common example involved mishaps with caskets at funerals. Normal damage rules (the casket's value as warranted minus its value as delivered) might be negligible or even zero. But the distress of seeing one's relative fall through the bottom of a casket justified some recovery. More recently, courts have expanded recovery for emotional distress slightly. It now includes some contracts where the plaintiff bargained for a performance that had largely emotional significance. For instance, when a vacation does not live up to the promises made, the effects are more emotional than financial. When plastic surgery does not live up to any warranties made by the surgeon, the effects are more emotional than financial. (Plastic surgery cases verge on the other two categories, but remain distinct. Liability for breach of warranty does not require professional negligence. Nor does the error need to qualify as an injury. Any difference between the promised result and the actual result constitutes breach.) The exception might stretch to cover breach of an insurance contact, where nonpayment seems particularly likely to cause distress. Most courts instead classify breaches of insurance contracts as torts, at least where insurers do not act in good faith. The extent of willingness to extend distress into contract recoveries varies widely. One court held that failure to pay disability insurance benefits did not involve a contract where distress was particularly likely. *Novick v. UnumProvident Corp.*, No. 01-CV-258, 2001 WL 793277 (E.D. Pa. July 10, 2001). Another court refused to dismiss claims for distress following improper foreclosure on a home. *Sinclair v. Donovan*, Nos. 1:11-CV-00010, 1:11-CV-00079, 2011 WL 5326093 (S.D. Ohio Nov. 4, 2011).

Constitutional Rights. Deprivation of a constitutional right may or may not involve actual losses. Some rights have substantive value—that is, depriving a party of that right causes direct damages. For example, wrongfully suspending a person's license to practice a profession causes lost income. The harm caused by the wrong provides a means to measure compensation. Denying procedural rights (such as a hearing or right to counsel) may have substantive effects, at least when proper procedures would have produced a different result (for example, no discharge from employment would have occurred if a hearing had been held). In these cases, damages for the substantive effects suffice—and usually fit within the other categories of damages. Damages for being fired remain the same, regardless of the wrong that caused the discharge. Lost income covers breach of contract, tortious retaliatory discharge, statutory discrimination, and denial of due process in considering the discharge.

Procedural rights may not affect the outcome. For example, the same result might have ensued even if a hearing had been held. Thus, the wrong did not cause harms that flow from the resulting decision (*e.g.*, suspension from school, discharge from a job, denial of a medical license). The wrong caused harms associated with the procedural default (*e.g.*, denying the hearing, limiting access to counsel, etc.). In these cases, identifying losses that flow from the harm poses more difficulty.

Some courts explored the possibility that deprivation of a right, in itself, constitutes a loss that courts can compensate even if no other losses result (or in addition to any other losses that result). The United States Supreme Court has rejected most claims that rights have independent, abstract value. *Carey v. Piphus*, 435 U.S. 247, 98 S.Ct. 1042, 55 L.Ed.2d 252 (1978). Where loss of the right is the only harm, plaintiff may recover nominal damages. Where loss of the right caused other losses, plaintiff may recover actual damages for those losses. Thus, distress caused by the loss of a right is recoverable. Evidence must link the distress to the loss of the right, not to the legal conduct of the defendant. For instance, in *Carey*, the plaintiffs proved distress, but did not prove whether the distress resulted from the wrong (denial of a hearing) or from conduct that was not wrongful (their suspension from school, which would have occurred even if the hearing had been held).

Damages for loss of the right to vote have been upheld. *Nixon v. Herndon*, 273 U.S. 536, 47 S.Ct. 446, 71 L.Ed. 759 (1927). The court distinguished these from the abstract value of rights, calling them "a particular injury—the inability to vote in a particular election—that might be compensated through substantial money damages." *Memphis Community School Dist. v. Stachura*, 477 U.S. 299, 106 S.Ct. 2537, 91 L.Ed.2d 249 (1986). *Stachura* rejected the suggestion that other substantive rights, such as the first amendment, justified damages aside from the harmful effects of the deprivation.

6. Wrongful Death and Survival Actions

Traditionally, most tort actions were personal to the victim. If the victim died, the right to recover for the injury died with her. Two independent methods prevent this injustice:

1. Survival actions, allowing the victim's action to survive her death; or

2. Wrongful death actions, allowing the victim's survivors to bring an action for causing the death.

States generally allow both, though they may differ in the line drawn between them.

Survival actions allow a deceased tort victim (through her estate) to recover for losses suffered between the time of the injury and the time of death—in some cases even if the time is a matter of minutes. Survival actions apply to torts that do not cause death. For instance, if a victim of defamation dies of unrelated causes before the case reaches judgment, the estate may continue pressing the claim. Because the case measures the loss suffered by the deceased, damages go to the deceased's estate.

Wrongful death statutes allow a deceased's surviving relatives to recover their losses resulting from the death. Most wrongful death statutes specify that survivors may recover only pecuniary losses. Originally interpreted to mean financial losses (expenses or income), the definition has expanded somewhat to cover other losses the death may cause.

The wrongful death action belongs to the survivors, not the deceased. It measures their losses, not losses to the deceased. Most states define the appropriate plaintiff by statute. While some specify the deceased's estate as the plaintiff, most specify a list of relatives. Spouses, children, and parents (in that order) generally may sue for wrongful death.

Out-of-Pocket Costs. Funeral expenses are recoverable in wrongful death actions. Other out-of-pocket costs caused by death are less common, but also may be recovered. (In theory, many of these costs would have been incurred eventually. Defendant caused the survivors to incur them now instead of later. That loss can be remedied by awarding the difference between the actual expenses and the present value of the expected future expenses. In practice, courts award the full costs.)

Loss of Support. Financial support that the deceased provided to the survivors is recoverable. Where support involved income, courts typically calculate recovery by assessing the deceased's full income, for the entire work-life expectancy, then subtracting amounts the deceased would have consumed for purely personal purposes. Thus, shared expenses, such as housing, utilities, vehicles, etc., would be recoverable by the survivors. But personal consumption, such as hobbies or vices, would not have been contributed to the family even if the deceased had lived. The wrong did not cause that portion of the income to be withheld from the survivors. Future lost support is reduced to present value.

Loss of support provides substantial recovery when the deceased held a paying job. It offers little or no recovery if the deceased was a child, a retired person, or an adult who did not work for a paycheck (such as homemakers). It may also provide no recovery if the deceased had no live-in dependents. Most expenses, in that case, would be personal consumption rather than support of others. As a result, courts have extended the definition of pecuniary losses beyond loss of financial support.

Loss of Services. Most states allow recovery for loss of services that the deceased provided to the survivors. To maintain their rightful position, the survivors must obtain replacement services. If they pay for those services, the loss is pecuniary, similar to out-of-pocket costs. In some cases, survivors do not (or cannot afford to) replace services in the market. In order to perform those services for themselves, survivors may need to give up other activities they once pursued. (Reduced leisure time is common. In other cases, education may diminish if an older child must leave school to take a job in order to support the family.) These sacrifices leave survivors worse off than if the death had not occurred, arguably requiring compensation. Giving up time, especially time that was not used to produce income, may not qualify as pecuniary loss. See *Hunter v. Office of Health Services*, 385 So.2d 928 (La.Ct.App.1980) (affirming a jury award that did not include loss of services because the survivors incurred no costs to replace those services). The cost to replace these services in the market offers a plausible measure of the loss.

Loss of services can be substantial, especially when deceased was a parent caring for children. Supervising the education of children, especially their moral education, provides a hook for some fairly large recoveries. Deceased children and retirees probably provided fewer services to their survivors. Similarly, deceased persons who lived alone probably provided fewer services.

Loss of Society. Fewer states, though a majority, allow recovery for loss of society. Loss of society includes intangible contributions of the deceased, such as affection, care, comfort, companionship, love, and protection. The absence of these leaves survivors worse off than before. Interpreting statutes that specify pecuniary losses to cover lost society seems problematic. Unlike services, survivors need not (probably cannot) pay to replace the deceased's companionship. Yet without compensation for these emotional components of a person, courts would struggle to find some recovery for the death of a child or retiree. Rather than leave these deaths uncompensated (or compensated at a very low level), courts often award these damages.

Grief and Distress. Very few states allow recovery for grief and distress caused by the death. Denying grief and distress gives some meaning to statutes limiting recovery to pecuniary losses. It also maintains consistency with rules denying distress over injury to others. A few states now allow recovery for grief. Grief remains the most obvious result of causing another's death. In some cases, grief is inevitable; the wrong merely accelerated its onset. In some cases, grief may increase because of the wrong (or the acceleration). The difficulties of evaluating grief and distress in general, combined with the heartlessness juries might associate with a defendant who probed the survivors' grief, limit the attention these issues receive in court.

Loss of Inheritance. Some persons save and invest in ways that produce an estate their survivors may inherit. Premature death reduces the size of the estate by decreasing the number of years the deceased contributed to it. Some states recognize this loss as compensable; others may follow. A history of savings offers a reasonable basis for estimating future estates, though some states reject this aspect of recovery despite a record of saving. The claim requires assumptions about future earnings, spending patterns, estate choices, and family stability that make awards border on speculation. (Would deceased disinherit these survivors or leave everything to charity?) Honoring the claim can produce additional speculation. Many Americans save nothing until later in life, permitting the inference that a deceased with no history of savings might create an inheritance. This component of loss seems likely to evolve over the coming years.

Deceased's Own Loss of Life. The deceased's inability to enjoy the remaining years of life presents perhaps the most direct loss caused by fatal wrongs. Where disability allows recovery for lost enjoyment of life, awarding the full loss following death seems a natural extension. Several states allow recovery for the nonpecuniary benefits the deceased would have obtained from continued life. In some cases, recovery occurs within the survival action, which compensates the estate for losses the deceased suffered. Others include it in a wrongful death action. Where wrongful death actions focus on the loss suffered by the survivors, including a loss felt exclusively by the deceased departs from the rationale. It also sits oddly with a rule limiting pecuniary recovery to the support the survivors would have received rather than the entire amount the deceased would have received. Placing it in the wrongful death action may avoid rules limiting survival actions to the period prior to the deceased's death. The convergence of these two forms of recovery may produce changes in the coming years.

Survival Actions. If a tort victim survives the tort, at least for a short time, her right to seek recovery for the wrong vests. The estate may assert that claim, even after the victim's death. Damages in survival actions cover the period before the victim's death. If the tort caused the victim's death, any subsequent losses generally fall within the survivors' wrongful death action. If the tort did not cause the death, then losses caused by the wrong would have ceased at the time of death anyway.

Damages in the survival action depend on the wrong involved. While survival actions often involve the wrong that killed the deceased, other torts that precede death also survive. Thus, a claim for defamation, fraud, or attorney malpractice might survive under these statutes, with the damages depending on the underlying wrong.

Plaintiffs often use survival actions to recover nonpecuniary losses against the tortfeasor who caused the death. As long as the deceased survived long enough to feel some pain, the survival action permits recovery of that loss. Pain and suffering may enhance, or even exceed, recovery for wrongful death—though payable to the deceased's estate, not the survivors. Other losses recoverable in a survival action include lost wages for any period before death and property damages (as where clothing or a vehicle were damaged in the accident that injured the victim).

7. Loss of Consortium

Loss of consortium is a cause of action. Physical injuries to one person (the victim) may cause losses to others (the consorts) who rely on that person for services and support. Losses may be pecuniary: replacing those services may involve expenses to hire a substitute provider. The victim usually cannot recover that expense. A reduction in the free services she provided to others may count as a benefit, not a cost. (If the inability to perform services to others distresses the victim, the victim might recover that distress.) In order to include lost services in the recovery against the defendant, courts created a separate cause of action for loss of consortium, allowing those who depend on the victim to seek their losses. Traditionally limited to spouses, some expansion has occurred recently.

Loss of consortium consists of three components: services, society, and sexual relations. It does not encompass grief, distress, or outrage at the injuries caused to another. As with wrongful death, some states have extended consortium to distress. In others, limits on the action for negligent infliction of emotional distress apply to these situations.

Services represent pecuniary losses to the plaintiff. When injuries to one spouse prevent him from performing household tasks, others must perform those tasks. Hiring others to perform the tasks clarifies the loss's pecuniary nature. As with wrongful death, even if the consort fills in by performing the services, that person's time has value. The loss is real, whether the time reduces remunerative activities or leisure.

Courts may measure the loss by the cost to replace the services in the market. This measure might be too low if the victim provided better services than those available in the market—or too high if professionals would provide better services than the victim. The market cost of services provides a practical measure of recovery, even if the plaintiff does not replace the services. A rational plaintiff will keep losses as low as possible: he will hire others if leisure is more valuable than the cost to hire others, but will perform the services himself if leisure is less valuable. Inability to pay others may explain a different choice. Issues of this nature sometimes lead courts to award more or less than the market value of services, even when they do not suspect that the hours spent on services have been exaggerated.

Loss of society covers other things that people provide each other, including affection, solace, comfort, companionship, assistance, and (between spouses) sexual relations. Unlike wrongful death actions, these losses may not follow from the wrong. An injury to a spouse need not make him or her any less loving, affectionate, or consoling. Only the most serious physical injuries—those involving comas or full-time care outside the home—necessarily produce these losses. Nonetheless, physical injuries can alter the emotional contributions a spouse provides, giving rise to some of these losses.

Society can be hard to evaluate, in part because it borders on emotional distress. There is little difference between the joy one felt conversing with the victim and the distress one feels now that the victim refuses such conversations (or is a less pleasant conversationalist). Keeping elements of distress and grief from entering the calculation of lost society can pose difficulties for the court. In some cases—especially those not involving spouses—courts reject recovery for these intangible components.

Permissible Plaintiffs. Loss of consortium traditionally applied only to spouses. At least 16 states now allow children to bring claims for loss of parental consortium, though many limit the claim to minor children or disabled adult children who remain their parents' responsibility during adulthood. Another 12 have rejected the right of children to recover for the consortium of a living parent. Several states now recognize parents' rights to seek loss of consortium for injuries to their children. Loss of filial consortium extends a parent's right to recover for loss of society following a child's death to include nonfatal injuries. Concern that filial consortium might abridge constraints on negligent infliction of emotional distress lead courts to confine recovery to lost services and society children provide, rejecting recovery for the parents' emotional distress.

A huge range of people may suffer losses as a result of tort injuries to another. So far, courts have resisted expanding the action beyond spouses and children—and many resist including children. Consortium claims brought by fiancés, domestic partners, roommates, and relatives outside the nuclear family have met with almost no success. That may change as domestic partner statutes entitle domestic partners to be treated as spouses for legal purposes. Recognition of same sex marriage may supplant consortium for domestic partners. As a practical matter, states may find it difficult to deny consortium to any person who could recover for wrongful death if the injury had been fatal. Once the relationship justifies recovery for death, denying recovery for nonfatal injuries seems inconsistent.

Procedural Aspects. Consortium claims risk inconsistent recovery, especially if the consortium claim is resolved separately from the victim's underlying tort claim. A jury hearing both claims can allocate the losses consistently to one plaintiff or the other. Separate juries may not know which losses the other claimant recovered. The risk of double recovery prompts some states to require that consortium claims be joined with the victim's suit.

G. LIMITATIONS ON RECOVERY

Concern that juries might overcompensate plaintiffs emerged in the nineteenth century. Doctrines limiting recovery emerged to avoid putting plaintiff in a better position than she would have occupied but for the wrong. These doctrines generally do not reject the rightful position standard, but seek to prevent juries from becoming too generous with other peoples' money. Nonetheless, the doctrines tend to err on the side of undercompensation.

1. Causation

The rightful position standard builds causation into its formulation: it limits plaintiff to the position she would have occupied if the wrong had not occurred. This rejects damages not caused by defendant's misconduct, losses plaintiff would have suffered even if defendant had not committed the wrong (or did not suffer despite the wrong).

Basic issues of causation—cause in fact, legal cause, etc.—tend to be covered in first year tort courses, not remedies courses. These rules relate to liability rather than damages. Here, we will focus on causation doctrines that affect damage calculation.

Mixed Motive. Motivation may be a key component of a wrong: conduct motivated by one reason would be perfectly legal, but the same conduct would be wrong if motivated by other factors. Employment offers easy examples. Discharging an employee for bad work is legal, while discharging an employee because of race, gender, or age (to name a few) would be illegal. Normally, a plaintiff must show that the illegal motive was a cause in fact (a but-for cause) of the wrong. *University of Texas Southwestern Medical Center v. Nassar*, ___ U.S. ___, 133 S.Ct. 2517, 186 L.Ed.2d 503 (2013).

Cause in fact fails when the evidence reveals multiple sufficient causes: when either of two (or more) reasons (one of them legal) would have produced the conduct independently of the other(s). In this setting, the result would have been the same even if the wrongful reason did not exist; the legal reason was sufficient by itself to produce the outcome. Thus, the wrongful reason did not cause the harm. For example, if an employee caught embezzling money is fired, defendant may testify persuasively that he would have been discharged regardless of any protected characteristic. Proof that the defendant also harbored a bias against people of plaintiff's description may establish a second possible reason, but is insufficient to establish cause. Even if defendant planned to fire plaintiff for wrongful reasons, if the rightful reason provides sufficient independent justification, the wrong did not cause the harm.

Pretext complicates arguments about mixed motives. A defendant accused of wrongful motivations often asserts a different, legal reason for the action. Plaintiffs must challenge whether the asserted reason really was a sufficient cause, in effect arguing that the legal reason is a pretext rather than a reason. If defendant would not have acted the same way faced with only the legal motive, then the illegal motive did in fact cause the harm. This may apply where defendant did not know about the legal reason at the time of the conduct or did not care about the legal reason—at least not enough to take the same action. Defendant's testimony about her state of mind can be hard to rebut. Similar situations where the defendant acted differently provide some evidence of pretext.

Difficulty rebutting defendants' assertions of legitimate reasons has produced a reduced test for causation in some cases arising under Title VII of the Civil Rights Act of 1964. Plaintiffs alleging discrimination based on status (race, sex, color, religion, or national origin) may obtain some relief if the protected classification was *a* motivating cause, even if it was not a but-for cause of the adverse employment action. 42 U.S.C. § 2000e–2m. Even if the employer proves that the decision would have been the same regardless of the protected characteristic, plaintiff may obtain some relief. Defeating but-for causation may protect the employer from reinstatement and damages for backpay, but would not defeat liability, thus permitting plaintiff to recover attorneys' fees and some injunctive relief.

The relaxed causation standard applies to a narrow range of claims: status-based discrimination under Title VII. Other employment discrimination claims, such as allegations of discrimination based on age and allegations of retaliation under Title VII, require plaintiff to prove but-for causation. *University of Texas Southwestern Medical Center v. Nassar*, ___ U.S. ___, 133 S.Ct. 2517, 186 L.Ed.2d 503 (2013); *Gross v. FBL Financial Services, Inc.*, 557 U.S. 167, 129 S.Ct. 2343, 174 L.Ed.2d 119 (2009). Cause in fact exists in cases involving multiple insufficient causes: when neither of two (or more) reasons would have produced the conduct independently of the other. The combination was essential to cause the conduct; the conduct would have been different if the wrongful reason did not exist. Thus, the harm was caused by the wrongful reason. For example, suppose an employer encounters employee misconduct that would not normally cause him to discharge the employee. (Consistent use of lesser sanctions for past violations may leave no doubt on this point.) However, because the employee also was active in organizing the union (an illegal consideration), the employer decided to fire the employee. The employer had not fired the employee before discovering the misconduct, suggesting that union activity was not sufficient to cause discharge. Nonetheless, the wrongful reason caused the discharge. Take it away and the employee would have been disciplined but not fired.

Illegitimate motives may lead to the discovery of the legitimate motives. For instance, an employer who observes minority employees more closely than others may discover misconduct by minority employees but not others. On one hand, it is hard for a plaintiff who deserved to be fired to argue that others should have been fired, too. If plaintiff got what she deserved, no wrong seems to require compensation. On the other hand, the different scrutiny may itself be a violation of law. (For instance, a law prohibiting discrimination in the terms and conditions of employment could be interpreted to prohibit scrutinizing some employees more closely because of certain characteristics.) If discriminatory scrutiny caused the discovery and hence the discharge, the wrong still caused the harm. The issue here may involve conflicting policies: one forbidding discrimination, another permitting discharge of poor or dishonest employees.

Physical Injury Requirement or Economic Loss Doctrine. With some exceptions, tort liability arises when defendant's misconduct physically injures the person or property of plaintiff, not when the misconduct causes only economic loss to the plaintiff. The rule limits defendants' duty: tort law requires due care to avoid injuring the person or property of others, but does not impose a general duty to use due care to avoid injuring purely economic interests. If, however, a tort injures the person or property of plaintiff, all losses caused by the wrong, including economic losses, are recoverable.

The rule limits which plaintiffs may sue for some wrongs. A defendant's negligence may affect one person directly, but have economic effects that ripple through a broad range of persons. Allowing each to sue for their economic loss allows recovery to parties far removed from the tort. For example, an injury to an employee may cause economic loss to the employer. The employee suffered physical injury and may sue in tort; the employer, however, has no tort claim against the tortfeasor. Similarly, a ship captain may negligently cause a collision with another ship. Damage to that ship is recoverable. But if the accident spilled toxic chemicals into the environment, every business in the vicinity that lost customers during the cleanup might sue. The economic loss doctrine rejects their claims. *Louisiana ex rel. Guste v. M/V Testbank*, 752 F.2d 1019 (5th Cir.1985).

In theory, rules limiting foreseeability and certainty would produce the same results, limiting recovery for remote effects. More remote plaintiffs are less likely to present foreseeable losses or to prove them with reasonable certainty. These doctrines, however, apply to the facts of each case, requiring discovery and judicial resources to resolve the matters—and perhaps even trial on the merits to a jury. If recovery eventually would be denied, the rule saves judicial resources and denies plaintiffs leverage to obtain settlement of claims that lack merit. In the process, the rule cuts off recovery by persons who could prevail despite challenges to foreseeability and certainty.

The rule also maintains the division between tort and contract law for warranty claims. Breach of warranty, whether innocent or negligent, reduces the value of a product. In contract, plaintiff can recover the difference between the value as promised and the value as received. But if plaintiff can prove negligence, suing in tort may prove more lucrative, avoiding contract clauses limiting recovery and perhaps including emotional distress. The economic loss doctrine precludes this option if the only loss plaintiff suffered was the economic loss of receiving a good worth less than promised. The bar may apply even if the product explodes. If the explosion damages other property of plaintiff, the property damage satisfies the physical injury requirement and a tort suit is appropriate. But if the explosion damages only the good itself, suit lies in contract for the breach of warranty.

Numerous exceptions qualify the economic loss doctrine. Most significantly, some torts do not inherently involve physical injury. Courts generally allow economic losses for these torts without proof of physical injury. Deception, attorney malpractice, defamation, invasion of privacy, and interference with contract rarely produce injuries to person or property and would virtually disappear if the economic loss doctrine applied.

Other courts have expanded (slightly) liability to remote plaintiffs by creating ad hoc exceptions. Especially if the doctrine might leave no plaintiff able to bring a suit, courts soften the limitation. These cases often involve environmental torts, where the tort damages property that no one owns, such as a river or ocean. Plaintiffs who use the river, such as fishers (commercial or recreational) and boaters, have been allowed to sue. Cases of this sort often limit liability to the most direct plaintiffs (*e.g.*, fishers), but deny liability for others affected (those who buy the fish, process them, sell them to restaurants, serve them in restaurants, or park the cars at seafood restaurants—and those who sell to the fishers, such as marinas, bait and tackle shops, and, for sport fishers, hotels, guides, etc.)

Statutory provisions also may expand liability beyond the physical injury requirement. For example, the Oil Pollution Act, 33 U.S.C. §§ 2701–2720, primarily allows recovery by landowners and lessees, but extends liability also to those who use the resource for subsistence and to states who lose revenue as a result of a spill. The provision allowing any claimant to recover "loss of profits or impairment of earning capacity due to the injury, destruction, or loss of real property, personal property, or natural resources" may open the door to expanded recovery. 33 U.S.C. § 2702(b)(1)(E). For example, it seems to allow recovery by one who depends on property or a natural resource even if the person has no legal claim to the property. Thus, an employee on a fishing boat that lost business following the Deepwater Horizon spill might claim lost earning potential from the destruction of a natural resource.

Loss of Chance is one of two doctrines aimed at wrongs that increase the risk of harm, but may not cause the harm. It applies where plaintiff had a chance of avoiding a harm, but defendant's wrong reduced the chance. Medical cases, where the failure to diagnose a problem earlier may reduce the likelihood of successfully treating the condition, offer the clearest examples. Defendants do not cause the condition and, thus, do not cause the harms attributable to the original condition. Thus, courts cannot award the full loss suffered by every plaintiff. But defendant's wrong did deprive plaintiff of opportunities that might (or might not) have prevented all or part of the harm. For example, an earlier diagnosis of an infection might prevent amputation; earlier diagnosis of a cancer might prolong life. Thus, zero recovery seems to underestimate the plaintiff's loss. Most states to consider the issue allow some recovery for loss of chance cases, even if the chances of avoiding the harm were 50% or less at the time of the negligence.

Proof of actual causation would avoid the issue. This would require courts to determine whether the particular plaintiff would have successfully avoided the harm but for the wrong. Usually that will be impossible. Medical testimony reveals the relative chances of success, but cannot say whether this plaintiff would have survived. For example, the chance of successful treatment might have been 65% if diagnosed earlier, but only 40% when actually diagnosed. Out of every 100 patients in this situation, 40 will survive despite the negligence. (Many of these will have no loss and will not sue. Others might suffer more expensive treatment because of the late diagnosis—a loss entirely caused by the negligence and not subject to the loss of chance doctrine.) Of the 60 who do not survive, 35 would not have survived regardless of the wrong, but 25 would have survived but for the negligent diagnosis. If the evidence permitted the jury to conclude that plaintiff would have been among the 25 who would not have suffered the harm, then actual causation would be established. Because courts often require reasonable medical certainty for causation, proof that an individual would have survived is nearly impossible to produce. Even applying the usual requirement of a preponderance, the likelihood that any given plaintiff would have survived is less than 50% (25 of 60 is 41.67%).

Proportional recovery offers courts a way to recognize defendant's wrong without overcompensating plaintiffs. Courts calculate the harm plaintiff suffered and multiply by the percent reduction in chance defendant caused. On the numbers above, plaintiff might receive 25% of total loss: defendant reduced plaintiff's chance of survival from 65% to 40%, a reduction of 25%. Alternatively, courts could focus on the odds that the loss would have occurred anyway. Taking the 60% who suffered the harm, 25 of them (41.67%) would not have suffered the harm but for the wrong. The latter formula assesses defendant's liability more accurately. If 60 misdiagnosed patients sue, the total recovery will equal the total harm of 25 of them. (Consider a simplified example, based on these numbers. If every misdiagnosed patient who suffered the result lost $1 million, total costs caused by the wrong would be $25 million—the harm to the 25 who would have been cured but for the wrong. If all 60 patients sue and recover 25% of their loss ($250,000 each), defendant will pay a total of $15 million. But if the 60 each recover 41.67% of their losses ($416,700), defendant will pay a total of $25 million, the loss caused.) The second formula forces defendants collectively to internalize the full cost of their wrong, providing more effective deterrence.

The loss of chance doctrine allocates some of the costs of the wrong to people whose wrong caused none of the loss. By hypothesis, many of the people affected by the negligence would have suffered the harm even if the condition had been detected earlier. Those physicians, though negligent, caused no harm. The inability to identify which of the negligent defendants caused the harm and which did not produces a compromise. To some extent, this approach resembles the wrongdoer exception to the certainty doctrine. *See* section G.6., *infra*. The defendant's negligence created the inability to discern whether the plaintiff would have survived if the diagnoses had been timely. (If timely diagnosis had occurred, plaintiff would have been treated and the success (or failure) would be an observable fact.) Having created the uncertainty, the wrongdoer may be held to a reasonable estimate of the amount of loss caused by the wrong, despite the inability to prove the loss with certainty. Loss of chance stretches this exception. Usually, the wrongdoer exception applies when the evidence permits a court to rule out the possibility that the plaintiff suffered no loss at all. Loss of chance, however, will allow recovery by many plaintiffs who suffered no loss.

Some courts treat loss of chance as a separate cause of action, requiring separate pleading, especially if the plaintiff died. To plead wrongful death, one must show the defendant caused the death, which is impossible in these cases. Plaintiffs may need to include a separate claim to recover for loss of chance.

Loss of chance can produce some odd results. A plaintiff whose original chance of survival exceeded 50% may recover the full loss. (More likely than not, she would not have suffered the harm but for the wrong.) That would be true even if the chance decreased by a small margin—say, from 51% to 46%. Of 100 persons negligently diagnosed in this way, 46 will survive (and probably not sue), 54 will recover their full damages—even though only 5 would have avoided the harm if properly diagnosed. On the other hand, if chances were only 49% when the diagnosis occurred, but diminished to zero when discovered, the plaintiff cannot show that the harm was more likely than not caused by the negligence. Of 100 plaintiffs in that situation, all suffer the harm and sue, each recovering a portion of the loss. Recovery based on how much the chance of survival decreased offers a more intuitive approach.

Potential Harm. Some wrongs cause little or no immediate harm to plaintiff. Instead, the wrong exposes plaintiff to a risk of future harm. For example, exposing defendant to a harmful substance may increase the risk that plaintiff will suffer from cancer much later in life. Many people exposed will not suffer the harm. A few might have suffered the harm even if not exposed. In these cases, plaintiffs have trouble proving that the defendant's wrong caused the harm. To compensate those who would have suffered the wrong anyway puts them in a better position than they would have occupied but for the wrong. But it may be impossible to determine which individuals developed cancer as a result of the wrong and which did not. Indeed, unless they postpone suit for years, they may not be able to prove that they suffered an injury at all.

Efforts to recover for the damage resulting from the potential harm raise different causation issues depending on when the claim is brought. While some plaintiffs might wait to see if they suffer the harm, potential harm poses more problems if plaintiffs sue immediately, before they know if the increased risk will affect them.

If exposure produces a risk of harm greater than 50%, then causation may be satisfied by all who are exposed. All can show that it is more likely than not that they will develop the harmful condition. (Applying a standard of reasonable medical certainty may alter the probability necessary to satisfy the causation requirement.) Future harms resulting from a prior injury may be included in the damage award. Losses may include cost of treatment, lost earnings, decreased life expectancy, and any other loss that would flow from the disease—reduced to present value, as the effects will be suffered in the future.

This result would produce significant overcompensation, forcing defendants to pay for far more harm than they actually caused. Some portion of those exposed will never develop symptoms. Their recovery will be pure windfall. Others might have developed the condition even if never exposed. If everyone exposed recovers, compensation exceeds justifiable levels.

One response is to deny recovery to persons who do not develop the harmful condition. Unless exposure produces an immediate harm, no injury exists that would require courts to consider the suit immediately. Those who develop symptoms related to the exposure can sue when those symptoms arise. (The statute of limitations does not begin to run until the injury occurs, which in this situation may be limited to the harmful condition. If exposure produces an immediate injury, it may be necessary to sue immediately and include a claim for future damages.) Limiting recovery to those who develop symptoms will not avoid compensating those who would have developed the condition even if not exposed. It will, however, address the most significant component of overcompensation.

Relatively few cases involve exposure that makes subsequent illness more likely than not. More difficult issues arise when exposure produces marginal increases in the risk. For example, exposure may increase the risk of heart disease or cancer from 2% to 8% (a 400% increase). But no one exposed is more likely than not to develop the disease. In these cases, plaintiffs cannot recover for the future disease by suing immediately. None of those exposed could establish that it is more likely than not they would suffer from the disease. Instead, postponing suit until the disease manifests would be necessary. Allocating damages among all who were exposed would dramatically undercompensate a few and overcompensate many. For example, if 100 persons were exposed, increasing their risk of cancer from 2% to 8%, 92 of those exposed would suffer no loss at all, but would share in the recovery based on their increased risk. Another two would have developed the disease anyway. They, too, would be overcompensated. But the six who develop the disease because of the exposure would recover only a very small portion of the costs they would ultimately incur. If, for example, total losses for those who suffer heart disease (reduced to present value) are $8 million ($1 million each), distributing the 75% caused by defendant ($6 million) awards each exposed person $60,000. The cost to defendant provides the right deterrent—and provides it now, reducing the risk that bankruptcy or other problems preclude future recovery. But the compensation for the people who actually suffer the disease falls far short of their actual loss.

Even if only those who ultimately suffer the harmful condition sue, causation can present problems. On the example above, where risk increased from 2% to 8%, all eight people who actually develop heart disease are likely to recover. Only six were injured by the defendant; two would have developed heart disease anyway. But each can show a 75% chance (6 out of 8) that the exposure caused his symptoms. This satisfies the preponderance of the evidence test. Allocating the losses among all eight plaintiffs (allowing each to recover 75% of the losses) overcompensates two plaintiffs and undercompensates six, but assesses exactly the right costs against the defendant. Smaller increases in risk, however, make causation hard to prove. If the risk of heart disease increased from 6% to 8% (a 25% increase), three fourths of the people who develop the disease would have developed it anyway. None of the plaintiffs can establish causation by a preponderance of the evidence. This scenario resembles loss of chance: the wrong reduced these victims' chances of avoiding the disease by one fourth. In this scenario, an allocation of loss (25% of damages for each plaintiff) may be more appealing.

In many cases, exposure will cause immediate harm. Exposure might produce minor injuries, such as nausea, difficulty breathing, or other modest physical consequences. If so, plaintiff must sue within the limitations period in order to recover for the immediate harm. The inability to prove that exposure will cause a subsequent disease precludes recovery for the disease in the action.

The risk of developing a disease may involve immediate harms. In some cases, exposure may produce distress over the possibility that the disease will manifest in the future. That distress is immediate, the result of physical exposure to the potentially harmful agent. It deserves compensation immediately. Some courts limit distress to those who develop at least one symptom of the feared condition. Others acknowledge the plausibility of the fear for all who are exposed.

The risk of developing a disease also may cause medical expenses before the disease actually manifests. Exposure may make it reasonable to incur the cost of medical monitoring, in order to detect the disease at its earliest onset and preserve the best chance for treating the condition. Monitoring following exposure may exceed the monitoring a plaintiff would have sought if not exposed. If so, the difference is recoverable as a loss caused by the exposure. Limiting recovery to reasonable monitoring costs reflects concern for the avoidable consequences doctrine. Plaintiff cannot recover for losses caused by her own unreasonable conduct following the tort— including unreasonable monitoring efforts.

Recovery for immediate harms can jeopardize recovery for the subsequent harms. Civil procedure rules present plaintiffs a dilemma. The injury has begun, starting the statute of limitations. Plaintiffs must sue within a relatively short time after exposure. Yet claim preclusion (res judicata) may preclude a later suit concerning the same misconduct. Plaintiffs must combine all claims arising from the same set of operative facts in a single action. A second suit generally is not justified merely because the injury proves to be more severe than first anticipated—or more severe than the evidence could prove at the original trial. A doctrine precluding recovery of potential future harms in the first suit in effect precludes them altogether. Some jurisdictions treat the subsequent effects as a new injury, permitting a new suit, even though the underlying misconduct is identical to that raised in the earlier action. The new injury triggers the start of a new statute of limitations once occurrence of the potential harm either is discovered or reasonably should have been discovered.

Harm to Others: Fluid Class Recoveries. In some cases, plaintiffs have asked courts to award a remedy to one group of people based on a wrong done to different individuals. This can apply to damage actions, where plaintiffs ask that defendant issue rebates to future customers in light of overcharges to past customers. It can also apply to injunctions, where a court may order conduct beneficial to subsequent persons like the injured persons. These issues usually arise in class action suits, where identifying the original injured parties and calculating the (perhaps minuscule) loss to each might be impossible or may cost more than the loss to each victim would justify. Identifying and compensating a class of similar people offers a more practical means of handling defendant's wrong, even though it might compensate people who were not defendant's victims. For example, a city that overcharges persons who bought monthly bus passes in July might be asked to discount passes for customers in a future month.

With rare exceptions, courts do not award remedies to persons who were not injured by the defendant's wrong over the defendant's objection. Courts have approved settlement agreements that benefit classes similar to those injured. Even if some victims will receive no compensation and some people who were not victims will receive compensation, a court may find that the settlement is in the best interest of the class. Discrimination statutes offer one exception. A history of discrimination against a racial group can lead a court to order the employer to hire a certain percentage from that racial group in the coming years. While court-ordered hiring quotas are not common, they have been accepted in some cases.

2. Avoided Consequences

Putting the plaintiff in the position she would have occupied if the wrong had not occurred requires compensation for losses the plaintiff suffered, but not for losses she did not suffer. Thus, any loss the plaintiff actually avoided should not be included in the recovery. More controversially, when a wrong bestows benefits in addition to causing losses, plaintiff should recover her net loss, after offsetting the benefits.

Avoided losses present little controversy. Plaintiffs often minimize their own loss. Awarding recovery for losses plaintiffs avoided borders on the silly, to the point that requests for such recovery rarely appear.

Although avoided losses are not recoverable, the cost of avoiding a loss is recoverable. For example, when an employer wrongfully discharges an employee, the employee may find a substitute job, thus replacing the wages the first job would have paid. The employee may recover for costs incurred finding the new job—for example, resumé printing and postage, cab fare to interviews, etc. None would have been incurred but for the defendant's wrong. (These expenses might be called incidental damages.) Similarly, a pedestrian hit by a car may obtain medical treatment to prevent permanent disability. She can recover the cost of the treatment.

Offsetting Benefits. In some cases, a plaintiff who suffers some harm also receives benefits as a result of the wrong. Typically, if defendant's tort benefits the same interest that it injured, the benefits will be offset against the harms in calculating damages, "to the extent that this is equitable." RESTATEMENT (SECOND) TORTS, § 920. While no similar rule is stated in contract law, the same principle is built into the damage rules. For instance, when a seller breaches, buyer is entitled to recover cover price minus contract price. Courts subtract contract price because, as a benefit of the breach, buyer no longer needs to pay the breaching seller. (If the buyer already has paid, it is entitled to a refund; then offsetting the full price is appropriate as an avoided loss. *See* UCC § 2–711.) To allow buyer to collect cover price without subtracting the retained benefit would exceed the net loss buyer actually suffered. Similarly, a seller may benefit by retaining the goods (or other promised performance) after buyer's breach. These benefits are not addressed by a separate rule governing benefits, but built into the damage formula. Tort, on the other hand, often involves duties that flow only one direction, making an express benefit rule more important.

Consider a simple tort example. Defendant defames plaintiff, who proves that she lost business as a result of the libel. But defendant proves that plaintiff, because of the wrong, was invited to give a number of lectures, for which she was paid. Awarding the full loss of business without offset for the financial gains of the lectures would leave plaintiff better off than if the wrong had not occurred. (But for the libel, the plaintiff would not have received income from the lectures.) Plaintiff's net losses will be awarded. In effect, awarding her the gross loss allows recovery for a loss she did not suffer.

The Restatement applies when the benefit to the plaintiff affects the same interest injured. Thus, a financial benefit would offset a financial harm. But a financial benefit would not offset an emotional harm or harm to dignitary interests (such as reputation). In the example above, both business income and lecture income involve plaintiff's financial interests. But if plaintiff also sought recovery for social ostracism resulting from the defamation, that recovery would not be offset by the financial benefits (even if those benefits exceeded the financial harm). If plaintiff claimed no business losses, but only loss of reputation, lecture income might not offset those harms at all.

The limitation to the same interest prevents courts from comparing apples and oranges. While financial losses are computed with some degree of certainty, nonpecuniary interests (pain, distress, indignity, reputation) often are the product of crude estimates. Offsetting a real financial harm with a somewhat speculative emotional benefit may prevent recovery in cases that seem to require compensation for the pecuniary losses. Limiting nonpecuniary benefits to offsetting the nonpecuniary losses prevents any inaccuracies in the estimation of distress or other components from overwhelming the relatively accurate (and sometimes much smaller) awards of pecuniary losses.

Some cases do not limit benefits to the same interest. Cases involving unwanted children offer one example. When defendant fails to sterilize a person (whether negligently or in breach of contract), the parents suffer the cost of raising an additional child. The emotional benefit they may receive from raising a child does not affect their pecuniary interests. Thus, the same interest requirement suggests no offset is required. Courts, however, rarely award the cost of raising a healthy child in these cases. Though sometimes discussed in terms of public policy, other courts express concern for awarding the full financial loss without offset for the emotional benefits. In effect, the nonpecuniary benefits are used to offset the pecuniary harms. (If parents claim emotional distress from raising the child, even a strict reading of the rule would allow the emotional benefits of raising a child to offset the emotional component of their claim.)

The Restatement suggests that in some cases it might be inequitable to limit recovery to plaintiff's net loss. Two situations seem likely to present this issue: (1) if plaintiffs actively sought to avoid the alleged benefits; and (2) if the defendant acted intentionally rather than negligently. The benefits rule should not license people to foist unwanted benefits onto others. Compare this with restitution, where a volunteer who bestows benefits on the plaintiff without giving plaintiff an opportunity to refuse or bargain recovers nothing, even though that leaves plaintiff better off than she deserves. A defendant whose tort bestows an unwanted benefit on plaintiffs may have even less claim to credit for the benefit bestowed, particularly if the tort was intentional. For example, if defendant paved plaintiff's farm and put up a parking lot, plaintiff might be entitled to the cost of restoring the land to farm territory, even if the wrong increased its net value.

Finding an offset inequitable poses more concern where benefits are mixed blessings. Consider the sterilization cases, where plaintiffs paid to prevent the very benefit that defendant now seeks to offset against recovery. An unwanted benefit establishes that plaintiffs are net worse off; they would not have incurred the costs voluntarily, despite the alleged benefits. But their choice does not necessarily imply the benefit is worthless, merely that the costs exceed the benefits. Ignoring the benefit completely overstates the amount of loss defendant caused. Thus, overzealous recourse to the inequity of offsetting benefits may undercut the purpose of the benefit rule.

The rules limiting benefits to the interest injured present some difficult calculation issues. The language of the rule suggests that where benefits to one interest exceed the harm to that interest, the excess benefit has no further effect; it should not offset harm to other interests. For instance, if the emotional benefit exceeds the emotional harm, plaintiff recovers nothing for emotional harm, but the difference will not carry over to offset part of the pecuniary harm. This result also removes any reason for plaintiffs to avoid pleading harms to one interest in order to avoid evidence of benefits to that interest. Nonetheless, some courts faced with these issues refused to apply the benefit rule at all. In other cases, they abandon the distinction between the interests, allowing total offset. Firm predictions are impossible at this time.

3. Collateral Source Exception

Traditionally, benefits bestowed by sources other than a defendant do not offset the plaintiff's recovery. RESTATEMENT (SECOND) OF TORTS § 920A. Defendant is entitled to a credit for benefits it provides—whether payments or other kinds of offsetting benefits under the preceding rule. But benefits provided by others do not offset defendant's liability. For example, in a personal injury case, defendant cannot claim credit for medical costs paid by plaintiff's health insurance.

When others pay the costs of plaintiff's injury, plaintiff does not suffer those losses. Thus, recovery may leave plaintiff in a better position than she would have occupied if the wrong had not occurred: she collects full damages from the defendant, but does not suffer some of the losses because others paid them. Sometimes the argument is false; excessive recovery does not occur. For example, health insurers often assert subrogation claims, recouping from the tort damages the amount they paid on plaintiff's behalf. Similarly, a plaintiff who chose to repay a person who provided assistance (even though not obligated to make repayment) would not be overcompensated by a damage award that included costs that others paid on behalf of the plaintiff. Even when overcompensation might occur, deterrence policies support making defendant internalize the full cost of the harm caused by the wrong. Regardless of who bore the loss in the first instance, the correct amount of deterrence depends on the cost ultimately being shifted to the defendant.

The deterrence rationale explains one variation on the collateral source doctrine. When recovery is sought from someone other than a wrongdoer, offset for benefits is more likely. For example, a party who suffered a hit and run automobile accident can seek recovery from their own automobile insurer, if the policy includes uninsured motorist coverage. If plaintiff seeks to recover amounts already paid by a health insurer, recovery probably will be denied. There is no deterrent value in imposing extra costs on the plaintiff's insurer, who could not have prevented the wrong no matter how many precautions it took. Similar variations apply to workers compensation cases and to claims against funds designed to help crime victims.

The possibility of double recovery has made this rule a target of tort reform. In at least 17 states, attacks on the collateral source rule have produced some changes. For example, New York now offsets the plaintiff's recovery by the amount of any compensation received from insurance and social security benefits, minus the premiums plaintiff paid for those benefits in the preceding two years. N.Y. Civil Practice Laws Revised § 4545. In other states, evidence of collateral sources is admissible, but the law leaves juries free to decide whether to offset the benefits. Several other variations on these rules have been adopted.

4. Avoidable Consequences

Often called mitigation of damages, the avoidable consequences doctrine limits the amount of damage a plaintiff may recover to the amount she could not have avoided by reasonable conduct. The rule may leave plaintiff worse off than if the wrong had not occurred. For instance, a discharged employee who makes no effort to find a new job may end up with less money than she would have received if she had not been discharged. If defendant can show that plaintiff would have found suitable work had she tried, the amount plaintiff would have earned will be subtracted from the amount defendant would have paid the plaintiff. (The cost plaintiff would have incurred in a job search probably will be awarded to plaintiff, since the reduction could not have occurred without these expenses, for which defendant would have been liable.)

The rule strives to treat avoidable consequences the same way courts treat avoided consequences. In effect, it treats plaintiff as if she did avoid the losses that she should have avoided. In part, the rule recognizes that defendant is not the only cause of avoidable losses. Because plaintiff could have avoided the loss, her unreasonable failure to avoid it is another legal cause of the avoidable loss. In addition, a policy to avoid waste urges courts to provide an incentive to prevent losses, when reasonable. The avoidable consequences doctrine provides this incentive.

The Rule. If the plaintiff fails to make reasonable efforts to minimize the loss, the losses she would have avoided by reasonable efforts will be denied. The rule applies in tort and contract. For instance, if seller breaches a promise to supply goods, a buyer who can obtain substitute goods elsewhere might avoid ensuing losses. If buyer fails to make reasonable efforts to obtain substitute goods, recovery for ensuing losses may be limited. Similarly, a plaintiff injured in an automobile accident might prevent the injuries from becoming a permanent disability by proper medical care. If plaintiff unreasonably refuses medical care, defendant may owe only the cost of the medical care, not the loss caused by the disability. In addition to common law claims, many statutory rights include the avoidable consequences doctrine, either expressly or by implication.

Defendant must plead and prove avoidable consequences as an affirmative defense. The defense involves two steps. First, defendant must show that plaintiff's efforts to minimize the loss were unreasonable. Second, defendant must show the amount of loss that would have been avoided had plaintiff made reasonable efforts. The second requirement protects a plaintiff whose efforts would have been futile. Defendant might prove it was unreasonable to do nothing. But if reasonable efforts would not have reduced losses at all, plaintiff still recovers the full loss.

If a plaintiff makes reasonable efforts to minimize the loss, no reduction in damages occurs even if those efforts failed. For example, a wrongfully discharged employee who makes reasonable efforts to find a new job may fail to find substitute work. She recovers the full salary defendant would have paid, plus the cost of the efforts to find new work. In effect, where plaintiff's reasonable efforts fail, courts conclude that reasonable efforts would not have prevented the loss.

Plaintiff need not choose the best means of minimizing the loss. Faced with alternative ways to minimize the loss, plaintiff may make any reasonable choice. Hindsight might reveal that a different choice would have been better. Nonetheless, a plaintiff that made a reasonable choice recovers the damages he actually suffered. *S.J. Groves & Sons v. Warner Co.*, 576 F.2d 524 (3rd Cir.1978). In effect, if defendant wants to specify how the loss should be minimized, defendant should negotiate with plaintiff instead of simply breaching and leaving plaintiff to deal with the losses.

Sometimes damages can be reduced by exceptional efforts. A discharged employee might find a new job by moving to a new town or state, by retraining in a different field, or by accepting work that affronts her dignity. Where minimizing the loss requires undue risk, burden, or humiliation, no reduction of damages results. RESTATEMENT (SECOND) OF CONTRACTS § 350(1). (The contract Restatement's reference to undue risk, burden or humiliation does not change the reasonableness test, but helps identify ways to argue that a particular effort was unreasonable. There seems little difference between saying an effort would have involved an undue burden and saying that it was reasonable not to make that effort.)

The rule requires reasonable efforts. In some cases, courts shade toward a less demanding requirement of good faith efforts. They resist holding plaintiff's efforts unreasonable by identifying ways that the plaintiff differs from the ordinary, reasonable person. For example, a plaintiff who refused simple, safe surgery almost certain to prevent disability received full compensation for her injuries. The refusal was deemed reasonable because the plaintiff suffered from a mental disorder that caused her to focus on the risks and underestimate the benefits. By taking into account the patently unreasonable aspects of plaintiff's character and concluding the decision was reasonable for her, the court in effect applied a good faith standard. *Small v. Combustion Engineering*, 209 Mont. 387, 681 P.2d 1081 (1984).

Religious objections to medical procedures pose difficult issues. Finding that a religious belief makes it reasonable to refuse care that would minimize the plaintiff's loss seems to endorse plaintiff's religion. Refusing to reduce damages rules plaintiff acted reasonably when conforming to the religious tenets—in effect, ruling those tenets reasonable. The effect allows recovery to a religious person that would not be allowed to someone whose faith did not espouse the same principles. The alternative, reducing damages, explicitly brands the religious practice unreasonable. The constitutionally protected status of religion makes it difficult for courts to rule on reasonableness in that setting. A good faith test says nothing about the reasonableness of the religion, addressing only the believer's sincerity. (A trial on the sincerity of the plaintiff's beliefs may contain other land mines.) In effect, a good faith test treats the religion like a mental disorder, which might make it reasonable for the plaintiff to act in a particular way even though it would be unreasonable for others to make the same decision. One court allowed a jury to apply the avoidable consequences doctrine, suggesting that the plaintiff is not entitled to demand that the defendant subsidize those religious beliefs by paying for harms that resulted as much from the religion (which prevented amelioration) as from the defendant's wrong (which created the need for amelioration). Another court has intentionally ducked the issue of whether the test is objective or subjective. Thus, reasonableness may mean something different under the avoidable consequences doctrine than it means when determining defendant's liability for negligence.

Exceptions, Real and Imagined. Lost volume sellers recover their full losses even though they seem to have avoided the loss by entering a substitute transaction. The exception applies if plaintiff could have entered two transactions—both the one defendant precluded and the one claimed in mitigation. In this situation, the second transaction does not offset the harm of the first. Rather, but for the defendant's breach, plaintiff would have had the benefit of both transactions. For example, car dealers often have virtually unlimited access to more new cars. If one buyer refuses to accept delivery, selling that car to another buyer may not offset the loss from the first sale. But for the breach, plaintiff could have sold two cars, not one. To obtain the benefit of both transactions, plaintiff should recover the profit lost on the first transaction (as well as any incidental costs incurred because of the breach). Cf. *Neri v. Retail Marine*, 30 N.Y.2d 393, 285 N.E.2d 311 (N.Y.1972).

The exception can apply in tort, especially in the employment context. Employees can moonlight, working two jobs instead of one. If a discharged employee takes a new job that would not have interfered with the original job, the court must determine whether the new job is a substitute job or an additional job—that is, whether the employee is a lost volume seller of services. If the plaintiff would not have entered the second transaction but for defendant's breach of the first, the second is a substitute transaction, not an additional transaction. But if plaintiff would have taken both jobs, defendant's breach left the plaintiff with less money than she would have had but for the wrong.

Courts typically assume that construction contractors are lost volume sellers, without evidence. By hiring more laborers, contractors can work additional jobs without increasing overhead. Thus, if defendant wrongfully throws a contractor off the job, the next job the contractor takes is not a substitute. The contractor could have worked both jobs and is entitled to the profit from two jobs, not just one. The assumption is so strong that at least one court has applied it where the contractor could not possibly have performed both jobs.

Sometimes defendants urge that plaintiff should have begun mitigation even before the wrong occurred. A plaintiff who anticipates a breach can take precautions to minimize the harm the breach will cause. In contract, a plaintiff who expects the other party to breach can minimize the amount spent preparing to perform its side of the bargain. In tort, a plaintiff who buckles a seat belt may reduce the harm he will suffer if an accident occurs.

On the whole, the avoidable consequences doctrine is not well suited to dealing with pre-breach precautions. Some courts expressly limit the rule to efforts a plaintiff could have undertaken after the breach occurs. Other doctrines seem better suited to addressing precautions that precede breach. In tort, comparative negligence allows juries to consider unreasonable conduct by plaintiff before the wrong occurred. In contract, anticipatory repudiation and adequate assurances of performance address when a party should prepare for the other party's possible breach. Nonetheless, some courts have reduced the amount plaintiff can recover by the amount that would have been avoided by buckling up. Many states have passed statutes rejecting this result, including states that require seat belt use by law.

Some courts recite an exception when defendant had the same opportunity to mitigate the loss that plaintiff had. The argument resembles an estoppel: having failed to pursue mitigation itself, defendant cannot complain that plaintiff failed to pursue mitigation. In most cases, the language is dicta, following a conclusion that plaintiff did act reasonably. If applied, it would create odd incentives for wasteful duplication of efforts to mitigate the same loss—or, worse, the failure of either party to mitigate the loss on the ground that the other party should have done so. It would be risky to urge application of this exception in any case where plaintiff really was unreasonable in failing to minimize the loss.

5. Foreseeability

The concept of foreseeability arises throughout the law, but means something a little different in each context. In tort, it may help decide whether a wrong proximately caused an injury or whether defendant owed a duty to the plaintiff. This section addresses foreseeability as a limitation on contract damages. A few cases have applied it to tort damages, particularly if the tort affects business income.

The Rule. Plaintiff cannot recover damages for loss that the defendant did not have reason to foresee as a probable result of the breach at the time of contract formation. RESTATEMENT (SECOND) OF CONTRACTS § 351. Where damages flow naturally from the breach in the ordinary course of events, defendant should foresee these losses without any special notice. Where damages are unusual, other circumstances may give defendant reason to know of these probable losses. Most commonly, plaintiff may reveal facts that give defendant reason to know that this type of loss is probable in the event of breach. *See Hadley v. Baxendale*, 9 Ex. 341, 156 Eng.Rep. 154 (1854) (mill was shut down pending replacement of a shaft; carrier misdirected the shaft, delaying replacement; no damages for lost profits because not foreseeable).

A few clarifications should help avoid the most common errors regarding application of this rule.

The rule requires that defendant have reason to know, not necessarily actual knowledge. A particularly dense defendant remains liable for the damages he should have foreseen, even if he did not actually foresee them.

Courts evaluate foreseeability at the time of contract formation. This protects a defendant's ability to bargain for a different allocation of risk. For instance, a defendant aware of the magnitude of the loss plaintiff might suffer may want to: (1) reject the deal altogether; (2) raise the price to compensate for the risk of loss; (3) include a clause limiting or excluding recovery of some or all of the loss; (4) buy insurance to cover the risk of loss; or (5) take extra precautions to reduce the risk of loss. Without reason to know that losses of this type are likely, defendant lacks a meaningful chance to bargain for terms like these.

The rule governs the foreseeability of losses if the contract is breached. The breach itself need not be foreseeable. Thus, defendant cannot avoid paying damages to plaintiff because, at contract formation, she had no reason to know that she would decide to breach. Rather, the court asks, hypothetically, what losses the defendant should have considered if she had considered the effects of a breach like the one that occurred.

Recovery is limited to losses that were a probable result of the breach. A mere possibility that losses of that sort might result will not satisfy the foreseeability requirement. Again, this helps protect the ability of parties to bargain. Defendant need not bargain over every remote possibility that might follow a breach. But if the loss was a probable consequence of breach, defendant should either bargain over the loss or pay damages for the loss. And if it is remote, plaintiff should either raise it during negotiations or accept the risk of loss. In some cases, courts find foreseeability only when the loss was nearly inevitable. This may read too much into the "ordinary course of events," limiting the ordinary to the inevitable and treating anything else as unusual. Once mentioned by plaintiff, however, defendant may have difficulty persuading a court that the loss was unforeseeable because not inevitable.

On different readings, the rule might require that defendant had reason to know the *type* of loss plaintiff would suffer or the *amount* of that loss. The first would allow recovery of lost profits if defendant had reason to know that plaintiff intended to resell the property. It is foreseeable that breach by defendant would prevent plaintiff from entering a profitable resale. The second allows recovery of lost profits only if defendant had reason to know how large the profit would be on resale. A defendant who knew that plaintiff intended to resell the property might expect the resale price to include a modest profit. If instead plaintiff negotiated an unusually high resale price, the fact that such large profits did not seem probable at the time of formation would limit recovery. Plaintiff could recover the amount of profit defendant had reason to expect, but not the excess. Reason to anticipate the type of loss generally will suffice to make damage foreseeable. While some cases require reason to know of the amount of the loss, these are less common.

Neither interpretation reflects the language of the Uniform Commercial Code, which allows recovery for loss "resulting from the general or particular requirements and needs of which the seller at the time of contracting had reason to know. . . ." UCC § 2–715(2)(a). This does not seem to require that the amount of loss (or even that the type of loss) be foreseeable as a probable result of the breach, only that the requirements and needs of buyer have been foreseeable. Nonetheless, courts often treat the UCC rule as identical to the traditional rule discussed above.

Consequential Damages vs. Market Value. The foreseeability rule applies to consequential damages, typically lost profits, but may not apply to other contract damages. By incorporating foreseeability into the definition of consequential damages, the UCC implies it does not affect other measures. Thus, when shortages drive the cover price to unusual levels, defendant cannot resist paying cover price minus contract price on grounds of foreseeability. The same might apply outside the sale of goods. For instance, a homeowner who refuses to deliver a deed after prices skyrocket might have to pay market price (at the time for delivery) minus contract price, even though she had no reason to know that prices would increase so much.

Consequential damages sometimes can be cast as market values, where lost profits affect the value of an asset. Depriving plaintiff of an asset (even temporarily) inevitably deprives her of the value of the asset. Thus, even if plaintiff cannot show how much profit she would have earned had the asset been delivered on time, she can recover the fair market value of the asset (or, for temporary deprivations, the fair rental value). Fair market value of income-producing assets depends on the profits people expect to earn from the asset. (Recall the discussion of capitalization of earnings.) This will not include unusual profits that only the plaintiff might have made, but will include the ordinary profits anyone could make. More importantly, because fair market value is assessed as of the date of delivery, the value of the property will include profits likely at that time, even if they were unforeseeable at the time of contract formation. In this way, damages may shift from consequential losses to market losses.

6. Certainty

Plaintiff cannot recover damages that exceed the amount that the evidence establishes with reasonable certainty. RESTATEMENT (SECOND) OF CONTRACTS § 352. The rule seeks to prevent extravagant or speculative awards. Requiring reasonable certainty has the effect of raising the standard of proof, requiring more than a preponderance of the evidence for some damages. In theory, the jury may be instructed to apply the certainty rule in deciding the amount to award. More commonly, the rule makes it easier for judges to intervene in damage decisions. Judges may reject some elements of damages (via partial summary judgment), precluding a jury from ever hearing evidence on those issues. Judges may remit a jury's award on the ground that the amount awarded exceeded what was reasonably certain.

The rule partially counteracts the traditional deference judges must pay to jury decisions on issues of fact. In reviewing a verdict, the court need not rule that no reasonable juror could have believed that amount was more likely than not. Instead, the court may rule no reasonable juror could have believed that amount was reasonably certain. This seems more modest, less invasive of the jury's role. The rule, then, emboldens judges by weakening the rhetoric required to intervene in jury awards. This shifts the balance of power between judge and jury.

The rule requiring certainty may be stated in different ways, depending on the context. In tort, the rule often is framed to require as much certainty as is practical. RESTATEMENT (SECOND) OF TORTS § 912. This statement recognizes the difficulty of fixing nonpecuniary damages (distress, pain, suffering, lost joy, indignity, outrage, loss of reputation) with any certainty. Generally, as long as the existence of these losses can be demonstrated, the requirements of the rule are satisfied. For pecuniary losses, in tort or contract, courts may expect somewhat more evidence establishing the existence of the loss. Even then, some courts are satisfied once the existence of loss has been established with reasonable certainty. Other courts, however, state that both the existence and the amount of damages must be proved with reasonable certainty. The difficulty of meeting this test is tempered somewhat by the application of the wrongdoer rule (more accurately, the wrongdoer exception to the certainty rule), which allows jurors some room to estimate the loss where the lack of certainty results from the wrongdoer's conduct. Each aspect is discussed below.

Plaintiff Must Prove the Existence of Damages with Reasonable Certainty. Where serious doubt exists as to whether plaintiff suffered a loss at all, the certainty doctrine precludes recovery, at least of that element of loss. Thus, where plaintiff's history of profits leaves doubt that it would have earned profits even if the wrong had not been committed, courts may reject lost profits as uncertain. New businesses suffer most under this rule. Many new businesses never earn a profit. With no history of profitable operation, the wrong may have prevented future losses rather than caused them. The inability to prove that future profits were reasonably certain precludes recovery of lost profits entirely. An established business, with a history of profitable operation, may satisfy the certainty requirement.

As long as courts are reasonably certain that lost profits exist, they usually allow a jury to consider how much profit the plaintiff lost. Thus, if plaintiff can demonstrate that lost profits were reasonably certain to equal or exceed $1, the certainty doctrine has been satisfied. Once the court is reasonably certain that $0 is the wrong amount of lost profits, it will not use the certainty doctrine to award $0, the one number that almost certainly is wrong. Thus, the jury will be allowed to estimate the amount of lost profit, subject to review on post-trial motion.

Plaintiff May Need to Prove the Amount of Damages with Reasonable Certainty. Some courts state the rule more strictly, requiring that both the existence of damages and the amount of damage be proven with reasonable certainty. In theory, a court stating the doctrine this way might strike a claim for lost profits even if plaintiff showed with reasonable certainty that lost profits were at least $100, but where no certainty existed concerning how much more the plaintiff lost. In practice, courts usually avoid this result by recourse to the wrongdoer exception, discussed below.

The rule applies to each component of a damage award. Thus, if plaintiff can show one component (say, cost to repair a building) with reasonable certainty, but cannot show other elements (say, the profit plaintiff would have earned from operating a business from the building during the period required for repairs) with reasonable certainty, plaintiff can recover the components proven. Defendant cannot avoid all damages because one element is uncertain.

Wrongdoer Exception. Where the defendant's wrongful conduct created plaintiff's inability to prove damages with sufficient certainty, courts usually permit the jury to estimate the amount of the loss, within reason. *See Bigelow v. RKO Radio Pictures, Inc.*, 327 U.S. 251, 66 S.Ct. 574, 90 L.Ed. 652 (1946). Taken literally, this exception would repeal the certainty doctrine. Defendant's misconduct always creates the uncertainty. If defendant had not committed the wrong, plaintiff would be in the position she would have occupied but for the wrong and, therefore, could prove what that position is.

Courts apply the exception to uncertainty concerning the amount of damages, not uncertainty concerning the existence of damages. If plaintiff cannot prove the existence of lost profits with reasonable certainty, courts deny lost profits regardless of the wrongdoer exception. But where plaintiff can prove some lost profits, even $1, with reasonable certainty, the court will recite the wrongdoer exception to permit the jury to estimate the amount of lost profits.

Reasonable Certainty Does Not Require Precision. Regardless of how they frame the rule, all courts note that plaintiff need not prove the amount of damages with precision. The rule does not require plaintiff to specify the amount of loss down to the penny. Rather, it precludes recovery of losses that exceed the amount proven with reasonable certainty. Once plaintiff overcomes the initial hurdle, courts allow juries to estimate the loss as well as they can. Courts object to pure speculation by juries, not to reasonable estimates based on evidence. (The court can always return to the issue via post-trial motions if the award seems excessive.)

Certainty does not demand that any one number be certain, but asks whether damages of *at least* this amount are reasonably certain. If so, that award satisfies the test. Thus, even if $100 is an unlikely number, as long as the court is reasonably certain that damages would have been at least that amount, a jury award of $100 would be sustained. As the amount of damages rises above the relatively certain minimum, the likelihood that damages would have been at least that amount declines. At some point, the likelihood of damages reaching that level diminishes below the certainty threshold. Any award greater than that amount would be rejected by the court under the certainty doctrine.

Proving Damages with Reasonable Certainty. Certainty does not preclude damages very often, as long as plaintiffs prepare their damage evidence carefully. Courts have shown increasing willingness to credit testimony by accounting experts, who use copious data and sophisticated techniques to estimate business losses. A party cannot assume a court will accept her own estimate of the profits her business would have made without some supporting factual material. Similarly, a plaintiff whose expert witness does not attempt to estimate the amount lost may fail.

New businesses still fall prey to the rule fairly often. Established businesses usually can point to some history of profits upon which to base an estimate of lost profits. Even new businesses may produce some indicia of success. For instance, a franchise might rely on the success of similar franchisees in other locations to provide some basis for concluding this business also would have earned some profit. Careful market studies and projections might permit a new business to show the likelihood of profits. Certainty tends to preclude recovery of only the most speculative ventures.

7. Public Policy

In some cases, strict application of damage rules may produce results that undermine the substantive policy objectives of one or more laws. When this happens, courts may reject or limit damages in a way that protects the policy objectives.

Public policy arguments usually involve three steps. First, identify a policy. Usually this requires a generalized statement of principle, not just a conclusion that a particular case should be decided differently. Second, support the existence of the policy. Just because a policy seems like a good idea does not make it the policy of the jurisdiction. Constitutions, statutes, or established judicial decisions offer legitimate sources of public policy. Courts can create or identify new policies, but usually show restraint. Unless the court can conclude that the public would be nearly unanimous in approving the policy, courts tend to let the legislature decide which (if either) side of divided public opinion represents the public policy of the state. Third, demonstrate how awarding a remedy will undermine the policy. At least two techniques for demonstrating inconsistency with policy are addressed below.

Undermining a Law's Policy Goals. A remedy may undercut the very policy that motivated creation of a law. In unusual cases, applying a law literally may cause the harm it sought to prevent. Courts may refuse to grant a remedy when doing so would undermine the policy goals that a law sought to promote. For example, plaintiffs sometimes ask courts to apply the antitrust laws in a way that would encourage less competition instead of more competition. In *Brunswick Corp. v. Pueblo Bowl-O-Mat*, 429 U.S. 477, 97 S.Ct. 690, 50 L.Ed.2d 701 (1977), buyers of bowling alley equipment defaulted on payments to the seller. Instead of repossessing the equipment (which no one else wanted to buy), Brunswick bought the bowling alleys and operated them in order to recoup some of its loss on the sale. Brunswick eventually owned enough bowling alleys that it nearly monopolized the industry. After another takeover, a local bowling alley sued Brunswick for antitrust violations. As damages, plaintiff alleged that if Brunswick had not bought a local competitor, it would have gone out of business and that plaintiff's business would have increased as a result. Because Brunswick kept the competitor open, plaintiff's business did not increase. The trial court held that Brunswick's conduct tended to create a monopoly, in violation of the antitrust laws. On appeal, the Supreme Court held that plaintiff's damages were not recoverable. The statute was designed to protect competition, but plaintiff's damages stemmed from too much competition (Brunswick keeping a bowling alley open instead of letting it close). That kind of loss was not what the statute sought to protect.

Conflicting Goals. In some cases, awarding damages may undermine one policy goal, but denying them may undermine a different policy goal. In these cases, courts may decide to reject or limit damages in order to prevent undermining one of the policies at issue. No rules govern which of the conflicting policies a court should protect.

In most cases of conflicting policies, both parties are wrongdoers. Thus, awarding damages to one allows them to profit from their wrong. In some cases, this prevents liability. Defenses such as *in pari delicto* and unclean hands preclude recovery by a wrongdoer. In cases where liability can be established, courts may reject damages. For instance, employers faced with union activity sometimes report undocumented employees to the Immigration and Naturalization Service. Discrimination based on union activity violates the National Labor Relations Act. The normal remedy for employees is reinstatement and back pay. Courts may balk at concluding that deported laborers' rightful position includes jobs in the United States; rightfully, they should never have been in the country at all, let alone employed. In addition, reinstatement means little to workers already deported. In effect, immigration policy requires rejecting a remedy for the workers, while labor policy demands a remedy. The Supreme Court has favored the immigration policy. *See Sure-Tan, Inc. v. NLRB*, 467 U.S. 883, 104 S.Ct. 2803, 81 L.Ed.2d 732 (1984); *Hoffman Plastic Compounds v. NLRB*, 535 U.S. 137, 122 S.Ct. 1275, 152 L.Ed.2d 271 (2002). No general rule describes how to choose among competing policies.

Unanticipated Implications of Rules. Good rules sometimes lead courts to unexpected conclusions. If the result seems unsavory, courts sometimes invoke public policy to avoid it. For example, medical malpractice sometimes results in the birth of an unwanted child. The elements of the tort may be clear; the application of damage rules (notably the benefits rule) may produce a recovery. Yet courts sometimes refuse to award damages, especially for the birth of a healthy child, but sometimes even when severe genetic defects motivated the effort to prevent the birth. *See Taylor v. Kurapati*, 236 Mich.App. 315, 600 N.W.2d 670 (1999).

Unanticipated implications pose the hardest justification for denying recovery. They usually arise without any established contrary policy. For example, damages in the birth cases would not undermine the policy goals of malpractice law. Nor do these cases involve two wrongdoers. The parents commit no wrong when they seek genetic counseling, sterilization, or even an abortion (if we confine wrongs to legally actionable wrongs). Thus, awarding damages to the parents would not encourage misconduct by them, but denying damages might reduce the deterrent on wrongdoers. Nonetheless, courts may identify and apply policies in an ad hoc manner when they find it appropriate to reject or limit damages.

H. AGREED REMEDIES

Parties to a contract may include terms intended to limit or to augment the remedies courts normally award. After early hostility to such provisions, courts have begun to enforce these contractual terms relating to remedies, within limits—at least when contract damages are at issue. Contract terms that try to alter tort remedies (*e.g.*, contracts with doctors) or statutory remedies (*e.g.*, contracts with securities brokers) receive somewhat greater scrutiny.

1. Limitations on Remedy

Limitations on remedy usually take one of two forms: (1) terms precluding recovery of some element of damages, such as consequential damages; or (2) terms substituting a different remedy for the ones provided by law, such as the cost to repair or replace promised property. Substitute remedies sometimes implicitly preclude consequential damages: if plaintiff can recover only the cost of repair, consequential damages are excluded. Some contracts include both kinds of provisions. Article 2 of the Uniform Commercial Code (covering sales of goods) treats these two kinds of limitations differently.

Excluding Consequential Damages. A term precluding recovery of consequential damages is valid unless unconscionable. UCC § 2–719(3). The code includes a rebuttable presumption of unconscionability if a contract for consumer goods precludes recovery for personal injuries. Clauses limiting commercial consequential losses are expressly authorized. The code never defines unconscionability, neither in this section nor in section 2–302. Courts use varying tests to determine whether a term is unconscionable. A term almost certainly will be held unconscionable if two elements are satisfied: (1) unfair surprise; and (2) oppression, sometimes stated as terms unreasonably favorable to the person who proposed them.

Unfair surprise implies that one party: (1) was unaware of the existence or effect of the terms; and (2) that party had no fair chance to determine the existence or effect of the terms before entering the contract.

Proving that a party did not read the contract (and thus did not know the terms) may not suffice. One who did not read the contract is surprised, but may not be unfairly surprised. If reading the contract would have alerted the party to the terms, then the surprise seems attributable to the person's failure to read, not any unfairness by the party who proposed the term. If, however, the terms were concealed in a manner that would have prevented a reader from recognizing their existence or effect—language calculated to confuse, misleading headings, fine print, etc.—perhaps the failure to discover and to understand them is excusable and the surprise unfair.

Oppression (or unreasonably favorable terms) implies that one party: (1) receives an advantage from having the terms in the contract; and (2) the advantage is unreasonable. Proving that the terms favor one party will not suffice; all terms eventually favor one party or the other. But if the terms provide an advantage that lacks a commercial justification, the term may be unreasonably favorable.

Because this two element definition of unconscionability is relatively strict and hard to satisfy, courts sometimes relax the definition. Occasionally, a court may find unconscionability based only on unreasonably favorable terms, without regard to surprise. More commonly, courts expand slightly the ways in which parties may satisfy each element.

Some states rephrase unfair surprise as lack of reasonable choice. Unfair surprise produces lack of reasonable choice. A party who does not realize a term is in a contract lacks any ability to bargain for a different term (because she does not realize there is any need to bargain for a different term). But rephrasing the rule in terms of meaningful choice may expand it to include other constrained choices, such as unequal bargaining power. Thus, a court may find unconscionability when a party would not have been able to persuade the other to change or to delete the term if she had tried to bargain. This approach, in effect, allows the weaker party to force terms on the stronger party—a result inconsistent with contract theories based on mutual assent. Courts using this definition always require some showing of oppression in addition to lack of reasonable choice—otherwise, unconscionability could be used to negate any term of any form contract.

Some courts redefine oppression to focus on the harmful effects to the plaintiff rather than the reasonableness of the term. Thus, a term that has harsh effects satisfies the oppression requirement, even if the other party had very good commercial reasons for insisting on that term. This approach is inconsistent with the UCC requirement that unconscionability be determined at the time of contract formation; at the time of formation, the effects are unknown, while the commercial justification of the term makes it seem reasonable, not overreaching by the proponent.

Substituted Remedies. The UCC allows parties to substitute remedies for those provided in the code. UCC § 2–719(1)(a). The remedies may expand rather than limit recovery. For instance, contracts that permit the prevailing party to recover attorneys' fees expand recovery. More commonly, contracts seek to limit recovery, often by specifying plaintiff's remedy is limited to repairs.

A substitute remedy may be either exclusive or optional. If optional, the plaintiff may elect to pursue remedies under the law instead of the substitute remedy. If the substitute remedy does not specify that it is exclusive, then it is optional. UCC § 2–719(1)(b). Most contracts seeking to limit remedies specify that their remedies are exclusive.

Unless the exclusive remedy fails of its essential purpose, it precludes recourse to remedies under the code. UCC § 2–719(2). A remedy fails of its essential purpose unless it provides plaintiff some minimally adequate remedy. For instance, an exclusive remedy limiting the buyer to repair would fail of its essential purpose if defendant cannot repair the item after sufficient opportunity to do so. The mere fact that the remedy is not as generous as those provided in the code is not sufficient to justify rejecting the contractual remedy. But the utter failure to provide the plaintiff with the benefit for which they bargained may permit the court to reject the limited remedy provided in the contract.

Combined Limitations. Contracts may contain both limitations: they limit the remedy to repairs and expressly exclude consequential damages. In those cases, courts must determine how the failure of one clause relates to the other. Specifically, when repairs are impossible, negating the substitute remedy, what happens to the exclusion of consequential damages? Some courts hold that the two clauses are independent: if the express term excluding consequential damages is not unconscionable, it is enforceable, without regard to the fate of the substituted remedy.

Others find that the failure of the substituted remedy should allow the plaintiff recourse to consequential damages: in effect, the failure of one limitation is the failure of both limitations. This view probably gives too little weight to the contract the parties made. Nonetheless, the animosity courts sometimes show to limitations that preclude effective remedies—those that honor plaintiff's rightful position—produce this result.

2. Liquidated Damages

Contracts may specify (or liquidate) an amount of damages, either as a fixed amount or by a formula. Liquidated damages clauses are not treated as substitute remedies: they do not reject the principles governing calculation of damages, but simply attempt to perform the calculation in advance.

Liquidated damage clauses are enforceable, but penalty clauses are void (against public policy). Courts differentiate penalty clauses from liquidated damages based on the substance of the provisions: merely calling a clause liquidated damages (or a penalty) will not ensure that the courts will treat it as such.

A liquidated damages clause is enforceable if it is reasonable. Factors considered in determining the reasonableness of a clause include (i) the anticipated or actual harm caused by the breach, (ii) the difficulties of proof of loss, and (iii) the inconvenience or nonfeasibility of otherwise obtaining an adequate remedy (say, through injunctive relief or restitution). UCC § 2–718(1); RESTATEMENT (SECOND) OF CONTRACTS § 356. (Amendments to the UCC, not yet adopted anywhere, propose to limit the second two factors to consumer contracts. If adopted, the relation between the clause and the anticipated or actual harm would be pertinent to any contract, consumer or commercial. Difficulty of proof of loss would be irrelevant to commercial contracts. The change may make clauses more easily enforceable in commercial settings.)

Anticipated or Actual Harm. Liquidated damage clauses are enforceable if the amount "is reasonable in light of the anticipated or actual harm caused by the breach." UCC § 2–718(1). The "or" is significant. A clause that wildly exceeds the actual harm is valid if it is reasonable in light of the anticipated harm. Similarly, a clause that wildly exceeds the anticipated harm is valid if it is reasonable in light of the actual harm. Thus, a clause the parties thought would be a penalty (because they underestimated how large the actual harm would be) may be enforceable.

The rule specifies the anticipated or actual *harm*, not the anticipated or actual *damages*. If the harm caused by the breach is great, it does not matter that normal damage rules might limit the plaintiff to damages much less than the harm. The liquidated damage clause allows the parties to include recovery for losses that the code otherwise would not allow, especially damages that might otherwise be unforeseeable or uncertain.

Some continued animosity toward liquidated damage clauses leads courts to apply the rule discussed here less generously than its language suggests. Courts may refuse to award damages if the amount seems unreasonable in light of the actual loss, no matter how reasonable the clause may have seemed at the time the contract was made. Other courts seem to apply an intent test: if the clause seems excessive at the time of its creation, the parties must have intended a penalty. This might justify rejecting clauses that capture the actual loss quite well based on an imputed intent to penalize. (Rather than impute punitive intent, courts could impute unusual foresight to the parties.)

Difficulty of Proof of Loss. At one time, courts required a party to prove that the loss would be difficult to prove as a prerequisite to enforcing a liquidated damage clause. If loss would be relatively easy to measure after the breach occurred, courts refused to enforce liquidated damage clauses regardless of their reasonableness. Most jurisdictions now reject that strict requirement. Difficulty of proof of loss is simply one factor to discuss in evaluating reasonableness—probably a secondary factor. It affects the degree of accuracy a court will require. Where damages are relatively difficult to assess after a breach (*e.g.*, profits are hard to estimate), a clause may be deemed reasonable even if it seems to miss the actual loss by a relatively large margin. On the other hand, if damages are relatively easy to calculate (*e.g.*, cover price and contract price are readily ascertainable in the market), a clause estimating damages may need to be relatively close to the actual or anticipated loss before a court will find it reasonable.

Inconvenience or Nonfeasibility of Other Remedies. In some cases, liquidated damages may seem unnecessary in light of other remedies, such as specific performance or restitution. A plaintiff's preference for damages under a liquidation clause over specific performance suggests the clause may be excessive—that damages would leave the plaintiff better off than if the contract had been performed. If so, the reasonableness of the clause might be questioned. That inference is weakened if other remedies pose difficulties. Those difficulties may be considered in determining the validity of the clause. In some cases, a liquidated damage clause itself may preclude other remedies by specifying that it is plaintiff's exclusive remedy. The argument is somewhat circular and may not prevail. In any event, the concerns this factor addresses are not entirely consistent with the increasing willingness of courts to allow parties to fix their own remedies, even if they may exceed (by a reasonable margin) damages a court would award.

Bonuses. Some bargains might achieve the same effect via a bonus clause instead of a liquidated damage clause. Consider two terms:

(1) A $20 million construction contract requires completion by July 21, but provides that the contractor will receive a bonus of $100,000 per day for early completion, up to a maximum of $2 million.

(2) A $22 million construction contract requires completion by July 1, but provides for liquidated damages of $100,000 per day for late completion, to a maximum of $2 million.

These two provisions provide the same payment, regardless of when the project is completed. The second might be called a penalty, unless $100,000 a day is reasonable in light of the actual or anticipated harm. The first, however, does not specify damages for breach at all. There is no breach on any day (until after July 21), so no clause attempts to specify the damages for breach. Analyzing the clause under this rule seems a stretch.

Some authorities urge that the rules governing penalties should apply to contract provisions that might circumvent the limitations, such as the bonus clause here. The rationale is suspect, but a complete analysis of bonus clauses might need to include a discussion of this possibility.

Alternative Performance. Contracts may specify alternative performances: they allow one party to perform in either of two ways, one of which may be more onerous than the other. For instance, a loan may allow the borrower to pay over the full life of the loan or to pay the full amount early, provided a fee for early payment is included. This is not a liquidated damage clause. There is no breach, so no damages for breach. Unless the additional charges are triggered by a breach of contract, the analysis here does not apply.

Similarly, take-or-pay provisions in oil and gas contracts usually are not analyzed as liquidated damage clauses. These provisions require the buyer to pay for gas whether or not she actually accepts delivery of the gas. Refusing delivery (arguably) is not a breach; refusing to pay is a breach.

Evolving Rules. It seems likely that liquidated damages will receive increasing acceptance over time. Legislation, restatements, and academics all urge enforceability—some even suggesting that penalties should be enforceable when agreed between capable parties. The traditional limitations identified here may diminish over time.

One state already has abandoned the rule prohibiting penalties. Instead, it asks whether liquidated damage terms are unconscionable. *Commercial Real Estate Investment v. Comcast of Utah II*, 285 P.3d 1193 (Utah 2012). This allows the court to uphold penalties that serve reasonable business purposes, at least when parties openly negotiated the provisions. The ability to strike oppressive penalty clauses may depend on how diligently courts apply the unconscionability doctrine.

3. Agreements Regarding Equitable Remedies

Contracts providing that specific performance or other equitable relief should be awarded receive less deference from courts. Equitable relief is discretionary. Courts do not treat these clauses as binding. At most, courts view these clauses as waivers of objections to equitable relief. More commonly, they view the contract as an invitation to use their discretion.

I. PUNITIVE OR EXEMPLARY DAMAGES

Punitive damages are not damages in the usual sense. They are a monetary recovery, but are not measured by the loss or damage the plaintiff suffered. Rather, they assume that compensatory damages have covered those losses completely and seek to impose an additional burden on defendant over and above the cost of compensating the plaintiff. While a few states refuse to award punitive damages at all, almost every state will award punitive damages in an appropriate case.

1. Rationale

Courts justify punitive damages on grounds of retribution and deterrence. While logically distinct, courts almost always recite them together. No consensus exists favoring either rationale as dominant. Those who think of compensatory damage awards in terms of deterrence also tend to think of punitive damages awards in those terms. Those who think in terms of corrective justice may see punitive damages as retribution. Choosing one rationale might affect how punitive damages are implemented. For example, vicarious liability for punitive damages (under, for example, respondeat superior) is harder to justify if they are deemed retributive than if they are intended as a deterrent. Retribution should be extracted from the party at fault, not from others, whose conduct was not subject to sanction, even though they were associated with the punishable party.

2. Liability for Punitive Damages

Scienter. Punitive damages are reserved for defendants whose state of mind suggests a need for deterrence or retribution. Mere negligence will not justify punitive damages; courts require some degree of reflection by the defendant before punishment becomes appropriate. The exact boundary varies among the states. All states that allow punitive damages allow them for actual malice, where defendant intends the harm. Generally, that includes imputed intent—not just the purpose to cause the harm, but also knowledge to a substantial certainty that harm will result. Almost all allow punitive damages where defendant's conduct implies malice—for example, if conduct is so outrageous that it seems likely defendant knew harm would result. Similarly, conscious disregard of an "unjustifiably substantial risk of significant harm" may justify an inference of malice. Many states also allow punitive damages for reckless disregard of a known risk, at least where the risk of harm is great. Whether the risk must be significant, probable, or substantially likely to occur varies among the states. Some states— fewer today than before—allow punitive damages for *gross negligence*, though the line between negligence and gross negligence is hard to describe in a rule. Juries determine whether the conduct was culpable negligence instead of mere negligence.

Some statutes allow recovery of damages that seem punitive without expressly requiring scienter. For example, the antitrust laws allow recovery of treble damages as a matter of course. Thus, compensatory damages are multiplied by three to produce the award, without regard to the defendant's state of mind. 15 U.S.C. § 15. Treble damages may have a compensatory purpose when antitrust damages are hard to prove. But courts also acknowledge a purpose to deter violations (a punitive rationale) and to remove any ill-gotten gain from defendants (a rationale sounding in restitution). The Racketeer Influenced and Corrupt Organizations Act allows plaintiffs to recover three times their actual loss. 18 U.S.C. § 1964(c). Liability under RICO—primarily a criminal law—often requires scienter. Patent statutes also permit, but do not require, a court to increase the damage award up to three times the actual damages. 35 U.S.C. § 284. Courts often limit treble damages to cases of willful infringement, though the statutory language does not specify that requirement. Similar provisions allow treble damages for trademark or copyright infringement. 15 U.S.C. 1117; 17 U.S.C. § 504. The Fair Labor Standards Act awards liquidated damages in an amount equal to the plaintiff's actual damages (effectively double damages), unless the employer can establish a good faith and reasonable belief that the conduct complied with the FLSA (a negligence standard). 29 U.S.C. §§ 216, 260. Some courts characterize the additional recovery as compensatory, acknowledging the many ways in which depriving an employee of full pay may lead to consequential losses that interest would not compensate adequately. The exception for employers who act in good faith links the liquidated damages to the employer's fault, a provision not completely consistent with a compensatory rationale. State laws also may allow treble damages, particularly where deceptive trade practices are involved. For example, Texas triples economic damages and allows recovery for mental anguish if a deceptive trade practice is committed knowingly; if committed intentionally, mental anguish damages also may be tripled. TEX. BUS. & COM. CODE ANN. § 17.50(b)(1).

Actual Damages. Punitive damages are unavailable unless the plaintiff establishes entitlement to compensatory damages. The rule reinforces liability rules that require injury. For example, punitive damages are unavailable against a defendant whose fraud caused no injury. Because no actual damages occurred, no liability for fraud attaches. On the other hand, where nominal damages are available, some courts have awarded punitive damages. For example, when plaintiff proves deprivation of a constitutional right, but cannot show actual injury, an award of nominal damages might satisfy the prerequisite for punitive damages. A few states, such as Ohio, reject punitive damages unless plaintiff recovers actual compensatory damages.

Noncontractual Liability. Punitive damages generally are limited to tort liability and statutory violations. Courts traditionally rejected punitive damages for breach of contract. Excessive liability for breach of contract might discourage people from making mutually beneficial contracts. (The traditional exception for breach of promise of marriage has been mooted by statutes repealing that cause of action in most states. It also represented an area where, at least at that time, people were unlikely to stop making promises.) Torts and statutes usually left no room for parties to opt out of the obligations.

Litigants seeking punitive damages sometimes find ways around this limitation. Conduct that constitutes a tort may justify punitive damages regardless of whether the conduct also breached a contract. A breach of contract does not negate a tort that arose from the same conduct. In addition, some breaches of contract have been redefined as torts. For example, many states now treat an insurance company's refusal to pay claims, if done without good faith, as a tort, not merely a breach of contract. Discharging an employee may rise to the level of tort (justifying punitive damages) if done in retaliation for protected activity, such as reporting the employer's illegal conduct or refusing an employer's request to commit perjury. Some attorneys plead ordinary discharge as intentional infliction of emotional distress in an effort to avoid the rule denying punitive damages in contract.

Vicarious Liability. When an agent or employee commits a wrong with the requisite scienter, punitive damages against the employee are available. Frequently, however, the principal or employer will not have acted recklessly or even negligently in connection with the wrong. While the employer generally will be liable for compensatory damages under the doctrine of respondeat superior, liability for punitive damages varies among jurisdictions. Some jurisdictions assess punitive damages against employers whenever their employees commit punishable wrongs within the scope of their employment. Others require some indication of wrongful conduct by the employer, though not always the same degree of recklessness or intent required to establish the employee's liability for punitive damages. Other jurisdictions require some indication that the employer was complicit in the wrongful conduct before assessing punitive damages against an employer. An employer's liability for punitive damages may be demonstrated in several ways:

1. the employee held a managerial position and was acting within the scope of employment;

2. the employee was unfit and the employer was reckless in employing him;

3. the employer authorized the doing and the manner of the conduct;

4. the employer ratified or approved the conduct.

See RESTATEMENT (SECOND) OF AGENCY § 217C. While the conduct of the employer need not necessarily satisfy the scienter requirement for punitive damages, some wrong (perhaps exceeding negligence) must be fairly attributed to the employer before these jurisdictions will authorize punitive damages.

The policies supporting punitive damages do not support automatically imposing punitive damages on the employer. Retribution against the employer would be appropriate if the employer acted with the requisite wrongful intent. In cases where the employer committed no wrong at all or, at worst, was negligent, punitive damages against the employer exceed the retribution rationale. Similarly, unless the employer committed some wrong that could be deterred, deterrence provides no justification for an award of punitive damages. While an employer's negligence might be deterred by punitive damages, typically courts hold that compensatory damages are adequate to deter negligent conduct. Respondeat superior serves a vital role in preserving compensation for victims injured by impecunious agents. Recovery of damages in excess of compensation seems to require a different justification.

The requirements for an employer's complicity may vary with context. For example, punitive damages for employment discrimination are not available when managerial agents make employment decisions that are contrary to the employer's good faith efforts to comply with Title VII. *Kolstad v. American Dental Association*, 527 U.S. 526, 119 S.Ct. 2118, 144 L.Ed.2d 494 (1999).

Insurability. Liability insurance policies generally exclude liability for damages expected or intended from the standpoint of the insured. Thus, where punitive damages arise from conduct the defendant intended, they will not be covered. Even if the defendant did not intend the harm, if the harm was expected (as in cases of implied malice), punitive damages will not fall within the coverage. In cases where the punitive damages arise from gross negligence or other conduct that falls short of intent, liability policies may cover the losses.

In many states, it is against public policy for an insurer to cover punitive damages, regardless of the policy language. Insurance weakens the ability of punitive damages to achieve their goals. Retribution should fall on the wrongdoer. Placing the burden on an insurer does not achieve that goal. (It would never fly in criminal cases; the perpetrator must serve the time, regardless of any contract she might have with another to serve it for her.) Similarly, deterrence is less effective if the cost is borne by the insurer. Even if the defendant ultimately pays higher premiums as a result of conduct that leads to punitive damage awards, punitive damages are aimed at the culpable defendant, not at the innocent insurer.

Policies prohibiting insuring against punitive damages vary in their scope. In a few states, the prohibition is general, applying to all punitive damages. New York even goes so far as to hold that New York residents cannot be covered for punitive damages, even if another state's court awards those damages. Other states reject insurance for the party whose conduct gave rise to the punitive award, but allow recovery by a person vicariously liable for the award. Thus, a driver whose recklessness justified punitive damages could not be insured, but the driver's employer might recover from insurance, if its conduct was not culpable. Other states preclude punitive damages when assessed for intentional conduct. To some extent, this restriction mirrors the way insurers write their policy coverage. At least three states allow recovery for punitive damages, but only if the policy expressly mentions punitive damages.

The differing policies on insurance may reflect differing views of punitive damages. The policies of retribution and deterrence suggest the critical point is to assess them against the wrongdoer, regardless of whether the victim actually collects them. The effect on the defendant is preserved by preventing the defendant from avoiding the impact. States allowing insurance, to some extent, give more importance to the plaintiff's ability to collect the recovery.

3. Measuring the Amount

No precise standard for measuring punitive damages has achieved general acceptance. Instead, states tend to list a number of factors juries may consider when determining how much to award. These factors include: (1) reprehensibility of the conduct; (2) defendant's wealth; (3) amount of compensatory damages; (4) amount likely to deter similar conduct by defendant and others.

Reprehensibility allows the court to differentiate the most culpable misconduct from other cases. Thus, wrongs that injure persons may be more reprehensible than wrongs that produce economic hardship alone. Repeated wrongdoing may be more reprehensible than a single wrongful act. The degree of scienter also affects the reprehensibility; intentional wrongs or conscious disregard of others may require larger awards than gross negligence or reckless disregard of others.

Taking account of defendant's wealth recognizes the marginal utility of money. While a $25,000 judgment would devastate many individual defendants, it might not be noticed by major corporations. The amount needed to punish or deter will vary with the defendant's wealth. Constitutional limitations on punitive damages may reduce reliance on defendant's wealth.

The amount of compensatory damages indicates the severity of the harm at issue. It establishes a rough proportionality test, helping evaluate whether the punishment is excessive for the wrong defendant committed. Where the damages are very large, the harm may justify a larger sanction. The approach is not universal. Criminal law often treats culpability as independent of the effect of the wrong: attempted murder is as bad as murder; the defendant deserves no credit for failing. Thus, where the potential harm to the plaintiff (if the defendant had succeeded in the wrongful endeavor) is very large, punitive damages may be larger even though the actual compensatory damages are not very large.

The amount likely to deter similar conduct reflects the overall enterprise. To the extent that punitive damages seek to deter, awards must be large enough to persuade the defendant and others to reconsider their conduct. This may encompass the other three factors. It focuses, however, on the message the award sends, increasing the award to avoid sending too weak a message (or decreasing it to avoid sending too strong a message).

4. Limitations

Concerns for excessive litigation draw attention to punitive damages, which can make claims for even small amounts of actual damages very lucrative. Legislatures and courts have considered a number of limitations on the availability and amount of punitive damages.

Statutory Limitations. Some state statutes limit the amount of punitive damages a jury may award. These caps resemble limits on the amount of pain and suffering or other nonpecuniary damages recoverable in litigation.

Some statutes allow the state to collect a portion of any punitive award. At the extreme, Nebraska requires that all penalties collected under state law (but not federal causes of action in state courts) be paid to counties for use supporting schools. As a result, plaintiffs' attorneys in Nebraska waste no time pleading and proving punitive damages. Ten other states allow plaintiffs to keep enough to cover costs and attorneys' fees, but collect a portion (35–75%) of the remaining punitive damages for the state. At least one court has rejected a sharing statute.

When the state receives a share of the punitive damages, the awards begin to resemble fines that might be challenged under the Eighth Amendment's excessive fines clause. The Supreme Court rejected challenges based on the Eighth Amendment because the states neither prosecuted the actions nor received a share of the proceeds. *Browning-Ferris Industries v. Kelco Disposal*, 492 U.S. 257, 109 S.Ct. 2909, 106 L.Ed.2d 219 (1989). So far, challenges under the excessive fines clause have been repulsed on the ground that the state still has no power to prosecute the action.

Constitutional Limitations. The United States Supreme Court has ruled that excessive punitive damages violate the due process clause of the fourteenth amendment. Due process requires that "a person receive fair notice not only of the conduct that will subject him to punishment, but also of the severity of the penalty that a State may impose." *BMW of North America, Inc. v. Gore*, 517 U.S. 559, 574, 116 S.Ct. 1589, 1598, 134 L.Ed.2d 809 (1996). The Court identified three factors that help determine whether an award satisfies due process: "(1) the degree of reprehensibility of the defendant's misconduct; (2) the disparity between the actual or potential harm suffered by the plaintiff and the punitive damages award; and (3) the difference between the punitive damages awarded by the jury and the civil penalties authorized or imposed in comparable cases." *State Farm Mutual Automobile Ins. Co. v. Campbell*, 538 U.S. 408, 418, 123 S.Ct. 1513, 1520, 155 L.Ed.2d 585 (2003). These factors closely resemble the factors state courts employ in deciding how much to award. The constitutional rule allows federal courts to review state court decisions for excessiveness. In addition, courts must review the constitutionality of a punitive award *de novo*, rather than applying an abuse of discretion test. *Cooper Industries v. Leatherman Tool Group*, 532 U.S. 424, 121 S.Ct. 1678, 149 L.Ed.2d 674 (2001). The combined effect gives judges considerable power and responsibility to limit punitive damages.

Defendant's wealth is notably absent from these factors. In *State Farm*, the Court appeared to reject evidence of defendant's wealth. When reviewing the constitutionality of a punitive damage award, "the wealth of a defendant cannot justify an otherwise unconstitutional punitive damages award." *State Farm*, 538 U.S. at 427, 123 S.Ct. at 1525. This language does not preclude a state from admitting evidence of defendant's wealth or allowing the jury to rely on that evidence. In reviewing the constitutionality of the jury award, however, the court cannot rely on evidence of defendant's wealth. Unless the other factors establish the constitutionality of the award, it will need to be reduced. In light of this, some states may decide to stop admitting evidence of defendant's wealth.

Reprehensibility. A defendant whose conduct is particularly reprehensible should have notice that courts might award large punitive damages. Factors a court may consider include the nature of the harm (physical injury vs. economic loss), the defendant's state of mind (malice or indifference to the safety of others vs. mere accident), the financial vulnerability of the plaintiff, and the frequency of the misconduct (repeated actions vs. isolated incident). States use similar factors when determining the amount of punitive damages. Any argument that makes the harm or the conduct seem more severe may contribute to the reprehensibility of the conduct.

Proportionality. A defendant whose conduct causes (or might cause) large losses to others should have notice that courts might award large punitive damages. Thus, if compensatory damages are relatively small, a large punitive award may be excessive. The Court in *State Farm* rejected any formula, but hinted that few awards could survive scrutiny where the ratio of punitive damages to compensatory damages exceeded 9:1. In calculating this ratio, courts may use the harm defendant's misconduct potentially might have caused to the plaintiff rather than the actual harm it caused. Thus, a defendant whose nefarious scheme fails may face a substantial punitive award, despite causing relatively little loss. In *Lompe v. Sunridge Partners*, 818 F.3d 1041 (10th Cir.2016), however, the court reduced an award from 11.5:1 to a 1:1 ratio even though the defendant's failure to control carbon monoxide in its apartments seriously injured plaintiff (and could have killed her). The court based the ratio on the actual losses, not the potential losses.

A larger compensatory award is more likely to deter misconduct adequately, without additional punitive damages. Punitive damages may be unnecessary or, if justified, a relatively low ratio (say, 1:1) may suffice. This argument seems unrelated to the notice rationale for due process review. Nonetheless, the U.S. Supreme Court suggested this approach in *State Farm*, hinting that $1 million might adequately deter the defendant. On remand, however, the Utah Supreme Court rejected the idea, instead allowing Campbell $9 million in punitive damages—a ratio of 9:1.

Punitive damages must be based on the harm the defendant caused the plaintiff. Harm or potential harm to others is subject to sanction in suits brought by others. But until those claims are brought and proven, defendant may not be punished for those wrongs. This does not prevent plaintiff from showing defendant's reprehensibility by introducing evidence of repeated wrongdoing or harm to others. But it does preclude inviting juries to award punitive damages to this plaintiff based on harms to others. *Philip Morris USA v. Williams*, 549 U.S. 346, 127 S.Ct. 1057, 166 L.Ed.2d 940 (2007).

The proportionality requirement poses puzzles for punitive damages when plaintiff recovers only nominal damages. Courts have found that nominal damages satisfy the requirement that plaintiff recover compensation as a prerequisite to an award of punitive damages. Strict adherence to a 9:1 maximum ratio, however, might severely limit the ability to assess an appropriate punitive award. In *Arizona v. ASARCO*, 773 F.3d 1050 (9th Cir.2014) (en banc), the court upheld an punitive award of $300,000 (the maximum allowed under state law, reduced from a jury award of $868,750) even though plaintiff recovered only $1 in nominal damages on her sexual harassment claim. The court relied in part on the developed state statutory scheme to provide due process notice of the amount of sanction defendant might face in light of its conduct.

Other Sanctions. A defendant whose conduct is subject to other serious sanctions, criminal or civil, should have notice that courts might award large punitive damages. Larger sanctions make it more likely a large punitive damage award will survive. Where penalties are smaller, the defendant lacks warning of the severity of the penalty that a state may impose. Deference to legislative decisions about the appropriate magnitude of a sanction may be appropriate. This approach may limit the usefulness of punitive damages as a means to rectify the legislature's failure to impose sanctions large enough to deter misconduct.

5. Punitive Damages in Arbitration

While a state can punish its citizens, punishment by a private arbitrator raises some concern. The challenges take different forms. Some argue that arbitrators should not be allowed to award punitive damages at all, that this power should be reserved for the government (that is, judges and juries). Others argue that arbitrators should not be allowed to award punitive damages unless a court would have been able to award punitive damages in the type of case. Thus, an arbitrator might lack authority to award punitive damages in a contract case, but retain that authority in tort cases. Each argument runs up against the general rule that arbitrators can fashion justice unconstrained by the rules that limit courts. Other challenges focus on the arbitration agreement, seeking to establish that it does not authorize the arbitrator to award punitive damages.

Federal Arbitration Act (FAA). The FAA governs arbitration clauses in contracts involved in interstate commerce. Under the FAA, federal courts have enforced arbitration awards that include punitive damages. These cases generally include some allegations of tort, such as fraud, even when the underlying dispute involves a contract. Thus, under the FAA courts seem to enforce arbitration awards that include punitive damages as long as a court could have considered punitive damages if the case had been litigated in court. In tort cases, an arbitration award including punitive damages seems likely to be enforced; punitive damages seem unlikely to survive in pure contract cases, where no tort is alleged.

Courts do not review an arbitrator's factual findings. Thus, an arbitrator's finding of malice may be beyond review. Courts required to apply constitutional limitations on awards of punitive damages de novo may need to reconsider the traditional deference to arbitrators. It remains to be seen whether the instruction to review the constitutionality of punitive damage awards de novo applies to district courts reviewing arbitration awards or only to appellate courts reviewing trial awards.

State Arbitration Laws. Some arbitration clauses are contained in contracts that fall outside the FAA. Many state courts have affirmed arbitration awards including punitive damages. Most of these awards arose from cases involving some allegation of tort. Some courts expressly note that in court plaintiff could have recovered punitive damages.

One famous (and much criticized) case appears to hold that arbitrators can never award punitive damages. *Garrity v. Lyle Stuart, Inc.*, 40 N.Y.2d 354, 386 N.Y.S.2d 831, 353 N.E.2d 793 (1976). The court stated that it violated the public policy of New York for private decisionmakers (arbiters), as opposed to public officials (judges), to award punitive sanctions—even if the parties expressly authorized the arbitrator to do so. While portions of the opinion are dicta, the breadth of the stated rationale casts doubt on any punitive award from an arbitrator. On the other hand, the opinion did not overrule precedent enforcing an arbitrator's award of treble liquidated damages (three times the estimated actual damages). That award is inherently punitive. The parties' assent to the formula for calculating the damages may have assuaged the court's doubts about private penalties. Nonetheless, the opinions are difficult to reconcile. In agreements under the FAA, federal law preempts *Garrity*, allowing arbitrators to award punitive damages unless their agreement clearly indicates the intent not to authorize arbitrators to award punitive damages. *Mastrobuono v. Shearson Lehman Hutton, Inc.*, 514 U.S. 52, 115 S.Ct. 1212, 131 L.Ed.2d 76 (1995).

The Arbitrator's Authority. Some courts consider whether the arbitration clause authorizes the arbitrator to award punitive damages. If the parties agreed to give the arbitrator this power, state intervention to protect people from their own agreement requires fairly significant justification. Arbitration clauses can be an important part of contracts, keeping the price down by reducing the cost of resolving disputes.

Courts draw different inferences concerning an arbitrator's authority. Some suggest a broad arbitration clause authorizes punitive damages unless it expressly excludes them. Others argue that an arbitration clause authorizes punitive damages only if it expressly includes them. Finally, some accept any indication that the parties intended to authorize arbitration of punitive damages.

The last approach often involves cases where one party submits a request for punitive damages and the other party does not contest the request in the arbitration proceeding. Whether viewed as course of performance (showing that the parties believed the clause permitted punitive damages from the beginning) or an implied modification of the clause (where the parties' conduct suggests mutual assent to arbitrating the issue of punitive damages), courts have enforced arbitration awards in these circumstances.

The parties' intent probably justifies allowing punitive awards when tort claims are arbitrated, but not when contract claims are arbitrated. In tort arbitrations, rejecting punitive damages converts the arbitration clause into a waiver of punitive damages. That may surprise an unwary party, even one who read the contract. In contract arbitrations, however, allowing punitive awards converts the arbitration clause into consent to punitive damages—again, without much notice to a party that the clause would have that effect. To avoid a trap for unwary parties, it seems fairer to assume the arbitration clause did not change the availability of punitive damages, but merely the forum in which they would be considered. Of course, courts could honor provisions that expressly alter the normal remedies courts award (that is, expressly authorize punitive damages in contract or expressly reject punitive damages in tort).

J. ATTORNEYS' FEES

The American Rule rejects recovery of attorneys' fees, leaving each party to pay their own counsel—even though other court costs are assessed against the losing party. It contrasts with the British Rule, in which the loser pays the winner's attorney, though fees assessed often do not equal actual fees incurred. The American Rule protects the ability of people of modest means to bring claims. Faced with the risk that they might need to pay for defendant's attorneys, even a fifteen percent chance of losing might deter many plaintiffs. The rich could afford to take these chances, as might the poorest members of society, who have no property on which defendants could execute a judgment for fees. But many people could not seek redress under a British Rule.

The American Rule, however, leaves the plaintiff worse off than if the wrong had not occurred. If damages accurately assess the plaintiff's loss, reducing them by 33–50% to cover the attorney's share (perhaps more to cover expert witness fees and other expenses) leaves plaintiff well short of the rightful position. In equitable actions, the problem is more stark. Even if the injunction prevents the wrong, the cost of an attorney falls entirely on the plaintiff, leaving her worse off than if defendant's action had not required the suit.

As a result, numerous exceptions to the American Rule allow prevailing parties to recover their attorneys' fees.

1. Statutory Exceptions

A number of statutes permit the prevailing plaintiff to recover attorneys' fees. Alaska allows partial fee-shifting in all cases, in effect the British Rule. Arizona and Texas allow fee shifting in contract cases, but reject or limit fee shifting in tort cases. State consumer protection laws often allow fees in suits for unfair business practices. Federal civil rights laws, such as employment discrimination suits and suits alleging constitutional violations, commonly allow fee-shifting. Antitrust suits and claims under the Racketeer Influenced and Corrupt Organizations Act (RICO) allow treble damages plus attorneys' fees to a prevailing plaintiff (but none for prevailing defendants). The Equal Access to Justice Act (EAJA) allows fees to some parties (individuals and small corporations) litigating against the government, if their net worth falls below specified levels (in the millions). The EAJA does not permit recovery of fees, however, if the government's position was substantially justified. Instead of drawing the line between winning and losing, the EAJA probes the reasonableness of litigation, almost a claim for negligent litigation.

Asymmetrical Fee Shifting. Fee-shifting statutes allow the prevailing plaintiff to recover fees as a matter of course. Denying fees to a prevailing plaintiff is an abuse of discretion, barring unusual circumstances. Some statutes, as interpreted, impose a higher burden on prevailing defendants, awarding them fees only if the plaintiff's action was frivolous. Defendants' rights to fees thus resemble a malicious prosecution action. Defendant recovers not because plaintiff lost, but because plaintiff should not have sued in the first place. Courts justify the asymmetry based on the purpose of fee-shifting provisions: to encourage plaintiffs to help the government enforce these statutes by bringing claims. The approach is equally consistent with compensating plaintiffs for the loss caused by the wrong. Defendant's wrongful conduct causes plaintiff to incur attorneys' fees as surely as it causes medical fees, and as foreseeably in many cases. Defendants' fees, however, are not caused by plaintiff's wrong unless it is wrong to bring the suit—applicable for malicious prosecution, but not for merely bringing a claim that loses.

Prevailing Party Requirement. Most statutes provide fees to the prevailing party. When a party wins a judgment in court on all counts, no problem arises. Difficulties arise whenever a lesser success occurs.

Plaintiffs may succeed on some but not all of their claims or against some but not all of the defendants named. In these situations, courts must decide whether to reject fees associated with the unsuccessful claims. Sometimes all hours spent on the case deserve compensation. Plaintiff may have sued too many people because defendants' conduct prevented plaintiff from discovering which of them was liable. Similarly, plaintiffs may need to include extra claims to cover contingencies that otherwise might allow defendants to escape liability. For example, even if plaintiff believes the misconduct was intentional, including a claim for negligence seems prudent. Losing on one claim does not exonerate the defendant, whose conduct remains wrongful. Plaintiff still prevails on its claim for compensation based on the misconduct. In *Arizona v. ASARCO*, 773 F.3d 1050 (9th Cir.2014) (en banc), plaintiff's recovered $352,000 in attorneys' fees despite recovering only nominal damages on only one of her three claims (plus a punitive award of $300,000). In some situations, however, plaintiff may be limited to the fees incurred pursuing the successful claims, especially where the other claims bordered on the frivolous.

When parties settle the litigation, entitlement to fees may depend on the way the parties embody their agreement.

A consent decree is a judgment entered by the court, with the parties' consent. Failure to comply with the court order is contempt of court. As a judgment, it represents a judicial resolution of the dispute. Thus, the party who successfully obtained the judgment qualifies as a prevailing party.

A settlement agreement is a contract between the parties. Failure to perform allows the nonbreaching party to sue the breaching party in contract. A settlement agreement, however, may not justify attorneys' fees. Settlements contain no indicia that the court approved the award. In fact, many settlements specify that the defendant does not admit any wrongdoing. Settlements may involve defendants paying to avoid nuisance suits, not paying to liquidate their liability for a wrong. Settling parties may include their fee arrangement in the settlement agreement. A settlement agreement, however, is not a judgment of the court. Thus, for purposes of federal attorneys' fees statutes, neither party has prevailed in the case. States are free to interpret their fee shifting statutes differently.

In some cases, filing a suit will induce defendant to change its ways unilaterally. The change may moot requests for injunctive relief. In these situations, plaintiffs have sought fees, alleging that their suit obtained the relief sought, even though no court order was entered. The U.S. Supreme Court has ruled that catalysts are not prevailing parties under federal fee-shifting statutes. *Buckhannon Board and Care Home v. West Virginia Dept. of Health and Human Resources*, 532 U.S. 598, 121 S.Ct. 1835, 149 L.Ed.2d 855 (2001). Catalyst awards still appear in some state court actions.

Lodestar Calculations. Courts awarding fees usually start by determining the number of hours reasonably spent on the action multiplied times the reasonable hourly fee. This starting point has been dubbed the lodestar. Lodestar calculations make accurate time records important even for attorneys who usually do not charge by the hour.

Courts have been asked to adjust the lodestar fee based on a number of factors that might justify a larger award. In *Johnson v. Georgia Highway Express*, 488 F.2d 714 (5th Cir.1974), *overruled on other grounds*, *Blanchard v. Bergeron*, 489 U.S. 87, 109 S.Ct. 939, 103 L.Ed.2d 67 (1989), the court collected a list of 12 factors:

1. the time and labor required for the case;

2. the novelty and difficulty of the issues involved;

3. the skill required to perform the legal services properly;

4. the preclusion of other employment by the attorney due to acceptance of the case;

5. the customary fee for similar work in the community;

6. whether the fee is fixed or contingent;

7. time limitations imposed by the client or circumstances;

8. the amount involved and results obtained;

9. the attorney's experience, reputation and ability;

10. the undesirability of the case;

11. the nature and length of the attorney-client relationship;

12. awards in similar cases.

488 F.2d at 717–19. These factors have been mentioned in the legislative history of subsequent fee-shifting statutes.

The *Johnson* factors may be an unnecessary gloss on the lodestar. Many of the factors will affect the reasonable hourly rate or the reasonable number of hours, elements already included in the lodestar calculation. For example, the reasonable number of hours will vary with the novelty and difficulty of the case, the time required, the amount at issue, and the results obtained. The reasonable hourly fee will vary with the skill required, the ability of the attorney to accept other work, the customary fee for similar work in the community, whether the fee is fixed or contingent, time limitations imposed by clients, the attorneys' experience, reputation, and ability, the undesirability of the case, and the nature and length of the attorney-client relationship. Especially in federal courts, additional adjustments based on these factors are unnecessary. They are more likely to distort the fee award than to improve its accuracy. The U.S. Supreme Court expressly rejected enhancement for contingency under federal statutes. *City of Burlington v. Dague*, 505 U.S. 557, 112 S.Ct. 2638, 120 L.Ed.2d 449 (1992). States remain free to interpret their own statutes.

The appropriate hourly fee can be difficult to set. Ideally, the market price for attorneys' fees will supply an appropriate rate. Identifying an hourly rate for plaintiffs' attorneys is complicated by the prevalence of contingency fees. Most plaintiffs do not pay a fixed hourly rate. Reference to the market rate for defense counsel offers an alternative. Plaintiffs seem unwilling to pay fees at these rates. On the other hand, defendant's counsel gets paid even if they lose. An attorney who will collect only if she wins might charge more per hour than an attorney whose fees are guaranteed. This might produce a sliding scale of attorneys' fees, with plaintiffs' counsel charging less for cases likely to succeed, but more for longshots. In this way, the market rate for counsel may begin to include contingency enhancement within the lodestar, though not as an independent enhancement.

2. Common Funds

When an attorney hired by one person succeeds in creating a fund that will benefit others in addition to her client, the common fund exception allows the attorney to recover fees from the fund. This rule does not shift the fees to the defendant, who still pays only the amount owed to the fund. Rather, it shifts the fees to other claimants on the fund, even though they had no relationship with the attorney and, thus, no contractual obligation to pay her. The rule resembles unjust enrichment: having bestowed a benefit on multiple parties (by creating the common fund), the attorney (or the person who paid her) deserves compensation from all the beneficiaries. Class actions and shareholder derivative suits often produce a common fund.

In common fund cases, courts sometimes award a percentage of the fund rather than applying lodestar. The common fund exception is a judicial creation, not a statutory provision.

Percentage recoveries pose challenges. When recoveries are dramatically large, fees may be enormous even if the percentage is quite small. Thus, when states recovered billions in tobacco litigation, a percentage would have allowed their attorneys hundreds of millions of dollars. That is the equivalent of hourly rates in the thousands, far higher than any attorney could charge on an hourly basis. On the other hand, when recoveries are modest, any percentage may be too small to make the case worthwhile. If damages total $50,000—an amount most individuals would find significant—even taking half the award may not make it worth the time an attorney needs to spend on the case. For example, in one case plaintiffs recovered less than $35,000 on a claim of discriminatory misconduct by police (including punitive damages). *City of Riverside v. Rivera*, 477 U.S. 561, 106 S.Ct. 2686, 91 L.Ed.2d 466 (1986). It took plaintiff's attorneys nearly 2,000 hours to unravel the case. A fee of $11,100 (a one-third contingency), would pay the attorneys only $8/hour; a 100% contingency would be only $24/hour.

3. Contract

Contracts may permit a prevailing party to recover reasonable attorneys' fees. Courts generally will enforce those provisions. Loan agreements and some leases often include fee shifting provisions. Contracts can specify their own measure of attorneys' fees, in the same way that they can provide a measure for other damages caused by breach—and subject to the same limitations on liquidating damages. Absent an express provision, "reasonable attorneys' fees" probably will be interpreted to allow recovery of a reasonable hourly rate times a reasonable number of hours, similar to lodestar calculations. Contract interpretation, reflecting the purposes of the parties, may not produce the same conclusions as statutory interpretation, reflecting the public policy goals of the legislature.

Attorney fee terms occasionally provide that one party (such as the lender or landlord) may recover fees, without mentioning recovery by the other party. By statute, California treats these clauses as mutual, allowing recovery by either party. CAL. CIV. CODE § 1717.

4. Contempt

When a party's violation of a court order forces the opponent to bring contempt proceedings, courts allow recovery of the fees incurred in connection with the contempt.

5. Family Law

In family law cases, courts often order the party with greater means to pay the other's attorney—without regard to who did or might prevail. In effect, this approach entitles each member of the family to pay an attorney from the assets of the family, regardless of which spouse has control of those assets at the time of proceedings. It resembles the division of property, which can redistribute assets from one spouse to another—though attorney fee awards may be interlocutory, before any judgment on how property ultimately should be divided. The effect resembles the common fund rule, in that the assets available to the parties diminish to pay the attorneys.

6. Collateral Litigation

In some cases, defendant's wrong forces plaintiff to incur expenses litigating against third parties. In these situations, expenses incurred in the collateral litigation are recoverable as an ensuing loss, like any other consequential loss. For example, a party buying goods might bargain for a warranty that the goods do not infringe anyone's intellectual property rights. If sued for patent infringement, the buyer's litigation costs (including attorneys' fees) are caused by the seller's breach of warranty. The buyer may recover these costs in an action for breach of warranty against the supplier. Fees incurred suing the supplier fall under the American Rule, but fees incurred in the collateral litigation are recoverable.

7. Litigation Misconduct

A party's lack of good faith in the course of litigation may justify an award of the other party's attorneys' fees. Torts such as malicious prosecution or abuse of process offer one avenue for recovery. (In some states, attorneys' fees are not recoverable in these torts—a result inherited from Britain, where the British rule made the tort unnecessary as a means of collecting attorneys' fees.) More recently, court rules, such as Rule 11 of the Federal Rules of Civil Procedure, imposed sanctions for bad-faith litigation. The wrong can involve the entire suit, but may involve a single motion filed in bad faith. Fees to respond to the improper motion are available to the party prevailing on the motion, even if that party may not prevail in the action as a whole.

Table of Cases

Index

References are to Pages

301